NUPE RELIGION

Traditional Beliefs and the Influence of Islam
in a West African Chiefdom

NUPE RELIGION

Traditional Beliefs and the Influence of Islam
in a West African Chiefdom

by

S. F. NADEL

SCHOCKEN BOOKS · NEW YORK

First published in Great Britain in 1954
Published in U.S.A. in 1970
by Schocken Books Inc.
67 Park Avenue, New York, N.Y. 10016
Library of Congress Catalog Card No. 71 114163

Printed in Great Britain

PREFACE

THIS book is intended as a sequel to my first monograph on the Nupe people, *A Black Byzantium*, the material presented there—on economic and political organization, and on kinship and the regulations of adolescence—being largely presupposed in the present volume. Here and there, however, the run of the argument necessitated a somewhat fuller reference to the data contained in the earlier book, so that repetitions and some overlapping could not altogether be avoided. Much the same applies to various papers which I previously published on particular aspects of Nupe culture.

In one respect the present account might seem incomplete; for it omits the full discussion of a topic not previously treated and one well suited to the context of a book on religion, namely, myths and legends. The reason for this omission is partly a practical one, since an exhaustive treatment of Nupe legends, which would inevitably lead on to ordinary tales and folklore, would have overburdened the present volume. But partly, the omission can be justified on the grounds that these tales and legends are of relatively little relevance for the understanding of Nupe religion, which point will be dealt with in due course.

As readers of *A Black Byzantium* will know, the Nupe people are today in great measure Mohammedanized, the influence of Islam steadily encroaching upon the indigenous form of worship. If, therefore, in this description of Nupe religion I were to take my lead from the actually obtaining state of affairs, I should have to assign equal weight to Nupe–Islam and to the traditional creed, if not indeed to give prominence to the former. In fact, I have done the reverse; more precisely, I have treated Islam in Nupe as an intrusion, as an instance (to use the familiar phrase) of 'culture contact', and the indigenous religion as my true or main subject-matter. I do not think that this viewpoint needs to be specially defended. The fact that the traditional observances had already disappeared from many parts of the country during my stay in 1934–6 and have probably receded even further since, far from detracting from our interest in the indigenous creed, only renders the task of recording and analysing it more important as well as pressing.

A purely technical point in conclusion. It is always difficult to decide, in books of this kind, just how much scope should be given to vernacular words and quotations. Clearly, in a topic like religion certain crucial terms must be given, or must at least be introduced, in the vernacular. But too generous a use of the indigenous language is both clumsy and confusing to the reader. I have therefore tried to reduce it to a minimum. Nor do I think that this entails a serious loss of accuracy; for even the most intricate vernacular terms are translatable, even though the translation itself might have to be specially explained and perhaps justified: which is precisely the procedure I propose to adopt.

CONTENTS

PREFACE   v

I. THE NUPE CREED   page 1

1. *Prolegomena.* 2. *Dogma and Myth.* 3. *Categories: God and the World; Ritual Force; Medicine; Body and Soul; Spirit Beings.* 4. *Religion and Polity.* 5. *The Nupe Cosmos.*

II. DIVINATION   page 38

1. *The mechanics of eba.* 2. *Nomenclature and Incantations.* 3. *Interpretation.* 4. *Social Implications.* 5. *The mechanics of hati.* 6. *Interpretation.* 7. *Conclusions: Dream Interpretation.*

III. RITUAL   page 68

1. *Preliminaries.* 2. *The Inland Village: Priestship; Movable Rituals; Fixed Rituals.* 3. *The River: Ritual Calendar; Priestship; Movable Rituals; Fixed Rituals.* 4. *Ritual and Culture Change.*

IV. RITUAL [continued]   page 99

1. *Form, Content, Validity.* 2. *The Promise of Ritual.* 3. *Symbolic and implicit Functions.* 4. *Solemnizations: Birth; Marriage; Death.* 5. *Solemnizations and Social Structure.*

V. MEDICINE   page 132

1. *Rational and mystical Procedures.* 2. *Pharmacopoeia Nupeana.* 3. *The Faith in Medicine.* 4. *The Personnel.* 5. *Cigbe and Morality.* 6. *Modern Influences.*

VI. WITCHCRAFT AND ANTI-WITCHCRAFT   page 163

1. *The Knowledge of Witchcraft.* 2. *Male and Female Witches.* 3. *Sex-Antagonism.* 4. *Symptomatology: Case Histories.* 5. *Countermeasures.* 6. *A ndakó gboyá Ceremonial.* 7. *On the Meaning of Witchcraft.*

VII. STRANGE GODS   page 207

1. *Adoptions and Rejections: The Hausa borí; the sogba cult; Yoruba influences; the gani of Kutigi.* 2. *On Motives.* 3. *The Character of Tribal Religion.* 4. *Conclusions.*

CONTENTS

VIII. ISLAM IN NUPE *page* 232
  1. *The Conversion to Islam.* 2. *Daily Worship.* 3. *Ceremonials.* 4. *The Moslem Way of Life.* 5. *Contact and Integration.*

IX. CONCLUSIONS *page* 259
  1. *On Types of Religion.* 2. *Weltbild: Morality.* 3. *Religion and Social Structure.* 4. *Assurance and Stimulation.*

X. INDEX *page* 279

ILLUSTRATIONS
(between pages 70–71)

1. Sacrifice before twin shrine
2. Sacred crocodile of Mokwa
3. Wall paintings in a Nupe house
4. *Eba* diviner
5. *Hati* diviner
6. *Žiba* sacrifice
7. *Ndáduma* sacrifice on the Niger
8. Scene from *gunnu* dance in Jebba
9. *Dzakó* sacrifice
10. The *zumácikã* medicine shrine in Jebba
11. Dressing the *mamma* mask
12. *Dzakó* dance
13. Cutting of tribal marks
14. *Dzakó* dance
15. Vendor of medicines
16. Circumcision operation
17. A bridal procession
18. Levelling the ground over a new grave
19. The Master of the *cigbeciži* in his 'dispensary'
20. A noted medicine expert and 'wise man' from Jebba
21. The dance of the *ndakó gboyá*
22. The *Sagi* of Kpatsuwa
23. *Gugu* dance of the Yoruba
24. The appearance of the *ndakó gboyá*
25. *Bori* dance of the Hausa
26. A *bori* dancer in cataleptic fit
27. *Sogba* sacrifice of the Gwari

28 Mask of the 'Great *elo*'
29 Dancer at the Bida *salla* with headdress modelled on the *elo* mask
30 The Nupe quarter in Lagos
31 The oldest mosque in Bida

I

THE NUPE CREED

1. PROLEGOMENA

THE title of this book, *Nupe Religion*, suggests a logical unity in our subject-matter which, at the very outset, might appear problematical. Two questions, in particular, might be raised. First, are we in fact dealing with *one* religion of *one* people, that is, with beliefs and practices which both form a coherent system and occur uniformly throughout the society? And second, how far are we dealing with 'religion' in the strict sense of the word, and with it alone, to the exclusion of 'magic', mere 'superstitions', and other, cruder forms of belief?

The answer to the first question cannot be given in the form of a simple 'yes' or 'no'; nor can all the issues involved properly be judged so early in the discussion. Let me, however, anticipate the relevant points. The religious beliefs and practices of the Nupe differ considerably in different parts of the country; we shall frequently meet with local cults and with forms of worship varying from region to region, even from village to village. Furthermore, the main acts of worship, their execution and promises, concern the single village community, and not that widest group, the Nupe people or tribe. Nor indeed is that widest group an unequivocal unit. The people who call themselves Nupe are internally divided in various ways—by ethnic descent, by tribal segmentation and, partly, political allegiance, by the cleavage between urban and peasant population, and by the barriers of social class. The bulk of the Nupe people is held together in the kingdom of that name, and in the following description we shall mainly be concerned with the politically united tribe or nation. Even so, certain of the internal divisions remain, and these, too, entail corresponding divergences in religious belief and practice.

It might seem, therefore, that in speaking of 'Nupe religion' we are merely employing a convenient descriptive phrase, a summary reference of the kind ethnographers find useful when they wish to state that such-and-such observances are found in a particular group or area. But the phrase is intended to mean more than this.

The varieties of belief and practice found in Nupe are at least roughly akin, both in their content and in what might be called their style; though they exhibit no conspicuous uniformity or even consistency, they yet hang together in relevant respects and also reflect an identical psychological tenor. Most important of all, the people themselves think of their religion in terms of such an underlying unity; indeed, as we shall see, they tend to exaggerate it. Thus, though the local observances may differ and the congregations in acts of worship be no larger than single village communities, there is a clear understanding that the diverse and separate practices are instances of a common creed. When the people performing one kind of ceremonial comment on the different usage in another part of the country, they yet imply that the two belong together or, more precisely, belong to something wider than both. So that, over and above internal divisions, the people draw the (to them) much more important distinction between the sum total of beliefs and practices in their tribe, and the different totals of this kind in others.

It must be emphasized, however, that for the people this over-all unity is not constituted by the intrinsic coherence of the religious usages that happen to occur in their tribe; it is constituted, rather, by the fact that these usages do occur in their tribe and hence are typical of and valid for a given people or society. That collective entity—the people called Nupe—is the basic premiss; the diverse beliefs and practices are construed into a common creed on that basis.

The precise relationship between the total society and the 'total creed' will occupy us at a later stage. Here we might note that the Nupe have no special, collective name for their religion. They have names only for particular conceptions, single practices, local ceremonials. As for the total creed, the Nupe can describe it only circuitously and enumeratively, as being concerned with the God *Sokó*, and not with deities named differently; with such-and-such rituals or 'medicines', and not with others; with spirits, but not anthropomorphous ones, and so forth. Yet it is for them a 'total creed' none the less. If it be argued that this cannot be so, since in this case the people would have found a way of summarizing all these aspects in a name indicative of their over-all unity (as we do when we speak of Christianity, Islam, or Buddhism), the answer is that they do not think of their creed in that way. As they think of it, it has no identity apart from its validity-for-a-society; so that it would be meaningless to define it by a separate concept. Differently expressed, Nupe religion is a tribal or national religion, and *one* inasmuch as a tribe or nation claims it as its own.

To turn to our second question, which, let this be stressed, is of a purely preliminary order. It is here raised, not for the sake of discussing the meaning or essence of religious belief or of separating its relevant varieties, but merely in order to outline the kind of data that have been included in this book and to justify their inclusion. The word 'religion' will here be understood in the widest and loosest sense. I have not, for example, made the familiar distinction between religion and magic a criterion for the selection or arrangement of the material. Not that the Nupe are without observances and concepts which merit the name 'religious', however narrowly understood. But other beliefs and practices, though they might not satisfy the criteria of 'religion proper', will not for that reason be excluded or kept on one side.

It does not seem very difficult to define our position in general terms. Convenient phrases are at hand, such as: By 'religion' shall here be meant all beliefs and practices implying communication with and control of the supernatural, whether this is attempted through appeals and prayers to some transcendental intelligence (in the manner of religion) or quasi-mechanically, by the manipulation of 'magic' agencies. But this equation of religion with 'supernaturalism' (as Lowie would say), convenient though it may be, only poses further problems of definition; and the familiar category of the 'supernatural' proves on closer inspection to be itself ambiguous.

When speaking of attempts at communicating with or controlling the supernatural we are clearly viewing the situation through the eyes of the people we are studying, imputing to *them* the thought of transcending the given reality; we should probably impute to them also definite attitudes and feelings relating to the things transcendental, such as awe or fear, humility or ecstasy, or the emotional concentration we call worship. Yet when we try to define the supernatural itself we are driven to assume the opposite viewpoint and to judge the transcendentality of things by our own way of thinking. Nor, indeed, can we avoid veering round from one viewpoint to the other, since neither is by itself fully satisfactory.

Consider that any definition of the supernatural must introduce the contrast with the domain of empirical and scientific knowledge; more precisely, when judging any action or notion to be concerned with the supernatural we assert by implication that it is concerned with existences or influences (beings, 'powers', 'forces') the assumption of which conflicts with the principles of empirical enquiry and verification.[1] And since these principles and

---

[1] It must be emphasized that the relevant conflict is with the *principles* of empirical knowledge and with the *methods* of scientific enquiry, not merely with the body of information extant at any given moment. For in the latter case any scientific theory in advance of existing ideas or techniques of verification would be 'supernatural'.

their potentialities have been fully explored only in our own modern science, and can certainly not be assumed to govern the intellectual efforts of primitive peoples, the separation of the 'natural' from the 'supernatural' can have a precise meaning only in our own system of thought. Thus, though we should hardly hesitate to call a primitive people's belief in spirits or witchcraft 'supernatural', we cannot in fact assume that these are considered less well proven, less 'true' or 'real', than the physical environment with which the people grapple in their everyday lives; and when we call a fantastic tale about the origin of the world a 'myth', this may well, for the believer, imply the same measure of credibility as he would assign to documented or witnessed 'real' history.

There is this further point. The very conflict between supernatural and empirical knowledge on which we base our judgments is likely to be absent in a primitive culture; so that our judgments are again valid only within our own system of thought. If people in our midst believe in guardian angels or the tale about the trumpets of Jericho, they do so in spite of the scientific knowledge current in our society and hence accessible to them also; in other words, these persons choose to accept one basis of credibility (faith) rather than another (knowledge), and our judgments on the supernatural character of such and similar beliefs rests on the possibility of this choice. But this mutual exclusiveness of the empirical and the mystic does not hold for less advanced cultures. The primitive who believes in guardian spirits or miracle tales does not do so in opposition to intellectual principles equally enunciated in his society; he is not facing a choice between faith and knowledge, having to set aside one when he accepts the other. Rather, he accommodates both, only distributing them over different provinces of life. He can believe that hard work makes the crops grow, but that on certain occasions guardian spirits do so also; that certain forms of illness come from eating the wrong kind of food, and others from the malevolence of witches; or that certain events in the past are authenticated by the memory of concrete individuals, while others are as credible even though (as the Nupe would say) 'no one has seen them'.

It would seem, therefore, that the category of the supernatural is of dubious value in anthropological description. This view has in fact been argued, to my mind very convincingly, by Dr. Bidney. We cannot, he holds, take it for granted that primitive peoples 'distinguish between the sphere of the natural and that of the supernatural, since gods and spirits are just as much a part of the order of nature as men and animals. The dichotomy of the natural and supernatural implies a scientific epistemology and critical, metaphysical sophistication which must not be assumed without indubitable evidence. And modern ethnography does abound in evidence that sacred as well as secular traditions are *equally* credible to the native mind and differ only as regards the motivations for belief'.[1]

Even so, it seems to me, we cannot dispense with the category of the supernatural, defined according to our own, the observer's, criteria, at least in a first approach to our subject-matter. In a sense these criteria alone enable us to mark out our subject-matter; for the very fact that primitive peoples give to spirits, witches, and mythical events much the same credence as to things 'true' and 'real', that is, that they reckon with and conceive of controlling phenomena which *we know to be imaginary*, clearly represents one of our most crucial problems. Yet it is clear also that this 'first approach' may seriously mislead us. Relying on our own criteria of the supernatural we should, for example, have to class as scientific (and hence non-religious) certain treatments of disease by means of exorcism or magic dances because, on the grounds of our own advanced knowledge, we understand these procedures to be psycho-therapeutically effective and thus empirically sound. Conversely, we should have to include in the category of the supernatural any technological processes which, without being 'transcendental' for the actors, prove from our standpoint to be empirically unsound, based on wrong reasoning or false premises; and the same would hold for any would-be science which we know to be mere superstition (such as astrology, folk-medicine, or weather lore). The 'supernatural' would thus come to include clumsy and fallacious science, while the 'natural' would extend over empirical facts misconstrued and as it were 'super-rationalized'. Differently expressed, we should be disregarding the intentions of the actors for the results they unwittingly achieve (or fail to achieve).

It will be seen that in order to point out the inaccuracies of our criteria of the supernatural we had to refer to something like the primitive's own criteria; our sources of error are such only because we do not expect our own distinction between empirical and transcendental aims to tally with some equivalent distinction drawn by the people we study. That we must credit them with this ability, no one today will deny. I am far from assuming a primitive mentality essentially 'prelogical' or dominated by 'mystic' thought. Nor did I mean to imply that in the primitive's conception ghosts, spirits, miracle tales, technological processes, the physical environment, and witnessed records of the past all belong to precisely the same category of reality. All I mean to imply is

[1] D. Bidney, *Meta-anthropology*, in Ideological Differences and World Order, ed. F. S. C. Northrop, 1949, p. 333.

that the *differentia* valid for the primitive is not coterminous with credibility, and hence with our 'sophisticated' dichotomy of faith and knowledge or things natural and supernatural.

What form, then, does this *differentia* take? Dr. Bidney suggests that the relevant distinction lies 'between secular, everyday experience and sacred, superhuman tales and traditions about gods and spirits, since (the natives) have *special terms to designate the different categories* of narrative'.[1] I would give much the same answer in somewhat wider as well as looser terms. The distinction we are after would seem to be twofold, bearing both on the assumption of particular 'existences' and 'influences' in the world, and on the means employed in reckoning with them. But since the assumptions entail the means, and both are implicit in the intent guiding the people's behaviour, we may formulate the distinction in the terms of the latter alone. Thus we shall place on one side behaviour of a public and everyday kind, understood (by the actors) to aim at 'normal' effects, that is, effects commensurate with ordinary human efforts and skills; and on the other, behaviour understood to aim at extraordinary and miraculous results, involving superhuman efficacy and achieved by esoteric (or 'sacred') skills. Our primary evidence will clearly be linguistic, being embodied in the statements and in the nomenclature of the people. It is probably futile to expect that the native language should always provide precise distinctions of the kind we require, words like 'normal' and 'non-normal', 'miraculous' or 'superhuman', 'sacred' and 'profane'. But as we shall see, the Nupe possess at least two concepts approximating to such precision, the word 'knowledge', meant to circumscribe all ordinary learning and skills, and the word 'ritual', which refers to a whole class of activities of extraordinary, miraculous, or sacred import. Secondly, there is the series of words naming specific existences or influences of such an extraordinary or superhuman character—the deity, spirits, ancestors, or the agency of 'medicine'. Finally, we shall find our evidence also in the visible attitudes of the people, in those signs of awe, fear, humility, and worship which we related at the outset to the sense of the supernatural, as against attitudes of ordinary concern and profane interest.

Let me emphasize that none of these criteria is by itself decisive. The Nupe word 'medicine', for example, is ambiguous in that it refers both to skills of an esoteric and miraculous kind, and to healing practices which are public, profane, and acquired by ordinary learning; but if the linguistic evidence blurs the distinction, the contrasting attitudes with which the 'medicines' are

---

[1] *Op. cit.;* the italics are mine.

handled re-establish it. Again, anthropologists are familiar with magic practices carried out in a prosaic, businesslike fashion, which reveals nothing of a sense of awe or worship; here the nomenclature or the invocation of named deities or spirits will demonstrate the transcendental aims of the procedure.

In assessing, as we must, the attitudes and feelings of the actors we are of course relying on evidence often so subtle that our judgment may easily be at fault. Nor will even the combination of all three criteria always separate unequivocally supernatural conceptions (or their equivalent) from empirical (or would-be empirical) knowledge. For among the Nupe as elsewhere we also meet with intellectual efforts which aim at penetrating to something like ultimate agencies or quintessences—the human soul, a life principle, and such like—which, for us, are simply mystical. For the people, this speculative knowledge is still 'knowledge' and 'learning', and not something that should be placed on the other side, with things sacred and miraculous. But neither is it 'ordinary' knowledge, going some way beyond it and being in some measure esoteric. We might say that it belongs to 'metaphysics' and not, strictly speaking, to religion; yet by all the criteria we can bring to bear no sharp division seems possible. For though these ultimate conceptions may be handled without conspicuous show of awe, fear, or reverence, these are not far removed; clearly, truths of this kind, attainable only to a few, are often approached in a spirit at least akin to the humility or thrill evoked by things truly sacred. Nor perhaps can we expect these ultimate speculations to bear no reference, however tacit, to the acts of deities, to the miracle of creation, or to a supreme will to be accepted in all humility: much as the assumption of a divine order of the universe could fuse with our own, rigorous science of earlier days.

To sum up. Whichever way we propose to circumscribe the province of things religious, we are bound to encounter a border zone which defies precise *a priori* allocation on this or that side of the boundary. To be sure, this residue of inaccuracy is entailed in the broad view of religion which we made our starting point. But no other starting point seemed feasible. Bluntly stated, what we set out to do is to describe everything in a particular culture that has a bearing on religion. And since 'religion is precisely one of those words which belong to the more intuitive portions of our vocabulary',[1] and hence cannot be given a sharp connotation, we have no choice, but to feel our way towards the meaning it should have in given circumstances. We must not risk omitting anything that might be relevant; the risk we have to take is that of including,

---

[1] Edward Sapir, 'The Meaning of Religion'; in *Selected Writings*, 1949, p. 346.

besides 'religion proper', also that 'border zone', composed of mere superstitions; of science misconstrued or all-too-crudely attempted; and of science aiming too high or incompletely severed from mystic thought.

2. DOGMA AND MYTH

The preceding discussion has to some extent laid down already what must be our first concern—to outline the basic categories in which the Nupe frame their transcendental knowledge and thus to express the crucial distinction between things religious and profane. This task clearly implies more than merely compiling a glossary and commenting on its items. These basic categories will embody already an essential part of the dogma or doctrine of the religion. For any dogma or doctrine, being a body of assertions and propositions, must employ the language of these basic categories; the significance we discover in the latter will already point to the tenets of the creed; while whatever further information might be derived from the doctrinal assertions, will in turn elucidate the terms of the 'glossary'.

In a sense, we cannot approach the dogma of Nupe religion in any other way. Like most primitive societies, the Nupe have not formulated their creed *ad hoc*, in a specific and coherent body of statements; nor is there any institutionalized teaching of doctrine on which we could rely. Rather, we must piece the creed together, from current sayings and from comments or arguments put forth in discussion, from the songs and prayers accompanying ceremonials and from the observation of the latter. There is, in many primitive societies, another source, again linguistic, which we could use, namely, the mythology of the people. Though dogma and myth are clearly not the same thing, they are akin in that both embody the tenets of the creed and the basic categories of religious thought: myths, of course, do so indirectly, through presenting (or concealing) the articles of creed in accounts of miraculous happenings, in narratives of some kind, which are meant to illustrate and exemplify rather than enunciate (in the manner of dogma). It has, in fact, been suggested long ago that in primitive religions, since they are without formulated doctrine, we must look for the 'key to ritual and practice', not in dogma, but in myth.[1]

None of this holds for the Nupe. To begin with, they do not separate 'myths' conceptually from secular traditions or 'historical' narratives, having the same term for both and relating

[1] W. Robertson Smith, *Lectures on the Religion of the Semites*, 1907, pp. 16–17.

both on the same, profane, occasions.¹ More important, Nupe mythology is altogether flimsy and rudimentary. It illustrates only two tenets of the creed, the conception of a supreme deity and the role of 'medicine', while others, for example, the equally basic conception of 'ritual', are given no such expression. Nor does the mythology concern itself more than scantily with cosmological speculations or with the justification of particular ceremonies.

Certain legends meant to account for particular practices or ceremonials will be quoted later, in that context. Let me here illustrate my point by relating the one cosmological myth the Nupe possess. It is, strictly speaking, only 'near-cosmological', being concerned, not with the origin of the world and of all the things and creatures in it, but only with the origin of man, of the Nupe people, and of one observance (which is incorrectly stated). The myth, incidentally, may not be entirely a Nupe creation; the names of the first human beings mentioned in it have a Mohammedan flavour ;² and certain details of the narrative (the bull who appears out of the water, and his strange language) occur in almost the same form among the Bororó Fulani.³ However this may be, the myth is far from well known, so that for this reason also it cannot be considered a relevant expression of the Nupe creed.

'In the beginning, there was a man called Ancestor Adã and a woman called Ancestress Adama. They had two children, one male, one female, who in turn begot two children, male and female. The male child died immediately after birth, while the girl stayed alive. When she grew up she spoke a strange language which her parents could not understand. But a bull who one day rose from the river when the girl was standing on the bank understood the language. He talked to the girl, and the two became friends. Later the bull became the girl's lover, and she bore him a male child. This child again spoke and understood the strange language. When the boy grew up, he used to go to the bank of the river to talk to the bull, until one day the bull climbed out of the river and followed the boy on dry land wherever he went. This boy was the ancestor of the "Cow Fulani", and the bull the first of the Fulani cattle.

'Ancestress Adama had a third child, a girl called Mureamu (Miriam or Mary), who had three children, two sons and a daughter. When they grew up the two young men both desired their sister. They quarrelled and one was killed. It was thus that

¹ The word in question is *etã*, meaning 'stories of old times', and these are told in daytime, not at night (as are stories meant for amusement), when people would be 'too tired to listen to serious things'.
² See below, p. 247.
³ See F. W. de St. Croix, *The Fulani of Northern Nigeria*, p. 8.

death and murder first appeared in the world. The couple who remained did not know what to do with the dead body. They carried the corpse on their shoulders for three days, lamenting and crying, but could not get rid of it. At last, God caused the earth to open, and they placed the body inside. Thus the practice of burial and of the three days' mourning for the dead began.[1] The couple now stayed together and begot a male child, who became the ancestor of the Nupe people.'

If, then, Nupe mythology is a very inadequate guide to dogma and doctrine, this inadequacy is itself significant, revealing the Nupe attitude towards their creed and indeed the whole tenor of their religious thought in their true perspective. Mythology, as we have said, illustrates and exemplifies rather than enunciates the creed. We may go further and say that it expresses the creed in a form less abstract and theoretical than does formulated doctrine. For myths borrow the phraseology of realistic accounts, dealing as they do with near-humans and near-natural events; thus they make less demand upon sheer credence, compromise with ordinary imagination, and as it were vulgarize the dogma. If, then, primitive religions rely on mythical narratives rather than on dogmatic assertions they seem to discard the more abstract contents of religious thought. Yet Nupe religion, which does not employ mythology either to any great extent, is clearly not of this kind. If the Nupe do not attempt a specific, coherent formulation of their creed, neither do they seek to re-phrase it in more concrete and would-be realistic language. In other words, Nupe religion forgoes the means of 'vulgarizing' the dogma. Thus, though its creed may be inarticulate, yet it is held in all abstractness.

3. CATEGORIES

(i) *God and the World*

The most basic concept of Nupe theology, that of the supreme being, is also the widest. In a sense it stands for the whole realm of religion, serving to separate all things that belong to that realm from others that do not. For in order to express this distinction the Nupe say of an object, phenomenon, or type of action that it is, or is not, *nyá Sokó*—'of God' or 'belonging to God'. There are two inaccuracies in this broad category of things religious. The clause 'of God' in the sense here understood is properly applied only in the context of discussions turning upon the dichotomy of the religious and profane. In a wider context the phrase loses its disjunctive implication; for ultimately everything is 'of God', that

[1] There is no such rule of 'three days' mourning'.

is, is his creation. But the relationship between God and the created world is once more viewed as a dichotomy. And in this final context only the forms of religious action which bear on the living, active powers of the deity are 'of God', while all others, having become part of his completed creation, are classed with the 'things in the world'.

We shall later exemplify this somewhat sophisticated point in Nupe theology. As regards the dualism of God and the World, it is aligned with yet another, of more concrete character, of the sky and the earth. Together, these four concepts describe the Nupe universe; for it contains no other cosmic entities, for example, no underworld or some yonder inhabited by the spirits of the dead; nor have the Nupe anything to say about the stars, the sun, or the moon. In all relevant respects the created world (*yiže*) is identical with the earth (*kin*); while the Creator is identified with the sky. Though the supreme being is also addressed or referred to as *tsóci*, 'Our Lord',[1] his proper name is *Sokó*, which is best translated as God-the-Sky, the same word also denoting the sky in the visible, physical sense.[2]

As God is identified with the sky, so he is also said to dwell in the sky. But this belief is vague and contradicted by other statements, as are most assertions on the nature of the supreme deity. In fact, nothing very definite can be said or is known about God. He is not on earth, and the most common and most strongly emphasized comment on the nature of the deity is *Sokó lokpá*, 'God is far away'. Yet in a different, more mystic sense he is present, always and everywhere; thus in a song I recorded it is said—

> God is in front,
> He is in the back.

God has clearly awareness, intellect, and some of the sensitiveness of man; for he is addressed and appealed to in everyday language. But he is hidden and cannot be seen; nor is he personified more concretely; indeed, no one knows if he is or is not like man.[3]

[1] The suffix -*ci* means 'our'; the word *tsó* occurs normally as a suffix of other words, denoting 'owner of' or 'master of', e.g. *kin-tsó*, Owner of the Land, *emi-tsó*, Family Head.

[2] There exists another word for 'sky', *sama*, which is of Hausa-Arabic origin and is used, at least today, when referring to the sky and firmament in the material sense, e.g. 'the sky is black', 'the sky is clear', etc. The word *Sokó*, incidentally, also indicates something big or great, the suffix -*kó* having that implication.

[3] Strictly speaking, therefore, there is no justification for calling the supreme deity 'he'. In Nupe language this issue does not arise since the personal pronouns have no gender and do not distinguish between animate and inanimate objects. For purely practical reasons, however, I shall continue to employ the personal pronoun in the masculine.

Characteristically, any thought of gaining more precise knowledge of the deity is regarded as absurd and may well be ridiculed, as in this somewhat slangy proverb: 'The thing that conceals God, go and buy it.'

Only these facts are positively and universally known and are often argued when the Nupe wish to compare their beliefs with those of other peoples: God is all-powerful, as he is all-knowing; there is only one God, and no other deities exist; God was in the beginning, before the appearance of man and the creation of nature, being himself the creator of all things. And here we must note that the phrase 'all things' is meant to include things good as well as evil, which article of creed appears, circuitously phrased, in various secular songs. Thus one song contains this phrase—'A being which God did not create, neither did the world create it'; and another runs thus—'Should you do anything that is beautiful, God has caused it to be beautiful; should you do anything evil, God has caused it to be evil.'

The Nupe deity, then, is something like the *causa causans* of mediæval philosophy, though the crucial problem of that philosophy, how to reconcile an omnipotent deity with the presence of evil in the world, is not really seen as a problem. Good and evil are both laid into the same creation, as are the various sources of evil —malevolent spirits, disease, witchcraft. Without further speculations about a Free Will, or the weakness of mind and matter, or Satan, the deficiencies of the world are taken for granted. The only problem in Nupe theology is the actual power of evil, not its origin. And this power is justified, once more without moral speculations, by accepting, simply, the aloofness of the deity. In other words, one does not wonder why God did not create a better world; but one attempts to answer the question—Why does God not better protect man, who has to live in this world? The answer, as we shall see, is that divine concern with the world is limited.

Here a slight correction is necessary. The Nupe do mention Satan or the Devil; but they only just mention him and no more. He is called *Abili* or *Jibililu*, and sometimes *Sheitán*. The last name is, of course, Arabic and a loan-word in Nupe. So is *Jibilílu*, which is the Nupe version of the Arabic *Jibríl*, an angel of the Qoran having been changed into an African Devil. Whether *Abili* is an original word or a further corruption of *Jibríl*, it is difficult to say; the Nupe use of the word in ordinary conversation seems to suggest the former. It is commonly employed to denote some unexpected evil turn of events, for example, a quarrel between friends or the discovery that an otherwise truthful person has been guilty of a lie. On occasions like these the people would exclaim—'Ah, the devil is at work' or, literally, '*Abili* is present'. But though the

Nupe firmly hold that the devil exists, that he is behind many (though not all) evil things, and that there is only one devil (while there are many evil spirits), their knowledge of Satan carries no further; nor does he play any part in religious observances. Only diviners might refer to *Sheitán* or *Abilí* in connection with a particularly sinister prophecy. Above all, the Nupe hold that God has created the devil, so that Satan, far from being a counterpart of the deity, is only one of his ambiguous creatures.

There is no doubt in the minds of the Nupe that God, as he created the world, so he can also control it and intervene in its course. Everyday speech is full of phrases such as 'with God's help', 'may God give this or that', or 'may God cause such-and-such to happen'. To describe, incidentally, this divine intervention one uses the ordinary causative mode and the same verbs that are applied to human actions. One also swears by God and lends weight to any assertion by adding *be Sokó nyi*—'by God'. But these allusions imply little certainty that God will in fact intervene; for 'God is far', aloof, outside the world; which tenet overrules all other notions.

This belief has an important consequence: one cannot approach God directly. Although every ritual act is accompanied by some phrase or blessing invoking *Sokó*, there are no prayers specifically addressed to God and capable of being employed freely and independently of the appointed ceremonial occasions. Rather, the approach to the deity is circuitous, that is, through the given ceremonials or rituals. If we call the belief in God-the-Creator the first article of the Nupe creed, the second would be this conception of ritual as an intermediary between God and man.

(ii) *Ritual Force*

The condition that God is approached implicitly in every ceremonial and solely in this manner is regarded, not as fortuitous, but as having been willed by God and embodied in his creation. Equally, it is regarded as peculiar to the Nupe form of worship. To quote a typical comment: The Mohammedans can pray to God directly; but *Sokó* is 'so very far from men' that he gave them the ritual as an intermediary—a 'thing-in-between'. The ritual is thus a gift of God or 'of God'—*nyá Sokó*; but being an intermediary, the ritual is also of this world. Now, the Nupe will readily quote an inventory of the world, thus: 'In the world there are these things—*zawangízi*, human beings; *ena gontází*, animals; *aljenúzi*, spirits; and *kuti*, ritual.' With one exception, this list fully accounts for the Nupe picture of creation, though the nature of animate beings is itself composite and requires a further list of attributes. For the moment we are concerned only with the last item on the list and with its twofold citizenship, among the 'things of God' and the 'things of the world'.

In translating *kuti* as 'ritual' we are not conveying the full import of the conception. We shall later speak of other acts of worship—invocation of ancestors, sacrifices to twins or medicine shrines, offerings to spirits; all these are ritual actions as we understand the word, and the Nupe too acknowledge the underlying identity by calling the crucial act, the sacrifice, offering or libation, by the same name—*labá*. But *kuti* means more, even though it always includes the phase of *labá* and in one form does not go beyond it. For the people the external procedure of *kuti*, the things you can see and hear and easily describe, stands for something more obscure and intangible, even unknowable. Nor is the nature of *kuti* exhausted by saying that it is a means of communicating with the deity. For there are many *kuti*, each with an identity and power of its own; each also has its individual name, and some are 'stronger' than others, and more or less dangerous. The *kuti* is called a 'thing', *enya*; it is also something that you 'make' or 'do'; equally it is said to know its priests and congregation, as though it were an intelligent being. The Nupe do not deny these contradictions and obscurities; they would simply hold that they are beyond human understanding. There is the Nupe saying—'Such-and-such *kuti*: a speech (explaining it) does not come first'; which means, you may learn the names and procedures of *kuti*; but as for the rest, no explanation must be expected. Ultimately, no one can see, hear, or know the *kuti*; to wit, these verses from the song cycle connected with the most important ritual of Nupe, *gunnu*—

> Do you know the *gunnu*?
> You do not know it.
> For can you hear it?

Yet though the nature of *kuti* cannot be fully grasped, the external procedures are known and can be learned. There are rules about performing a particular *kuti*, guarding it, keeping away from it or protecting it from illicit knowledge; and by means of these procedures, which are both delicate and on occasion dangerous, humans are enabled to tap some mysterious but in essence divine force. Also, the procedures belong to humans, much as material possessions belong to their owners. Thus it is considered a general and important characteristic of the Nupe people, which gives them a distinct position in *rebus sacris*, that they collectively 'own' the ritual called *gunnu*, while different sections of the tribe possess other rituals besides, and different tribes rituals of other kinds. Mostly, however, this 'ownership' is understood more narrowly, being ascribed to single village communities; and as these 'own' such-and-such *kuti*, so they can exercise a certain mastery over the universe on given occasions and for given aims. Generically, *kuti* is a portion of cosmic power, which is in itself unspecific but is capable of being harnessed and canalized into specific efficacy in particular rituals; or more briefly, *kuti* is the Force-that-is-in-ritual.

We have noted the twofold nature of *kuti* as a thing-in-between God and man. In one sense, it plays the part of a gesture or utterance whereby man brings his wishes to the attention of the deity; but in another it is also a thing-in-between man and the power which, we must presume, God normally wields when he makes or remakes the world. Let me argue this point from the Nupe point of view. Men, they would hold, cannot hope to move the remote and aloof deity by prayers alone; but they possess, in *kuti*, a means of drawing directly upon the power that is God's. There is this saying: 'The human being, he makes *kuti*; God, he causes it to come', that is, to have the desired power or efficacy. In a way, it is as simple as that—a matter almost of pressing a button. But the fact that human beings can thus simply summon divine action, is itself due to an act of divine providence. Paradoxically speaking, the Nupe deity, concerned over the limits set to his concern with the fate of men, bestowed upon them, not the efficacy of prayer (which might not reach him), but a portion of his own force. In this sense, then, the ritual is a shortcut as well as an intermediary and has the greater effectiveness of such a direct access to the causes that move the world. This notion too has been formulated, if more elliptically, in these verses from the *gunnu* cycle of songs—

(*If someone said:*) 'Give me for the sake of God',
    I should give him nothing.
(*If someone said:*) 'Give me for the sake of the *gunnu*,'
    There it is—I give him.

Which means, in simple language: While it is of little avail to invoke God, the performance of the *gunnu* (or any other *kuti*) is always effective.

This, incidentally, is a somewhat optimistic view, as we shall discover later, when discussing the occasions for ritual and the precise expectations that go with them. We may anticipate this, however. As *kuti* are vested in, or 'owned' by, communities, so the aims and occasions of their performance essentially bear on the problems of community life.[1] These are the ubiquitous and perennial

---

[1] This is true of the 'fixed' rituals, which have their firm place in the Nupe calendar. Certain of the 'movable' *kuti* can on occasion be performed for the sake of individuals, though their performance is still in the hands of the community priest (see below, p. 87).

problems of survival which face, not this or that individual, but the collectivity, such as droughts, epidemics, the fertility of the land, and the fertility of the population. The close association of *kuti* with the well-being of the whole community is convincingly expressed in the concluding formula of every ritual, whatever its occasion—*Sokó lá eži u ge*: 'May God grant that the village (or town) prospers.'

Let me make it clear that the efficacy of the ritual lies in the whole of the procedure and not in any of its elements, not even in the language employed on such occasions. Though invocations and prayer-like formulae play their part in ritual, they are not peculiar to it; like the act of *labá* they also occur, in much the same form, in other observances and are by themselves without any power. Significantly, they are often couched in language which is nondescript or takes the form of riddles and parables representing comments upon the ritual rather than crucial stages in the procedure. Also, the language can be varied without affecting the efficacy of the rite; thus I could record songs in one ritual which were borrowed from another, the people's comments being that 'it made no difference'. Nor yet are there material objects, effigies and the like, which might be said to contain the supernatural power. Most rituals have their customary places, and some of the sacred songs speak of the 'initiates entering the house' of the *kuti*; but this is a mere metaphor, for no Nupe ritual has a 'house' or 'temple', or indeed a locality which is on all occasions 'sacred', barred to the uninitiate, or avoided by the people. On occasion, the localities are changed without further ado, for example, when a village grows and encroaches upon the grounds hitherto reserved for the ritual. The cult objects, if they exist at all, are usually things of no sacred association—boughs or leaves carried in the dances, unimportant animals killed in the sacrifice, and pots and dishes used for cooking and eating.

There are exceptions. In a few places I found rituals associated with stones, either ordinary rocks in the ground or (in two instances only) round stone balls supported on carved wooden posts. Sometimes the rituals are even named accordingly, for example, *fĩtákuŋ*, 'The Stone drinks' (a ceremonial from Doko and Pichi), or *takúŋžiko*, 'Black Stone' (a ritual from Katcha). Other cult objects seem to be of alien origin, such as the masks of the *elo* ritual of Mokwa, which betrays Yoruba influence, and the 'thunderbolts' used in a fertility cult known to come from Gwari. The most elaborate cult objects in Nupe, certain bronze figures in human shape, occur only in the Niger valley, in the two villages Jebba and Tada, and are again said to be of alien origin; they also belong to a very special series of rites, associated with the mythical founder of Nupe kingdom and serving the interests of the state. We shall later deal with these 'exceptions'. Let me here stress that in calling them that I am taking my lead from the people. Indeed, the Nupe would altogether disregard these lapses from a wholly abstract creed, which seems to require no effigies or visible symbols; for when comparing their religion with that of other peoples, the Nupe will always emphasize that they have no sacred emblems, idols, masks, or 'little likenesses' (*zazagízi*).

It is perhaps not surprising that so abstract a conception as that of *kuti* should not be held with equal clarity by everyone. In particular, I met with two as it were heterodox notions; one was the idea that *kuti* represents a part of *Sokó*, or a *Sokó tetengi*, a 'Little God' (which, in Nupe language, is a contradiction in terms); according to the other, God was 'up above', but *kuti* was somehow of the earth, being a 'thing' buried in the ground, very likely in the places of ritual. These notions were always put tentatively, and were moreover voiced by individuals who could not claim the fullest knowledge available in the society, that is, by younger men or by Nupe under the influence of Islam; the older men, and especially the priests of *kuti*, declared such views to be false. But supernatural power understood more concretely and associated with specific material objects also has a place in the Nupe universe. This notion is embodied in the third tenet of the religion, which concerns the existence of *cigbe* or 'medicine'.

(iii) *Medicine*

Let me say, first of all, that 'medicine' is the literal translation of the vernacular term, which is applied not only to 'magic' substances but also to medicinal herbs or drugs of any kind, native as well as European, whose properties are assessed essentially empirically. Of the relation between the two we shall speak in a later context. Here we must note that the Nupe inventory of the 'things in the world' does not mention 'medicine', although in some respects it is an exact counterpart to *kuti*, that is, an agency meant to aid man in a universe governed by an all-too-distant deity. But unlike *kuti*, 'medicine' is not thought of as being part of the creation and a primordial gift of God. If it now exists in the world, it does so because of man's own endeavours. There is a legend, well known throughout the country, expounding this view.

'There was a certain younger brother, called Kpara, whose elder brother was Tswasha Malu. They lived in the time of *Etsu* (king) Shagó.[1] There existed a certain medicine, called *cekpyeca shina*

[1] The two brothers are mentioned in no other myth. The name of the king, Shagó, occurs also in the myth describing the origin of the

shina buburukun (meaningless words). On the day when the two brothers were making this medicine, Kpara wished to climb up into the sky. Kpara explained to the king that he needed a chain. The king summoned the blacksmiths of the whole country and they forged a chain of seven links. Then Kpara tied the chain round his waist and went straight up, higher and higher, until he reached the sky. It took him three years to travel up to the sky, and people thought they would never see him again. At the end of the three years people beheld the chain dropping slowly down to earth, and 19 days later, Kpara himself dropped from the sky, sitting down, bang, on top of the chain. The people asked—Had he seen God? Kpara answered (this part is sung):

> God is far away,
> God is far away,
> But medicines are applied on earth.

"The person who tries to eat porridge while shouting at the same time will get nothing into his stomach" (i.e. one must not attempt the impossible). Kpara then said to all the people that they must try and make medicine of ingredients. "For God is not watching man." This Kpara was the elder brother of the father who begot us—our tribe, that is.'

This legend or myth introduces two crucial features into Nupe doctrine. One is the assertion that 'God is not watching man', or literally, *Sokó nw' á yelé à*, 'God is not seeing'; the other is the notion that that powerful agency, *cigbe*, has been produced or discovered by man's own initiative. The two clearly hang together, both following logically from the root concept of the supreme being. The assertion that God 'is not watching' only expands and sharpens that other idea, that God, though creative and omnipotent, 'is far away'—too far away to follow closely his handiwork, and too impersonal to concern himself closely with all that happens on earth. And it is this extreme aloofness of the deity which justifies the further notion of human self-help. God, as we know, cannot be reached by prayers and invocations alone. Thus there have to be intermediaries, of which *kuti* is one and *cigbe* the other. But there is this difference. Only the *kuti* is 'of God'; equally, it provides only for the collective and unvarying needs of a people, not for the more variable and particular troubles of individuals. As regards these, God seems even more remote; for he has not thought of giving man the appropriate aids: rather, they had to be discovered by man left to himself. Here, then, we have

anti-witchcraft cult *ndakó gboyá* (see below, p. 173). Shagó is probably identical with the mythical hero and deity of Yoruba religion, Shangó, who, in Yoruba mythology, is described as a man or king of Nupe.

something like a Free Will, though crudely conceived and devoid of ethical implications. All the Nupe concept implies is that man can attempt to correct creation, and is compelled to do so by his knowledge (as the myth has it) that 'you cannot have everything' —live on earth and have the full protection of God.

This is a naïve and, if you like, cynical philosophy. Within its frame of reference, however, everything falls into place and *kuti* and *cigbe* appear complementary in many ways. We said before that the *kuti* is understood both as a means of reaching the attention of the deity and as a means of drawing more directly upon the divine (or cosmic) force, as an 'intermediary' as well as a 'shortcut'. Now *cigbe* is a shortcut much more than it is a medium of appeal. If in *kuti* the invocation of the deity and the harnessing of a cosmic force are made to merge, in 'medicine' that force is more independently effective and works in the manner almost of a machine. In preparing or administering 'medicine' the name of *Sokó* is often mentioned; but now it occurs, not in the context of a prayer-like appeal, but in a *spell*, every word and phrase of which is important and unchangeable. At the same time the mastery of *cigbe* is strictly technical; the Nupe say that it is *kpeyé*, 'knowledge', and nothing else. This knowledge no longer refers to total procedures embracing prayers, localities hallowed by the occasion, the occasions themselves, songs, dances, and all the phases of the ritual performance; rather does it refer to highly specialized *skills*, primarily to the skill of *gbá gbèrè*, 'using ingredients', that is, to a skill in manipulating and manufacturing material things. For the *cigbe* is always material, some object or substance whose efficacy is communicated by physical contact or therapeutic administration. We note the ambiguous role of medicine, which is opposed to ritual both as another (more 'machine-like') form of supernatural control and as an altogether different kind of mastery, through technical-empirical knowledge. For the Nupe, the latter alignment counts more heavily: if they were to use our phraseology they would say that the practice of medicine is less 'religious' (or 'supernatural') than ritual, and in many instances entirely non-religious.

Again, the conception of ownership differs fundamentally in the case of *kuti* and *cigbe*. The former is 'owned' corporately by groups, and the question of acquisition does not arise (save in mythical speculations). Though the ritual procedures can be learned, and are learned by every new generation, this is a secondary feature, incidental to the right or title to the ritual knowledge; which title is vested, inalienably, in the tribe or village community. It makes no sense, in Nupe, to ask whether strangers can learn and put themselves in possession of a *kuti*. If they are adopted into the community, they will also learn about the ritual and share in its possession; otherwise they remain without the crucial title, even though they may conceivably come to know all about the technical procedure. In *cigbe*, the latter is everything: who learns, possesses, and the learning is open to any individual who can find a teacher. Admittedly, certain medicines are today owned by families and passed on from generation to generation; but with few exceptions this vested ownership is only of the kind that applies to trade secrets, and everyone understands that, originally, the knowledge of such family *cigbe* had again been taught and learned, perhaps even bought. Medicines of all kinds can still be purchased, regularly and openly, from their makers; you might also purchase the knowledge of how to prepare them, though this would be done only occasionally and in secrecy. Finally, both the medicine and the recipe may be brought in from another country. Now, it would once more be nonsensical to think of a *kuti* that can be bought; and though a few rituals are said to have been introduced from abroad, this was the work either of immigrant groups, which 'owned' the *kuti* by right and are still called its 'owners', or of mythical figures and heroes. In brief, the *kuti* is part of the traditional estate of communities; the *cigbe* is individual property, fortuitously acquired and held. With the different title of possession goes the corresponding conception of the benefits conferred by the possession, which are once more collective in the case of ritual and individual in the case of medicine. This contrast is thrown into relief in the invocations accompanying the two practices; for the prayer formula invariably voiced in all Nupe rituals, 'May God grant that the village prospers', is as invariably absent in the *cigbe* spells.

Here we are touching upon a final difference between *kuti* and *cigbe*, which goes deep into the ethical foundations of the Nupe creed. The *kuti* is, *ex definitione*, good; it always serves to secure benefits—prosperity, health, success—and to combat evils or ills —disease, drought, barrenness. Many 'medicines' do the same; but some may also serve evil purposes, that is, they may be meant to further the egoistic aims of individuals while harming the rest of the people. *Cigbe*, then, is potentially 'anti-social'; and, logically, the force of evil *par excellence*, witchcraft, is by many attributed to the efficacy of *cigbe*. Now, as God is the indifferent creator of things both good and evil, *kuti* and *cigbe* represent the two sides of his nature. Not all that is evil or ill in the world is due to *cigbe* or witchcraft; indeed, various evils and ills may be diminished by the agency of *cigbe*. But 'medicine' remains a supernatural agency which men might wield for disaster and harm. Thus the conception of 'medicine' reflects, on a smaller scale, the ethical

THE NUPE CREED

indifference which the Nupe ascribe to divine creation. Yet since the world contains both things, *kuti*, which is good, and *cigbe*, which is both good and evil, the good would seem on balance to preponderate. As we shall see, various other religious thoughts confirm this impression of a cynicism tempered with optimism.

(iv) *Body and Soul*

We turn to the other 'things in the world' and first to the animate beings. Each of these possesses, to begin with, a body, *nakã*. The Nupe word means precisely what we mean by 'body'—the flesh and blood of living creatures, resulting from procreation, parturition, and natural growth, and decomposing after death. The biological processes of procreation and parturition are fairly well understood, though this empirical knowledge is not free from fallacies. Thus no one misunderstands the connection between coitus and conception; one understands, too, that both women and men can be infertile, and that abortion can be brought about by strong laxatives or overstrain. At the same time the Nupe also use certain purely 'magical' cures for barrenness and charms or magic belts to prevent conception. More surprisingly, the Nupe fail to distinguish between semen and male urine, or have to borrow a word from Hausa to describe the former. Nor finally is the precise length of pregnancy known. To quote one of my informants, a diviner and knowledgeable old man: 'It all depends; it may take anything between seven months and a year; a strong and fit child will be born after eleven months or so, a weak one after a shorter period.'

The biological processes as such, one believes, produce only a lifeless body, as death in turn leaves the body lifeless but still physically intact. The living being thus has further attributes, of soul-like nature, which are three in number: *rayi* or 'anima'; *fifingi* or 'shadow soul'; and *kuci* or 'personal soul'.

The word *rayi* is used generally to denote the living state; the pulse, for example, is called *rayigi*, 'little life'. Everything animate possesses *rayi*, while stones, pieces of wood, and similar inanimate objects are without *rayi*; growing trees and plants, however, are counted among the animate things. Life comes from God and exists with God, in the sky, when it is not incarnate. At death 'God takes it away'; at birth it is sent down by God, more precisely, it appears already when the child first moves in the womb. The new life is thus at first tied to the life of the mother, and in a sense remains so tied for a period even after birth. For the mother who has borne one child must not risk another conception before the child can walk and is 'sufficiently strong', lest it would never grow up; so that its *rayi* would seem to be diminished by the other life that is growing in the mother.[1] Though this notion is not fully thought out, this much is clear: the *rayi* is a quantity, which increases with growth and diminishes with old age and in all forms of illness; it is impersonal, without sex or individual features; it is common to and infinitely divisible among all animate beings. It is a life principle or life soul, the Latin *anima*, and nothing more specific or personal. All that is peculiar to the individual human being, his appearance, his character, his particular spirit and intellect, comes from the two other entities, *fifingi* and, especially, *kuci*.

As death represents the complete severance of body and *anima*, so disease weakens the link and attacks the life principle. In sleep, body and life soul are separated temporarily and more lightly; normally, the *rayi* will return to the body; but one cannot predict that this will always happen, so that a person may die in his sleep. It is then, incidentally, when the life soul is loosened from the body, that it can be harmed by witches, who, as we shall hear, 'feed' on the *rayi*. When I dream, my *rayi* wanders about and sees all the things that come to me in the dream. But the *rayi* does not wander alone; it takes something with it that is, though not of the body, yet of bodily shape; for I may appear to others in their dreams, as in turn I dream of other persons. It is not, of course, the real, full person that is met with in dreams (for the real person may be away in other parts, or asleep at home), but only his or her image or shadow—the *fifingi*.

Fifingi means 'shadow' much as we understand the word, that is, the shadow thrown by men and animals, not the shade caused by inanimate things. But the word has a second, mystic, meaning, best translated as 'shadow soul'; for when a person dies and his body decomposes the *fifingi* continues to exist and will still be visible (as in our dreams of dead people). Normally, nothing further can be said about the *fifingi*; beyond appearing in dreams it has no effectiveness. It is not identical with the dead whose disembodied souls may act as the guardians of the living or be invoked in sacrifices: these souls or spirits represent that other entity, the *kuci*, to which we shall presently return. But in certain cases the *fifingi*, too, are active after death; they are said to find no rest, to haunt houses or localities, scare travellers, and to cause nightmares when they visit people in their dreams. This happens when a person, having died an unnatural death or in a strange place, was buried without the proper rites; in which case a symbolic burial *in absentia* will lay the ghost. More vaguely one also believes that evil persons are similarly condemned to wander about restlessly after death. In either case, however, it is not really

[1] This rule refers specifically to conception, not to sexual intercourse; for the parents may practise *coitus interruptus*.

the *fifingi* which acts in this fashion, although one may loosely use this term; for in the cases just described the shadow soul turns into something else—a *fará*, a ghost or spirit.

As I have already suggested, the *kuci* corresponds to something like a 'personal soul'. But this is an obscure conception, and all informants will at some stage of the discussion plead ignorance or the presence of a final mystery. The Nupe believe in reincarnation, the souls of the dead being re-embodied in their offspring; it is these transmuted souls which are called *kuci*. One does not in this connection think of distant and perhaps unknown ancestors, but of great-grandparents or even grandparents reborn in their children's children. The rebirth can occur in either line of descent, which fits well into the Nupe kinship system with its strong emphasis on bilateral descent. Whether the ancestors are paternal or maternal, as they are reborn, so their personal qualities, of character (good or bad) as well as physical likeness, reappear. The body, *nakā*, is thus partly shaped by the ancestral soul or *kuci*, which is said to 'enter' it much as a fluid or substance enters a vessel (while the *rayi* does not 'enter' the body but merely gives life to it).

The *kuci* appears in the act of birth, that is, it 'enters' a body already possessing life, and the new-born is in fact called 'a *kuci*', unnamed. For a time body, life soul, and *kuci* are not yet firmly united. Body and life soul merge fully when the umbilical cord is cut; but the *kuci* will not be in full harmony with the other two until it has been identified by divination and the infant's name (which is the name of the reincarnated ancestor) has been pronounced for the first time. The crying of the babe, too, will cease at that moment, since it is only a sign that the new-born senses the initial disharmony. In other words, the three components of the living being become reconciled when the link between human vessel and ancestral soul is acknowledged socially, that is, by the symbol of a name. Only then does the *kuci* lose its other-worldly nature and become fully of this world; while the infant is from then on a person, and not only a breathing body. Henceforth it will be called *egi*, child, and no longer *kuci*, disembodied soul or spirit. The *kuci* therefore adds to the *anima* or life soul a 'personal soul', which is also the carrier of heredity and of kinship continuity.

It is difficult to say just how personal this soul concept is. It is certainly specifically human; for animals have no *kuci*, as they have no names or kin groups. Yet the relationship between the ancestral *kuci* and its reincarnation is not of a one-to-one kind. The same ancestral soul may animate numerous progeny, all living at the same time; indeed, it is said that there 'is no limit' to the number of simultaneous incarnations of the same *kuci*. Here, then, the *kuci* appears as an impersonal principle of descent and heredity, even as something like a biological strain mystically interpreted. It is consistent with this latter conception that the *kuci* should be held to be sexless, so that the soul of either grandparent may appear in offspring of either sex. This theory, however, is belied in practice; for I have found few personal names that can be given both to males and females; rather are male and female names sharply distinguished, which would presuppose the opposed assumption of a sex-linked reincarnation. And once, when I was present during the divination of the *kuci* of a new-born child and commented on the likely identity of the *ndakó* (grandfather) in question, the diviner corrected me, pointing out that the child was a girl and that her soul would therefore come from a *nnakó* (grandmother).

The two conceptions, of a 'personal' and of a 'kinship soul', conflict, above all, in the beliefs concerning their fate after death. At death, the *kuci* is said to leave the body and to return to God, if only temporarily, until it finds a new incarnation. Yet it is also said to stay on earth, watching over its kinsfolk in the manner of a guardian spirit and ready to come to their aid in various ways. The *kuci*, incidentally, does so indirectly, having no power of its own, but acting in some fashion through *Sokó*. To enlist the aid of the *kuci*, one performs special sacrifices (*labá*) in the house or on the grave of this or that ancestor. Now, such a belief in the souls or spirits of the dead which, while not at the time incarnated, interest themselves in their surviving kin, would seem to reconcile satisfactorily the two conceptions of a personal soul and one bound to lines of descent. But Nupe belief failed to work out a consistent solution on these lines. Thus the ancestral sacrifices are performed both on the grave of the grandfather most recently dead (and hence hardly yet reincarnated) and on the grave of the most remote known ancestor (who will surely have found a new body). And if, in the latter case, one knows of one outstanding person among the ancestors, the sacrifice will be addressed to him. On the other hand, one need not sacrifice to any particular, named ancestor at all; often, the people address an anonymous *kuci*, that is, the souls of the dead in a generic sense. This is done invariably, in an informal fashion, whenever one drinks beer; then a small libation is poured on the ground, for a *kuci* no further defined.

There is no orthodox answer to the question how the *kuci* can be 'with God' and on earth at the same time, or how it can influence God when it has already entered upon another incarnation. When pursuing this point I received these diverse replies. A first informant made the revolutionary suggestion that there might be two *Sokó*, one in the sky, the other on earth; needless to say, this notion was rejected by everybody else. A second view was more widely held, namely, that the *kuci* remains on earth but is watched by God, so that your appeal to the *kuci* will yet reach God; the *kuci*, then, would be 'with God' only in a metaphorical sense. A third informant argued as follows, with somewhat dubious logic: Since you cannot see either God or *kuci*, it follows that they are together. Finally, there was the unprofitable but incontrovertible reply, that here we have a mystery of which 'man is ignorant'.

If the Nupe failed to work out a clear and consistent conception of this survival of 'personal souls', they equally failed to exploit its potentialities. The belief in souls of the dead which remain concerned with the fate of their living kin and are reincarnated in progeny would seem to lend itself ideally to an ethical interpretation. Yet there is no trace of this. There is no conception of the *kuci* being angered by the sins or offences of the living, perhaps refusing its aid or sending punishment. In appealing to the *kuci* the suppliant expects help, not rewards, and help untempered with justice; the help may not come; but this only means that the circumstances were unfavourable or the difficulties too great. Nor is the fate of the soul after death affected by the deeds or character of the living person. It is the same for good men and evil, and the idea that the two might fare differently in the beyond is simply not understood. 'When a person dies, we no longer see him', is all the Nupe find to say on this topic. Which is another facet of that ethical indifference we noted before.

The *kuci* is invariably invoked in the ceremonials surrounding the crucial events of kinship life—birth, marriage, death. Apart from this, *kuci* worship has no special domain, nor is it subject to any regular routine. The sacrifices to ancestors represent casual appeals, performed *ad hoc*, for a variety of reasons, and nearly always on the advice of diviners. Of ten informants one had performed the sacrifice three times in the last four years, because of his ill-health; one had sacrificed twice, first because his horse was sick, and then because his child had smallpox; six informants had sacrificed once during that period—three because of illness, two because of a drought, and one for no particular reason and without consulting a diviner. One informant had performed no *kuci* sacrifice for seven years, and another had sacrificed regularly every year; but he was a village chief, and in his case the sacrifice, addressed to the ancestor who was also the founder of the village, had merged with a *kuti* 'belonging' to the community.

This fusion of *kuci* worship with another type of observance is not an isolated case. As we shall see, it is also entailed in the possession of certain 'great', hereditary medicines, which similarly absorb the appeals to ancestors. This is only another aspect of their lack of a special 'domain'. And even where *kuci* worship does not lose its independence so completely, it yet has little autonomy; for the kind of supernatural aid it promises can equally be procured by other forms of worship or sacrifice. But of this, too, we shall speak later.

Let me conclude the present account with the brief mention of a further ambiguous practice, a form of sacrifice which stands halfway between an appeal to *Sokó* and the appeal to *kuci*. It is performed by families in which there are or have been twins and is known by that name, *bakomba*. Such houses will possess a special shrine, consisting of a number of small earthenware pots built into the outside wall of a hut, which the women will regularly fill with beer and porridge. Once a year, on the birthday of the twins, the family head will bring a sacrifice of beer and blood of fowl. Now, twins are lucky and a sign of divine benevolence; equally, they represent a special incarnation, a concentration as it were of the 'kinship soul'. In this sacrifice, then, one addresses *Sokó* as well as (an anonymous) *kuci*; and the people who have such a twin shrine will perform all their sacrifices to *kuci* there, and not over the grave of an individual ancestor.

(v) *Spirit Beings*

In the preceding discussion we touched upon certain beliefs in spirits—in 'ancestral spirits', which are an aspect of the personal soul, and in 'ghosts', which are transmutations of the shadow soul. But when the Nupe mention 'spirits' among the things that make up the world they do not mean either of these; they mean immaterial beings which exist in their own right and are not derived from humans, although they have some quasi-human attributes and inhabit the same earth. It is possible that this belief is not an original tenet of Nupe creed; for the Nupe call these spirit beings by a Hausa–Arabic name, *aljénu* (pl. *aljenúži*), and may well have borrowed certain of their aspects from Islam. However this may be, the Nupe do not regard this belief as in any way alien or 'borrowed'. And whether the name for spirits is Nupe or Arabic, it is a name, sharply distinguishing this class of beings from all others.

Though circumstantial and readily expressed, the spirit beliefs are fluid and far from uniform. The most varied opinions will not be thought unorthodox, but will be taken as evidence for the multifariousness of the spirit world. A first group of spirits, vaguely anthropomorphous but without distinct individualities, is said to inhabit the inanimate parts of nature, hills, trees, watercourses, the bush, and so forth. These spirits have sex, and according to some informants the female variety lives in the water while the males prefer the land. The sex of the spirits does not influence their character, which may be either friendly or hostile. The people know where 'good' spirits dwell as well as the places haunted by 'evil ones', and may perform sacrifices to keep their friendship or to ward off their malevolence. Small gifts to the spirits (called *efu*), consisting of a little food, honey, a few kolanuts or cowrie shells, are often left on the roadside, placed beside a spring, or dropped in the river. The behaviour of the good spirits is nondescript and consists in not doing evil or mischief rather than in doing anything positively beneficial. The hostile spirits act erratically and unpredictably, their actions ranging from meaningless pranks (such as throwing stones or making frightening noises) to the infliction of serious harm (causing lunacy or fever, or making pregnant women bear a deformed child). Any locality showing unusual or unnatural features, such as an unexpected clearing in the bush or a grassless patch in a meadow, is likely to be the dwelling place of a spirit; so is any uncommonly large tree in the bush. A woodcutter who is unable to fell a tree, a fisherman who loses his nets in the river for no apparent reason, would equally suspect the presence of an *aljénu*. At midnight, when there is 'no noise and sound', the spirits are likely to be abroad. But on the whole one pays little attention to these 'nature spirits', which can easily be foiled by simply avoiding the haunted locality and against which sacrifices are ample protection.

Only in the Niger valley have I recorded nature spirits ascribed more momentous power as well as names and individualities and worshipped in proper, full-scale rituals. We shall in due course speak of two of them, the spirit *Ketsá*, inhabiting the steep rock of that name which rises in mid-stream near Jebba Island, and the spirit suggestively called *Ndáduma*, 'Father Niger'.

A second group of spirits is vaguely associated with animals. I recorded only two isolated instances of fully-fledged beliefs in animal spirits. The first concerns a spirit called *Bukpe* which lives, in the shape of a crocodile, in a stream near Mokwa. It is supposed to be a male spirit, 'black' or evil, causing disease and drought. Yet its malevolence can be controlled by means of an annual ritual, known by the same name, and by means of a pact concluded between the people of Mokwa and the crocodile spirit. It is part of the pact that the people of Mokwa must never kill or annoy this or any other crocodile, while they in turn will not be harmed by any member of the species. This belief, however, is not willingly put to a test; when I visited *Bukpe* in his lair, my Nupe companions were very careful not to come too close. Some time after my visit the crocodile in fact killed a child; whereupon the people of Mokwa, true to the fiction of the 'pact', held a formal court, trying the animal for breaking the pact and passing sentence of death.[1] The power of Mokwa over crocodiles is well known all over Nupe country and, today at least, unrivalled. The village of Katcha, on a tributary of the Niger, apparently had a 'sacred crocodile' in the past; but the charm had failed to work and, less faithful to their cult (or less optimistic) than the people of Mokwa, the people of Katcha abandoned the practice.

My second instance comes from Pichi, a small village near Bida, and concerns a spirit said to be embodied in the leopards of that locality. Surprisingly, it is identified with one of the early chiefs of Pichi, many generations back, and known by his name, *Ndakó Yisa*, Grandfather Yisa; but since all Nupe invariably refer to leopards in this circuitous and respectful manner, and since Yisa is an extremely common name, I am inclined to regard this quasi-totemic interpretation as apocryphal. Nor is the belief very positively stated or accompanied by special rituals. The people believe, however, that no leopard will attack a person of Pichi, and in turn refrain from molesting the animal, even if it kills their dogs or goats.

If animals ever played a more momentous role in the Nupe universe, there is little evidence of it today. Some disconnected 'superstitions' and a few suggestions in folklore are the only instances of this kind. Thus the Nupe believe that animals, like men, have 'spirit doubles' (of which more presently) and that certain animals are also possessed of quasi-human or superhuman faculties. The attitude towards leopards is a case in point. Most villagers are convinced that if the respectful, indirect reference to 'Grandfather Yisa' were omitted, the leopards in the neighbourhood would be annoyed by this 'lack of courtesy' and would surely attack the village (though strict observance of the rule would not make them more amenable or friendly); but no attempt is made to explain the belief or to relate it to some other, more fundamental, tenet of the creed. Much the same applies to 'Father Tortoise', *Ndakpa*, who is the hero of numerous tales, in which he plays the part of a would-be clever fellow who runs into various adventures, either amusing or containing a moral. A small red beetle which appears at the beginning of the rains is called *Sokó*, which odd nomenclature elicits only this comment: 'Since the

[1] The people told me afterwards that the crocodile had in fact died; when I pointed out that I had since seen it in the stream, I was assured that it was 'a different one'. The people of Jebba Island, incidentally, claimed that the river ritual *ketsá* similarly protected all riverain people from crocodiles; which claim was ridiculed by the proud owners of the crocodile cult in Mokwa, who at once recalled that three years previously a Kede man from the river had been killed by a crocodile.

insect heralds the season, it must surely be sent by God.' We may mention finally that the decorations of houses and the ornaments on leather or carved wood frequently display the outline figures of the 'mythical' animals leopard, tortoise, or crocodile; again, no deeper significance attaches to them; also, today at least, the figures of 'ordinary' animals as well as other designs are as often employed, being all meant 'for amusement only'.

The most interesting variety of spirits is also the one least clearly conceived. This is the personal spirit or spirit double, which belongs to every person from birth until death and cannot be shed or changed. Men have male, women female, spirit doubles, and both can be either good or evil; there is no accounting for the latter fact, which rests entirely 'with God'. The spirits are also of unequal strength and often jealous of one another, forcing their own feelings of hostility upon their human counterparts. The success of a marriage, for example, will be determined by the manner in which the spirit doubles happen to agree. But the spirits are responsible only for the luck and fate of their human twins, not for their character or morals. A friendly spirit will protect its human twin; it will, for example, betray to him in sleep or dream the name of witches who try to harm him. More generally, the 'good' spirit can give wealth, prosperity, and success in everything, at least as much as its strength permits; a weak spirit might well fail in all these attempts; while 'bad' spirits would intentionally make their twins suffer nightmares, illness, and misfortune of all kinds.

Not every illness is of spirit origin; the illness which readily responds to treatment or has a well-understood physical origin (breaking one's leg, food poisoning, and the like), has nothing to do with spirits. Only stubborn or frequent ailments of obscure origin, and especially mental diseases, are ascribed to the spirit doubles. But again, this does not apply to every form of mental disorder. Thus the Nupe define idiocy in what are to them rational terms, as a mere 'deficiency' (*eti a gbà o*—'the head is insufficient'), and point out that it often goes together with bodily deformities. Like the latter, mental deficiency 'simply happens', for example, owing to some carelessness of the expectant mother. 'Raving lunacy', however, is invariably caused by spirits; and, let us note this, since the spirit doubles are part of divine creation, lunacy, being their gift, is ultimately a gift of God. Yet madmen are in no way vessels of divinity; rather are they instances of the misfortunes and evils which God inscrutably dispenses.

The belief in spirit doubles leads to curious consequences. If the power and morals of the spirit determine the success in life of its human double without determining also the character or morals of that human, it follows that good spirits can be wedded to evil persons and vice versa. 'Good' spirits might therefore grant success to the most evil machinations, and 'bad' spirits frustrate the best intentions of their human twins. Also, a good person, tied to a good but weak spirit, cannot hope to escape misfortune; while the misfortunes of an evil person who happens to possess an evil spirit double would be as blindly bestowed. All this fits well into a universe which *ab initio* contains good and evil, fortune and misfortune, without moral reasons. But here, in the realm of concrete personal fate, the amorality of the creed is most clearly noticeable. Yet it is so only for us; the Nupe worry little about the ethical issues. Only in one respect do they face these issues and resolve them by admitting this exception to the general rule: Witches always have evil spirit doubles, and these exercise their power, not against their human twins, but against the victims of the latter. But this modification of the spirit belief is slight; for the evilness of the spirit does not make the witch a witch; his or her evil nature is simply given and only aided by the congenial spirit.

A few of the men with whom I discussed these questions seemed prepared to reinterpret the belief in personal spirits more thoroughly. They held that all spirit doubles were 'good', not morally, but in the sense that they served their twins as best as they could. As the spirits were weak or strong, so they would be capable or incapable of gaining success for the human beings, whatever the morals of the latter. These were the views of a minority, and far from correcting the moral ambiguity of the creed they only added to its cynicism. But they seem to indicate a desire to correct another weakness in the creed, which strikes us as forcibly, namely, the supererogatory character of the spirit belief. Clearly, there is no need to make the spirits good and evil as well as weak and strong; the former distinction adds nothing in the way of explanations which the latter does not already furnish.

In a wider sense, the whole conception of personal spirits seems redundant since it accounts for nothing that is not already accounted for by other agencies. Owing to the spirits the human beings meet with fortune and misfortune; but the same fortuitous dispensation of good things and bad is ascribed to the very nature of the created world. The spirit doubles account for nightmares or helpful dreams, but so do the *fifingi* and *kuci*; they bring about illness, but this may equally be due to the weakening of *rayi*, to the attacks of witches, or (as we shall see) to acts of God. The spirit doubles cause afflictions of the mind, but these may again come from God or be rooted in the human body. Altogether, the Nupe creed seems without economy; diverse agencies are introduced to explain the same phenomena, and diverse supernatural aids are made to overlap in their aims or concerns. Thus one sacrifices to spirits, twins, kinship souls, and, through rituals, to God himself; or one uses *cigbe*; and one does so for the same reasons—to secure prosperity, to protect oneself from illness, or to safeguard fertility of man or nature. Even so, there is some design and order in this confusing picture; the Nupe universe is not entirely a random array of entities and mystic forces, but something of a cosmos. We shall, by way of a summary, try and outline its features.

4. RELIGION AND POLITY

First, however, I must mention an important figure in the Nupe creed which falls into none of the categories so far discussed—Tsoede or Edegi, the legendary first King of Nupe. The tradition of Tsoede and its essentially political symbolism has been discussed elsewhere, so that here a few remarks will suffice.[1]

Tsoede's memory survives in an elaborate cycle of myths, the only instance of this kind in Nupe; several rituals and sacred objects (an iron chain, brass bangles worn by chiefs, the bronze figures mentioned before) are said to have been his creation; and a specific cult also bears his name. Similar observances also exist, here and there, in the villages, relating to the ancestors of hereditary chiefs; they, too, are sometimes regarded as the founders of their communities or as the initiators of particular cults, their *kuci* being invoked in regular ceremonials. But Tsoede is much more than an ancestor chief magnified, and the rituals called after him do more than merely summon up his memory. Nor is it the *kuci* of Tsoede which is invoked. The concrete ties of descent, implicit in the worship of *kuci*, are obviously absent between the ancestor king and the vast, nation-wide congregation of his cult, while his 'personal soul' has no part in any cycle of rebirth.[2] In the rituals of Tsoede it is he himself who is invoked, so that he may intervene with *Sokó* on behalf of his people. The precise circumstances of this intervention are neither explained nor pictured in any way; yet one knows that it is more powerful as well as active than that accessible to *kuci* (which are merely 'watched by God').

If Tsoede is not a *kuci*, neither is he a 'spirit' nor *aljénu*. He represents, in fact, a figure outside the general framework of Nupe religion and a conception both anomalous and unique in Nupe

---

[1] See *A Black Byzantium*, pp. 72–76, 141–2.
[2] Tsoede is said to have been harelipped, and every Nupe child born with a harelip is still named after him. But this custom only serves to keep his memory alive; for it has no further consequences and does not imply any belief in Tsoede's reincarnation.

thought. He is a man-become-deity (though there is no pantheon where he could find a niche), a national hero turned into an ancestral being (though again, there are no named ancestors to whose ranks he might be added). Tsoede is the ancestor only of a line of kings; but in a wider and vaguer sense all Nupe within the kingdom regard themselves with pride as his 'offspring', in the sense, that is, that they were born in a country he founded and made great and come of stock which, originally, lived under his rule and supernatural protection. This protection, which still endures, bears on certain problems of life which are resolved also by means of other rituals or appeals to *Sokó*, namely, the ubiquitous problems of illness and fertility. But these are only incidental effects of Tsoede's mystic power; its main efficacy used to bear on political interests—the maintenance of the 'king's law', the punishment of criminals, and the protection of the 'King's Highway' on the river Niger.[1] Even the 'incidental effects' of the Tsoede cult are bound up with political interests, being embodied in material objects which are at the same time the paraphernalia of secular power. Let me only mention the 'Chain of Tsoede', which is believed to cure the sterility of women but which was formerly also used to strangle political offenders and to uncover crimes in the manner of an ordeal.

In brief, the Tsoede cult is essentially a State religion superimposed upon a pre-existing creed. The cult ties the people to supernatural benefits granted not simply by God, nor by a God who commands his own rituals, but by a God who listens to kings. And its rituals, no longer 'owned' by communities or kin groups, are aligned with the growth and pride of a nation.

5. THE NUPE COSMOS

I spoke before of the supererogatory character of certain Nupe beliefs. In a sense, the greater part of Nupe doctrine has this character. Consider that the Nupe hypothesize a deity who creates the world and then leaves it to itself—uncertain, full of obscurity and accident, and embracing good and evil in entirely fortuitous measure. With such a conception of the relationship between God and the world, the Nupe need not have speculated further about some deeper meaning behind the features of the universe. Anything that exists or happens in it would be sufficiently explained by that key concept of an aloof and non-ethical deity. One might, for example, imagine a religion starting from the same premisses which would leave all further explanations to the crude realism of naïve common sense. Whether so unambitious a theo-

[1] See my article on the 'King's Hangmen' in *Man*, 1935, 143.

logy is ever likely to arise, I will not venture to discuss. The point is that Nupe theology is more ambitious; the Nupe do speculate further, and reckon with a great many additional (or 'supererogatory') existences and influences. They seem to feel the need to do justice to the particular features of the world by means of particular conceptions, over and above its broad justification in terms of divine creation.

This proliferation of thought is, of course, not peculiar to Nupe religion, though we may note that the Nupe ignore many 'particular' features which other religions feel compelled to acknowledge and elaborate. Thus the Nupe find nothing to explain about the heavenly bodies, do not concern themselves specifically with lightning, thunder, or rain, and speculate only vaguely about animals or natural features. Instead, their attention is focussed upon health and disease, birth and death, fertility, misfortunes, dreams, that is, upon things human. The Nupe elaboration of the universe, we might say, is anthropocentric.

Yet it concentrates on natural man, not on the moral being. Again it neglects all features which might serve this kind of conception, such as an after-life promising reward or retribution, or natural catastrophies that might signify divine anger or warning. Even where the ethical interpretation suggests itself forcibly it is ignored; thus the metamorphosis of the soul stands apart from any ethical design; the powers of good and evil spirits descend on man at random, and the success or failure of supernatural appeals, to ancestors or even to God, do not reflect upon the moral worthiness of the suppliants. There are a few vague notions of divine retribution. Thus it is admitted, but never spontaneously vouchsafed, that incest is punished by barrenness and blindness, and that persons guilty of concealed crimes may be punished by the *kuti* (in an unspecified manner) or killed by lightning (in the case of theft). But these half-hearted concessions do not alter the picture of a creation devoid of moral purpose.

Are, then, all the 'additional influences' which the Nupe read into creation and all their 'further speculations' merely attemps to 'do justice to the particular things in the world', and no more? It may well seem so. There seems to be no other, ulterior, motive behind the readiness to ascribe the contrariness of a tree or the uncanniness of a locality to spirits rather than to nature just-so created; behind the belief that certain ailments betray the machinations of spirits or witches over and above the weakening of the *anima*, and perhaps natural causes; or behind the subdivision of mental afflictions, which are traced to spirits, to the vagaries of the body, and to God. But consider also that these diverse explanations are not kept apart, by some economical parcelling-out of the universe;

rather, they mostly represent alternatives and overlap for the same phenomena. And since each explanatory conception entails a different notion as to the controls or remedies applicable to the phenomenon in question, the multiplication of the former means also a multiplication of the latter. In other words, you have several strings to your bow. Indeed, this is doubly true. For as we know, the overlap in explanatory conceptions is matched by the overlap in the supernatural aids themselves; like the appeal to the *kuci*, which has 'no domain', ritual and even certain forms of medicine have a wide and multifarious efficacy. The lack of economy of thought thus means first, that the map of the universe is drawn in greater detail, and second, that in coping with its forces one has the chance of several trials.

Now, the 'details' in the universe are not multiplied at random. Rather are they ordered in the sense of two principles. The first reflects the organization of human society as the Nupe see it. Thus there is the sphere of the fate of communities, governed by influences irreducible beyond the givenness of creation and anonymous beyond their ultimate origin in God, which influences are controllable by the collective efforts of *kuti*. Then there is the sphere of individual fate, governed by the specifically named agencies of life soul, shadow soul, witchcraft, and spirits (personal or otherwise), and controllable by *cigbe* and individual sacrifices. There is, further, the sphere of kinship fate, governed by the agency of *kuci* and controlled by sacrifices to ancestors and twins. And there is, finally, the sphere of the kingdom and political fate, with its special rituals of Tsoede. Admittedly, these various spheres are not as neatly separated, the social appropriateness of supernatural aids like the social import of supernatural influences overlapping at many points. Certain nature spirits also affect the fate of communities and hence call for the effort of ritual, while a drought, though it threatens the community, can also be dealt with by an invocation of *kuci*. Certain medicines are owned by kin groups, and certain *kuti* can be invoked by individuals; the twin sacrifices are addressed to God, like the *kuti*; witchcraft, though it attacks individuals, may be treated as a threat to the community or state; and the 'royal' cults of Tsoede also serve to meet the needs of individuals. If there were no such overlap, the chance of 'several trials' would not be as great as it is. But neither is it unlimited, being subject to that hierarchy of social appropriateness, which is only a little blurred by these ambiguities.

The second principle is purely theological and integrates the speculations about the 'details' of the universe with the basic dichotomy of God and the World; for this is carried even into the realm of things found in the world. Thus certain things come directly from God, such as the power of *kuti* or the life principle, while others indicate his presence only indirectly or ultimately, in that they are part of creation or happen in it. This is true of *cigbe*, of the nature spirits, and of various diseases and misfortunes. We might say that God willed certain things, while he permits or suffers others to exist. In other religions, a similar dualism might follow from the assumption of divine omnipotence, serving to vindicate the latter in the face of the evils in the world. In Nupe, it follows from the belief in a single act of creation, performed by an aloof creator disinterested in the progress and day-to-day fate of his work. For the two things which are most conspicuously 'willed' by God are also exceptions to this tenet; that is, they vindicate, though not the goodness of the deity, at least his continued concern with the world he called into being.

First, there is the conception of *kuti*, by means of which man can break through the aloofness of the deity. That this is so, is part of God's willed creation; but through investing man with this supernatural tool, God is committed to further acts upon the world he already fashioned once and for all. These renewed acts are only intermittent and in a sense casual, being contingent upon the human appeals; furthermore, man is also competent, and permitted, to fashion similar tools for himself. Thus the created world has some independence and some development of its own, as its human creatures have some inventiveness and will of their own. The second exception goes much farther, implying the continuous creative activity of God. The renewal of life on earth, more precisely, the bestowal of *rayi* upon animate beings, is conceived of in this fashion. This was made clear to me by means of a parable meant to elucidate the relationship of *rayi* and *kuci*. On the surface, the two seem alike, both leaving the human body at death and 'returning to God'. But in one case it is like throwing an object skywards which will soon afterwards drop down again by itself; in the other, you must imagine someone up above who would catch the object, so that it stays in his hands; so the *kuci* goes up to God and returns to find a new incarnation, while the *rayi* goes up and is 'held by God'. The life soul, then, returns to God in the sense that it is re-absorbed in the process of creation; every time it appears on earth, it is a new, separate manifestation of the divine will. The personal or kinship soul, which returns to God only for a while, is independent of this continuous creation; it is as it were continuous in its own right, having its own cycles or chains of existence, which essentially correspond to the empirical cycles or chains of generations. So that it stands, once more, for the world 'left to itself'.

Yet let me admit that in all other respects the dualism of God and the world is less sharply conceived than we have phrased it. It is blurred, above all, by the ambiguity of that crucial phrase 'of God'.[1] We can now define it more sharply: The Nupe will generally assert that only certain things in the world are *nya Sokó*, and that others are not; but, when pressed, they will admit that even these 'independent' entities are yet known to God and must in some sense be by his will. Nupe theology, in other words, has not refined its conceptual tools sufficiently to carry this dualism to its logical conclusion. The contrasted concepts which we employed, of things 'willed' by God as against those he only 'suffers' to exist, is beyond its capacity or intentions. Yet the Nupe do express something of the kind in a different way, by default as it were rather than in positive statements, for they leave the share of God in the creation of these 'independent' things of the world unemphasized, like matters that are unimportant and of no consequence. Thus it is important and always stressed that God gave life and ritual to man; and it is unimportant and not normally mentioned that in some fashion divine creation also includes *cigbe*, illness, the shadow soul, evil spirits, lunacy, and witchcraft.

I would read a further meaning into this unequal emphasis of the divine share in creation. It suggests, it seems to me, an attempt to gloss over the philosophical difficulties entailed in this conception of a creation which is imperfect and neutral with regard to good and evil. These difficulties might have been resolved in a more sophisticated theology by some pseudo-Thomist doctrine, equating the divine design of the world with perfection and making the world 'left to itself' the source of all imperfections and evils. Yet though Nupe doctrine fails to furnish any such vindication of divine providence, the failure can at least be concealed by the manner in which the doctrine is handled, through emphasis here and 'glossing over' there. These attempts are never more than crude and half-hearted; but the motives behind them are, I think, unmistakable. Indeed, in one instance they even intrude upon the formulated doctrine; and this relates, significantly, to the one form of evil which is specifically and unreservedly ascribed to the deity.

The two most dreaded diseases are in this sense 'of God'—sleeping sickness (*kpatsŭgi*) and leprosy (even called *Sokó 'gŭ* or *sokogŭci*—the 'Illness of God'). Now, God did not pre-ordain them in their deadly form; he created only their possibility, while the actual evils are a consequence of the 'world left to itself', that is, of accident and unpredictable circumstances. When creating man, God placed leprosy and sleeping sickness into every human organism, but he created the two diseases both in male and female form, and an organism possessing one form only remains healthy and

[1] See above, p. 10.

normal. The actual disease materializes when the two forms happen to be combined in the same person, and the prospects of a cure depend on which 'germ', male or female, is the stronger. Predominantly male leprosy is curable, predominantly female leprosy, fatal. In the case of sleeping sickness everything depends on the treatment, though the prospects are bleak in either case; if a *cigbe* expert succeeds in killing the male 'germ' only, the disease will take its fatal course; in the opposite case death at least will be avoided, though another incurable disease, lunacy, will result.

This is once more a half-hearted vindication of divine providence; all it attempts to prove is that creation is not necessarily evil and that evil things slip into it by chance. Fundamentally, the whole Nupe universe is thus ruled by accident. Such benevolent design as is discernible in it is all too vulnerable and all too easily vitiated by the coexistence of evil. Yet neither are evil and malevolence more securely established. It is true that there is no real struggle between the two, as between opposed wills or destinies, but only the casual share-out of fortunes and misfortunes. Even so there are grounds, if not for an inspiring faith, yet for its cruder version, optimism. And to this, as we shall see, the Nupe firmly cling.

This is not, however, the whole picture. Our view of Nupe religion is still one-sided, based as it is on the doctrine alone, on ideas asserted, taught, and learned as such. Another kind of faith or assurance, less articulate but perhaps more powerful, may spring from the concrete acts of worship, that is, from the psychological stimulations and experiences gained in ritual and other observances. With these the following chapters will deal.

For the moment we need point out only one of the consequences of the Nupe conception of the universe. Clearly, it vouchsafes little certainty or guidance for action. Even the promises of supernatural aid only add to the uncertainties, for as they offer the chance of several trials so they confront the user with the problem of choice, which problem is not always readily solved. But the Nupe universe holds out some promise of certainty and some guidance for action. Both are mechanical and of a case-to-case kind; in other words, they are such as divination can offer. And since this guidance is required both for the problems of everyday life and for the handling of the supernatural tools meant to aid man in these problems, divination becomes a prerequisite, not only of provident action in general, but also of religious actions. It seems logical, therefore, to turn to divination first, and afterwards to ritual, medicine, and to all the other 'supernatural tools'.

II

DIVINATION

WE shall deal with two methods of divination, both of which are known throughout the country and applied on all occasions, trivial as well as serious. The first, called *eba*, consists in throwing strings of shells and resembles in technique the *ifa* divination of Yoruba; the second, *hati*, is of Mohammedan origin and involves drawing mystic patterns in the sand.[1] The two methods appeal to a somewhat different public, the former being practised mainly in the villages and pagan districts, the latter in the sophisticated capital, Bida. The division, however, is far from rigid; also, as we shall see, the two methods share certain essential features in spite of the difference in technique and religious background.

Two other types of divination, which are used infrequently and mainly on minor matters, and which are known only in the river area, may be disregarded. One, called *evo* ('cowrie shells'), is a simplified version of the method of *eba*. The other, called *kpápagi* ('tortoise'), employs the dried, hollowed-out body of a tortoise, which is made to slide down a taut string. This is a crude oracle, permitting only three answers—'yes' (if the tortoise glides down quickly), 'no' (if it does not glide down at all), and 'doubtful' (if it glides down slowly).

I. THE MECHANICS OF EBA

The method of *eba* is far from uniform. Although the divining apparatus itself and the principles of interpretation are the same everywhere, the 'key' used by the diviner, his invocations, and his minor paraphernalia may differ from locality to locality, even from one person to the other. This scope for variety does not extend to the attitude assumed in the act of divining. The eight men I observed all went through their act in a serious and tense mood, their gestures and utterances from time to time rising to an excitement which lent to the proceedings a thoroughly dramatic atmo-

---

[1] The Nupe term *hati* appears to be a corruption of the Arabic *hatim*, 'seal', 'magic square'; cf. the corresponding Hausa term *hatimi*.

sphere. One diviner, indeed, behaved in an almost hysterical manner. The clients in turn were shy, spoke little, and behaved in the presence of the diviner with the same visible restraint and, occasionally, awe which the Nupe bring to the esoteric part of a religious ceremony.

The diviner's apparatus includes two sets of objects, the divining strings themselves, and a series of marked slabs which serve as the 'key' for interpreting the throws. The former consist of eight cords of hemp, each strung through four perforated, hollow half-shells, placed equidistantly along the cord, about three inches from one another. The cords end in four strands, covered with small rings made of hollowed-out berries and cowrie shells; these cord-ends have no importance in the actual divining, being merely ornamental tassels, though it seems significant that they are again four (or eight) in number. The divination fastens upon the four half-shells, which are called *kpyekpya* and are made either of the shell of sheanut or of the kernel of the dompalm; in either case the bundle of eight cords is referred to as *vúnkpara*, 'white shell' (of sheanut). The diviner starts the proceedings by placing the eight cords on the ground, in parallel rows and pointing away from him, all shells being turned open side down. He then picks them up at the middle, two at a time, holding one in each hand, and throws them down again, once more in parallel rows. When this has been repeated four times, that is, when all the cords have been picked up and thrown, the diviner will interpret the pattern of shells as they happened to fall, open side up or closed side up. The procedure is called *sa 'ba*, 'to cast the *eba*', or for short, *esa*, 'the casting'. The diviner himself is known, accordingly, as *ebásaci*, 'One who casts the *eba*'.[1] The interpretation of the pattern thrown does not, however, consist merely in counting up the shells, but involves a more complicated calculation which requires certain aids to memory and a definite 'key'.

These are provided in the second set of objects, which is included in the generic name for the whole divining apparatus, *eba*. It consists of eight small, roughly square slabs cut from gourds, each of which bears a different series of point-like marks. The point-designs are known as *emi* or *kata*, that is, 'house', which nomenclature will become clear presently. The diviners employ two further paraphernalia, which play no part in the actual interpretation of the *eba*, a hippopotamus tooth, and a round or wedge-shaped stone about the size of a fist. Throughout the proceedings the diviner will poke the tooth or stone at the divining cords as though he wished to prod them into activity or to aid some process that

[1] The diviner is also called, by the Hausa name, *boka* or (the Nupe-ized version) *boci*.

is going on in them. This act is in fact intended to 'bring out the truth' and to help the shell cords to 'give speech'. The hippopotamus tooth is sometimes replaced by the tooth of a warthog, but no reason can be quoted why it should be one or the other; nor have these two animals any mystic or mythical connotation. The stone, on the other hand, is known as *sokógba* ('stone of God' or 'thunderbolt') and is always claimed to have 'fallen from the sky'; when pressed, however, the diviner will usually admit that he either simply found the stone or obtained it from a friend. Its round shape and smooth surface seem to be the main reasons for the choice, the nature of the stone being unimportant. Several diviners of my acquaintance used ordinary pebbles; one had a piece of quartz, another a piece of iron ore which, I discovered, came from disused iron ore workings in the neighbourhood. The diviner is also free to add to these paraphernalia at his own discretion; one of my diviner friends who had been working, in the conventional manner, with a hippo tooth and stone, had added a chameleon to his apparatus when I visited him after an interval of a few months. He had found the animal in the bush, which meant that it 'must be a gift from *Sokó*', claimed that it understood what he said, and employed it by throwing it from time to time at the divining cords. Judging from the behaviour of the onlookers, he had indeed acquired an impressive and uncanny tool.

The sketch opposite shows four different sets of *eba* slabs used by Nupe diviners. They are numbered from right to left, and are shown in the order and position in which the diviner places them on the ground, with the lower edge towards him. Series (*a*) and (*b*) are used in Bida and the surrounding district, including the Beni village of Doko; series (*d*) comes from another Beni village, Pichi; series (*c*) from Jebba Island.

The fourth slab in each series is sometimes placed face down on the ground, since it indicates misfortunes which the diviner wishes to ignore if not to spirit away. Although the markings differ widely in the four series they are supposed to be merely different versions of the same thing. One diviner used both set (*a*) and (*b*), considering that the latter set was simpler to read', since it showed only the marks that 'counted' and omitted those which had no significance.[1] Equally, the diviners will insist that there is a close correspondence between the markings on the slabs and the patterns of open or closed shells thrown in the strings, and will go to great length to prove it. They would argue, for example, that each pair of holes on the slabs corresponds to one shell thrown open

---

[1] The same diviner also taught me the art of *eba*. He first used set (*a*) but later brought along the second set, since he 'could see that I found the other too difficult'.

DIVINATION

side up, and each single hole to a closed shell; or that only the upper (or lower) halves of the slabs count in this calculation. None of these explanations, however, proves correct; in reality, the markings are entirely irrelevant and cannot even by a *tour de force* be harmonized with the varying combination of open and closed shells. What counts is not the markings on the slab, but the order

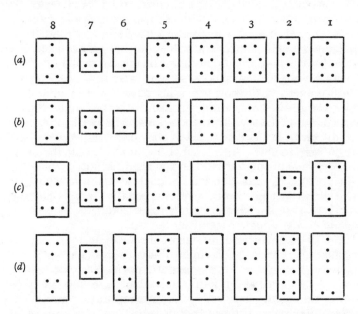

of the latter and the significance attached to each of the eight positions in it; for it is this position which is linked (quite arbitrarily) with the various possible 'throws' and gives the 'key' to their meaning. This connection is illustrated, for series (*a*), (*b*), and (*c*), in the diagram below; the position in the series of eight is indicated by the respective numbers; shells falling with the open side up are shown as rings, shells falling with the closed side up, as dots.

2. NOMENCLATURE AND INCANTATIONS

Though the markings on the slabs and the corresponding patterns of open and closed shells vary so widely, the significance attributed to their numerical order and the names given to them in that order are largely identical in all forms of *eba* divinations. To begin with, the shell patterns are called, generically, *etsuži* (sing. *etsu*), that is, 'kings' and are usually referred to by their number in the series, for example, '*etsu* three is a good *etsu*' (i.e. propitious), and so forth. Then there is a name for each 'house', that is, for the position which the slabs or shell patterns occupy in the series of eight. Two names, finally, refer to the slab markings themselves and to the corresponding patterns of open and closed shells. These last two names represent a sort of code, indicating the meaning attributed to the markings and shell patterns. One refers to the upper half of the slab and to the respective shell pattern lying 'straight' (i.e. as shown in our diagram); the other, to the lower half of the slab and to the shell pattern turned upside-down. Normally, only the first 'code' name is quoted; and when any shell pattern appears in reverse it usually changes not only its name but also its meaning, sometimes assuming, by a simple symbolism, the opposite significance.

The eight combinations of open and closed shells shown in our diagram are those the diviner would first demonstrate when explaining the system, the 'standard positions' as it were. But since for each string of four shells there are sixteen different throws, the eight standard positions represent only half the number of possible throws; that number, then, is completed by allowing for the reversal of the 'standard position'. By the same means the diviner can also double the range of his interpretations.

Even so, certain additional rules and provisos must be brought in. Certain slabs, for example, have symmetrical markings, so that their 'upper' and 'lower' halves coincide; in this case the second name, which corresponds to the reversed throw, refers to the (blank) back of the slab. Again, two strings in their standard position—Nos. 6 and 3 in (*a*) and (*b*), and Nos. 8 and 6 in (*c*)—show the same shell pattern when reversed; here the 'reversed pattern' is obtained by counting open shells as closed and *vice versa*. Furthermore, series (*a*) contains among its standard positions two throws (Nos. 1 and 8) which are the reverse of one another; they also have roughly opposite meanings, prophesying good fortune and disaster respectively. Since here one particular combination and its reverse are both included among the eight standard positions, another possible combination of shells must obviously be missing; if this missing combination occurs in a throw

DIVINATION

it remains meaningless in this series. Let me note finally, that not every shell pattern in reverse has a special meaning; in other words, the range of interpretations utilized by the diviner lags behind the mathematical possibilities of his system.

We need not point out specially that one series includes among its standard positions throws which do not occur in the other or occur there only in reversed position. It will be agreed, I think, that there is a great deal of arbitrariness and even haphazardness in this system of divination. The cause may well lie in the manner in which the rules of divination have been transmitted from generation to generation or spread from one community to another; this arbitrariness would thus reflect errors in the learning and memory of individuals and perhaps unwitting variations which crept into the practice. As we shall see, the system of divination is in fact taught, learned, and handed on in a purely practical and often fortuitous fashion, with none of the sacred or ritual sanctions which would make for strict adherence to given rules. However this may be, in the following discussion I propose to ignore the different variants and exemplify the method of divination on one series, that marked (*a*) in our list.

These are the names of the eight 'houses' and the 'code names' for the markings and throws, both in 'standard' and 'reversed' position:

	8	7	6	5	4	3	2	1
Name of 'House'	*Kuti*	Road	Man	Woman	House of Diviner	Town	House	*Sokó*
Code name stand. pos.	Crowd	Arab	Wretch	Hole	Offerings	Monkey	Witchcraft	Divination
Code name rev. pos.	Hiding	Wound	Receiving (gifts)	Needle	Danger	Begging	*rusu*	Rain

The translation of the 'code names' entails considerable difficulties since the words are often given an unusual or cryptic meaning; nor can the diviners themselves always state it in more than tentative fashion. The code name for No. 8 in reversed position, for example, is *shikã*, which means normally 'dirt'; but the diviner suggested that in this context the word represents a contraction of two verbs, *shi*, meaning 'to be dark', and *'kã*, to 'hide from sight'. Again, the name for No. 4 in standard position is *nyikã*, 'fish'; but here it is taken to refer, not to the zoological species, but to the ritual offerings of fish. The name *rusu* for No. 2 is altogether untranslatable, though the diviner held (without any etymological evidence) that it meant 'foreknowledge of evil things'. I suspect that much of this is pure speculation, put forth to disprove the apparent arbitrariness of the names. The diviners are certainly convinced that there is a definite logical connection between the names for the 'houses', the code names for throws and markings, and the prophecies based on both, and in order to demonstrate it they will resort to the most far-fetched and circuitous explanations. Here is one such glossary, alleged to prove the connections underlying the threefold terminology.

No. 1: Both divination and rain come from *Sokó*.

No. 2: A house (*emi*) has a family head (*emitsó*), who wields 'power'; witchcraft equally gives power; and people also have foreknowledge of witchcraft (through dreams).

No. 3: The monkey is an animal, that is, one of many; in the 'town' there are many human beings, some of them beggars.

No. 4: The diviner often receives gifts of fish, while his craft entails certain mystic dangers.

No. 5: The 'hole', like the eye of a 'needle', stands for the vagina and hence for 'woman'.

No. 6: The 'man' consulting the diviner is often 'wretched', that is, worried over his possessions; while the prophecy connected with this 'house' bears on personal possessions (i.e. on what one 'receives').

No. 7: 'Arabs' are mostly traders and thus travel on the roads; on the roads, there are also robbers who may attack and wound travellers; thus the prophecies connected with this 'house' bear on trade and highway robbers.

No. 8: At the *kuti* there are 'crowds', and the *kuti* is also 'hidden'.

From the nomenclature we may briefly turn to the incantations which accompany the art of divining. 'Incantation' is not quite the right word; the Nupe speak of *emisa*, which is the term for the set and often elaborate forms of address required by Nupe etiquette.

Similarly each pattern of shells has its appropriate 'greeting', which the diviner utters when it appears among his 'throws'. Mostly he mumbles it as though speaking to himself, and the listeners cannot possibly catch what he says. Nor could they make much of it even if they were interested (which they are not); for the meaning of these phrases is no less obscure than that of *eba* nomenclature. But now the diviner himself will admit this difficulty. Even my most knowledgeable informants, when trying to explain the *emisa*, gave up after a few attempts, saying that these were 'just greetings', and hence meaningless. Interspersed with meaningless words, however, one usually discovers decipherable phrases, which take the form of proverb-like sayings of nondescript character and of no striking appropriateness. Few of these sayings, incidentally, are today in common use or widely known. Their connection with the names for 'houses' or divining strings, if it exists at all, is vague, often purely verbal, and sometimes quite haphazard; the impression of haphazardness is further strengthened by the considerable diversity that occurs between the sets of *emisa* used by different diviners. A few examples will illustrate the character of these 'incantations'.

Throw No. 1, standard position: 'Fire of witchcraft, though red, will not burn the house'. This 'greeting' would seem to fit throw No. 2 much better; in another series it is replaced by the altogether cryptic allusion 'The devil is hungry.'

Throw No. 2, standard position: 'Dampness quietly causes the house to collapse.'

Throw No. 5, standard position: 'A burglar will not fall into a hole, though he may stumble on a slippery place.'

Throw No. 8, standard position: 'A large boat that would go into a narrow creek, you cannot build it: a crowd cannot go into a narrow place.' Replaced in another series by—'When the knees bend, the mouth should not joke' (i.e. you cannot work and play at the same time).

Throw No. 1, reversed position: 'The gown of a poor man will not (by itself) catch indigo; if he pays money, people will dye the gown for him. The poor man who becomes a grave-digger must hang his hoe on his back and walk from house to house' (i.e. even as a grave-digger, a poor devil will have to beg for custom).

Throw No. 2, reversed position: 'The leader who quarrels while pretending he wishes to prevent quarrel (is as bad as) a man who stabs you in the back.'

Throw No. 5, reversed position: 'He can sew but not wear (what he has sewn); when war eats a horse, the vulture is pleased' (which means, 'evil deeds find you out).

Throw No. 8, reversed position: 'A bushfowl breaks away from the birdlime; the only thing for it to do is to run fast' (and hide).

3. INTERPRETATION

We have, so far, been dealing only with the preliminaries of divination; this obviously consists in more than reciting the names for the 'houses' and divining strings or in knowing the appropriate formulæ of address. Nor is the diviner's skill exhausted when he is able to interpret the shell patterns in their fixed numerical order, rather is this only the first step. This order (illustrated in our diagram) shows each possible shell pattern in its appropriate place or, as the Nupe would say, 'each king in his own house'. It represents a model or 'key' series, on the basis of which the diviner must compute the meaning of the actual throws. These, of course, may fall anyhow, so that any one of the eight cords may show any one of the sixteen possible shell patterns; in other words, a particular shell pattern may appear in a 'house' other than its 'own'. The main problem of the diviner, therefore, is to interpret these irregular, transposed, throws, and it is here that the series of slabs acts as an aid to memory; for having the slabs before him in their fixed numerical order the diviner is kept aware of his 'key'. To quote one diviner: To know the names and 'greetings' and to interpret the throws 'in their own house' is easy—only a matter of 'remembering'; what is difficult and demands a 'good head' is 'to know the speech of the cords when they fall in a strange house'.

I have called this part of divining a computation; for such in essence it is. The diviner knows the meaning of the various places in the series of eight; he also knows the meaning of each possible shell pattern in the key series. In divining any actual throw he considers the juxtaposition of place and shell pattern, and arrives at an interpretation combining in some reasonable fashion the two meanings. If, for example, shell pattern No. 3, which, in the key series, means 'fortune', occurred in the seventh cord (or 'house'), which has the meaning 'road', then the diviner would argue that the actual throw must mean 'fortune acquired on the road', that is, in travel or trade. It is not easy to say how far the diviner reasons anew in this fashion every time he interprets an actual throw, or merely follows some remembered rule governing this and all other possible permutations. It is most unlikely, however, that he relies on remembered rules alone, since these would have to be far too numerous.[1] When demonstrating the system of divination for my benefit the diviners did in fact cite a number of

---

[1] To cover all possible permutations, there would have to be 112 such rules, ignoring the 16 rules for interpreting the key series.

possible permutations with striking readiness, which suggested that they were relying on well-memorized rules. But in the concrete case, when divining for clients, they sometimes arrived at different interpretations for identical throws. Sometimes, too, the diviner would repeat certain throws twice or three times before he seemed satisfied. The reasons for doing so were explained to me by this analogy: 'When you are told something important once only, do you believe it? No—you would wish to hear it twice or three times before you are satisfied that it is the truth. Similarly you must consult the cords several times.' But I suspect that by means of this repetition the diviner merely tries to obtain an arrangement he can more readily interpret. I would conclude, therefore, that the diviner relies on a number of remembered rules, covering certain set permutations, and interprets all others by *ad hoc* reasoning. In either case, he would also be guided by the questions put to him by his clients and by such knowledge as he happens to have of his clients, their interests, and the like.

To some extent, this kind of guidance is fully admitted; for in actual divining the different 'houses' and shell patterns vary in relevance according to the nature of the questions put by the client and the interests he is likely to have. When dealing with a trader, for example, the 'house' called 'road' will be the most important; in the case of a person concerned about the birth of a child 'house' No. 5 ('women') and shell pattern No. 2 (referring to fortunes or misfortunes befalling a family head) will be the most significant. Furthermore, the timing of the prophecies differs for the different shell patterns. The first three shell patterns have unlimited validity, bearing on the near as well as distant future; the prophecy of shell pattern No. 4 includes only the actual day of the divination, shell pattern No. 5, the next two days, shell pattern No. 6, an indefinite future, and shell patterns Nos. 7 and 8, the near future. The interest of the diviner in all the possible throws is thus narrowed down, and he will in fact acclaim the appearance of the relevant throws with much aplomb, while lightly passing over all others.

I have listed below all the interpretations referring to throws in the 'key' position and a number of interpretations of 'transposed' throws. The list is based on 'key' series (*a*), which I recorded in Bida.

Key position

Shell pattern 1—A great man, someone well known in the town, will die. Reversed—The nobility will be angry with the White Man.

Shell pattern 2—Some misfortune will befall the family head. Reversed—The family head will acquire greatness.

Shell pattern 3—Smallpox will visit the town in the rainy season, but there will be no deaths.

Shell pattern 4—The diviner will receive gifts. Reversed—Misfortune will threaten everyone, in the whole country.

Shell pattern 5—The women will quarrel. Reversed—Everyone in the country will enjoy good business; the women will have children.

Shell pattern 6—All the men (not the women) of the town will have grounds for distress, for example, because of the death indicated in shell pattern 1.

Shell pattern 7—Trouble on the highway.

Shell pattern 8—All the important people in the town will be happy.

Transposed position

Pattern 1 in house 2—Happy relations between the nobility and the White Man.

Pattern 1 in house 3—Many deaths.

Pattern 1 in house 5—Refers to menstruation.

Pattern 1 in house 7—There will be fights on the road, possibly death or murder.

Pattern 2 in house 1—Rain will fall; or—Happy relations between the nobility and the White Man.

Pattern 2 in house 4—Many deaths.

Pattern 2 in house 7—Pregnancy.

Pattern 3 in house 4—The diviner will receive a gift of a goat or sheep.

Pattern 3 in house 5—The women will quarrel among themselves.

Pattern 3 in house 6—Highway robbery.

Pattern 3 in house 7—War.

Pattern 4 in house 1—Many deaths.

Pattern 7 in any house other than 5—A guest will arrive.

Pattern 7 reversed in any house—A case of death.

Pattern 7 in house 5—Pregnancy.

Pattern 8 in house 1—There will be greetings and gifts for the nobility.

Pattern 8 in house 2—The client should stay at home and not travel.

Pattern 8 in house 3—Success in trade.

Let me note that different diviners, using a different key series, will also interpret it somewhat differently. Mostly, this merely means that the interpretations are moved about, from one place

DIVINATION

on the list to another, while the list as a whole remains unchanged. Sometimes, however, the lists themselves differ; though these differences are few, they bear relevantly on the social background of the diviner and the interests current in his setting. Thus the diviners in the villages interpret shell pattern 3 as meaning, on occasion, a 'good hunt', which interpretation does not occur at all in the list of the diviners in or near Bida town, where there is no hunting. Again, in the villages shell pattern 8 is sometimes taken to mean 'a council in the house of the chief'; the connection with the 'important people' mentioned in our version is clear; but in that version, coming as it does from the capital where there are no councils of elders or chiefs, the reference to a 'council in the house of the chief' would clearly be out of place. Conversely, shell pattern 1 reversed has in Bida a meaning which hardly affects the life in villages remote from the political difficulties and tensions of the capital; characteristically, in the villages the same pattern reads 'rain will fall', a prophecy which in turn has less importance for the townspeople. In one instance at least—the transposed pattern 2 in 'house' 1—the diviner's key allows for both these interests. I need not point out especially that it allows also for modern conditions and problems of a thoroughly topical kind.

Let me finally quote two examples of complete divinations. The first was performed for a canoe-man who was about to set out on a trip up the river. The cords fell as follows:

Cords	1	2	3	4	5	6	7	8
Shell patterns	6	2 rev.	4	7	3	4	2 rev.	1
Prophecies	The people will foregather	Refers to evening	A pleasant trip	Good trading	The women will pick quarrels	The men will be pleasant	Gifts for the chief	The *kuti* is friendly

The advice to the client was to be of good cheer: he should start out in the evening, take along gifts for the chief, and be careful in his dealings with women; he would return, after a successful trip, in four or five days (which last prophecy was nowhere indicated in the cords). The second divination was concerned with identifying the *kuci* of a boy just born to the client (a man). Here the diviner was interested only in the first two 'houses', the first referring to 'God', the second to 'House', that is, to the client's position of a family head. After several throws the diviner obtained this combination:

Cords	1	2
Shell patterns	4	6

whereupon he announced: 'The grandfather who begot your father—his name is that of the child.' The diviner would not explain his reasoning more precisely beyond saying that pattern 4 in 'house' 1, meaning 'many deaths', must relate to a *kuci* five 'deaths', i.e. generations, removed, while pattern 2 in 'house' 6 indicated the male sex of the *kuci*. Since the Nupe usually regard a great-grandfather as the most remote ancestor likely to be reincarnated, the diviner's reference to an additional generation would seem to be a plausible interpretation of a throw meaning 'many deaths'.

4. SOCIAL IMPLICATIONS

The names of the 'houses' and the meanings attached to the various throws, even in the simple key series, clearly illustrate the close connection between divination and social life. Among the names and meanings we find represented, not only the universal problems of men and communities (death, birth, rain, illness) or particular religious notions (*Sokó, kuti*, performance of sacrifices), but also the mundane interests typical of Nupe society. Events on the high roads and travel and trade; the ever-present social issue of 'greatness', that is, of success in the struggle for rank and status; and the equally ubiquitous interest in matters politic, chieftainship, councils of elders, the actions of the ruling class—all these have their place in the scheme of divining and partly even in its basic vocabulary. Similarly, each relevant social grouping is explicitly referred to: the 'house', that is, the large extended family under a family head (*emi*); the 'town' or village (*eži*); the 'whole country', that is, the kingdom of Nupe; and the class of the 'great men' and nobility. As we have seen, the diverse social settings of the capital and of the villages are reflected in certain variants in the rules of divination. These affect the individual case as well; for a diviner would interpret the prophecies referring to 'gifts' or 'greatness' differently when dealing with a *talaka* (a commoner or peasant) than when dealing with a member of the aristocracy. In the former case 'gifts' mean bowls of food and 'greatness' the favours of a nobleman; in the latter case the gifts turn into more valuable presents, and 'greatness' bears on promotion in rank and title. We have seen, too, that the rules of divination are far from static, having been successfully adapted even to recent conditions and to political problems only some forty years old. We can even point to a typical, transitional phase in this process; for the choice mentioned before, of interpreting the same throw as meaning either 'rain' or 'friendly relations with the White Man', means nothing else.

It is easy enough for the diviner to guess the status and background of his clients, and hence their likely interests, even if they are strangers to him. For dress and general behaviour reveal a good deal in Nupe; and the questions put to a diviner are usually sufficiently specific to give him such clues as he may need. Wellknown personages, incidentally, such as members of the high nobility, never consult a diviner in person; they send messengers who are not supposed to divulge the names of their employers. But these messengers are usually servants or retainers of the nobleman in question, and as well known as he.

Generally speaking, the Nupe diviner tends to be optimistic; if some trouble is forecast, the suggestion of a ready remedy or some warning easily observed would accompany the prophecy. I have, in fact, not met with any prophecy which was outright disastrous. Nor is the Nupe diviner given to cryptic statements; ambiguous though his technical vocabulary may be, his communications to clients are clear and straightforward. Occasionally he makes use of symbolic allusions, which are, however, readily understood; thus the mention of 'dark' or 'black' things means that the prospect is bleak or frightening; 'white' means luck and good prospects, while 'red' indicates wealth, ampleness, prosperity.

In order to gain a clear picture of the variety of problems on which diviners are usually consulted, I employed a crude statistical technique. I supplied four diviners with sheets of paper on which I drew rough pictures representing certain expected topics and instructed them to mark, underneath, their visitors, day by day for one month—a stroke for a man and a circle for a woman. Cross-strokes were meant to indicate repeated visits, while space was left for additional topics. It must be noted that all four men had a high reputation in their locality so that the size of their clientele, which proved to differ widely, did not reflect their unequal renown. Rather surprisingly, the largest and most regular clientele was that of a diviner in Bida, where I should have expected the competition of sand-divining to have spoiled the market for the pagan variety. The next best clientele was that of a diviner in Saci, a small hamlet near Bida, while the custom of two diviners in the heart of the country, in Kutigi and Jebba, was markedly smaller. The season of the year, incidentally, did not seem to affect the diviner's business.

The Bida diviner had thirty-seven male and twelve female visitors in a month (in March); of these five men had come twice, and one man three times. The diviner knew personally only one of his clients, who was his brother-in-law and came from Doko. The diviner in Saci was consulted twenty-eight times by men and twice by women (in January); three men had come twice, four men four times, and one woman twice. Again, he knew few of his clients personally, though he knew that they came in about equal proportion from Bida and from the hamlets nearby. The diviner on Jebba Island had six male and five female clients (in June), one of the women coming twice. Though Jebba Island is a small village it lies close to an important river port with a considerable floating population of traders, canoe-men, and other strangers. It is understandable, therefore, that, with two exceptions, the diviner's clients were all strangers. The diviner in Kutigi, finally, had four male and two female clients (in March): all were local people and well known to him.

The reasons for which the diviners were consulted varied characteristically with local conditions. In Bida, consultations about prospects of trade came first (in the case of both men and women); only a little less important were enquiries about projected journeys—when to set out, whether to travel at all, and so forth—and about the well-being of distant relatives whom the client thought of visiting; there were a few cases of men who consulted the diviner about marriages they had in mind, of men and women who desired children, and of others who wished to divine the name of a new-born child; very few consultations were about illness, and even fewer about favours which men of high status were anxious to obtain from the king. Excepting the last topic, the diviner in Saci had to deal with almost exactly the same set of problems. In Jebba, the order of topics was as follows—journeys and distant relatives; childbirth and naming of a new-born; trade; illness and enquiries as to the appropriate 'medicine' or sacrifice; and some unspecific requests for fortune-telling. In Kutigi much the same topics occurred, with the exception of enquiries about trade, which were absent in this predominantly rural community; enquiries about projected journeys and distant relatives were at the bottom of the list, which tallies with the geographically much more limited range of Kutigi marriages and movements in general. We note the absence of enquiries about projected marriages both in Jebba and Kutigi; the reason seems to be that in the villages marriage is much more rigidly laid down by custom and more firmly controlled by the kin group; the restriction of individual choice, then, obviates the need for the diviner's services.

A final reason for consulting the diviner, on matters of communal ritual, does not appear in our lists, mainly because they are based on random periods and hence apt to miss these relatively infrequent occasions. Consultations of this kind are the responsibility of the village chief or the *kuti* priest. They take place, less often on the occasion of the fixed, seasonal *kuti*, than at times when an unexpected misfortune threatens the community; in the former case, too, it is sometimes considered advisable to make sure of a propitious day; but in the latter case divination may be the only means for discovering the appropriate religious remedy. Let me mention in passing the widespread conviction that even the Emir of Nupe consults diviners (of the Mohammedan variety), in large numbers and 'for whole weeks at a time', to aid him in his multifarious problems: which belief, in spite of its circumstantial nature, is unsupported by such evidence as I could muster.[1]

One more word about the frequency of the visits one pays the diviner. For the townspeople no rule can be laid down; persons who seek advice on trade, travels, promotion in rank or other specific questions will obviously consult the diviner *ad hoc*, whenever the need happens to arise. It is somewhat different in the villages, where people also go to the diviner simply to have their fortunes told. Here individuals would pay fairly regular visits, once or twice a month, or at least once in two or three months. I have, however, spoken to villagers who had not been to the diviner for as much as five or six months.

The diviner is paid a small fee every time he is consulted. The fee is neither rigidly laid down nor claimed in advance. In Bida, the diviner is usually paid in money, though a bowl of rice or a few kolanuts may be thrown in, the client paying according to his ability, between a penny and sixpence. In the village one mostly pays in food or kolanuts. The diviners themselves regard the payments as 'gifts', and would strongly deny that they are divining 'for money'. No diviner could in fact live on what his skill earns him; nor does a diviner's reputation add in any way to his status in this rank-conscious society. Divining is merely an additional vocation, prized for the mystic wisdom and power it implies rather than for material or social gains.

This brings me to the last point, the social position of the diviner himself. Divination is essentially 'learning'—a skill that can be acquired by anyone having a 'good head'; if it is hereditary in a family it is so only incidentally. A great many diviners learned the art, in their youth, from another expert, paying for the tuition. One Bida diviner, for example, a man of about sixty-five, had learned divination when he was fifteen, studying for ten months, 'every day as in school'. Another had learned the craft from a stranger he met on his wanderings when a young man. Two diviners made an exceptional and unorthodox claim; while admitting that they had to acquire the skill, they maintained that they had 'learned it from God', by inspiration as it were. The majority of the diviners I met were also farmers; one was a barber by

[1] According to tradition, the old kings of Nupe had numerous official diviners among their retinue; this practice has certainly disappeared.

profession; the diviner in Kutigi was the head of the small group of 'hunters' in that community; while the diviner in Jebba held a high rank among the village elders and the priestship of an important *kuti*. Several diviners are medicine experts at the same time, so that they can treat as well as diagnose illness; those who are not must send their clients to a 'doctor' for the appropriate *cigbe*, unless of course their diagnosis reveals the kind of illness which only sacrifices and similar observances can cure.

Being a learned 'skill', divination is irregularly distributed. Bida, not unnaturally, has a great many diviners (though the majority are Moslem sand-diviners), both in the town itself and in the farming settlements outside. Doko, a moderately large village, has three diviners; Kutigi, a much larger place, and Jebba, a busy thoroughfare on the river, have only one each. Some villages have no resident expert; here the people would go to diviners in the neighbourhood, the diviners themselves being apparently unwilling to go 'on tour'.

Every diviner, apart from advising clients, also divines for himself and his family, either when confronted with some particular problem or on regular days (for example, every Friday in Kutigi). Furthermore, before his first divination of the day, the diviner must go through a particular procedure which in a sense consecrates his tools. Without at first using the marked slabs, he will throw the cords as often as is necessary to obtain the full key series. As each shell pattern appears in its proper place he puts the corresponding slab on the ground. In due course, the *sokógba* is placed between the 4th and 5th slab, that is, beside the slab referring to the diviner's own 'house'. While proceeding with his throws, the diviner mutters a kind of running commentary, thus—'Figures of the *eba*, join each other. Are your words (or signs) sufficient? They are not sufficient. There are three *etsu*, now there are four *etsu* . . . I have not yet extracted *etsu* (number) three . . .' So it goes on until the series is complete. At this stage the diviner says—'*To, Sokó da bo*', 'Good, God is there', turns all cords with the open shell face down, and is ready to begin the real divining.

In no other way does the diviner stand under special rules, restrictions or observances, with two exceptions. If he happens to refresh himself with beer while divining, as he often does, he would pour a little on his slabs, saying that this is 'for God', while the normal practice is to pour a little beer on the ground for the *kuci* or 'grandfather'. Again, while the *efu* gifts to spirits made by ordinary people are harmless, the diviner's gift harbours great danger for any person who would first catch sight of it after it had been placed on the wayside. To avoid this danger, the diviner would place his *efu* underneath some large tree in the bush where people are unlikely to pass. These two rules, then, and the 'consecration' of the diviner's tools with its reference to the presence of God, demonstrate the mystic power that attaches to divining and to those who handle it, and the sacred provenance of the skill. As we have seen, however, this evidence of sacredness does not content every individual; so that some will also claim that their whole knowledge is divinely inspired or that their paraphernalia are gifts of God.

Whatever status the diviner will claim for himself, for his art he will always claim the perfection of a well thought-out system, governed by rigorous, consistent rules, even though he must resort to far-fetched arguments to prove his case. Let us consider this point for a moment. The diviners clearly represent a selected group of individuals, not a random sample; for only those with particular leanings and aptitudes—those with a 'good head'—will choose this profession. Now, comparing the manner in which the Nupe generally are apt to discuss religious topics with the attitude shown by the diviners in their field, we find that one of the variants of the former constitutes the norm of the latter. The layman discussing religion may or may not be inclined to embark upon speculation: the diviner discussing divination does so as a matter of course if by this means he can force his facts into a more convincing order. Equally, in the act of divining, he is capable of a tense and dramatic mood. The first attitude only satisfies the diviner's own leanings; for his public takes no interest in these speculative refinements and cannot appreciate them. But his public does expect the diviner to be tense and excited, and is visibly impressed by his excursions into drama. In either case, we may conclude, the diviner's role offers a congenial niche to individuals of that religious bias or, more generally, of that temperament and intellectual predisposition.

5. THE MECHANICS OF HATI

Although we are not at the moment concerned with the influence of Islam on Nupe religion, it is convenient to discuss the Mohammedan variant of divination in this context. For in the main it is only the technique which is novel in this system of divining, while its topics, interpretation, and social aspects coincide with those typical of the pagan system. Partly, too, the two techniques share various points of resemblance, such as the designs of the 'key' figures or the use of series of eight, so that it would seem that the new, Mohammedan, practice has been assimilated to the older, indigenous method.

Hati or sand divination is even more fully a learned skill than is the system of *eba*. Its performance is prosaic, without any show of excitement or drama. Even its links with things sacred are reduced to the level of strictly occupational accomplishments since *hati* is one of the skills which 'mallams' alone can acquire, that is, men who have studied the Qoran and acquired at least the rudiments of Moslem learning. Most of these mallams-cum-diviners are found in Bida. They include men of widely varying status, learning, and reputation. Two of my diviner friends will illustrate the extremes. One was a highly educated scholar, who could read and write Arabic, possessed a number of books, and had some knowledge of Islamic doctrine. The other could read a little, though without much understanding; he could not write more than the cryptic cypher the diviners put on the sand table before starting to divine; and he neither knew the Qoran nor possessed any knowledge of Islamic doctrine. The first case, however, was an exception; for the true Islamic scholars (by Nupe standards) do not normally engage in divining; while the diviners are not infrequently men who had been unsuccessful in the scholarly profession. Thus one diviner had studied the Qoran but, earning too little as a mallam, later became a beadworker, supplementing his earnings by divination and the sale of charms. Another diviner was at the same time a trader in a small way, a third a hatmaker. Some of the sand diviners (including the scholarly mallam) seemed to be doing very well, having one to three clients a day. Less successful ones would still have two or three a week. Only one of the five diviners I knew had had no customers for a month, though he claimed that this was exceptional.

Like the *eba* system sand-divination has its 'key' and key series, though these are not embodied in a separate set of objects but are carried entirely in the diviner's head. A more substantial 'key' does in fact exist; it is contained in a book on divination, written in Arabic and amply illustrated with diagrams, the relevant pages of which are in the possession of most diviners; while actually divining, however, this book of rules is never consulted. The diviner's apparatus is simple, consisting only of sand, flattened out on the ground so that it forms a square, smooth surface, on which the various signs are impressed with the tips of the fingers. Before he begins, the diviner draws a cypher in the sand, which looks vaguely like an Arabic sign but which I was unable to identify; it is said to be the 'sign of the king', but fits neither 'king' nor 'Allah', nor any other word I could think of in this connection. To the right and left of the cypher certain of the 'key' signs are impressed, varying with the day of the week. On Friday, for example, the diviner puts sign 14 on the left and sign 7 on the right; on Sunday he draws signs 15 and 9; on Monday, signs 4 and

DIVINATION

5, and so forth. Saturday alone has more than two signs, namely, the four signs 6, 8, 10, and 13. No reason is quoted why this arrangement rather than any other should be chosen. Having completed this preparatory task, the diviner wipes the surface clean again and starts with the real divining.

He impresses small dots into the square of sand, one beside the other, starting from the left bottom edge and describing an arc up and down again to the right side of the square. He produces sixteen such dotted arcs, one underneath the other, which are considered to fall into four sets of four arcs. Having completed this fourfold set, the diviner wipes out every second dot in each arc, now starting from the right, down to the left bottom edge; where the last dot to be wiped out would be the last dot of the arc, that dot is left intact, so that in this case a double dot remains. As a result, the diviner obtains four patterns of dots lying along the left bottom edge and consisting each of four single or double dots.[1] These four patterns, as will be seen, are obtained entirely by chance. Once they are obtained, however, chance ceases to play a part; for the subsequent procedure is purely mechanical and rests on computations and manipulations all ultimately based on the four initial dot patterns. First, the sand table is once more wiped clean. Then the diviner draws the four patterns into the right upper space, the pattern which was originally farthest to the left being placed farthest to the right, and so forth in that order. In this new position the four patterns are drawn upright and symmetrically, and now represent the proper 'signs' of *hati*. From this first group of four signs the diviner derives a similar second group, which he draws into the left upper space; he does this by converting each horizontal line of dots in the first group into a corresponding upright column in the second, thus:

	2nd group					1st group			
••	•	•	•		•	•	•	•	a
•	•	••	•		••	••	••	•	b
••	••	••	•		••	••	•	•	c
•	••	••	•		•	••	••	••	d
d	c	b	a						

Underneath this row of eight signs a second and then a third row are drawn, now numbering four signs each. The lower rows are obtained by coupling adjacent signs in the next higher row and reducing each such pair of signs to a single sign in the row below. In the case of the top row each sign is coupled once only, that is, in accordance with this schema—*ab, cd, ef, gh* (if *a–h* are the eight

[1] Sometimes the diviner draws only eight arcs at a time, in which case the process just described has to be repeated.

signs). In the second row each of the four signs is coupled both ways with its neighbour, so that again four pairs result, thus—*ab, cd, ad, bc*. In reducing a pair of signs to one, the diviner adds up the dots which appear horizontally, on the same level, in the two given signs and considers whether the total for each level is two, three or four; if the total is two or four, the resulting sign in the next lower row will have a double dot on the corresponding level, if the total is three, a single dot. For example:

upper row	• •	• • •	— level 1 — level 2 — level 3 — level 4
	• •		— level 1
lower row		•	— level 2
		•	— level 3
		• •	— level 4

Having thus obtained sixteen signs in three rows, the diviner performs a further calculation. He adds up the total number of dots appearing on the top level of each of the three rows and deducts twelve from the total or, if the difference exceeds sixteen, twice twelve. The balance gives him the key series number of a particular dot pattern, which he must then locate in his sand drawing and use as a starting point for the interpretation. The proviso, that the difference must not be more than sixteen, is explained by the fact that the key series itself consists of sixteen signs, so that a number larger than this would be useless. It is possible, however, that the number so obtained might be that of a sign which happens to be missing in the sand drawing; if so, the diviner will look instead for one of the six 'kindred' signs, which will be discussed presently.

The diagram opposite illustrates the key series of *hati* divining; with two exceptions its general design is also that of the actual sand drawing. The first exception is of a minor order and refers to the lay-out of the third row which, in the key series, is broken up into three-plus-one signs. The second exception refers to the principle upon which the key series is constructed. This bears no relation to the procedure just discussed, whereby the diviner derives his whole drawing from an initial group of four signs; rather, the key series seems to be put together almost at random, though we may note (a point strongly emphasized by all diviners) that the total number of dots in each group of four signs is always twenty-four. As we shall see, this discrepancy in the construction of the two designs does not prevent the diviners from explaining both by an identical analogy.

DIVINATION

We note the resemblance between the dot patterns and certain of the markings on the *eba* slabs. In the case of *hati*, however, the key series is complete, its sixteen signs including every possible combination of single and double dots grouped in this manner. Let me mention some other similarities. The correct name for the signs in their key position is 'stars', which is consistent with the vaguely astrological background of sand-divining; in spite of this, the diviner will usually refer to them as 'houses', that is, in the phraseology of *eba* divination. A single dot in any sign is called

```
 8       7       6       5         4       3       2       1
· ·     · ·     · ·     ·         · ·     · ·     ·       ·
· ·     · ·     ·       ·         · ·     ·       · ·     ·
· ·     ·       · ·     ·         ·       ·       · ·     ·
·       · ·     · ·     ·         · ·     ·       · ·     ·

 12              11              10              9
· ·             · ·             ·               ·
· ·             ·               · ·             ·
·               ·               · ·             · ·
·               · ·             ·               · ·

       15              14              13
       ·               · ·             ·
       · ·             ·               ·
       ·               · ·             ·
                       ·               · ·

                                       16
                                      · ·
                                      · ·
                                      · ·
                                      · ·
```

'open' and a double dot 'closed', as though the diviner were again dealing with shells falling face-up or face-down. The actual divination, finally, rests once more upon considering the varying positions (or 'houses') in which any one sign may appear and upon combining the meanings of place and pattern.

This procedure, however, is backed by a different theory and a much more elaborate set of rules. To begin with there is the astrological background of sand-divining. The signs in their key position (the 'stars') have long, Arabic-sounding names, said to be the names of constellations.[1] In each sign the four levels of single or

[1] These are too complicated for regular quotation, so that the diviner uses the key-series number instead. I could identify only a few of these names, which would seem to refer, not to constellations, but to diverse Islamic concepts. *Almayika*, the name for pattern 2, is probably *Mala'ikah*, 'Angels', which is also the name of the 35th *Surah* of the Qoran. *Atariki*, pattern 5,

double dots (counting from top to bottom) represent the four elements—Fire, Air, Water, Earth. Equally, the key series as a whole is taken to symbolize the four elements; these are so distributed over the sixteen signs that the three groups of four in the first and second row each contain three of the elements, one of them twice, while the group of four in the bottom row includes all four elements in their proper order (reading from right to left), thus:

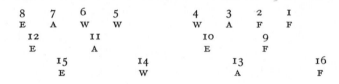

The analogy with the four elements plays no further part in the interpretation of the key series. Here their spatial arrangement alone is important and its meaning is explained with the help of a different analogy, with procreation and kinship. The first group of four signs (1–4) is called the 'mother-group'; the next group (5–8), the 'children' (there being no corresponding 'father' group); the four signs in the second row (9–12) are called 'grandchildren', and the three signs in the bottom row (13–15), 'great-grandchildren'. Sign 16, which contains the largest possible number of dots and stands apart in the design, also has an independent meaning in this pseudo-genealogy: it represents the 'mother' of all the other signs, and in the divination bears a prophecy concerning the diviner himself. The four 'mother' signs in the first group are said to 'give birth' to the 'children' signs, these to the 'grandchildren' signs, and so forth. The latter analogy is once more applied to the drawing of the design in actual divination; for when the diviner derives the second group of signs from the first, and similarly the lower rows from those above, this procedure is again described as signs 'giving birth' to signs. The same procedure also establishes other, more specific links of 'kinship' between the signs; for all those signs which, by means of this procedure, would produce the same resultant sign (or 'give birth' to it) are regarded as that sign's 'kin'. In demonstrating this connection repetitions and signs appearing in reverse are ignored, so that each sign has

seems to be *Tariq*, 'Way' (of belief) and the name of the 86th *Surah*. *Nasuralharaja*, pattern 9, and *Nasuraldahili*, pattern 12, may mean *Nasr al kharaj* and *Nasr al dakhl*—'Luck on leaving' and 'Luck on Entering' (?). The name for the last and fullest pattern (No. 16), *Jim'a*, is Arabic for 'assembly', 'congregation'. *Almanku*, the name for pattern 8, seems to be the Nupe word *Mankó* arabicized, meaning 'Great Scholar'.

six 'relatives'.¹ The diagram below illustrates this for the first sign in the key series. The example also shows, incidentally, that the 'kinship' so derived conflicts with that other, genealogical, schema, since now a sign of the 'mother' group is assumed to be 'born' of signs belonging to the offspring generations. The logical conflict, however, has no further consequences; only the 'kinship' between signs is made use of in the practice of divining, while the genealogical schema remains pure 'theory'.

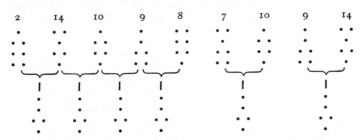

6. INTERPRETATION

Let me now list the meanings attributed to the various signs in the key series and hence to any sign in its own 'house'. Each position in the key series has a brief name, this time quoted in Nupe not in Arabic, which corresponds to the 'code' names of *eba* divining and similarly alludes to the respective prophecy.

No. 1. Good health; the client will have a son. Code name 'Life and War'; the latter allusion is, as it were, per contra, war being the destroyer of life and sons.

No. 2. Some day the client will be rich ('Wealth').

No. 3. The client will some day have a large family and receive many gifts ('Kinship').

No. 4. The client's wife, or a female client, will become pregnant ('Father and Mother').

No. 5. As No. 1 ('Child').

No. 6. Recovery after illness ('Illness').

No. 7. The client will find a good wife or husband ('Marriage').

No. 8. The whole town will be thrown into strife and upheaval ('Uproar', 'Commotion').

¹ The 'mother' sign 16, which consists wholly of double dots, is equally ignored. Bearing in mind the rules for reducing two signs to one, it will readily be seen that sign 16 cannot be derived from any other pair of signs. In this sense it is rightly placed apart from the rest of the design. There is a further kind of 'kinship', which is however unimportant. It links each sign with the one showing the same pattern in reverse, and sign 1 (which is entirely 'open') with its opposite, sign 16 (which is entirely 'closed').

No. 9. A successful journey ('Voyage').
No. 10. All the leaders of the town will meet in consultation, but will arrive at bad decisions ('Nobility', 'Office Holders').
No. 11. God will listen to all prayers and cause all 'medicines' to work successfully ('Doubts').
No. 12. Success in love against rivals ('Enemy').
No. 13. Success in every enterprise ('Writing', 'Prayer').
No. 14. Financial success ('Trade' and 'Money').
No. 15. Fear and worries will disappear ('Barbers'; the allusion is to the many barbers who are also doctors and thus make illness 'disappear').
No. 16. The diviner will find many clients ('Mallam').

In the actual divination not every sign is located, identified, and interpreted in accordance with its varying position; this would clearly be immensely complicated, and the diviner does not even pretend to do it. Rather does he greatly simplify the procedure by various means. Thus he assesses and interprets the combination of place and sign only in the case of the one sign which serves as his starting point. Assuming, for example, that this happens to be sign 12 in the key series, meaning 'wealth', and that in the actual design it appears in 'house' No. 2, which in turn means 'enemy'; the diviner would then conclude that 'people are jealous of the client's wealth' or that the client 'will rival the wealth of others', according to which divination seems more plausible in the case of a particular person. The diviner's next step consists in tracing the six 'kindred' signs; and now he no longer considers the precise position of the signs but only their relative order, that is, whether they occur in a place with a higher or lower number. The sign occurring in the place with the higher number (that is, further to the left or in a lower row) is said to 'eat up' the 'kindred' sign in the place or places with the next lower number; which means that the prophecy of the former will overrule the prophecy of the latter. For example, sign 13 ('Prayer') occurring to the left of the 'kindred' sign 8 ('Uproar') is taken to indicate that 'prayer will eventually overcome the strife'.

Furthermore, the sixteen signs are allocated to four series on the grounds of their allegedly similar meaning. The first series includes all signs referring to wealth, success, health and high social position, (signs 2, 4, 7, 10, 11, 13, 14, 16); the second series includes all signs referring to poverty, misfortune, ill health, and other worries of the moment (signs 1, 3, 5, 6, 8, 9, 12, 15); the third series is said to concern men—(signs 2, 5, 6, 8, 10, 11, 13, 16), the last series women (signs 1, 3, 4, 7, 9, 12, 14, 15). The main merit of this arrangement, which incidentally does not quite tally with the interpretations listed before, seems to be that it operates with two pairs of broadly contrasted categories of wide applicability and with four series of eight, which are relatively easy to remember. In interpreting these series, the diviner will always take into account whether his client is a man or a woman. Thus, if the sign to be interpreted belongs to series 1 (meaning 'success') and series 4 ('concerning women'), and occurs in the consultation of a man, the diviner will conclude that his client will be successful in finding a wife. If the same combination occurs in the case of a female client, it will probably mean that she will be prosperous in business. If the sign belongs to series 1 and 3 ('concerning men'), and occurs in the case of a male client, the latter will 'gain reputation and rank'. If the sign belongs to series 2 (meaning 'misfortune') and 4 ('concerning women') and occurs in the case of a female client, it might mean that she will have a difficult pregnancy, and so forth.

It is clear that in this flexible system of divination the diviner will be guided by the particular case of his client much more fully than is his pagan colleague; in fact, the system of divination itself acknowledges the importance at least of the sex of the client. Also, the diviner has several methods of calculation at his disposal and is free to choose the less complicated one provided it still offers a plausible prophecy. This is borne out by the existence of an optional, final rule which reduces the whole system of divination to a simple mechanical procedure. This rule lays down that all signs which have a single dot at the top and a double dot at the base, so that they 'point away' from the diviner, bear an adverse prophecy; while all signs of the opposite design, 'pointing inward', are propitious. If the diviner uses this simplified method exclusively he will consider only the 'houses' that bear on the client's question and phrase his reply accordingly. In a consultation I watched the diviner was asked if the client would recover some goods that had been stolen. The diviner looked at 'house' 2, meaning 'wealth', at 'house' 9, meaning 'voyage' (since the goods had been 'carried away'), at 'house' 12, 'enemy', and at 'houses' 13 and 14, implying 'success'. The signs at 2 and 13 were inconclusive; the signs at 9 and 12 pointed outward; only the sign at 14 had a propitious meaning. The answer was, quite plausibly, that it was no good looking for the thieves; the client might be successful if he could follow them; but this was difficult since they had by then left the town with their loot.

Perhaps the most striking feature of Nupe sand-divining is the contrast between its pretentious theoretical framework and its primitive and slipshod application in practice. In some respects the 'theory' simply evaporates in the 'practice', as in the high-sounding Arabic nomenclature which gives way to common Nupe expressions or in the astrological notions of which no use is ever made. The practice is clearly meant to cope with the relevant problems and interests of Nupe social life; and these, let us note, are now typical, not only of a Mohammedan community, but also of a highly urbanized one. There is no longer any mention of rain, of the prospects of hunting, or of the influence of *kuti*; instead, we find references to 'writing and prayer', to mallams and barber-doctors, to 'the whole town in strife', and the strong emphasis on travel and trade, including travel and trade 'concerning women'.

The discrepancy between the theoretical framework of *hati* and its practical application suggests once more an attempt to assimilate the Mohammedan system to local conditions. The attempt is crude and unambitious, stopping far short of anything like a true synthesis; rather, any feature which cannot readily be assimilated is left on one side and only nominally acknowledged. Occasionally even this bare acknowledgement is discarded, as is shown in this example. One diviner, able to read his Arabic book on divination, discovered in it a new rule which distinguished between 'fixed' and 'movable' stars and operated with series of seven and the corresponding permutations. The diviner frankly admitted that he did not fully understand the rule: consequently he simply ignored it, not even borrowing the new nomenclature.

7. CONCLUSIONS: DREAM INTERPRETATION

I have called the guidance offered by divination mechanical and of a case-to-case kind. The preceding discussion will have borne out this description. Nupe divination is concerned less with foreknowledge in its own right than with resolving the problems and obscurities of the moment. The diviner can discover and disentangle some of the hidden influences which are at work always and everywhere, and can to that extent predict—piecemeal, and illuminating only the immediate future: he cannot uncover any more embracing design. Indeed, as we know, there is no such design in this non-committal and fundamentally amoral religion. Yet within the limits set to it divination has a part to play, providing some of the certainty and guidance required for provident action. We may call Nupe divination a concession or compromise; for as its scope is so restricted by the logic of Nupe religious thought, the fact that it exists at all, is a concession exacted by the practical needs of human life.

Let us note that religion itself adds to these needs. We spoke of the 'proliferation' of Nupe religious thought which crowds the universe with supernatural agencies overlapping in their effects and multiplies the supernatural aids, so that their appropriateness can only be discovered by trial and error. Once more divination is needed to reduce the uncertainties which must arise; it is thus that it becomes a 'prerequisite' of religious no less than of practical action.[1] And here, I think, we find the explanation for a somewhat puzzling point of Nupe doctrine. Although Nupe divination is marked off as being 'of God', it is not numbered among the other, similar 'things of the world', that is, of creation. Nor are there any legends explaining its origin or appearance on earth. This ambiguity seems in keeping with the peculiar role of divination in Nupe religious practice. Divination is clearly one of the tools bestowed by God upon man so that he may be better fitted to cope with the practical problems of life on earth; but these include also the problem of handling successfully all the other transcendental tools. And just because divination is such a twofold 'prerequisite' and so basically indispensable, its presence is simply taken for granted.

The role of divination in Nupe life, however, must not be exaggerated. It is far from all-important; the Nupe, for example, do not practise divination as regularly or consistently as do many other primitive societies. When I asked my informants if they consulted diviners daily or perhaps weekly, they simply laughed. In a great many walks of life one can carry on without this mystic advice; for daily life has its own routine and its own practical rules, on which one can safely rely. Medicine, too, has its routine side. So has religious life: the seasonal rituals, fixed by the calendar of the country, are performed largely without the aid of diviners. Only when the routine of everyday life breaks down and when its rules prove inadequate in the face of choice, that is, when anxieties and uncertainties arise, divination comes into its own.

Among the topics handled by the Nupe diviner we should perhaps expect to find also dreams, especially since they offer so important clues to witchcraft and to the activities of spirits and *fifingi*. Yet this is not so. Certain rules for interpreting dreams exist, but their knowledge does not appear to be widespread, being altogether absent in certain parts of the country. Even where it exists, it is shared by diviners and laymen alike and is never made the subject of divining proper. The Nupe do puzzle about their dreams and suspect that a curious dream may have a message or purport something important; in this case the dreamer might discuss his experience with others, and together they would speculate about the likely meaning. Or, where there are individuals knowledgeable about dreams, the dreamer would look for one of them among his friends or fellow villagers, the 'expert' claiming neither payment nor special status.

[1] See above, p. 37.

Generally speaking, there are three kinds of dreams. If your dream is accompanied by pains and nightmares, then it betrays the presence of an evil *aljénu*, which must be dealt with by the appropriate gifts to spirits. If you dream that some other person is about to kill you, then this is evidence of witchcraft. In neither event is it necessary to consult any book of rules since this kind of dream is obvious to everyone. If, however, your dream is merely unusual or odd, then it requires interpretation according to the rules, which would usually also suggest certain observances meant to secure the promise of the dream or to ward off its veiled threats.

Thus, when you dream of herds of wild animals, it means that witches threaten you; when you dream of herds of cows, you may expect wealth and success, though you should make a gift of milk to a mallam. A man who dreams of women or girls in the water will marry well, provided he presents some honey and millet to the unmarried young men of his acquaintance and some fish to the married men; the same applies (suitably adapted) to the corresponding dreams of women, though in their case omission of the gifts would bring on severe and painful menstruation. A man dreaming of a black snake will prosper in his enterprise provided he sacrifices a white cock to the *kuci*; in the case of a woman the dream means pregnancy. If you weep in your dream, you will be successful; if you laugh, you will die, and no sacrifice and the like will help you. A fish freshly caught means the birth of a child; a dried fish, the death of an acquaintance or relative. The latter meaning is also attributed to dreams about digging out yams, since this suggests the digging of a grave. Both fire and water indicate witches, and such dreams must be followed by sacrifices to *kuci* or by alms to the poor. Excrements mean sickness; so does blood in a man's dreams; in a woman's dreams it may mean childbirth (if it is 'good' blood, that is, from menstruation) or abortion (if it is 'bad' blood, from a wound). No dreams, incidentally, tell a woman anything about her prospective child: this is simply 'God's will'. Finally, if you dream about a person being killed, then this is the truth, and you will warn that person, who must in turn consult a diviner.

In these dream interpretations Mohammedan ideas (alms, gifts to mallams) and pagan ones (sacrifices to the *kuci*) are employed quite indiscriminately. So are diverse principles of interpretation; some, as we saw, fasten upon contrasts, others upon analogies more or less close or suggestive. Certainly, we find no consistent symbolism, nor yet any of the 'universal' symbols cited by psychoanalysts. More important, the prophecies attributed to dreams are much the same as those dispensed by the diviner, so that the interpretation of dreams (which one can do for oneself) and professional divination in some measure duplicate one another. If this means that the diviner has no monopoly of prophecy, it equally means that one need not be very seriously concerned over one's dreams, since the message they might hold would also transpire in some other way. Normally, in fact, the people are not inclined to take their dreams very seriously, even in the localities where there are experts versed in that lore. I used to record all the dreams of the Nupe men with whom I was in daily contact; though they were quite often puzzled about their dreams, they performed sacrifices and so forth only when their dreams referred to dead relatives. Dream interpretation, then, represents another 'supererogatory' element in Nupe religious thought, another 'additional' notion about the meaning of the things in the world, and now one conspicuously treated as such.

Let me add that in other respects, too, the diviner holds no monopoly of prophecy. If he pronounces upon lucky or unlucky days, some knowledge of this kind is common throughout Nupe. Thus two months, the seventh and thirteenth, are held to be unlucky, and people will avoid travelling or having wedding feasts and other celebrations at these times. In all other months certain days are specially lucky—the second, seventh, twelfth, seventeenth and eighteenth day; so is the time of full moon, while moonless days are unlucky and dangerous for all tasks.[1]

If divination and the interpretation of dreams represent supernatural aids which overlap in their efficacy but are of different ease of access, this is true also of the knowledge, shared by everybody, of propitious and unpropitious dates. In other words, for much the same kind of guidance you can rely on your own knowledge, on what you or your friends know about dreams, and on the professional advice of diviners. Once more we note the 'proliferation' of Nupe religious thought and that tendency to multiply the mystic tools, that is, to have 'several strings to one's bow.'

[1] It is usual in Nupe to refer to months and days in this way, by numbers rather than names. The interval of five between the lucky days, incidentally, plays no further part in Nupe thought or religious observances.

III
RITUAL

1. PRELIMINARIES

ON the grounds of time and occasion the Nupe rituals fall into two sharply distinct groups. On one side we have rituals occupying a regular, fixed place in the calendar of the country; on the other, rituals which, as the Nupe say, 'have no month', that is, whose performance is contingent upon the variable needs of the moment. A few 'fixed' rituals which can also be performed out of season and others which, originally 'fixed', have become 'movable' represent intermediate or transitional forms. But even here the twofold division is not obscured. For in the case of rituals performed both regularly and contingently, the latter performance is clearly marked off as an adaptation to particular circumstances; it is on a much smaller scale and lacks the festive features which accompany the regular ceremony, being as it were only concerned with the business in hand.

Surveying Nupe country as a whole the number of different rituals is strikingly large and their geographical distribution irregular; the chart on p. 69 lists a number of them by name and locality, and also shows their varying times of performance. Only one ritual, *gunnu*, occurs everywhere; others are common to one or two tribal sections only or even to a few villages, where special local conditions appear to justify the special cult. In the extreme case a particular ritual may be restricted to a single village community. We met already with instances, such as the Mokwa ritual of the sacred crocodile, the rituals called *ketsá* and 'Father Niger' in the riverain area, and the worship, once more on the river, of the sacred bronze figures associated with Tsoede. Let me add some further examples: in the kolanut-growing district of Labozhi we find the special cult of an ancestress reputed to have introduced the planting of kolanut; a somewhat similar cult, concerned with the cultivation of the oilpalm, occurs in the village Kutiwengi, in the 'oilpalm belt' to the north; Jebba Island possesses a special ritual, unique in Nupe country, which is meant to ward off smallpox; while Mokwa and a few villages in the neighbourhood practise the similarly unique masked dance *elo*.

CHART OF NUPE RITUALS

		LOCALITIES—INLAND								LOCALITIES—RIVER		
Month	Doko	Sakpe	Kutigi	Etsu	Labozhi	Ewugi	Wuna	Mokwa	Jebba	Leaba	Gbajibo	Bele
1 (13)	[navũ]	gunnu [navũ]	[navũ]					[navũ]				
2												
3			gani	lugba*								
4												
5	žiba											
6 (Fixed Rituals)	sakó				gunnu	gbara		gunnu				
7						sara	dakunu			gunnu	elo	
8										mamma		
9	žiba		[sallagi]		nnakógba	gunnu*	gunnu*	elo				gunnu
10								sara; bukpe	mamma; dzakó; ndáduma	ndáduma	mamma	žiba; ndáduma
11	gunnu	mamma		gunnu			fufobo		gunnu			
12			[sallakó]									
Movable Rituals	Dibo Saba; fitakũ	sara; žikinta	gunnu; žikinta	tidzana	gunnu	dzanavu; žikinta	žicigbã	sara; bukpe	tidzana; žikinta; ketsá; ndáduma	žikinta	sara; žikinta; ndáduma	žikinta

Note: Names in square brackets indicate Moslem observances (see chap VIII). Rituals marked by a star are performed triennially; as these are isolated cases they are disregarded in the text.

With so much variety it is impossible to select a particular community whose rituals would be 'typical' of Nupe practice; rather, each village cycle of rituals is typical (or atypical) in its own way. Yet neither is it possible to describe every variety of Nupe ritual (several of which I only knew from hearsay or from informants' reports). What seems more important is to examine some such cycle of rituals within the setting in which it operates, that is, within the corporate life of the community for which it is primarily valid or, in Nupe parlance, by which it is 'owned'.[1] As regards the question, which particular cycle of rituals to select, I propose to resolve it by taking two instances, one from Doko and the other from Jebba Island. This compromise seems the most expedient both since I have actually observed the majority of rituals in these two places and since these represent an interesting contrast, Doko being a 'typical' inland village, with hereditary chieftainship, and Jebba Island a riverain community where chiefs are elected. Let me add that, from other points of view, both communities are also 'atypical'; Jebba, because it is one of the two villages possessing major 'relics' of Tsoede; and Doko, because it formerly belonged to a federation of villages (or 'towns' as the Nupe would say), which type of political organization is unique in Nupe country. As regards the two communities themselves, a full description has been given elsewhere and need not be repeated.[2]

One further point of more general import may be anticipated. In spite of the great variety of local cults the number of rituals performed and their place in the year's cycle do not differ greatly in the different communities. Usually there are one or two movable rituals, rarely more, and two or three fixed rituals, only a few villages having four or five; and though the dates of the fixed rituals vary somewhat from place to place, they fall more frequently in certain months (e.g. the 9th and 11th) than in others (e.g. the 3rd or 5th).[3] The corresponding months in our calendar, incidentally, can only be calculated approximately since the Nupe reckon in lunar months, the year beginning with the onset of the rains, and insert a 13th month every five years. In other years the 1st month is usually also called the 13th, especially when the rains are late, which not infrequently leads to confusion, some localities being temporarily a month out in their reckoning.[4]

[1] I am here using the phrase 'primarily valid' since certain rituals imply an additional, wider validity (or 'ownership') which extends to the whole sub-tribe or even tribe. This point will be examined later (see below, p. 103).
[2] See *A Black Byzantium*, pp. 19, 25, 35.   [3] See the chart on p. 69.
[4] In 1934, for example, the 1st month was taken to have begun on March 15th in the eastern part of Nupe, but at the end of April I found that the people of Mokwa, in the west, had just started with their 1st month. For a fuller description of the Nupe calendar, see *A Black Byzantium*, Appendix V.

1. Sacrifice before twin shrine

2. The sacred crocodile of Mokwa

3. Wall paintings in a Nupe house

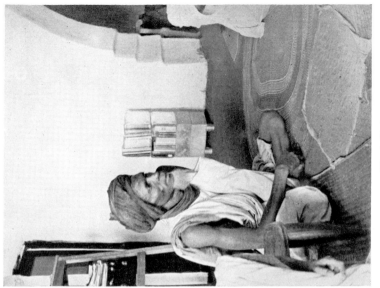
5. *Hati* diviner

4. *Eba* diviner

7. *Ndáduma* sacrifice on the Niger

6. *Žiba* sacrifice

8. Scene from *gunnu* dance in Jebba

9. *Dzakó* sacrifice

10. The *zumácikā* medicine shrine in Jebba

11. Dressing the *mamma* masks

12. *Dzakó* dance

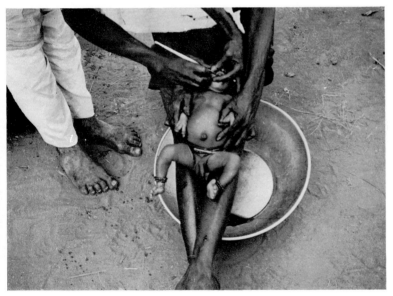

13. Cutting of tribal marks

14. *Dzakó* dance

15. Vendor of medicines

16. Circumcision operation

17. A bridal procession

18. Levelling the ground over a new grave

19. The master of the *cigbeciži* in his 'dispensary'

20. A noted medicine expert and 'wise man' from Jebba

21. The dance of the *ndakó gboyá*

22. The *Sagi* of Kpatsuwa

23. *Gugu* dance of the Yorubu

25. *Bori* dance of the Hausa

24. The appearance of the *ndakó gboyá*

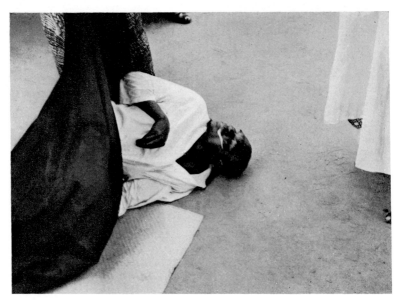

26. A *bori* dancer in a cataleptic fit

27. *Sogba* sacrifice of the Gwari

28. Mask of the 'Great *elo*'

29. Dancer at the Bida *salla* with headdress modelled on the *elo* mask

30. The Nupe quarter in Lagos

31. The oldest mosque in Bida

This roughly uniform timing of the fixed rituals might suggest that they are bound up with important seasonal events, farming activities and the like, which are similarly uniform throughout the country. The 9th month, which is so regularly accompanied by rituals, in fact represents a crucial phase in the life of a farming people, coinciding with the end of the rains and the time of the sorghum harvest, the staple crop of the country. But the 11th month, which falls in the middle of the dry season, coincides only with a minor agricultural activity, the harvesting of the last bean crop. Conversely, an important agricultural phase, the 1st (or 13th) month, when rains and planting begin, is infrequently accompanied by ceremonials. Other dates marked by rituals in different communities coincide with the first millet harvest (5th month), with the first yam harvest (7th month), or fall in the early rains (3rd month), when nothing in particular happens.

The Nupe rituals are thus neither firmly linked with important agricultural activities nor yet concentrated in the season when farmwork is at a standstill, when the granaries are full, and when the people have both food and time to spare. But there is a nexus of a more general kind; for the Nupe rituals tend to be associated with the reaping of the crops more than with the planting, with 'ends' more than with 'beginnings', bearing upon the renewal of the fertility of which one has just received a token rather than upon attempts to secure it at the outset. The subsequent discussion will bear out this view. Here we must note that the ceremonials which happen to coincide with this or that harvest are in no way strict first-fruit rites, meant to signal the proper time for reaping or to control the first consumption of the new food; nor yet are they special feasts of thanksgiving. Rather is their religious import more unspecific, bearing on fertility, the thriving of crops, and health in general, irrespective of the particular occasion.

2. THE INLAND VILLAGE

(i) *Priestship*

The list of Doko rituals is brief. There are two movable ones —*fitakŭ* ('The Stone drinks') and *Dibo Saba* (named after an ancestor chief),—and three fixed rituals: *žiba*, which is performed twice, in the 5th and 9th month; *sakó*, performed one month after the first *žiba*; and *gunnu*, performed in the 11th month.[1]

The ceremonials are in the charge of different officiants. The ritual *Dibo Saba*, addressed to an ancestor chief, is also performed by the chief. The ritual *sakó* concerns only the small group of

[1] In our calendar the 5th month corresponds roughly to July–August, the 9th to December, the 11th to February.

hereditary hunters in Doko and is performed by the head of that group. The two ceremonials, then, have no special 'priests', being entrusted instead to particular individuals in virtue of some other office or position they hold. In addition, there are two priests in the strict sense of the word, men specifically invested with the religious office and holding no other official position. One has charge of the rituals *žiba* and *fitakū*, the other of the *gunnu*. Both men must have the status of full adults, that is, must be married, before they can assume the religious duties. In all other respects their qualifications differ fundamentally.

The first priestship is traditionally vested in one of the reigning chief's younger brothers (real or classificatory), who must not be his prospective successor. This division of the two offices, one political, the other religious, also includes the guardianship of the sacred bangles of Tsoede which, in Doko, represent the insignia of the chiefly office; they are kept, not by the chief, but by his priest brother, the chief himself being allowed to wear them only on three ceremonial occasions—at his investiture; when he performs his 'own' ritual, *Dibo Saba*; and when he pays a visit in state to the *Etsu* Nupe. The peculiar relationship of ruler and priest is traced back to the first chief of Doko and represents, for the people, something in the nature of a complementary arrangement, at once uniting and separating secular and religious authority. Logically, the two offices bear analogous names, the chief being called *Žitsú* ('king of the town') and his brother *Žigí* ('priest of the town').[1] The priest is, however, addressed by another, ceremonial name, *Ndákatsa* of uncertain derivation.

The *gunnu* priest is known as *Gunnukó* (Great *gunnu*) or, more specifically, as *Ndazo*, and is addressed by that name. *Ndazo* means the 'rare man' or the 'man difficult to find', which name already indicates the unusual manner of his election. For only an individual born with a tuft of hair on the top of his head can become (and in fact must become) a *gunnu* priest. That this birthmark is rare need not be specially emphasized; during my stay in Nupe only one village in the whole country (actually Doko) had a true *Ndazo*, and he was as yet too young to officiate. In the frequent periods of interregnum the office becomes hereditary in the family of the last *Ndazo* who had the miraculous qualification, his successors cutting their hair so as to imitate the tell-tale tuft. When a true *Ndazo* is born, the man who previously took his place will train the youth in his future responsibilities, take him to all ceremonials even while he is a babe in arms, and eventually surrender the office to him. Should the *Ndazo's* family die out before

[1] The latter name means literally 'One who eats (in the sacrifice) for the town'.

a new priest is born, the village must temporarily cease to perform the ritual altogether and join instead in the celebrations of a neighbouring, more fortunate, locality.

The *gunnu* priest is also in other ways elevated above common mortals. In everyday life there is little to distinguish the *Žigí* or *Ndazo* from the average Nupe peasant. The only visible distinction lies in their manner of dress; for the two priests may only wear a loincloth and a piece of cloth slung across the shoulder, never the more elaborate flowing gown and trousers of Nupe, and must always walk bareheaded. Both the simple dress and the uncovered head are also obligatory for anyone attending the rituals in question (and indeed most rituals), so that the priests are as it were always 'on duty' and constantly display their association with things sacred. In the case of the *Ndazo*, his very life is sacred: he is inviolable, and no one may lay hands on him, even if he committed some serious offence. Also, when the *Ndazo* dies, the usual funerary rites are replaced by a performance of the *gunnu*. Concerning the priestly dress, the usual explanation is that the *Žigí* and *Ndazo* must not wear anything 'tied round the waist' (as they would if they wore trousers); but the people do not speculate further, and the *Ndazo's* birth-mark is taken to mean simply something that is rare and lucky, and attaches to the most vital part of the body, the head. Characteristically, another lucky birth-mark, once more on the head, is linguistically associated with the *gunnu*: children born in a caul are called *Ndagunnu*, 'Father *gunnu*'.

Of the three fixed rituals of Doko the *gunnu* is undoubtedly the most important, representing the peak of ceremonial life and being thought of as harbouring the strongest force of *kuti*. Equally, it is the only ritual bearing so conspicuously the stamp of the miraculous. Somewhat surprisingly, the greater importance of the *gunnu* has not helped to protect it from the impact of cultural change. On the contrary, the *gunnu* is usually the first ritual to disappear or at least to lose its character of a 'fixed' ritual, surviving only as an occasional, 'movable' ceremony. Now several of the villages which abandoned the *gunnu* altogether did so when their 'born' *Ndazo* died or the family of hereditary priests became extinct. Whatever other influences may have tended to weaken the hold of the *gunnu* ritual, the difficulty of finding a successor to this unique priestship must have hastened the process; so that the link with the miraculous, as it helped to raise the cult above all others, also made it more vulnerable.

(ii) *Movable Rituals*

These are quickly described; for they are simple and businesslike, devoid both of elaborate proceedings and complicated paraphernalia. The 'business' of *fitakū* is to break a drought or to combat illness. I witnessed the ritual in July, during the so-called 'little dry season', when the usual spell of dry weather lasted unexpectedly long. The ritual took place at midday, in a clearing in the bush a few minutes walk from Doko. The place formed a rough circle whose entrance was flanked by two fresh mounds of earth. In the centre of the clearing, under a big tree, there was another, old, mound, said to cover the sacred stone from which the ritual derives its name; a small pot was half buried in the mound. The congregation consisted of the *Žigí*, who performed the sacrifice and spoke the prayer, and of family heads and other old men, the village chief not being present. In the sacrifice the blood of the slaughtered animal (a ram) and some beer were poured into the pot in the mound, thus making the 'stone drink', after which the meat was cooked, divided among the men present, and consumed there and then together with the rest of the beer. The priest ate and drank first, the others following in order of rank and age; a share of both meat and beer was kept for the chief, to be taken to his house after the ceremonial. In the prayer which accompanied the sacrifice the beer was referred to as *nuwā*, 'water' (as is usual in all Nupe sacrifices), so that the stone was made to 'drink' the fluid of which one stood in need. The prayer was brief and addressed to both *kuti* and God, thus—

'*Kuti*, the thing we are pouring, drink this water. *Sokó*, cause rain to fall, *kuti*, cause rain to fall. *Sokó*, cause that the whole town may prosper, that everyone may (have things) to eat, that everyone may have health.'

Finally, some leaves were plucked from the tree and stuck into the mound of earth underneath. This action was merely meant as a sign that the ceremony had been performed and had no ulterior or symbolic meaning. The whole ceremonial lasted a little over an hour.

According to Doko tradition Dibo Saba was the village chief who ruled at the time of Tsoede's advent, and the second in a long and (until recently) uninterrupted line of chiefs. It was he who received, at Tsoede's hand, the sacred bangles, and of all the graves of more remote ancestors his alone can still be identified. It lies outside Doko, on the old, now abandoned, site of the village, and today forms a narrow uncultivated space surrounded on all sides by farmland. The ritual is performed whenever some grave danger threatens the community, especially illness or, again, drought. The present chief of Doko performed it in 1930, during an outbreak of smallpox, and again in 1932, when a horse sickness attacked Doko. It was not performed either in 1934 or 1936, during my stay in the country, so that my description is based on the account of informants. But their account tallies with the ancestral sacrifices I had seen elsewhere; and the *Dibo Saba* ritual is, in essence, nothing but a sacrifice to the *kuci* of an ancestor, though both the ancestor and his invocation are here matters of public concern. This double significance of the ritual is clearly expressed by the people, who would say that, on this occasion, the chief is performing two sacrifices at once, one for his own 'house', and the other for the 'whole town'. It is interesting to note that the present chief of Doko does not come of the dynasty of Dibo Saba but of a new family, which came to power two generations ago; even so, he continues the sacrifice to this alien ancestor. In other words, the transformation of the chief's private kinship rite into an official and public ceremonial has become complete. In the ceremonial the chief, accompanied by the older men, sacrifices beer, a goat, or some other food over the grave of Dibo Saba and addresses both the *kuci* and *Sokó*. The choice of the sacrificial animal depends on the diviner's instruction. The formula of prayer is of the usual kind, mentioning the need of rain (or whatever the cause), of food in abundance, and ends with the stereotyped wish that 'the whole town may prosper'.

(iii) *Fixed Rituals*

Let me start with the simplest of the three, the ritual called *sakó* (meaning 'Great Deer'). As already mentioned, it is 'owned' by the hereditary hunters of Doko, that is, by a small number of families, all kinsmen of the *Majī Egbe* ('Master of the Hunt') and descended from some earlier holder of that office. In Doko everybody is also a hunter, or can be one if he is so inclined, and every house has its bows and arrows, traps, and hunting nets. Conversely, all the hereditary hunters are also farmers. But it falls to them to organize the large-scale drives carried out in the dry season (now increasingly rarely since the bigger game is fast disappearing), and it falls to the head of this group to ensure, by ritual means, success in hunting. He receives a share of the big game killed by any Doko man; he also keeps the horns of buck and deer killed by his own group in a small hut in his house, while other people would throw these trophies away. Whenever the Master set out on a large-scale hunt or desires to invoke his ancestors, he pours a small libation of beer outside this hut, addressing an anonymous *kuci*. In his case, then, the hut containing the trophies replaces the ancestral grave or shrine of other families. Once a year, the same offering is brought in order to secure good hunting for the whole community, the ritual being now performed in the Master's sleeping hut. No particular secrecy surrounds the sacrifice, though it must not be seen by women. I saw it late in August; it was attended (as is the rule) only by the Master and his adult sons, and consisted in pouring beer on the ground, drinking the rest, and breaking some reeds over the place of the libation. The Master spoke thus—'*Sokó*, may the town have health, may everything be prosperous (now that) we are breaking the reeds finally'. The breaking of the reeds was explained to me as follows: 'Reeds grow in the bush, and game is found in the bush'; which devious analogy seems to have little bearing on the very general character of the prayer formula. As regards the latter, let us note that here again a private ceremonial is linked with the well being of the whole community.

Of the two *žiba* rituals I only saw the earlier one, performed in July; I understand, however, that the two performances are exact replicas. The name is explained as meaning *eži bà*, i.e. the 'town prays'; but this interpretation is somewhat doubtful since the same phrase can also be read as *eži 'bà*, 'the place' or 'ground of the town', which would tally with the name of a very similar ritual in other places, called *žikinta*—'the ground (or soil) of the town'. The early *žiba* coincides with the harvest of bullrush millet, the first crop of the year. On the eve of the ceremonial the priest cuts a bundle of millet on his farm and has gruel made from it. About noon the next day he goes to the place of the sacrifice, which closely resembles that of *fitakū*, accompanied by much the same congregation. A black she-goat is killed (contributed by the chief), blood and beer are poured on the mound of earth (now concealing no sacred 'stone'), and the food is eaten by the people present; a share is once more sent to the chief. In this as in the other ritual in his charge the *Žigí* is assisted by his sons and brothers. The *Žigí* prays twice, first while killing the animal and again when making the offering of beer and blood:

(1) 'May the whole town have health; may it have to eat, may it have to drink, may the whole town have health'.

(2) '*Tsoci* (Our Lord), what we are giving this year, (what) we are doing thus: God may give health (for that reason); the doing of new (things), may it come (to prosper) also next year, also (in) a thousand years.'

When the sacrificial meal is over, the *žiba* assumes the new aspect of a public ceremonial and festivity, which sharply distinguishes it from the *fitakū* and all other movable rites. The congregation walks back to the village, stopping at the chief's house. The priest alone may enter the chief's sleeping hut, where the latter has been awaiting his visitor, while the others stay in the entrance hut. The priest informs the chief that the ritual has been completed and the chief replies—'It is well; (after) what has been done, may God give that we pass through (endure) this year, and that the next years may pass (in well being).' From the chief's house the congregation repairs to the home of the priest, where they stay to drink the rest of the beer. Meanwhile women and young men, who were not allowed to see the earlier part of the ceremony, have gathered outside the house and drums have been brought out. A dance begins in which the old men alone are supposed to perform; actually, the younger men (not the women) join in later, but they are only suffered to take part and are sometimes stopped, though not very seriously. Later the whole crowd walks in procession through the village, 'saluting' on the way the houses of the various family heads and finally stopping at the dancing ground. Here the dance is resumed, in an unexcited fashion, until nightfall, when both the dance and the ceremonial come to an end.

We noticed, in the *žiba* prayer, the emphasis on 'this year and next' and on 'new things', that is, on the completion of a phase, and on continuity and renewal. This idea is even more concretely expressed; for immediately after the ceremony the skin of the goat that had been sacrificed is sewn into a sack, shaped like bellows, to be kept in the priest's house until next year's ritual. There it will serve as an instrument of ordeal, anyone accused of a crime being able to protest his innocence by touching the bag: if he lied, his body would swell up ('like the bellows'). Thus the protection of the law and the punishment of crime are renewed year by year by the force of this *kuti* concerned with the 'doing of new things'.

The *gunnu*, unlike most other Nupe rituals, has its special myth, which relates how the ceremonial originated and also explains, if only in an elliptic and cursory fashion, one or two features of the actual practice.[1] It tells of a mysterious stranger who, many generations ago, came to live among the Beni, in a small hill village in the north, close to the border of Gwari country. After a while he developed leprosy, was looked after by the kind-hearted villagers, and eventually died. As was the custom, the body of the leper was abandoned in the uninhabited bush on the top of the hill. Later, it was found that the body had miraculously disappeared and that in its place there had appeared a patch of pure white sand. The villagers then realized that the stranger had been no ordinary mortal and that God himself had buried him. They planted a tree on the place and instituted a big ceremony to be performed annually, so that the *kuci* of the dead should be propitiated and duly worshipped. The ritual, which is said to have

[1] A much more detailed description of the ritual and the full texts of the *gunnu* songs are given in *J.R.A.I.*, 1937, vol. LXVII.

spread in the course of years through Beni country and the whole of Nupe, is the *gunnu*; the hill is known as *Gunnu* Hill; and the white sand is said to possess special healing properties (a claim which chemical analysis did not confirm). The *gunnu* priest of that village is regarded as the senior among all other *gunnu* priests, almost as the spiritual head of their fraternity; for at the beginning of the month of the *gunnu* celebrations every born *Ndazo* of Beni country makes a pilgrimage to *Gunnu* Hill, travelling by night and in secrecy, to salute and consult the local priest, and to collect a little of the sand and a few pebbles from the sacred place. The sand will later be used as medicine and for divining (in *hati* fashion); the pebbles will be placed on the place of sacrifice, and when the *Ndazo* opens the *gunnu* dance he will put one of the pebbles in his mouth.

These are all the tangible links between the myth and the ritual practice. We note that they apply only to the Beni sub-tribe, a section more closely united by kinship ties as well as politically,[1] so that the collaboration of the *gunnu* priests goes together with co-operation in other, secular spheres. In the rest of the country the religious collaboration and the myth sustaining it are alike unknown; at least, the myth might be known only sketchily, and would be quoted merely as a curious tale of no real consequence.

Apart from these few references to details of procedure, the myth offers only a vague and incongruous pedigree for the ritual itself; it merely relates certain mysterious happenings in the distant past, which seem to have no bearing on the aim or the general design of the ritual, and then concludes summarily—'And this was the beginning of the *gunnu*'. This kind of jumpy logic is of course not unfamiliar in the mythology of primitive peoples; its incongruity in the present case can be seen from these three instances. To begin with, so unique a feature as the *Ndazo* priesthood is completely omitted in the mythical account. Conversely, the arrival and death of the stranger and the whole notion of this saint-like personage, buried by God Himself, are in no way touched upon in the ceremony; indeed, they represent utterly alien features in the conceptual framework of Nupe religion. Characteristically, when the Nupe tell the story they have no other term to describe the character of the stranger than the Arabic word *wali* ('saint'). Finally, the crucial motif in the myth, leprosy, is without bearing upon the aim and design of the ritual. There are certain indirect and tenuous links: everywhere in Nupe (not

---

[1] I am referring to the old federation of the twelve Beni 'towns', which in some respects survived to the present day. See above, p. 70, and *A Black Byzantium*, p. 25.

only among the Beni) the burial of lepers is the responsibility of the *gunnu* priests; and leprosy, as we know, is considered a 'disease of God', as the *gunnu* is a '*kuti* of God.' In their speculations about the meaning of the myth the Nupe indeed seize upon this last point. But they would only enlarge upon the terrifying aspects of leprosy and its divine preordainedness, being content to draw the parallel with a *kuti* equally powerful, dangerous, and divinely preordained. Their interest does not go further; none of my informants, for example, referred to the male-female principle believed to govern leprosy (and unrepresented in the ritual); nor did they attempt to relate the name *gunnu* to the name for leprosy, *Sokó 'gũ*, an etymological speculation which, from my knowledge of the Nupe ways of thinking, I should have expected. The Nupe, in brief, do not feel the need for any closely argued 'mythical charter' of their religious practices; and indeed, as I have stressed, the *gunnu* myth is altogether an exception.

A few informants offered me their theories about the derivation of the name *gunnu*. According to one the ritual was so called because of *egũ na dã miní 'nu ō na*, because of the 'red earth that is inside (the furrows) of hoeing'; according to another the reason was that, in the ritual, 'one reaches the end of the wandering, it is accomplished', *àgũ 'nu mã, nwa dà zo*; in a third interpretation *gunnu* was taken to be the word *nugũ* ('boundary', 'limits'), reversed.[1] The first version would merely bring out the character of the *gunnu* as a farmer's ritual; the other two versions go more deeply, alluding to the characteristic concern of the ritual with the completion of a phase, and with 'end' and 'renewal'. Even so, the arguments are specious ones, ignoring, for example, the tone structure of Nupe language. Let us call them what they are, a play upon words and mere speculation.

To turn to the ceremonial itself. It lasts for three to five days, according to the amount of food and drink which the people are able to accumulate. The celebration I observed in Doko started on the 17th of February and lasted until the 19th.[2] Like the *žiba*, the *gunnu* has an esoteric part, performed outside the village, in the secrecy of the *gunnu 'bà* ('*gunnu* place'), and a public one, performed on the village dancing ground. The congregation of the esoteric rite includes both older men and youths, the youngest being about 15. The *gunnu* place looks much like the places of

---

[1] Such reversals of bisyllabic nouns occur quite often in Nupe language; they turn the noun into the corresponding verb, so that *nugũ*, 'limit', would become *gũ(e)-nu* 'reaching the limit', 'accomplish'.

[2] The date is not inflexible; in the same year the nearby village of Pichi celebrated the *gunnu* almost a month later, since the people had no 'leisure' before that, being kept busy by the collection of tax arrears.

sacrifice previously described; again, there is a big tree in the middle, this time adorned with a strip of white cloth, which is renewed at each ceremonial; if the village has a 'born' *Ndazo*, he will wear the new cloth round his waist while officiating, and put it back on the tree afterwards. Also tied to the tree are two tortoise shells, which will serve as drinking vessels during the sacrifice and afterwards as musical instruments, being beaten with small sticks. The other musical instruments used in the *gunnu* are as unusual and are employed on no other occasion; they consist in two large and two small pot drums (of Gwari manufacture), and a raft-zither made of reed. During the year they are stored in the house of the *Žigi*, who has, however, no other function in the *gunnu*.

On the day of the *gunnu*, before dawn, the *gunnu* drums begin to play. This is the signal for the boys and young men to leave their homes and to go to some secret place in the bush, led by the *Ndazo* and the *Ndakotsu* (the appointed leader of their age grades), Arrived in the bush, where they may only talk in whispers, they remove their caps and everyday clothes and dress in *gunnu* fashion, that is, in a loincloth of striped cloth such as the women wear round the waist. They break off twigs of the *nūbeci* tree, which will later serve as the 'whips of the *gunnu*'.[1] Then the novices are taught the deportment required of them at the ceremonial—to keep their heads bent, eyes on the ground, as one does in the presence of superiors; equally they are taught the *gunnu* salute, which consists in a fierce yell, accompanied by the throwing-up of both arms and a rhythmical stamping on the ground. During these proceedings the novices at least are visibly frightened, while the older boys try to show their unconcern. Finally, they leave the bush, walking in single file, the tallest first, to the place of the sacrifice; throughout the ceremonial the young men will move thus, in a long file, 'whips' in hand, led or sometimes driven by the priest and the *Ndakotsu*.

At the *gunnu* place they join the older men who have meanwhile assembled. The musicians sit under the tree and have started drumming and singing. Everyone is stripped to the waist and sits on leaves or branches, since it is sacrilege to sit on the bare ground of the *gunnu 'ba*. The older men form a circle round the place of the sacrifice; the youths sit some distance apart, though they will from time to time jump up to 'salute' late-comers or to drive away strangers who might trespass on the secret site. Soon the sacrifice follows, which varies from year to year, according to the advice of

---

[1] This tree has no further ceremonial significance, though its twigs are sometimes stuck into the ground outside a house as a charm against thieves.

the diviner; in the ritual I observed it consisted of fish-and-porridge and the ubiquitous libation of beer. The *Ndazo*, on his knees and using one of the tortoise shells for a vessel, pours some beer on the ground, speaking thus:

'Lord God, take this. The *Etsu Daži* (chief) ordered us to make *gunnu*. *Gunnu*, may the town have health. The food of the soil, may it thrive greatly. The women, God give them children. May the town have health. Rain may fall, yam may thrive, corn may thrive. God may cause that everything shall prosper.'

Then the priest drinks, and more beer is handed round in gourds, first to the old men in order of age and rank, then to the musicians, and lastly to the young men. The sacrifice and invocation are repeated, now with a dish of food. Throughout the proceedings the *Ndazo's* younger brother acts as his assistant. At the end of the meal everyone washes his hands, in the same order of seniority, and the gourds which served as dishes are broken in pieces and left on the ground.

The sacrifice over, dancing begins, still in the secrecy of the *gunnu 'ba*. The older men dance singly, the young men in a group, the novices being taught and shown the dance steps by others who are more experienced. But while the older men can pause whenever they are tired, the youths must dance without a break, and are driven on to greater and greater exertions by their leaders. The excitement is visibly mounting, and may indeed go too far, for the young dancers will suddenly start using their 'whips' on one another. Though flogging with the whips of the *gunnu* has its place in the ritual, its premature introduction, at the place of the sacrifice, is a serious breach of discipline, and the culprits are made to kneel before the *Ndazo* and beg forgiveness. The incident is taken as a sign that the dance had lasted too long already (it had lasted about three hours); silence is ordered once again, the dance stops, and the congregation moves in a long procession to the village.

The secret part of the *gunnu* is now over; what follows is done publicly and before a crowd of onlookers. The youths race each other to the village, half running half dancing. They will beat anyone standing in their way, and this liberal use of the whips continues when they all arrive at the village. They lash out at each other and at strangers or women, although both strangers and most women are allowed to watch this stage of the ceremonial. This episode does not last long, however, and gives way to a general dance begun by the *Ndazo* in slow, dignified fashion. He is followed by other old men and the chief himself, who only now joins in the proceedings. Eventually everybody joins in, congregation and onlookers, men as well as women, and all join also in the singing.

The dance frequently rises to feverish excitement, when the youths will suddenly resume using their whips, violently and against anyone. The flogging now has a purpose: when directed against male adolescents it is thought to promote growth and maturity; when directed against women, fertility. But there are also phases of calm as well as humorous episodes, acclaimed by general laughter. One episode, in particular, may be mentioned: now and again, the young men will imitate, with comic exaggeration, a typical women's dance or caricature the walk and gestures of women.

I will not describe the dance further: it fills the rest of the *gunnu* festivities, being interrupted only for a brief night's rest, and ends when all the beer is exhausted and everyone too tired to carry on. I will only note these important and partly unique features. Some time during the dance the young men form themselves into a procession led by the *Ndazo* and march and dance through the village, still singing the *gunnu* songs, to give the 'salute' in front of the houses of high-ranking elders. On the way they also visit the childless women of the village; for these are strictly forbidden to watch the *gunnu* dance and must hide in their huts until the ceremonial is over. These women may be unhappily barren; or they may be suspected of avoiding childbearing and family duties so that they might lead the immoral life of female traders and prostitutes (which, in Nupe, means one and the same thing). In either case the *Ndazo* will enter their house and encourage or admonish them, as the case may be; the woman, kneeling before him, will receive two lashes with the *gunnu* whip, administered by one of the young men, which is both a punishment and a promise of fertility. Women who have no taste for either will have to leave the village or hide in some other house during the critical period, as indeed quite a few are doing.

Again, few other Nupe rituals include a mixed dance of the sexes; in the *gunnu*, this is not only permitted but considered a relevant part of the celebration, as is the whole excited and abandoned tone of the dance. Always, when describing the *gunnu*, the Nupe will use some such phrase—'we make merry, we drink, we dance, men and women together without order, until we talk without sense'. This excitement is in no small measure sexual; not only is the attention of the young men constantly drawn to the other sex (even by the fact that they wear an item of women's dress), but the week preceding the *gunnu* and the whole period of the celebration are also marked by a severe prohibition of all sexual intercourse, lest death visit the community. Only when the dance is ended and everyone has bathed, the men in a nearby stream, the women at home, is the rule of chastity lifted; the same night men and women will again sleep together, matrimonially or promiscuously—no one cares. Which final aspect of the *gunnu* is once more emphasized in all statements.

The ceremonial is thus full of allusions to procreation and fertility. But we noticed also the emphasis on male adolescence, more precisely, on the role of the age grades, on the respect relationship between youth and old age, and on the teaching or initiation of the novices. In the ritual I described this last aspect was only lightly touched upon. But in a fuller version of the *gunnu*, which disappeared in Doko some ten or twenty years ago, the emphasis on initiation was much stronger. The short prelude in the bush was then expanded to a full night; and the youths were made to dress up in elaborate fashion and to paint their bodies red and white, so that everybody should see that they were '*gunnu* men'. All through the night the novices were kept in a state of nervous excitement and fear by tales of the spirits that haunt the bush; often the dreaded apparition of the *ndakó gboyá* would materialize to punish any youth who had, in the preceding year, offended against this or that rule of custom, and especially against the rules of filial respect. We shall hear more of the *ndakó gboyá* later on; let me say here that its part is acted by a member of the secret society of that name, and that it is also referred to as the 'policeman of the *gunnu*', which epithet aptly summarizes its functions.

Today this episode has fallen in abeyance in Doko as elsewhere. The reasons are not the same in all places. In Kutigi, a relatively recent and pseudo-Moslem ceremonial has absorbed the initiation aspect of the *gunnu*, so that the more elaborate version of the ritual came to lose its particular appeal.[1] In Mokwa, the vigil in the bush fell in disfavour with the young men, who refused to suffer any longer the threats and punishments that go with that episode; the remonstrations of parents and elders were met by the argument that even young men were nowadays earning money and paying taxes, and had hence become the equals of their seniors. In Beni country, the attractions of Bida town were seducing more and more adolescents away from the 'crude' village celebrations, so that eventually the greatly reduced attendance made the whole initiation rite seem futile. About that time, too, the Government suppressed the *ndakó gboyá* secret society, the drama in the bush thus losing its main actors. These varied causes reflect the multifarious changes assailing traditional Nupe life, in the political and economic sphere, in family relations, and in recreation as well as in religious belief. That the changes were so effective in truncating the *gunnu* (while falling more lightly or tardily upon other ceremonials) is not due only to the force behind the new influences; rather is it in large measure due to a factor touched upon before,

[1] See my article *The Gani ritual of Nupe*, Africa, 1949, vol. XIX, p. 183.

84   RITUAL

the greater vulnerability of the *gunnu* ceremonial. For the very ambitiouness of its scope exposes it, on too many sides at once, to the impact of change.

3. THE RIVER

(i) *Ritual Calendar: Priestship*

In Jebba Island I recorded the fullest repertoire of rituals anywhere in Nupe country, including three movable and five 'fixed' rituals, one of the latter being also performed 'without a month', whenever the need arises. Not all, however, are still in use, so that the ritual calendar of the island now approximates more closely to that of other communities. Though the people quote specific rational reasons for the discontinuation of the respective rituals, I suspect that the 'repertoire' itself proved too large and simply became unworkable under modern conditions. Jebba Island owes its rich list of ceremonials essentially to two facts; first, to its double livelihood, derived from the land as well as from the river, and reflected in the religious institutions; and secondly, to the possession of the sacred emblems of Tsoede, which are scattered mainly along the old highway of the Kingdom—the river valley.

Today, the Jebba people perform two movable and two fixed rituals, one which serves both purposes and one which, formerly fixed, has now become 'movable'. The movable rituals proper are the *ketsá*, previously mentioned, and the *tídzana*, a sacrifice to the sacred 'Chain of Tsoede'. The fixed ceremonials comprise the rituals *mamma* and *dzakó*, both performed in the 9th month (November–December). The *gunnu*, traditionally performed in the same month, is nowadays celebrated as a movable rite, though in a different sense it still retains its compulsory character. The ritual *ndáduma*, finally, is performed both as a fixed rite, again in the 9th month, and as a movable ritual. Another movable ritual, the *žikinta*, concerned mainly with success in hunting and fishing but also with childbirth and health, is now hardly practised; and a fixed ritual, *sokokó*, was discontinued some twenty years ago. To some extent the observance of the ritual *mamma* has also been affected by the changed conditions; for most of the grass masks worn in the ceremonial were destroyed in a fire some years ago and have not been replaced; the people now husband their two remaining masks and perform the ritual only in years when there is a special reason. Even so, the ceremonial cannot be moved to another date, and has for this reason been included among the 'fixed' rituals.

The different rituals are again in the charge of different officiants.

Two of these are priests in the strict sense of the word—the *Ndazo* of the *gunnu*, whose office has the same miraculous connotation as elsewhere, and the hereditary priest of the *ketsá* ritual. The priestship of the remaining rituals goes with secular status, that is, with certain ranks vested in family heads and with the appropriate positions on the council of elders. Yet while the large majority of the Jebba ranks (eleven out of thirteen) are non-hereditary, being based on election and promotion, only one of these (a minor rank) entails a religious office, the rank *Ndace*, whose encumbent officiates in the *dzakó* ritual. The two hereditary ranks, on the other hand, *Ejukó* and *Tswanya*, are both linked with duties of priestship. The *Ejukó* is the guardian of the Chain of Tsoede and officiates in the corresponding ritual; he is at the same time an important member of the village council and was formerly its chief 'legal officer' as well, since the Chain of Tsoede figured prominently in the legal machinery of the country. The connection between religious and political office is even more pronounced in the case of the *Tswanya*. In the religious sphere he takes charge of the ritual *mamma*; in the secular sphere it is his privilege and duty to deputize for the (non-hereditary) village chief during an interregnum and to name the successor. In other words, he is an hereditary 'king-maker' who, as I have explained elsewhere, appears in all Nupe communities which are without hereditary chieftainship and whose investiture with a sacred office replaces the religious connotation which otherwise attaches to chieftainship itself.[1] As in Doko, then, religious and secular power are at once united and kept distinct, though in Jebba the separation is the more marked.

If the priestship of several rituals is thus linked with secular ranks, the same kind of link applies to the rituals as such. For two of these, the *gunnu* and *dzakó*, also form part of the funerary ceremonials for titled elders, being added to the rites known as 'Three Days' (after the burial) and 'Forty Days'.[2] Thus the *gunnu* is performed at the death of the chief, the *gunnu* priest, the *Tswanya* and *Ejukó*, and at the death of seven other elders; the *dzakó*, for the *Ndace* and two other elders. Only one rank is left out, that of *Kpotuŋ*, which was introduced relatively recently, having been copied from the hierarchy of ranks in the capital; being an innovation, it is also unconnected with the traditional usage.[3] When thus employed in the funerary ceremonial, the *dzakó* is greatly reduced in scale; the scale of the *gunnu* varies with the importance of the rank held by the deceased; the death of the chief, *Ndazo*, *Tswanya*, and an elder styled *Cece* commands the

---
[1] See *A Black Byzantium*, pp. 52–3.   [2] See below, p. 122.
[3] This rank was not included in the thirteen mentioned above.

full-scale performance, while in the remaining cases there is a mere suggestion of the ritual.

This association of two fixed rituals with the funerary ceremonial presents several puzzling features. To begin with, the distribution of the two rituals among the thirteen ranks of Jebba is strikingly uneven, ten ranks being linked with the *gunnu* and only three with the *dzakó*. This, I was told, was not always so; but a more even distribution was upset in the course of time, when certain ranks originally linked with the *dzakó* were allowed to lapse because at the death of the incumbents there happened to be no suitable successors. This may be so; during my stay in Jebba, for example, three minor ranks of the *dzakó* group (not counted among the thirteen) were in fact vacant, and several more may have completely disappeared. Even so, the fact remains that no attempt was made to even out the inequality, though this would present no difficulty in this non-hereditary rank system. Furthermore, the dual division on the grounds of the suitable funerary ceremonial extends, not only to the men holding the respective ranks, but to their whole 'house' (i.e. lineage); thus the Jebba people generally class any individual or family as belonging either to the *gunnuciži* or *dzakociži* (the '*gunnu* people' or the '*dzakó* people'). This fits in oddly with a rank system based mainly on election and promotion; for it would imply that whole kin groups might have to change their religious affiliation if their titled head is promoted from a rank belonging to one section to a rank belonging to the other, or if a new family head is elected to a rank, say, of the *dzakó* group while his predecessor belonged to the *gunnu* section. Such promotions and elections do in fact occur and, as might be expected, entail considerable confusion. Most puzzling of all, this comprehensive division of the population into ritual moieties seems to have no relevant consequences, religious or otherwise. At least, the only consequence ascribed to it is both incongruous and obscure. It was claimed by most informants that the sons of *gunnuci* families alone were formerly allowed to join in the esoteric part of the *gunnu*, while no such rule applied to the *dzakó*.[1] One informant, an old man of high rank belonging to the *dzakó* section, maintained that that ritual was similarly exclusive. Since the rule concerning the *gunnu* is no longer in force (if it ever existed), it was impossible to verify the respective information; the *dzakó* ceremonial I witnessed certainly failed to

---

[1] If this were true it would obviously mean that boys and young men originally admitted to the secret part of the *gunnu* might be excluded from it when their family head changed his rank, or that boys not previously admitted might suddenly acquire the necessary qualifications. Either contingency is difficult to credit.

substantiate the other 'theory'. Indeed, I suspect that it is mere 'theory'—an attempt to lend neatness and logic to an unconvincing and haphazard division.

It should perhaps be added that there is no trace in Jebba of an original ethnic division of the kind which, in other Nupe communities, accounts for the divided 'ownership' of particular rituals. Nor does the situation elsewhere in Nupe furnish any clue. The association of rituals with the funeral ceremonial for elders occurs, so far as I can judge, only in the river valley. But the puzzling dual division does not occur outside Jebba. In Bele, a small village up-river belonging to the same sub-tribe, Gbedegi, the two main local rituals, *gunnu* and *žiba*, are performed together at the death of all elders. In Mokwa, another Gbedegi town, a short distance from the river, the majority of rankholders are given a *gunnu* funeral; at the death of the *Sheshi* (the hereditary 'king-maker') his 'own' ritual is performed, and at the death of the *Samaza* (a non-hereditary rank), the masked ceremonial *elo*, which is in the charge of that elder. In neither case are the two men or their families excluded from the *gunnu*. Thus, as regards the Jebba version of that custom, I can only conclude that it represents an isolated attempt, neither thorough nor ultimately successful, to divide two of the main rituals evenly among the community. And this seems consistent with the general predilection of the Nupe for dichotomous arrangements.

(ii) *Movable Rituals*

A novel characteristic of these rites in Jebba is that they can be performed also at the request of individuals, even of strangers and non-Nupe, who wish to invoke the powerful 'magic' of the island or have been advised by diviners to do so. Indeed, the movable rituals are meant to benefit a much larger population, that is, all the groups living on the river. The *ketsá* sacrifice, more particularly, has made Jebba Island almost a place of pilgrimage.

The man in charge of the *ketsá* is called *Ndádoro*, 'Father of *doro*' (which is another name for the ritual). A priest in the strict sense of the word, like the *Ndazo*, he also walks about bareheaded and always wears 'ritual' dress. The *Ndádoro* I knew was old and blind, so that his actual duties fell to his son and future successor, though the father would still lend his presence and authority to the ritual performance.

There is a story connected with the origin of the ritual. Once a disastrous flood of the Niger destroyed all houses and farms and brought famine to the river valley. The *Kuta* at Muregi, the chief of the 'Downstream Kede', had learned from Tsoede how to combat floods and prevent their recurrence. Following this advice, the

Kuta sent a white cow to Jebba, instructing the island people to add a white cock and some honey, and to sacrifice all these at the foot of *Ketsá* Rock. This was the beginning of the ritual, which is today repeated, still by the *Kuta's* order, whenever there is a danger of floods, and also when a new Kede chief assumes office. The story thus closely supports the actual practice so far as it bears on the welfare of the riverain people and on the strong political link between Jebba Island and the Kede sub-tribe.[1] But the story tells nothing of the origin of the *ketsá* priestship; nor does it refer to the much wider application of the ritual. For anyone on the river can request its performance—chiefs for their communities, individuals for themselves or their families—and can do so for widely different reasons; equally, the sacrifices will vary widely, according to the advice given by diviners. But while the ritual performed in the name of the Kede chief and for the whole river population is on a large scale, involving the usual sacrificial meal of all the elders as well as drumming, singing, and dancing, the 'private' rituals, strictly 'businesslike', consist only in the sacrifice itself, performed by the priest and his close kinsmen. In 1936, for example, the following 'private' performances took place: the *Etsu* of Patigi sent a fowl, requesting it to be sacrificed for the general well-being of his community; the chief of a small riverain village did the same; a Hausa man offered a goat for good fishing; a Kakanda man a goat for 'health'; two Nupe men offered fowls to secure the birth of children; and there were other, similar, requests. A final instance concerned me personally. I had gone down with a severe attack of dysentery, and my Jebba friends, who visited me regularly, advised me to sacrifice a fowl in order to recover. The sacrifice was duly performed, though unhappily I was too weak at the time to attend it: and this was the closest I ever got to seeing the *ketsá*, which was performed so irregularly as well as promptly that the news of its performance never reached me in time.

The second movable rite is concerned with the 'Chain of Tsoede' and is called by that name, *tídzana*. In appearance, this is an old slave chain, with fetters for arms and legs; it is kept in the *Ejukó's* house and is invariably covered with dried-up blood and beer from the sacrifice. In 1936 three of these sacrifices were performed, all small-scale and 'businesslike', and invoked by local people.[2] One sacrifice was for a man who offered a goat to recover from a fever;

[1] For fuller information on the Kede sub-tribe see my chapter on 'The Kede: A Riverain State in Northern Nigeria', in *African Political Systems*, 1940, ed. M. Fortes and E. E. Evans-Pritchard.
[2] Strangers, too, may invoke the *tídzana*, though this is said to happen relatively rarely.

the second for the chief, who was worried by the numerous cases of illness in the village; and the third for a young man who sacrificed a fowl so that his wife might bear a child. We note that the *tídzana* is appealed to for much the same reason as the *ketsá*; let me note also that the third suppliant came of a family which 'owned' a particular medicine reputed to cure sterility, even though he himself had invoked the sacred chain instead. In his case as in all others the sacrifice had been indicated by the diviners, who are the final judges of the appropriate supernatural remedy.

I mentioned before that the Chain of Tsoede formerly also served as an ordeal of deadly efficacy and as an instrument of execution.[1] It may seem puzzling that a tool of death should be believed to restore health and fertility. Yet even as a tool of death the Chain of Tsoede is a *kuti*; indeed, it is used to kill because it has the supernatural power also to purify the executioner and sanctify the deed. And as the *kuti* is always a force, divine in origin and unspecific in nature, so it can, by definition, be made to do many things.

We may add the ritual *ndáduma* to this list of movable rites although it figures equally among the fixed ceremonials. In its movable form, it is concerned with the rise and fall of the river and is performed when the seasonal floods are late or of threatening dimensions (though not sufficiently grave to warrant the performance of the *ketsá*). The name of the ritual, 'Father Niger', refers to a whole species of spirits inhabiting various localities on the river. The most powerful of these river spirits is said to live at Bazumagi, a small village up-river from Jebba. Here the local priest performs a special version of the ceremonial, which takes place only when ordered by the *Kuta* of the Kede. In the course of this ceremonial the priest wades into the river and throws a stone ashore, the place where the stone drops being believed to show that year's highwater mark. In Jebba, the ritual is in the hands of the *Tswanya*, who sacrifices a white cock, some beer, and a little honey (a favourite food of all river spirits). I did not witness the movable ritual but only the fixed version, which is the last in the cycle of rites falling in the ninth month; it was performed on 5th December, succeeding the ritual *dzakó* by two days. The actual observance, however, is the same in both rituals, though the fixed form bears not only on the river floods, but also, more generally, on health, prosperity, and childbirth in the village. In neither case can the *ndáduma* be made to serve the private interests of individuals or

---

[1] See above, p. 32.—The name *tídzana* is said to mean 'head (*eti*) of Dzana', Dzana being the name of the legendary first victim of this method of execution.

strangers. Indeed, it is not supposed to be seen by strangers, and these are driven away with much shouting and angry gestures; the contingency arises quite often, for the place of the sacrifice is fairly public, being situated on the open bank of an arm of the Niger, close to the landing place of a canoe ferry.

The ritual takes place in the morning and lasts about four hours. Eight elders accompany the priest to the *kuti* place, where a mound of earth has been thrown up close to the edge of the water. Water, fetched from the river in gourds, is first poured over the mound, followed by a little honey, the rest of which is thrown into the river. Then the white cock is beheaded over the mound so that his blood drips on to the earth; the head is left lying on the mound and the feathers are planted around it in a circle; this is done as a sign that the ritual has been performed and as a suggestion to passers-by to leave a gift to the spirits. A libation of beer follows, the rest of the beer being passed round among the elders. Meanwhile the preparation of the meal has begun, the cock being cooked in corngruel over an open fire; while this goes on, the old men chat freely, without any signs of awe or restraint. When the meal is done, the priest throws a few morsels on the mound and into the river, and the rest is eaten by all present. Finally, all wash their hands in the river and a last gourd of river water is poured over the mound. At each offering the priest repeats the same brief prayer, which is of the usual informal kind; one prays that God may give health, that there should be plenty of food, and that the women may have children. Though the prayer starts with the invocation of 'Father Niger' no further mention is made of the river. During the sacrifice I witnessed a sentence was added *ex tempore*—'God give health to the White Man', a reference to my recent illness. Such special appeals, I was told, were quite in order; though no individual could order the *ndáduma*, the health or fate of any member of the community (which status was accorded to me) can suitably be brought to the notice of the river spirits and of God.

(iii) *Fixed Rituals*

The *kuti mamma* is supposed to start the cycle of rites linked with the 9th month. Once more, however, the ritual time table is not rigid; the performance I saw, for example, fell on the 16th November 1934, i.e. in the middle of the 8th month in Nupe reckoning. Also it lasted one day, more precisely one night, instead of the traditional week. The ritual, which is again in the charge of the *Tswanya*, includes two distinct observances which appear to have been merged in a purely fortuitous fashion. The first, called *zumácikã* ('Back of the Bush'), is concerned with the sacrifice to a *cigbe* shrine of that name, said to ward off smallpox; the other, the *mamma* proper, consists mainly in the appearance and dance of masked figures called *nãgbe*. The masks themselves are referred to as *kũyi* ('full garment') or simply as *ewo* ('dress'), and their appearance is meant to cleanse the village of evil influences. These are not further specified save negatively, in that they exclude witchcraft. The *zumácikã* is said to have been introduced by an old woman who, many years ago, happened to arrive in Jebba during a smallpox epidemic and taught the people the secret of the appropriate medicine; nothing further is known about her, about the manner of her death, or about her burial place. The medicine is contained (so it is said) in an earthen pot which now stands under a low grass roof in the middle of the village. It is in every respect an unusual version of *cigbe*. It cannot be utilized at will but only at this ceremonial; it belongs to the village and not to any individual owner; nor yet is it used in the manner of other medicines. For the substance in question is neither drunk nor otherwise applied to the body, since its effect would be deadly if it were so used; indeed no one has ever seen it. It is hidden inside the vessel, being periodically increased when blood and beer from the sacrifice are added, and its mere presence is magically effective. This effect bears on the prevention of the disease rather than its cure: smallpox is being 'kept away as you keep away a stranger'; which preventive aspect is also reflected in the date of the ritual, which falls towards the end of the cold season, while outbreaks of smallpox are believed to occur only during the hot season, in the 10th and 11th month.

The masks of the *kuti mamma*, on the other hand, are attributed, with so many other things, to Tsoede. They are made of dried grass, consisting of a skirt and a kind of veil covering face and chest, and during the year are stored in the houses of various elders. While the *cigbe* vessel stands on a public place and is in no way concealed, the masks must be kept hidden and may be put on only in a safe and secret place. The whole ritual is similarly veiled in secrecy; it takes place at night, the women having been warned to keep indoors, and out of the sight of strangers: if women or strangers were to see this *kuti*, they would be killed by its 'force'.[1]

The ceremonial I saw started about 8 p.m. on a moonless night,

[1] The fear of the *mamma* is a very real one. At the time of the performance here described the District Head from Mokwa, a Fulani nobleman, happened to stay in Jebba. He heard that a 'feast' was going to take place, and when he learned that I was going he decided to come also. He arrived when the dance was already in progress, gave one look, and literally fled. His hurried retreat was received with much hilarity by the men present, who added: 'This is how all strangers run away when they hear the *mamma*.'

and was performed to the light of a hurricane lamp and a number of grass torches. About forty men were assembled in front of the *cigbe* shrine. The beating of drums and a high-pitched screech of the men announced the beginning of the ritual, giving also a final warning to women who might still be abroad. The *cigbe* pot had been decorated with a strip of white cloth tied round its neck, which was referred to as the 'dress' of the vessel, that is, by the same name as the masks worn by the dancers. These appeared later, accompanied by two older men, one of them the *Ndakotsu* of the senior age grade, and some youths, all carrying sticks to drive away and beat intruders. There were two masks, worn by young men of the senior age grade, who had dressed in the presence of the *mamma* priest while he spoke this brief prayer:

'Our Lord God, let us go out (as masks); men and women (who must not see the masks), God will kill them. Now the *kuti* enters (into the masks). May God cause that the thing (i.e. smallpox and evil in general) does not stay here (in the village).

At the place of the *cigbe* shrine, the masks keep at first in the shadow without moving. The officiant kneels down in front of the *cigbe* vessel, whose lid has been removed, while the rest of the men sit around him in a triple halfcircle, the old men on the inside, younger men in the middle, youths on the outside. The man who actually performs the sacrifice is the *Ndakotsu*, since the *Tswanya* is too old and weak; but he sits immediately behind the younger man and from time to time instructs or corrects him. Throughout the proceedings the drums continue playing, and repeatedly the congregation breaks out in a high-pitched scream or calls out '*gengebaru*' (a meaningless word)—the 'greeting' of the *cigbe*.

The officiant pours some beer into the *cigbe* vessel, saying— '*Kuti*, we brew beer, we give thee water (i.e. beer), so that the town may have health, everyone may have sweet things, the women may have children, everything may prosper'. The libation is repeated three times, then the officiant drinks a little of the beer and pours the rest into the *cigbe* vessel. He kills a black male kid, slitting its throat, and lets the blood run into the vessel. The body of the animal is removed to be roasted over an open fire while the libation of beer is repeated, the same prayer being now spoken by the old men, one after the other. Finally, the beer goes round according to age and rank, the *Tswanya* drinking first. The men clearly enjoy drinking the beer and behave much as they would at any ordinary drinking party. This concludes the first phase of the ceremonial; the proceedings that follow belong to the *mamma* proper.

They begin with singing and a slow and dignified dance of a few old men. The masks soon join in, being acclaimed with shouts of '*mamari*', the 'greeting' of the *mamma* masks. Later the masks, accompanied by all the young men, set out on a dance-procession through the village, where they beat with their sticks on the doors of houses, to frighten all evil persons (and all women). On the way they 'salute' the houses of chief and elders and also look out for strangers who might have strayed into the village. The dance procession is repeated several times, and on every return the masks join in the singing and dancing, which become more and more general. Let me stress that the dance preserves its restrained and quiet character throughout, the occasional shrieks notwithstanding. Altogether, the general mood is neither excited nor severe. The men who stay behind at the *cigbe* shrine, if they do not dance, talk in whispers but quite informally, about previous performances of the *kuti*, about old times, and so forth; one of the elders takes the opportunity of telling me about the meaning and rules of the *mamma*. Some time during the dance the meal has been prepared and is eaten by the congregation after some morsels of food are dropped into the *cigbe* vessel. It is by then 11 o'clock. There is no washing of hands, and no other formal conclusion of the sacrifice. Singing and dancing, and the drinking of beer while it lasts, go on in the same manner until dawn, though some old men, tired out, have fallen asleep. In the morning, the men return to their houses to sleep, while the womenfolk, now released from the night's prohibition, set about their day's work. Formerly, I was told, this went on for a whole week, with dancing at night and rest during the day.

The songs sung during the *mamma* refer, on the whole vaguely and obscurely, to the ceremonial and its rules, though the text is interspersed with meaningless words.

1

> The person who offends the *mamma*,
> He (the *mamma*) will hear it and tell it
>   (i.e. the person will be punished with death).

2

> The *mamma* instructs the masks;
> it is closed to the uninitiated.

3

> The masks, *woro woro*,
> The masks kill (evil) people,
> *Eyeh*——

4
Arato, one makes the *mamma*,
Arato, the drum of *mamma* (is playing).
By night, the drum of *mamma* is speaking.

5
They are making the *mamma* with it together,
They are making the *mamma* with it together
('it' refers to the *kuti*, the phrase meaning—
in the ceremonial masks and *kuti* are one).

The people have no theory why the cult should be particularly frightening to the women; on the contrary, they emphasize that the *mamma* is meant to frighten all evil doers and deny that it has any bearing on witchcraft (which is wielded essentially by women). Yet the cult is clearly the men's secret and seems to express male dominance and some antagonism between the sexes. Oddly enough, one of the ritual paraphernalia, the smallpox medicine, is described as a woman's gift. But let me leave this point for the moment and only point out that the *mamma*, which cleanses the community from evil influences, fittingly initiates the cycle of rites meant to procure more positive benefits—timely floods, as in the *ndáduma*, or health and fertility, as in the *dzakó*.

The latter ritual is supposed to succeed the *mamma* by ten days, though the performance I witnessed took place seventeen days later, on 3rd December. The *dzakó* is performed in public, without secrecy, in front of the sacred relics of Tsoede, two bronze figures of a man and a woman. Special musical instruments are used, two gourd rattles, and three drums hung with brass bells and other ornaments again attributed to Tsoede. The congregation during the sacrifice itself consists of the thirteen elders of Jebba, as usual bareheaded and stripped to the waist, and carrying long staves; but other men and women, even children, may watch and will later join in the dance. The officiant of the ritual is the *Ndace* (the 'Father of Hunting'), though the ritual has nothing to do with hunting. Nor has the rank itself this particular connotation. In Jebba, it is an elder's rank among others, though one specifically connected with the relics of Tsoede; for the *Ndace* is one of the four men who serve (or used to serve) as the 'executioners' wielding the Chain of Tsoede.

The ceremonial starts in the afternoon, with a sacrifice in front of the bronze figures, during which the officiant has the two rattle players on his right and left. The place on the priest's left, opposite the female figure, signifies 'birth', the place on his right, opposite the male figure, 'health'; which symbolism of right and left is unique in Nupe religious practice.[1] First, water is sprinkled on the ground and a little beer poured out; immediately afterwards the priest kills a white cock, cutting off its head and letting the blood drip on the earth. The head of the cock is left lying there while the body is taken away to be cooked later in the evening. Before the meal, in which only the elders share, a further offering of a few morsels of the meat is placed before the bronze figures. During each offering the *Ndace* utters this brief prayer—'God, may the town have health; may the (several) towns prosper; may the women bear children; the children, may they be plentiful.[2] The killing of the cock concludes the sacrifice proper: what follows is '*dzodzo*', '*jī raha*', mere 'playing' and 'merry-making'.

Even during the sacrifice an old woman and later an old man did a few dance steps. Afterwards more old women (bareheaded like the men) and all the old men, carrying their staves, join. Even very old men, who can hardly stand on their legs, try a few shaky steps. Later still, young women and girls form a ring round the musicians, singing and swaying rhythmically with the music without moving from the place; this motion is called the 'dance of the female bronze figure'. The two sexes never truly join in the dance; for the younger men do not dance at all, and the girls keep to themselves. Only old men and old women dance together, occasionally holding hands and behaving with jocular amourousness, almost like grandfather and grandmother remembering their youth; some such comments in fact come from the onlookers, who are greatly amused seeing 'the old people playing young couples'. Throughout, the dance is strikingly calm; nor is there any time for a more excited mood to gather force, for at dusk, after three hours, the ceremonial comes to an end. The songs sung at the *dzakó* are irrelevant little ditties, which have no bearing on the ritual.

About the *gunnu* I can be brief. I saw it in its small-scale version, as part of the funerary rites for the *Ejukó* who died during my stay in Jebba. It included only the sacrifice of a fowl (on the village dancing ground), the mixed dance, and the playing of the *gunnu* drums; the young men carried their whips, and the dance was a close replica of the one in Doko, though the funeral version omits the sexual taboo and loses much of the hectic excitement typical of the true *gunnu*. From the description given me of the full-scale ritual I gather that it used to correspond closely to the one I saw elsewhere, being, however, more elaborate, comprising the vigil in the bush of the adolescents as well as the appearance of

---

[1] *Eba* divination provides the only parallel, the slab called 'man' lying to the right of the slab called 'woman'.
[2] The plural in the second sentence is unusual; it refers to all the 'towns of Tsoede', that is, to all the settlements on the river possessing Tsoede relics.

the *ndakó gboyá*. As mentioned before, the practice was abandoned apparently in the early twenties. But it was since revived once, in 1931, at the death of the village chief, when even the *ndakó gboyá* society played its part (in spite of the official ban).

4. RITUAL AND CULTURE CHANGE

This seems an opportune place to consider the impact of changed conditions upon Nupe ritual, at least in its negative, disruptive aspects. The changes undergone by the Jebba rituals do not of course stand alone; in the last generation or two numerous pagan rituals all over Nupe country have been disappearing or have suffered more or less radical modifications. But the conditions in Jebba are in some respects unique and hence capable of illuminating factors and processes obscured elsewhere.

Let me, to begin with, say a few words about one of the abandoned Jebba rituals, the *sokokó*, whose name suggests a ceremonial of uncommon importance. It belonged to the cycle of rites performed in the 9th month; it was concerned with fertility, health, and prosperity in general and centred upon a sacrifice performed on the top of a hill overlooking the river valley. It is said to have been discontinued in 1914, when the residence of the Governor was built on the site of the sacrifice.

Now, similar reasons, similarly fortuitous, are also quoted in connection with certain other changes of ritual practice. In each case, my informants maintained, the disappearance of the *bà žiko*, the 'black' or 'secret place', led to the disappearance of the respective ceremonial or at least to some radical change in the observance. It is true that the place formerly chosen for the esoteric part of the *dzakó*, which used to lie on an uninhabited bank of the river, is today occupied by a riverside camp of Hausa fishermen; the old *gunnu* grove and the place in the bush where the *mamma* masks used to dress in secrecy have similarly lost their former seclusion, being now close to crowded thoroughfares. Yet it is equally true that suitable adjustments could be made: the *dzakó* is still regularly performed, with a programme only slightly changed; the *mamma*, though performed irregularly, has suffered this change for different reasons, and the masked dancers can still dress in secrecy, now in the privacy of an elder's house. Only the observance of the *gunnu* has been altered in a more far-reaching manner. These facts bear out a point made previously, that sacred places and the like are of relatively little importance in Nupe religion. If, then, a ritual is abandoned altogether or radically modified, this must be due to factors other than the loss of the customary locality and seclusion, inconvenient though the loss might be.

One such change, affecting the *gunnu*, has already been discussed. The changes that occurred in Jebba, however, show a new and interesting aspect in that they reduced an unusually rich repertoire of rites to dimensions both more moderate and more common. This levelling-down of the ritual schedule would seem to imply two things. First, it suggests that Jebba, which had clearly for a great length of time carried on happily with its numerous rituals, reduced their number in a crisis which did not as seriously affect other communities, whose ritual programme was less ambitious; secondly, we may assume that this levelling-down amounted to a reduction to essentials.

(1) The first assumption repeats, on a more general plane, what we previously said about the *gunnu* and its 'vulnerability' under changed conditions; if this seemed to attach to the ambitious scope of a single cult, the ambitiousness of a whole repertoire of ceremonials now proves to have the same effect. As regards the 'crisis' which precipitated the disruption, I already suggested its nature: the over-rich repertoire proved unworkable under modern conditions. More precisely, its demands upon time, interest, and resources must in many ways have clashed with the increase in trade and production, with the more severe economic competition as well as the new forms of economic stress, and with the many new interests, aesthetic, recreational, and political, which emerged in recent years. These influences, too, have been felt throughout Nupe country. Comparing Jebba and Doko in particular, it may be said that both have been exposed to much the same impact, as they were similarly fortified against it. In Doko, the impact of change came from the proximity of Bida, the centre of trade and political activity, of a new religion, and of a new metropolitan culture. In Jebba the river and the railway, with their large cosmopolitan traffic, exercised a comparable influence. The Doko people are sustained in their traditional way of life by the knowledge that they are neither alone nor isolated, but belong to a large, closely knit group, the Beni sub-tribe, sharing the same institutions, intermarrying, and looking back upon a common history. In Jebba, the links with the riverain communities and the tangible evidence of the past, embodied in the Tsoede emblems, help to buttress the traditional values. If these weakened in the religious field, they did so, not because of the greater weight of changed circumstances in that community, but because of the greater 'vulnerability' of its religious institutions.

(2) The last remarks also suggest the sense in which the changes in the repertoire of rituals can be called a levelling-down to 'essentials'. As we have seen, the association of Jebba with the river and the figure of Tsoede is behind a large proportion of the

Jebba rituals; and these remained unaffected by the general reduction in number. Jebba, then, abandoned (or abandoned first) the rituals of more general appeal and more common occurrence, and preserved those bearing on its peculiar geographical and historical position. The 'national' rites as it were gave way before those of local importance. Equally, the rituals which gave way—*gunnu, sokokó, žikinta*—had in essence been concerned with benefits of a very general order, with fertility, health, livelihood and prosperity at large; while those which were preserved voice much more specific aims, bearing on the river floods, on ordeals, smallpox, and the expulsion of 'evil things'. Let us note that, when the former were abandoned, relatively little was lost, since the same aims were common to most other rituals; while the second group of ceremonials, which were not so duplicated, could not be discontinued without a serious loss of this kind. It fits into this picture that the Jebba *gunnu* was preserved in its more specific form, as a funerary rite for titled elders, and not as an annual ceremonial meant to renew fertility and well-being.

This process of change clearly presupposes that 'overlap' in the efficacy of religious observances which we noted so frequently. It is now thrown into relief from a new angle. The 'overlap', as we see, is not irreducible: it may give way, in a crisis, before the assessment of essentials.

A last question remains: do fixed and movable rituals resist change to a different degree? The fact that a movable Jebba rite, the *žikinta*, disappeared together with other, fixed, ceremonials would suggest a negative answer. Yet we also know that certain originally fixed rituals only survived in movable form, or at least in a form no longer rigidly bound up with annual performances, such as the *mamma* in Jebba and the *gunnu* there and elsewhere. By means of this conversion the loss of the religious rite was minimized; though it disappeared as a regularly repetitive institution it remained available as a possibility, to be utilized 'when the need arises'; which compromise seems adequately explained by the lesser demands upon time, energy, and resources of the movable ceremonials, especially when the conversion goes together with performance on a lesser scale and in 'businesslike' manner. But another factor is probably also at work. For we can understand that people who have abandoned or neglected many of their traditional religious institutions will revert to them in sudden emergencies or times of stress, that is, in precisely the conditions for which the movable rituals are designed. The sudden, single revival of the Jebba *gunnu* after a pause of many years seems a case in point; and similar evidence also comes from other Nupe communities.

IV

RITUAL (*continued*)

1. FORM, CONTENT, VALIDITY

WHEN we speak of 'ritual' we have in mind first of all actions exhibiting a striking or incongruous rigidity, that is, some conspicuous regularity not accounted for by the professed aims of the actions. Any type of behaviour may thus be said to turn into a 'ritual' when it is stylized or formalized, and made repetitive in that form. When we call a ritual 'religious' we further attribute to the action a particular manner of relating means to ends which we know to be inadequate by empirical standards, and which we commonly call irrational, mystical, or supernatural. And one of these means, perhaps the most crucial one, is constituted by the very formalism of the action. If its rigidity no longer strikes us as incongruous, this is so because we are so thoroughly familiar with the notion that the supernatural efficacy of behaviour is bound up with rigid formalism. Whatever the psychological roots of this notion, it is clear that it furnishes the motive for this particular way of acting and underlies the actor's expectations; for the performers of a ritual do not behave purely mechanically in the rigidly repetitive manner (as some sufferer from compulsion neurosis might do): they behave in the given manner because they trust in its efficacy. This trust in turn rests on the body of organized beliefs, on doctrine and the tenets of the creed, which sanction the (ritualized) behaviour and warrant its relevance.

In analysing religious rituals, then, we are always dealing with two sets of facts: the *form* of the action (since without the set form it would not be a 'ritual'); and its content of ideas and aims (since without the mystic aims it would not be 'religion'). The 'content' is again twofold. It includes, first, the desired effect or end result, that is, the professed 'aim' of the ritual; and second, the items of the creed relevant to the 'means' employed. This latter knowledge clearly goes beyond a guarantee of isolated manners of acting; rather is it of a general and systematic kind, and amounts to a frame of reference bearing upon every kind of action which a group of people will regard as 'religious'. In Nupe, this frame of reference is given in the conceptions of the deity, of the universe, of the force of *kuti* or *cigbe*, and so forth. We need not again expound it, and can therefore take this aspect of the 'content' of rituals for granted.

Yet understood thus widely, the category of 'ritual' would include also various other observances, which the Nupe hold apart from *kuti*—sacrifices to ancestors and twin-shrines, to certain 'great' medicines, and even the minor offerings to spirits. In another sense, too, these practices do not stand apart, but merely extend the Nupe conception of ritual. Its two forms, 'fixed' and 'movable', clearly supplement one another: where one is bound to time and occasion and involves enterprise on a considerable scale, the other is freely available and capable of being employed readily as well as economically; and where one (as we put it before) anticipates the ubiquitous and perennial needs of communities, the other bears on unforeseen events, which must be dealt with quickly and *ad hoc*. Together, they fit communities to meet, on the supernatural plane, all the problems and threats that might face them. But in one or two instances the movable rituals are made to include even such problems or threats as may face individuals or single families. And if this private validity of ritual, as the Nupe understand it, represents an exception, it becomes the rule in those other observances, sacrifices to *kuci* and so forth. They thus complete the hierarchy of social appropriateness of which we spoke before, and which has two of its grades or steps already within the practice of ritual.

This hierarchy need not concern us further; nor is there any need, in the present context, to revert again to the other observances, save in passing: the employment of medicine will form the subject of a special chapter; the sacrifices to *kuci* will be mentioned in connection with kinship ceremonial, that is, with the one 'domain' they command; as for the casual offerings to spirits, there is no more to be added. But let me note this. The circumstances and actions characterizing these three practices all occur also in the movable ritual—sacrifice, prayers or invocations, the private character of the appeal, and its concern with contingent needs. Much that will be said on the latter therefore also applies to the former rites, even though, in Nupe eyes, they do not constitute 'ritual', but an essentially different kind of appeal.

Reviewing the professed aims of ritual we find them to be strikingly uniform. Mostly they are composite as well as unspecific (without special 'domain'); almost every ritual is meant to ensure the same series of benefits—health, ample food, fecundity of the women, and general prosperity. In the movable rites the aim is usually adjusted more narrowly, bearing on the specific need of the moment. The fixed rituals, too, may, by their date or particular associations, be related to a more specific purpose; even so the more general bearing will be voiced at least in the final phrase of the prayer formula. Again, the professed aim nearly always bears on the village community; occasionally that scope is widened, so as to include a whole tribal section, or (more rarely) narrowed down, so as to benefit individual suppliants. Finally, the professed aim is always conspicuous, being openly stated, both in the prayers and in relevant comments. This is not equally true of the songs that accompany certain rituals: where the songs are not altogether irrelevant, they usually refer only to the general characteristics of the religious rite, its secrecy, power, the dangers that lie in mishandling it. It falls to the songs, therefore, to affirm those 'items of the creed' which relate to the position of the *kuti* in the conceptual framework at large. Thus it is not puzzling that songs belonging to one ritual should on occasion appear in another.

To turn to the formal features, which are once more widely uniform. The general plan of the ceremonial, especially, varies little. There is the same sequence of esoteric and public events, usually accompanied by a change of scene, and the same series of episodes—the sacrifice and prayer, the libation of beer and the sprinkling of blood; the communal meal, and the final dance and general festivity. The separateness of the various phases is reflected in the nomenclature which assigns to each a particular name. The sacrifice and prayer is called *labá*; the communal meal *biki*; the scene of the esoteric part is known as *kuti ba* or *ba žiko* ('secret place'), and the final, public and festive, episode as *dzodzo* (playing, dancing) or *jï raha* ('merry-making'). There are certain differences. Most movable and a few fixed rites are without the final phase; the *gunnu* alone includes a dance in which both sexes join and, preceding it, a sexual taboo; the *mamma* alone involves the utter secrecy of a performance in the dark of the night. Within the set framework of phases or episodes the various component actions are again fairly uniformly standardized. Thus the officiant always kneels when bringing the sacrifice; the congregation always appears bareheaded and stripped to the waist; and beer and food are always passed round in accordance with age and rank. Occasionally, too, there is a triple repetition of the prayer formula. Yet the formalism is not over-strict: as we know, time and place of the ritual are subject to change; the performance of the sacrifice implies no peculiar, stereotyped gestures; above all, the invocation is loosely phrased, without any insistence on a rigid rote. Indeed, we might call the very fluidity of the formalism part of the 'typical' form of Nupe ritual.

In spite of this fluidity and uniformity each *kuti* represents, for the people, a procedure possessed of a distinct and unmistakable identity. We need not mention especially certain external details marking off one ritual from another, such as the different trees in places of sacrifice otherwise closely alike, different musical instruments played with songs which themselves may be interchangeable, or one or two objects peculiar to particular ceremonials. More importantly, the person of the officiant varies from ritual to ritual, only very few sharing the same priest. We spoke of him as being 'in charge' of a ritual; the Nupe would say that he 'owns' the ritual: and for them no reference to a *kuti* is complete without the mention of this relevantly varying 'ownership'.

Now, this is a new conception of the ownership of rituals. We have met with two others—an ownership vested in the village community, as part of its corporate estate, and one vested in the whole tribe or nation, as an attribute of its collective identity. The former comes closest to 'ownership' in the conventional sense of the word, since the village community in fact views its cycle of rituals much as one does some concretely held source of benefits. In the priest's ownership of 'his' ritual this notion disappears; for he 'owns' the ritual only as a task or duty (if a privileged one), which falls to him by virtue of his descent or rank. In either case, the village community, as the true 'owner' of the ceremonial, delegates its execution to one of its segments (the priest's kin group) or to one of its individual members. This notion is in fact carried to the extreme; for neither the priest nor his family derive any particular benefits, secular or mystic, from the religious office: the priest is merely the one individual entitled and expected to exercise it 'for the whole town'. The unique priestship of the *gunnu*, which sanctifies the person of the incumbent, is only partly an exception. The priest is distinguished from other mortals only inasmuch as he is a vessel of a force working miraculously; but he is not expected to be blessed with children because he officiates in a cult of fertility nor to be better off than others because the cult alsc promises prosperity. Indeed, like any other person due to assume a public office, he must prove that he is 'strong enough', that is, he must first acquire the full adult status of a married man and family head.

The individual 'ownership' of ritual thus implies no special validity of the thing owned for the owner. The two forms of group ownership imply precisely this. Here 'ownership' is coterminous with validity for a group so-and-so constituted. Where this group is the society at large, the tribe or nation, that is, the widest group on which behaviour is normally oriented, the validity of the ritual also ceases at the group boundary; which is merely saying that

Nupe religion is 'national', not 'universal'. Where the group equals the village community, the coincidence of validity and group is no longer entirely true. More precisely, the validity of the ritual holds on two different planes, both coinciding with and extending beyond the group boundaries. Thus every ritual is valid for the community which actually performs it, promising its various benefits to that congregation; and every ritual is further valid for the wider or widest group of which the congregation forms a part. This wider validity may again be of two kinds. First, the group performing the ritual may regard it as a task (a privileged task) apportioned to it within the embracing social unit, so that each performance is understood to contribute to the welfare of that unit and also affirms its existence; as we have seen, this is true of several rituals in the river area and, on the widest plane, of the rituals associated with Tsoede and the kingdom of Nupe.[1] Secondly, the community performing the ritual may merely know that other villages in the tribe or perhaps sub-tribe 'own' an identical observance; so that every performance will recall and confirm the existence of a larger human aggregate of like customs and beliefs. In the first case, then, the single village community sees itself as belonging to an embracing association in which it has a part to play; in the second, as belonging to a particular species of humanity. In either case the purely religious aims merge with notions of group existence and relationships.

2. THE PROMISE OF RITUAL

The discussion of the validity of rituals, which is bound up with the promises they hold out, leads us at once to the crucial questions—how do rituals fulfil their promise? and how do they convey the hope, or perhaps certainty, that their professed aims will in fact come true?

Consider that the rituals are being performed incessantly through the generations and have undoubtedly, at times at least, been followed by the desired results; thus there must be in existence a body of knowledge, empirical if misconstrued, bearing out the believed-in efficacy. Consider further that the fixed rituals are concerned mainly with 'ends' and 'new beginnings', that is, with the overall repetitiveness of natural life—with the cycles of the seasons, with birth, with the growing of crops, with the rise and fall of the river. This repetitiveness is well known empirically, independently of any belief in supernatural agencies. The

[1] We note the same principle of 'delegation' which also underlies Nupe priestship, though the 'privileged task' now falls, not to individuals, but to sections of the society at large or to groups within groups.

traditional Nupe calendar shows this clearly, naming as it does the various parts of the year 'First rain', 'Nothing-but-rain', 'Growing-time', 'Hot time', 'Cold time'. If the rituals are meant to ensure that life goes on being what it has always been, they merely aim at preserving a normality which one knows to be such. In other words, if you accept that there should be such rituals, then you will find that their aims come true. Purely practically, the rituals would seem to be supererogatory efforts; yet just because they are so supererogatory they are also self-confirming. But the question of supererogation does not really arise; for the Nupe, like all people, are capable of thinking on different planes. On one plane, there is an empirical 'normality', valid for all ordinary intents and purposes. On another, this normality is part of divine creation, which includes, with the natural order of things, also that mystic order of which ritual is an item. It is not a question of one conditioning the other or being necessary for the other; the two belong together and to the same design; both exist, and fit. And from this fit, so conceived that it demonstrates itself in the familiar regularities of life, one derives, not merely hope or confidence, but certainty.

This is still an incomplete view both of the universe as the Nupe picture it and of the efficacy of their rituals. The former also contains accidents, and the latter are meant to secure also benefits beyond those vouched for by some summary 'normality'. This is true especially of the movable rituals which deal with unforseen contingencies; but the fixed rituals, too, aim at such things as freedom from illness, prolific childbirth, prosperity, the disappearance of evil, that is, at the control of uncertainties. Here the ritual efforts, no longer self-confirming, can only convey a hope or strengthen confidence.

The nature of ritual as the Nupe conceive it betrays the same wavering between hope and certainty. As we know, it is a procedure, a rule of acting, which actuates a portion of cosmic force. In this sense, then, it is a macnine, set in motion and working towards predetermined results. At the same time the procedure belies its own efficacy; for part of it is a *prayer*, not an automatically effective spell, that is, an invocation and appeal. One begs God to bring about what the performance of the ritual acts are themselves trusted to bring about. I do not think that I have misread the paradox in this situation. The *mamma* ritual would seem to express it most clearly. For there one employs a 'medicine' which is in itself automatically powerful and masks which are equally charged with some autonomous force; yet one also prays— 'May God cause . . .' Nor can this ambiguity be reduced by calling the prayer a request for divine blessing, without which the ritual procedure would remain powerless. The notion of a blessing is quite alien to the Nupe: they say 'May God cause so-and-so to happen', not 'May God make our efforts successful'; the prayer simply duplicates the other features in the ritual performance. Nor yet is there any conception of moral worthiness, of 'showing reason' why God should grant success or give his blessing. The paradox remains, and the only way to dissolve it is to call the Nupe ritual a bow with two strings.

This viewpoint fits well into the conceptual framework of Nupe religion, where different rituals and even different forms of supernatural appeal appear as alternatives which may replace each other, one being effective where the other happened to fail. Their possible failure is thus to some extent anticipated. The efficacy of the 'fixed' and more general rituals, especially, may be corrected by that of the 'movable' and more specialized ones. As we know, divination will suggest the suitable alternative, while the wide overlap in the ritual aims makes such choices and changes feasible. There is some hierarchy of power among the rituals, some being definitely 'stronger' than others; nor are they all interchangeable. The supreme or unique rituals, therefore, such as the *gunnu* or *mamma*, may suffer a failure which is irreducible. But even this failure does not assail the confidence that is placed in them; for there are the loopholes which we know well: the ultimate unconcern of the remote deity, and the evil forces he suffers to exist.

The fact that the failures of ritual can in this fashion be explained away does not, however, account for the initial source of the confidence which is thus protected. It might be argued that no special explanatory hypotheses are needed; since people, after all, believe in what they practice, the assurance found in the practice is likely to be implicit already in the belief. Differently expressed, the confidence in the ritual would simply be part of its conceptual content. Undoubtedly, this must be true, in some measure, of all rituals, and wholly true of the movable rituals and all the other casual observances, whose aims are not self-confirming and whose procedure is prosaic and businesslike. Here the rule holds—if you believe, then you will find assurance in the practical application of this belief; if you do not, the practice will carry no conviction; for the application itself offers nothing further in the way of persuasion. The ritual, as it were, draws upon faith but does not add to it, save accidentally, when its professed aim happens to come true.

It is different in the fixed and more elaborate rituals; for here the belief is affirmed by the practice, and the content of the ritual sustained and reinforced by its form. Let me explain this more fully. The form of the ritual clearly implies more than an external procedure composed of such-and-such invocations, music, and manners of eating, sitting, or walking. These items and others also produce a certain mood, made up of emotional tensions and satisfactions, and of given expectations. Upon this mood fall the words which voice the aims of the ceremonial, so that they gain weight through the very context in which they are spoken or sung; and this mood is further effective as any stirring experience is effective, in offering stimulation and catharsis, in providing sensory pleasures, and, ultimately, in leaving a mark upon experience. Many—not all—of these stimulations are also normally sought and felt satisfying, apart from ritual contexts, in dances, songs, festivities of all kinds. The rituals add the thrill that goes with secrecy and uncommon occasions. Above all, one knows that the ritual *is* a special, sacred occasion, which has a name and a given aim: so that the stimulations and satisfactions that lie in the ritual behaviour blend with the promise for which it stands. One is not *proved* by the other; but one is emotionalized by the other, and the promise made or sought in this mood gains, though not in intellectual certainty, yet in persuasiveness. One *feels* the import of things so announced. They are, of course, things one also wishes to believe. If any person simply said, say, 'May God grant you children' or even 'You shall have children', the faith put in this pronouncement will depend partly on the prior faith in the role and powers of the speaker, and partly on the strength of the wish and hence on its capacity to predispose the audience towards a ready belief. But if there is, in addition, the stirring atmosphere of the full-scale ritual, this predisposition is itself created. To be sure, it is not created *ex nihilo*: the important thing is that the ritual does not merely draw upon faith but also adds to and reinforces it.

It is true that the crucial pronouncements are made before the full emotional force of the ritual can be felt. But there is some anticipatory effect; for one knows the ritual to be a whole, with given phases, and any earlier phase carries within it the expectation of its sequels. Indeed, the sequel may protrude into the preceding phases (as in the anticipated episode of flogging in the *gunnu*). Again, the crucial pronouncements are made before a smaller congregation than that for which the promise is to hold; but the wider community knows, at least in general terms, all about the things the ritual is supposed to do. It is possible, however, that the public phase, with its sensory and aesthetic appeal, might become dissociated from the esoteric phase, which contains the intellectual kernel of the ceremony. The Nupe ceremonial shows clear traces of this. The singing and dancing sometimes assume the role of pleasures sought and found satisfying in their own right; and jokes or horseplay, which seem quite out of place, are inserted in the programme of 'merry-making'. If the dissociation were complete, the ritual would cease to be one and turn into a mere festivity. Normally, this is not permitted to occur; when economic stress or similar circumstances make it necessary to curtail the ritual performance, it is the 'merry-making' which is so shortened or even omitted altogether. But I have met with one instance of the opposite change. The people of Mokwa have a ceremonial called *elo* which has a great many of the essential features of the Nupe ritual: it has its 'month' (the 9th); a titled elder who has charge of it and can alone sanction the performance; and it employs masks and special dresses normally stored away and used on no other occasion. But it is without sacrifice, esoteric phase or prayer; nor is it (today at least) credited with any aim beyond *dzodzo*, 'play'. There is no evidence that the *elo* has been truncated for any particular reason; the evidence merely shows that the dissociation of the esoteric from the public episode can become complete, the latter coming fully into its own.

3. SYMBOLIC AND IMPLICIT FUNCTIONS

Normally, even the public episodes are permeated with significance or continue to convey the ideas primarily expressed in the esoteric rite. A familiar method of keeping ideas in sight is by means of signs or symbols, that is, by means of objects or ways of acting understood to point beyond themselves, to some 'referent' or *significatum*. This reference may be of a general kind, merely indicating that the situation is of a religious nature or part of a particular ceremonial. Think of the dress obligatory in the esoteric sacrifice but worn also during the public episodes, of the *gunnu* whips or the staves of the old men in the *dzakó*, of the yells or shouted words which are understood to be a salute of the *kuti*, or of the musical instruments which are known to belong to this or that ritual. These symbols, then, act as reminders that even the 'merry-making' has its peculiar, more solemn context. The symbols may be more specific reminders in that they refer to the professed meaning of the ritual performance. Thus the *gunnu* whips and the flogging indicate fertility; the masks of the *mamma* secrecy and a knowledge hidden from women and strangers; and the cult objects of Tsoede stand for the whole past and unity of the tribe and kingdom.

Symbols, of course, also play a part in the esoteric rites. The river water poured on the ground in the *ndáduma* indicates the character of this river ritual; the white cloth, annually renewed in the *gunnu*, signifies the 'end and renewal' sanctified in the cult;

the freshly cut grain eaten in certain sacrifices points to subsistence and the continuation of fertility which the ritual is meant to secure. The meaning of all these symbols is fairly obvious and in a sense 'natural', being based on a commonly known nexus between the sign and the thing signified. Symbols of a more artificial kind, resting on some specific and perhaps esoteric convention, are rare in Nupe ritual. The only clear instance is the symbolism of right and left in the *dzakó*, which, as I have said, has no parallel in any other Nupe cult. The sacrifice of fish in one version of the *gunnu* is a more doubtful case; for though fish are associated with fertility (in dream interpretation) and welcome gifts (in divining), that knowledge is far from general. The use of tortoise shells in the same ceremonial reminds the congregation of the Father Tortoise stories, but does no more. The rule that the *Ndazo* must not wear anything 'tied round his waist' evokes no association, say, with constraint inimical to growth and fertility. And though it may be tempting to speculate on the rule of calling the sacrificial beer 'water', that is, by the name of the fluid which (as rain or semen) is linked with the fertility of nature and man, the Nupe attach no ulterior meaning to this metaphor.

Whether these and other details of the ritual procedure do not perhaps involve symbolisms of a more subtle and unconscious nature, I will not discuss. In my view uncomprehended 'symbols have no part in social enquiry; their social effectiveness lies in their capacity to indicate, and if they indicate nothing to the actors, they are, from our point of view, irrelevant and indeed no longer symbols (whatever their significance for the psychologist or psycho-analyst). But let us note that certain modes of acting may be significant for the actors without constituting symbols, merely because they represent a rule, a formalism of acting, that is, a *ritual*, and not accidental or random behaviour. This is true, for example, of the choice of the sacrificial animals. To begin with, they are in every case 'ordinary' animals, without sacred associations and neither rare nor avoided in workaday life. Though most rituals prescribe the sex of the sacrificial beast, males and females are chosen in random manner, suggestive of no symbolic link with the purpose of the ritual. The *ketsá* is perhaps the clearest example; the legend, as we remember, mentions the sacrifice of a cow; yet the actual ritual, when performed at the request of the Kede chief, requires the killing of a bull. In other rituals the sex as well as the species of the animal simply depend on the outcome of divination. It might seem that at least the specification of white or black animals, which is fairly common, must have a symbolic significance since black colour is generally associated with secrecy and evil things, and white colour with prosperity. But again, both kinds are irregularly employed; all that can be said is that the sex, colour or species of the animals is *laid down*, and hence stands for a rule significant as such.

A few words must here be said about the whole conception of the Nupe sacrifice. It seems anomalous that a non-personified deity or an abstract 'cosmic force' should be offered food and drink. But the prayer formula accompanying the offering speaks concretely of 'giving' these to God or *kuti*, just as the name of at least one ritual implies that the *kuti* (or the stone representing it) 'drinks' the fluid offered. The name for sacrifice, *labá*, offers no further clue; denoting the actual offering as well as the prayer accompanying it, it does not separate the former from the general act of worship. The offering is thus a gesture among others: like the prayer formula, meant to break through the aloofness of the deity, the sacrificial gift serves to attract and hold his attention. In either case the gesture used is borrowed from everyday life, the prayer employing ordinary language, the sacrifice items normally offered by clients to patrons. And this conception of a 'normal' gift is once more consistent with the notion that the various *kuti*, precisely like persons of rank and standing, command their special 'greetings'. If the offerings are anomalous, they share this character with all the other forms of addressing God and *kuti* and indeed with the very conceptions of the deity and of the Force-that-is-in-ritual.

Let me note briefly that the same anomaly also holds in the case of sacrifices made to ancestors or over the vessels of 'great' medicines. The former, as we remember, are brought to the disembodied souls which are 'with God'; mostly, too, they are accompanied by invocations addressed at once to God and *kuci*. The sacrifices to medicines again involve the invocation of God; and though they consist in offerings of beer, morsels of food, and the blood of the sacrificial animal, they are, as we shall see, also understood to strengthen the impersonal force that is imputed to the substance of medicine. Nor are the offerings to spirits, de-humanized beings that they are, any less anomalous; indeed, in a different context I recorded the positive assertion that 'spirits do not eat'.

The first two observances may, like ritual proper, include the sacrificial meal of the congregation; the sacrifice to ancestors does so in most cases, the sacrifice to 'great' medicines only where it has fused with a *kuti* or with *kuci* worship. Invariably, however, the inclusion of the communal meal, even where it means merely a sharing-out of beer, entails the invocation of God, and not only of ancestors or of the 'force' of medicine. Yet the sacrificial meal has in no way the significance of a sacrament. The meal undoubtedly represents a sacred occasion, although it may show little trace of awe or emotional thrill.[1] But there is no conception of consuming things sacred in themselves and hence of sharing bodily a token of divinity. The crucial aspect of the sacrificial meal lies in the fact that here God and his worshippers eat and drink together; and if this is a symbolic act, its symbolism merely points to, and confirms, the 'fellowship and mutual social obligations' between deity and congregation. Much the same point was made by Robertson Smith in his discussion of the ancient semitic sacrifice, and I can do no better than quote from him: 'The one thing directly expressed in the sacrificial meal is that the god and his worshippers are *commensals*, but every other point in their mutual relations is included in what this involves. Those who sit at meat together are united for all social effects; those who do not eat together are aliens to one another, without fellowship in religion and without reciprocal social duties'.[2]

Here we are no longer dealing with symbols in the strict sense of the word but with a new type of significance, bearing on things of very general social import and established by means of a relevant parallelism between the form of ritual and the norms governing social relationships. Before turning to this aspect let me mention another border zone of symbolism in ritual, where the symbolic function of modes of acting overlaps with their direct, causal, efficacy. The modes of acting, in other words, both 'point to' a state of affairs relevant to the aims of the ritual, and also cause this state of affairs to materialize. The instance I have in mind is the sexual taboo of the *gunnu*, followed by a period of licence. The fact that normal sexual relations are first suspended and afterwards conspicuously resumed must clearly focus attention upon sex and procreation, and upon the sequence of 'end' and 'new beginning'; so that this rule of acting comes to symbolize the central theme of the cult. Equally, however, the prohibition, rendered more severe by the provocation of the 'mixed dance', and its subsequent lifting produce both tensions and catharsis, and generally add to the stimulations generated in the ritual: and in this sense they simply engineer or create the required mood and expectations.

Generally speaking, then, strict (and comprehended) symbolism plays no great part in Nupe ceremonial. In a different sense, however, all ceremonials operate with modes of acting which 'point beyond themselves' in a manner analogous to signs or symbols. They no longer serve merely as 'reminders', nor do they bear upon

---

[1] This is borne out by the usual translation of the Nupe word *biki* into Hausa-Arabic; using the latter phraseology the Nupe would speak of *walima*, 'sacred feast'.

[2] *Lectures on the Religion of the Semites*, 1907, p. 269.

or underline only the professed aims of the ritual; rather do they express additional aims in an implicit and incidental fashion. Consider that the ritual procedure acknowledges distinctions of rank and seniority (for example, in the order in which the congregation is seated and receives food and drink); that it draws a sharp line between those admitted to the esoteric ceremonials or to the ceremonial altogether (certain age sets, men, members of the community), and those excluded from it (other age sets, women, strangers). Again, among the youths admitted to the esoteric rite there are the novices and those already initiated, each group being expected to behave differently, to show fear or not, to teach or to be taught, and so forth. Among the women who may join the public phase the girls might have to keep apart from the old women, as in the *dzakó* dance. Both in the *gunnu* and *mamma* the leader of the age grades assumes the special duty of supervising and organizing the youths. And in all larger ceremonies there is some procession through the village, when one 'salutes' the houses of chiefs and elders.

Now all these instances refer to behaviour valid and meant to be valid also in everyday life. If, then, respect towards elders, awareness of one's place in the society, the very notion of being of it, are given expression in the ritual procedure, this comes to demonstrate, in the manner of a model, the obtaining social norms. Needless to say, it is a very special model since it is presented in the context of stirred-up emotions and to a consciousness artificially heightened. Rarely is this model also explained in so many words; nor does it seem necessary: the norms of ritual behaviour simply parallel or duplicate the norms of 'real' life in a conspicuous manner, the ritual mobilizing the group as it should normally function. And since this 'normality' is an aimed-at state and represents goals or values governing secular life, we may here speak of aims or functions super-added to the professed aims of the ritual, or, with Radcliffe-Brown, of 'social values' rendered visible in the ritual. The important thing is that they are rendered visible *incidentally*, being implicit in the procedure of a ritual overtly directed towards quite other aims. In other words, the form of the ritual adds to its content, and this tends to be cumulative, absorbing a variety of aims.

Yet though these represent ways of acting generally desirable and important in social life, the ritual, in virtue of its professed aims, has its own importance. So that one importance is sustained or thrown into relief by the other. This circle is true of most or all religious rituals. But let us note two things. The additional aims conveyed in the ritual need not be merely implicit in its procedure; they may equally be made explicit by formal pronouncements occurring in the course of the ceremonial. In Nupe, this is the case only in the *gunnu*. We remember the exclusion of barren women from the public celebrations: this attitude is not merely left to emerge from the procedural rules but is also laid down in the form of an explicit warning voiced by the *gunnu* priest. Similarly the general obligation of respect towards elders and, especially, of sons towards their fathers is put into words, during the vigil in the bush, when the *ndakó gboyá* catechises the adolescents. Thus the Nupe can rightly say (in one of the *gunnu* songs) that the '*gunnu* teaches men', though in a more indirect fashion this would be true of all their rituals.

Furthermore, the 'desirable and important ways of acting' demonstrated in the ritual, implicitly or explicitly, may be held up as desirable and important in the ritual alone, not having the same weight in everyday life or not appearing in it at all. The ritual would then present, not a duplication or model, but something else—an ideal rarely met with in practice or even a reversal of the practice. This is true in varying degree of four features of the Nupe ritual, all concerned with the relationship of the sexes. There is, first, the rigid exclusion of women from the esoteric rites, which sometimes goes together with intimidation and threats. Yet women play an important part in Nupe social life, in many ways equal to that of the men; many women are influential and wealthy, and ranks and titles are open to them.[1] In no sense are they the 'weaker' or more timid sex. If, then, it is 'important' in the ritual that women should be kept in their place and forcibly reminded of their inferiority, this seems to imply a redress of balance, a compensation for the loss of male prominence, and something in the nature of a wish-fulfilment. The issue seems conspicuously summarized in the *mamma* ritual, which admits the power of women (since the 'medicine' employed is a woman's gift) yet is also meant to subdue and terrify them. The sex antagonism here apparent has a much wider bearing and will occupy us again in the discussion of witchcraft.

Secondly, the ostracism of the childless woman in the *gunnu*, though it does not contradict the norms valid in 'real' life, greatly exaggerates them. The Nupe men will always moralize about the impropriety of contraception and the shameful conduct of mothers who behave as though they had no children, becoming professional traders and, incidentally, prostitutes; equally, everybody will decry the misfortune of barrenness. But the fact remains that a great many women, childless or not, happily live in this 'shameful' state and are able to choose it without necessarily incurring the

[1] For a fuller account of the position of the women, especially in the economic sphere, see *A Black Byzantium*, chap. IX.

risk of divorce or even of their husbands' serious anger. The ritual alone seriously and publicly brands immorality or subjects barren women to a 'cure' which is indistinguishable from punishment.

Thirdly, the hectic mood of the *gunnu* dance is a model 'in reverse'. For this kind of abandoned behaviour is never permitted or thought of in ordinary life, and any open reference to sex is severely shunned by the rather prudish Nupe. Sex and privacy go together; and no ordinary dance permits a mingling of the sexes. Indeed, in all ordinary dances and in most ceremonial ones the whole mood is one of calm and restraint. Perhaps, then, we may call the *gunnu* (and one or two similar ceremonials) a safety-valve, a licensed compensation for otherwise rigid self-control; certainly, it puts a premium on a mode of behaviour otherwise not only improper but unthinkable.

The final instance, again taken from the *gunnu*, is of a slightly different order. I am referring to the masquerading of the boys as girls. 'Masquerading' is possibly too strong a word, for all that happens is that the boys wear a piece of woman's cloth.[1] But this aspect of the *gunnu* dress is always specifically mentioned, and in the general dance the boys are encouraged to imitate and caricature female steps and mannerisms. Now in 'real' life boys or men are never expected to behave like the opposite sex. From the time when children put on any dress at all (when they are about six or seven), they are dressed differently. As soon as the boys form themselves into the earliest age grade (at the age of eight or nine), the occupations, interests, and codes of conduct of the sexes differ sharply, and this is true also of songs, dances, and pastimes of all kinds. Male homosexuality, which would blur this dividing line, is severely condemned and, in fact, denied to occur. The exceptional behaviour at the *gunnu* thus appears to have a symbolic significance (though it is not stated more explicitly), the temporary change of roles pointing to a more permanent one. The boys who are admitted to the *gunnu* are on the threshold of manhood, the very admission to the ritual being a first token of the new status. Before that they were something else—children, still looked after by their mothers as much as by their fathers, and being with women more often than with men. Later, this ambiguous position will come to an end, which change roughly coincides with admission to the *gunnu*. The symbolic identification with the female sex on that occasion thus emphasizes the transition through concentrating it into something like 'a last time' when boys can be confused with girls. It is not literally a 'last time'; for even before this event boys did not walk about dressed like girls or behaved

[1] In the *gani* ceremonial, to be described later, this 'masquerading' is much more elaborate and definite (see below, p. 218).

like them; and after the first admission to the *gunnu* there will be repetitions of the same ceremonial and masquerade. The *gunnu* thus exaggerates the change of roles and presents it in a manner not exactly true to life; but just because it does so it becomes a means of dramatizing a crucial crisis of life which, in reality, is neither as conspicuous nor as dramatic. So that the *gunnu*, through this part of its procedure, assumes the relevance of a *rite de passage*.

To summarize. By its professed content, the ritual applies and partly affirms the system of religious ideas; and by its form, it becomes part of the machinery which maintains the efficient working of a society of a given structure. By its form, too, the ritual 'accumulates' further aims and ideas, bearing on codes of conduct, on social roles, and hence on the values of 'good' and 'bad'. Surveying all the various Nupe rituals we find that the *gunnu*, as it is considered the paramount ritual, so it is also the richest in 'cumulative' content. There is practically no manner of acting which is not referred to and evaluated in its procedure; furthermore, the *gunnu* alone goes beyond implicit references and contains also express pronouncements upon these 'additional' aims.

As I previously tried to show, it is not paradoxical that a cult of such far-reaching importance should be the first to disappear or to be truncated under the pressure of change; rather, its very ambitiousness exposes it 'on too many sides' to disruptive influences. Let me rephrase this assertion in terms of the 'content' and 'form' of rituals. The disappearance or radical alteration of the ritual clearly implies some weakening of its appeal. The professed content of the ritual would lose its appeal only if the whole conceptual framework of the religion were disrupted, as it would be by the impact of another religion, in this case Islam. Yet this was certainly not true (or not yet true) of the many Nupe communities where the *gunnu* alone of all the various rituals had disappeared or broken down. The form of the ritual, however, since it absorbs so many of the general norms of social life, would be weakened by any change affecting the latter, by any remodelling of the relationship between the generations, by any new attractions seducing the younger people, and by all changes in moral or educational standards. It is precisely dislocations of this kind which have spread most widely through Nupe country; and it is thus the *gunnu* carrying within its 'form' a mirror of the traditional way of life, lost its appeal and indeed its very relevance as its picture ceased to be true.

4. SOLEMNIZATIONS

We now turn to ceremonials which do not stand on their own, as so many efforts to wield supernatural power for particular ends, but which surround or merge with certain critical mundane events, birth, death, and marriage. For the Nupe, these ceremonials do not represent *kuti*, rituals proper: they do not move the force that is in the universe; nor do they belong to the tools which God granted man for this purpose. The ceremonials of birth, death, or marriage are merely observances, customary ways of dealing with the events in question or, as the Nupe say, 'ways of doing things'. If we call them 'rituals' or 'rites', we are applying our own nomenclature for such procedures. Even so, these 'ways of doing things' involve appeals to God and some link with the whole system of religious ideas; that is, they are *solemnizations* of mundane acts.

(i) *Birth*

The observances bearing on childbirth begin already with conception and culminate, some time after the actual birth, in the naming ceremonial, so that the event of birth is treated, not as a climax, but as one in a series of events or stages. This concern with pre- and post-natal phases corresponds closely to the Nupe conceptions of life and of body and soul; several of the respective observances, however, are neither specifically 'religious' nor explicitly fitted into the 'natural philosophy' of the people, belonging rather to the more indefinite range of notions we commonly call superstitions.

Thus the most auspicious time for conception is laid down, in typical Nupe manner, by numbering the day in question, which should be the fifth after the mother's menses. The night should be young, for a child conceived in the dark of the night, when spirits and witches are abroad, might easily be born misshapen. As soon as the pregnancy is noticeable (in the third month, as the Nupe calculate, or at the latest in the fifth), the parents must discontinue sexual relations; the mother must avoid places inhabited by spirits as well as certain kinds of food which might harm the child: honey would give it adenoids, and a certain fish cause it to have six fingers on one hand. I have already mentioned that the avoidance of cohabitation continues for about three years after the birth of the child, since a new conception and pregnancy might stop the growth of the infant. In addition to these general rules and avoidances, which everyone knows, there may be special ones, ordered by the diviner, whom the expectant father will at once consult.

He will consult the diviner again at the beginning of the confinement and before the child is named. The father will also buy 'medicines' to facilitate the birth and buy or collect herbs with which to prepare the new-born's first food. During the delivery itself the father keeps away, leaving the scene to his elder sister, mother or aunt, and to his father or father's brother, who is called in to cut the umbilical cord and dispose of the afterbirth (which is buried outside the hut). Even afterwards the infant's grandfather plays a more conspicuous part than does the father; while the latter goes quietly about his business, the grandfather loudly announces to all friends and visitors that a grandchild has been born to him, and it is to him that all congratulations are addressed. The delivery and the treatment of the new-born represent essentially practical procedures devoid of ceremonial. We may mention only that for four days the infant is fed on a boiled infusion of the herbs which the father has collected and given the mother's milk only on the fifth. On the same day the father sends gifts of kolanuts to all relatives and friends, with the announcement that the naming ceremony, meanwhile fixed, will take place on such-and-such a day.

This ceremony, known as *suna* ('name'), usually takes place eight days after the birth, and is traditionally preceded, on the seventh day, by a libation of beer to the ancestor thought to be re-born in the child. The ceremonial is brief and takes place in privacy, usually in the hut where the reincarnated ancestor lies buried, being attended only by the child's father and his nearest male relations. The father kneels down, a gourd with beer in his hand, and speaks this prayer (to quote a concrete instance):

'I am praying to *Sokó*. The child that has entered, Lord God, it is Landu returned (the grandfather's name). *Kuci*, hold him (the child) securely, do not permit that he falls sick. May he live, cause him to grow old'.

The ceremonial ends when beer is poured on the ground and the rest drunk in silence by the men present. As this brief ritual summarizes the whole conception of reincarnation, so it also betrays its ambiguity; for the *kuci* which is believed to have returned to the living is yet asked to take care of the living; and though one sacrifices to a particular ancestor, one yet invokes God.

The naming ceremony itself makes no further mention of these mystic notions, being concerned exclusively with formally announcing the name and identity of the new-born. This is done before a gathering of guests as large as the host can make it. The guests are relatives, friends, neighbours, and such important personages as the child's father may happen to know; they are expected to bring small gifts and will in turn be furnished with food and drink. Traditionally, it is the child's grandfather who announces his name, simply and without ceremonial. But today the ceremonial has been widely remodelled in Mohammedan fashion, the announcement now falling to a mallam among the invited guests. The child's grandfather merely whispers the name to the mallam, who will then offer up prayers, in the usual mixture of crude Arabic and Hausa, and invoke divine blessing upon the new-born. It would seem that this innovation preserves the specifically religious aspect of the ceremony while shifting it from the preamble, the ancestral sacrifice (which is omitted in the strictly Mohammedan version), to the public announcement. But since a great many families still observe both the pagan sacrifice and the prayer of mallams, the religious emphasis is doubled. And this, too, seems fully warranted. For the public ceremony, at least, in the lavish style to be presently described, with singing and dancing, is itself an innovation, originating in Bida and among the wealthier classes of the capital. This festivity might well obscure the religious connotation of the naming ceremony; so that the doubling of the religious emphasis preserves the balance and hence the aspect of solemnization.

In the next and last phase of the *suna* this aspect once more disappears, giving way to purely secular interests. The infant is now brought outside, leaving the mother's hut for the first time, to be exhibited to the assembled guests. It is carried by the paternal grandmother, who also holds it when, presently, barbers will cut its hair and scratch the tribal marks on its cheeks and forehead. Traditionally, a male child's head should be shaved completely, while in the case of a girl the hair on the top of the head is left standing; this, incidentally, is the only feature in the *suna* ceremonial which varies with the sex of the child. Today, however, it is the fashion, especially in Bida, to cut the hair of boys *à la* mallam, that is, to leave a tuft of hair in the middle of the head as pious mallams do. The hair which has been shaved off is treated with some care; it is collected in a bowl and later buried inside the house, though there is no notion of evil consequences if these precautions were neglected. The facial operation is sometimes postponed for several days if the infant is too weak to stand it at once. To the observer, indeed, its cruelty seems the outstanding feature: the babe cries and squeals, and blood is running all over its face and body. The crowd, however, hardly takes notice, eating, drinking and chatting as before. The barbers perform the operation in a businesslike manner and leave as soon as they have finished, had some food, and received their fee. In wealthy households several barbers will be called in, though one man is quite sufficient for the job, and the father will try to secure the services of a famous barber-doctor. In wealthy households, too, drummers and professional musicians will be engaged to entertain the gathering and a women's dance, executed by the younger female guests, will conclude the festivities. Some of the food left over will be sent to relatives and friends who were unable to come; the father may also make gifts to the blind or the poor, or to the children of the town, if the diviners so advise him.

In the pagan ceremonial and in the *suna* of the poor the sumptuous feast is replaced by a modest meal of meat-and-gruel offered to friends and relations, without the added attractions of music and dancing. The shaving of the infant's head and the cutting of the tribal marks is the same in either case. We note, then, that the ceremony establishing the individual and kinship identity of the new-born also demonstrates his social identity in a wider sense, that is, the membership of tribe and sub-tribe into which the child is born and whose physical marks he will bear for life.

A similar idea, though more ambiguously expressed, would seem to underlie also male circumcision. This custom is universal throughout Nupe, so that having been circumcised must be considered a mark of tribal membership. Yet circumcision is never quoted when one enumerates the things that 'make a Nupe'; indeed, one knows that other tribes do the same and that circumcision is also typical of Islam. The observance presents several other puzzling features. It is called *zũ 'ba*, 'cutting the penis', which open reference to private parts is strikingly uncommon. Nor is the performance of the operation any less realistic and businesslike. It is once more in the hands of the barbers, especially hired and paid sixpence or a shilling for their work, and is accompanied by no ceremonial; the only rule affecting everyday family life is that the women must be out of the house on this occasion. The operation coincides neither with birth nor with puberty, that is, with an obviously important event or phase of life. It is performed at the age of eight to eleven and individually for every family, whenever the father thinks fit. The operation is, incidentally, even more repugnant to watch than the cutting of the tribal marks. The boys are terribly afraid; they have to be held down by the barber and his assistant, and severely feel the pain. Yet this shock experience seems again to serve no purpose; it is certainly not linked with any other experience that might be impressed upon the victims after or in consequence of their ordeal: they are neither segregated from the community nor made to feel that they have now passed a vital crisis and acquired some relevant qualification. Nor yet will the operation ever be referred to again. Through it, the boys have been made like other men of the tribe—that is all; but it is difficult to see why it should take place at this time of

their lives rather than at any other, and with so little formality.
The people can offer no explanation save the non-committal 'it is
the custom'. It is, then, a custom whose general 'content' of aims
seems clear, but whose particular 'form' appears arbitrary if not
ill-chosen.

(ii) *Marriage*

Including all the various preliminaries, the wedding ceremonial
is a long drawn-out affair, occupying twelve days, divided into
three phases of four days. It begins when the bride puts on (or
'enters') the veil, which she will put aside only on the twelfth day,
after the consummation. Even afterwards she will continue to
wear the veil whenever she leaves the house or meets strangers (for
another month in the villages, for three months in Bida), but may
remain unveiled in the company of her husband and relations.
During the first four days the bride's house is the centre of activities. The bride will bathe, stain hands and feet with henna, and
don her wedding dress. Thus attired she and her family will receive
visitors, and the bride's young female companions will sing and
clap hands, the typical accompaniment of girls' songs and dances.
The feast reaches its climax on the fourth day, when professional
drummers and musicians are hired for the occasion and the bride's
father offers food and drink to numerous guests.

Among them will be two envoys of the bridegroom, his brother
and his best friend, who have come to accompany the bride to her
future home. Among the pagans, the two men also attend the
sacrifice performed by the bride's father on that day. This sacrifice
(of beer and a cock) is intended for the *kuci* and is performed
privately at the usual place for family sacrifices—over an ancestral
grave, a twin shrine, or in front of an hereditary *cigbe*. The bride's
father briefly invokes *Sokó*, asking for a prosperous marriage,
blessed with children. Among Mohammedans, the religious rite
involves the presence of a mallam, and every family will try to
secure the offices of a famous one. The mallam, in front of all the
guests, will announce the marriage, offer up prayers for bride and
bridegroom, and recite the names and titles of their fathers and
grandfathers as well as (having been carefully primed) the details
of the brideprice and dowry. In the Mohammedan version a public
ceremonial thus again replaces the private sacrifice, and secular
ostentation is mingled with the religious rite. Let us note that in
Mohammedan practice this solemn announcement of the marriage
also establishes, formally and legally, the marriage bond, the episode
being in fact referred to as *pá yawó*, 'tying the marriage'; while the
pagan ceremonial replaces this precise, single act by a more circuitous procedure, of which the sacrifice to the *kuci* is the first step.

Afterwards the bride is taken to her new home by the bridegroom's envoys, accompanied by her girl friends, her father's younger sister, her mother's brother, as well as some drummers and musicians. If the marriage is between families living in the same village or town, the procession will start after nightfall since it is 'shameful' for the bride to be seen on this occasion (her veil notwithstanding). If the marriage is between villages too far apart for a short walk after dark, the procession starts at daybreak the next morning. Should the bride be then seen by others, which can hardly be avoided, she must kneel down and sob realistically to show 'how ashamed she is'. In Bida, it is now customary for the bride to ride on a more or less beautifully caparisoned horse to her new home—another Mohammedan innovation and another chance for displaying wealth and status.

In the next phase the scene shifts to the bridegroom's house. The bride is received by her parents-in-law and taken to her sleeping hut, which has been decorated and painted. Here she will stay in seclusion, in the company of her aunt, her girl friends and a married woman from the bridegroom's family (usually his mother's younger sister). The women and girls take no share in the 'merry-making' which will presently start in the other parts of the house, but pass their time chatting and singing womens' songs. On the morning after the bride's arrival the bridegroom's father performs a sacrifice to the *kuci*, which is an exact replica of the one previously performed in the bride's house and is again attended by an envoy from the other family (now the bride's mother's brother). This ritual is clearly meant to affirm the acceptance of the bride into the new family and lineage and, in duplicating the previous sacrifice in the bride's house, to 'tie', or complete in tying, the marriage bond. It is not surprising that the Mohammedan ceremonial includes no counterpart to this double ritual; for there can be no need to 'tie the marriage' again; while the public announcement of the marriage by the mallam, coupling as it does the names of the spouses as well as the names of their fathers and grandfathers, also obviates the need for a separate ceremonial of 'acceptance'.

On the same day the festivities begin, to which all the friends and relatives of the bridegroom's family are invited. Neither this nor the concluding phase of the wedding feast include any specifically religious features. During the 'merry-making' the emphasis is on the male participants, among whom the bridegroom's age mates figure prominently, typical men's songs and dances being alone performed. The bridegroom himself, in his finery, sits stiffly among the guests without joining in the general fun. The festivities end on the ninth day, and with them ends the segregation of the bride. On the tenth day she will for the first time sweep the hut, having until then been waited upon by her companions, and join the other women of the house in the routine of household work. But she may not yet leave the women's part of the house and hence still remains separated from her husband. The same evening she sits down outside her hut, where she is visited by all the relatives and friends of her new family, receiving a small gift of money or kolanuts from each. This custom is called the 'buying of shame', since the bride will no longer need to feel ashamed when meeting the strangers among whom she is to live. On the twelfth day the concluding observance takes place. In the morning the bridegroom sends two fowls, one cock and one hen, to the bride's mother or, if she lives in another village, to his bride's aunt who has come with her. This woman will cook the fowls, adding various spices, and take them at midday back to the bridegroom. The hen is then sent to the bride, who will offer a small portion to her mother-in-law and eat the rest together with her companions. The cock is cut in two, the bridegroom and his best friend eating one portion, while the other is eaten by his father, alone in his hut. Afterwards the bride's companions finally depart, leaving her by herself in her new home. Now, as the Nupe put it, the 'path is open at last', that is, the marriage will be consummated the same night.

No religious significance is attributed to the observance just described, which pagans and Mohammedans alike perform; it is merely taken to express or affirm, in the manner of an obvious gesture, the new, friendly relationships which are henceforth to obtain between the husband and his wife's family, and between the bride and her in-laws. In this sense the observance represents the last step in the circuitous traditional procedure of 'tying the marriage'. That this exchange of food includes both a male and a female animal would seem to throw into relief the crucial nature of the occasion, the union of man and woman. But the fact that men eat the cock and women the hen appears to harbour also a further meaning, namely, an expression of that sharp dualism of male and female which pervades the whole of Nupe philosophy.

(iii) *Death*

Of the three 'crises of life' death is most heavily weighted with ceremonial. This seems consistent with the trend of Nupe religion, to emphasize 'ends' rather than 'beginnings'. But it does not reflect the more sinister nature of the event, doubly sinister, it might be thought among a people ignorant of after-life and knowing only the vague chance of reincarnation. For though death itself is always felt to be uncanny and disturbing, the ritual elaboration is heaviest at the death of old people, in which one sees nothing tragic, and is meant to meet social demands as much as metaphysical fears. The ceremonial surrounding death differs somewhat in different communities; mostly, these variations are of a minor character (concerning, for example, the precise duties of the grave-diggers), and can be ignored.

The full funeral ceremonial includes a whole series of rituals, beginning with the burial, called *mba*, and spun out over three funerary rites, performed after eight days, forty days, and one hundred and twenty days, and called after these time intervals. Poor families may be unable to perform the last rite, which is altogether absent in the riverain area and in a few pagan inland villages. Several informants maintained that the Hundred-twenty Days' rite was an innovation, though long since established in many parts of the country (both among pagans and Mohammedans), and that it had come to Nupe with Islam. This last assumption is without foundation since the Mohammedan funeral customs include no such observance. Yet it does seem likely from the present distribution of the ritual that it originated in the Mohammedan capital and then spread to the pagan villages. The villagers, of course, show in a great many ways their readiness to imitate the 'superior' way of life in the town; and there need have been no stronger reason for an innovation otherwise congenial to the traditional outlook. But in the town the addition of another funerary feast fits more specifically into the social conditions.

To some extent it merely reflects the greater preoccupation, in the town, with occasions for the display of wealth and status. But there seems to be this also. When discussing the final funerary rite the Nupe always stress that it is 'important for the women' or concerns 'the women especially'; as we shall see, it does in fact bear specifically on the end of widowhood and on the parentage of posthumous children. In the villages which do not perform this rite, these questions are settled, three months after the death, in an informal family council. The last funerary rite thus ceremonializes the same occasion as well as postpones it. Now, this occasion is much more important, the issue being more uncertain, among the townspeople than among the peasants in the villages. Only in the town, among the aristocracy and the wealthier classes, does large-scale polygyny occur, so that the re-marriage of widows becomes a complicated matter; equally, levirate and marriage of the mother's brother's widow which, in the villages, greatly simplify the problem, are disappearing among the Mohammedans of the town. The postponement of the decision by another month would thus seem to be a useful expedient; while the added ceremonial lends moral weight to an occasion grown more critical.

The number as well as the scale of the funerary rites vary with the age, sex, and status of the deceased. The full series is performed only for married men; in the case of old men who are not survived by widows the last ritual is omitted. Children, young men who are as yet unmarried, and most women are accorded only the Eight Days; only old women, married or widowed, who hold the position of *nŭsako* (the 'Great-old-one') are entitled also to the Forty Days. This position goes to an eldest surviving sister in the oldest generation, and the nature of this qualification, referring as it does to the woman's own descent and not to her status by marriage, is also reflected in the arrangement of the ceremonials; for in the case of widows who returned to their own family after the husband's death (as many do), both rites take place in that house; while if the woman died in her husband's house, the Eight Days is performed there, and the Forty Days in the house of her kin. Differences of age and kinship position also determine the burial proceedings and the choice of the burial place. Old men and family heads, and old women, are buried in their sleeping huts, beneath the floor, and a sacrifice is performed over the grave; everyone else is buried, without special ceremony, in the space between huts or by the compound wall, or perhaps in a disused, roofless hut. At the death of old people, finally, the Eight Days' and Forty Days' rites include (among pagans) drumming, singing, and dancing, while this festive aspect is absent in the case of younger people; for their death makes 'the heart ache', while old people 'have seen the world', and there is no cause for grief.[1]

At the death of chiefs or priests the performance of the particular *kuti* they 'owned' may replace the funerary rites of the Eight Days and Forty Days. Similarly, the hunters will perform their own rituals on these occasions. But the rules differ widely; in some communities, as we know, the *gunnu* is the ritual appropriate to the funeral of chiefs and elders. Whichever solution is adopted, the combination of the funeral ceremonial with a fully-fledged *kuti* once more exemplifies the Nupe view of death as warranting the heaviest ceremonial.

The general rules are further modified when the death has been

[1] The qualification of old age cannot be stated more precisely. Old women who do not also hold the position of *nŭsako* are sometimes treated like younger people. And in the case of men one always considers these three things—ripe age; possession of an elder's rank and title; and headship of the family. When these three qualifications coincide, there can be no doubt as to the appropriate ceremonial, burial place, and so forth. When only one or the other applies, there is some latitude, the final decision depending mainly on practical considerations, such as the economic position of the family and the likely number of mourners. Thus the observances appropriate to 'old' people do not always form an unbroken series; a person may, for example, be buried in the sleeping hut, with a sacrifice, but without the subsequent festivities of the Eight Days or Forty Days.

of an abnormal kind. Lepers, we remember, are buried in the bush, by the *Ndazo*; people who die of smallpox are buried in the normal manner, though their body is wrapped in dirty rags instead of a new piece of cloth, and there is no ceremonial or mourning. In most parts of Nupe death by lightning does not affect the ceremonial; but in the north and east, apparently under Gwari influence, such persons are buried by the priests of the *sogba* cult, which flourishes in Gwari country.[1] When a person dies on the farm or in one of the outlying hamlets, the body is taken to the village for burial, and all ceremonies are performed there. A person who dies on a journey or in another part of the country is buried locally, without ceremony, all the rites being performed at his or her home; but if the deceased's kinsfolk are not certain that he has been buried at all (say, in the case of people killed in the war), they will perform a fictitious burial with a shroud representing the body. Criminals who have been executed used to be buried, without rites, by the executioners; but in the case of unconvicted criminals, even if they are known to have been guilty of the most hideous crimes, the usual ceremonial is observed: as moral depravity does not count in the beyond, so it ceases to be important on the threshold.

Let me begin with a few words on the technique of burial. The grave is oblong, square, and shallow, only about two feet below the ground. There are no marks on the grave; on the contrary, the ground is carefully levelled and repaired so that it looks like any other place. If the grave is inside a sleeping hut, the latter remains in use after the burial, the same hut often containing two or three graves of successive inhabitants. The body is placed in the grave lying on its side, 'as though asleep', and, among Mohammedans, facing east. The grave chamber is kept clear of earth by a roof of wooden beams, covered with a white grass mat; the body rests on another mat of the same kind. Among Mohammedans, fresh leaves and boughs are in addition scattered over the floor and roof of the grave chamber.[2] The grave-diggers are called *goro*, and are charged also with preparing the body and performing a first sacrifice over the grave. Their duties, ritual already in their secrecy, are usually hereditary in certain families which hold no other religious function. Among Mohammedans the body is prepared by four male or female relatives, according to the sex of the deceased, and mallams are grave-diggers.

[1] See below, p. 211.
[2] I was told of an older form of burial, in which the grave chamber is dug into the side of a circular shaft five to six feet deep. This practice has now disappeared, though the people of Doko assured me that chiefs would still be buried in this fashion. I have seen burials of this kind only in the neighbouring country of Gwari.

The burial is marked by extraordinary haste, the *goro* being sent for immediately. If possible, the dead are buried within three or four hours, at all times of the day, even at dawn or dusk, if only there is sufficient light to see by. There is no articulate fear or concern behind this haste, say, fear of the ghost of the dead or concern with the fate of the soul; rather is it the presence of the corpse as such which the Nupe find disturbing. The people in the house especially, who must stay with the body until the grave-diggers take over, are anxious to see it go; for 'the person who sees a dead body, his heart sinks'. For the same reason children are at once sent out of the house and not allowed to return until after the burial. When the *goro* arrive (usually three or four men) they wash the body with soap and water, rub it with aromatic camwood, wrap it into a new indigo-dyed cloth, and pull a cap (in the case of a man) or a kerchief (in the case of a woman) over the face of the deceased. Men of rank are today buried, in Moslem fashion, in a white gown, with a turban on the head. The grave is dug, the body placed in it, and the grave covered with loose earth, without ceremony. If the deceased was an old man or woman, the *goro* perform a libation of beer over the closed grave and speak a brief prayer, thus:

'Grandfather of the *kuci* (i.e. the deceased) who is returning to the earth, (thy) grandchild is now coming. (When) he arrives, spread (thy) two hands, receive him to your heart.'

All this is done in secrecy, no one watching; the mourners stay away, and when the *goro* leave the grave they will shut the door of the hut with a curtain or bar the access to the burial place with branches placed across the path. On the next day the ban will be lifted, the earth over the grave will be beaten down and levelled by the young women of the house, and if the grave had been dug in a sleeping hut (that is, for an old man), his heir will at once move in. When the grave-diggers have completed their task they join the mourners, being offered refreshment and a small fee, and leave shortly afterwards.

The news of the death travels fast, and an hour or two later the house will begin to fill with guests. Men and women stay apart, the former in the entrance hut of the house, the latter in the women's huts. All are dressed in old clothes, simply and without ostentation, and sit about stiffly, with expressionless faces. Only the chief mourners among the women—the mother, sisters, and the widows of the deceased—are expected to express their grief more violently, by loud sobbing and an occasional high-pitched wail (called *tigi*) which is the conventional expression of deep sorrow. The nature of the gathering will vary with the status of the departed; if he is a titled elder, all the other village elders will come to mourn him; if he is a young man, all his age mates will be present. Messengers have also been sent to nearby hamlets, and if visitors live too far to arrive on the day of the burial, they will come later and stay for the first eight days. The family head (or his heir if it is the former who died) will receive the guests and offer them food and drink. Every new visitor, before joining the mourners, kneels down before the family head and speaks the conventional formula of condolence, *okú be hákuri*—'Hail with Compassion'.

The mood of the mourners, which must be kept up for eight days, is rigidly conventionalized, though the convention is maintained with varying success. Also, it differs for the sexes. The men keep a severe, dignified and calm countenance; there must be no irrelevant chatting, only subdued talk, one topic alone being allowed, the dead person, his achievements and qualities. But the rule is often broken; on one such occasion I heard the mourners discuss farming prospects and taxes (if in whispers), and one man, whom I had some time previously presented with a watch, thought nothing of asking my wife, in the middle of the mourning, to wind up his watch for him. However, as soon as a new visitor enters, everyone at once puts on the rigid look that passes for a show of grief. Nor is the violent mourning of the women uninterrupted; now and again they may cease their sobbing and wailing and rest for a while. Female relatives who come from distant places will join in the wailing for one day and afterwards stay as ordinary guests. They, too, sit together and talk in whispers, but do not omit their more prosaic duties; for young mothers come with their babies, who must be fed and looked after, and others will help with the work in the house.

For eight days the relatives of the deceased may not wash, dress their hair or change their clothes. None of the older people may leave the house, and the women not even their huts (save for calls of nature). The men observe this rule for four days only, so that afterwards they may help with the preparations for the Eight Days' feast. But even before that household work has been going on all the time, being shouldered mainly by the younger folk. The young men will continue to go to the farms or to the market, joining the mourners in the evening, while girls and young women look after the house. These are least affected by the duties of mourning; when, the day after the burial, they level the floor over the grave, they exhibit no signs of grief, but laugh and joke freely. This, the Nupe will tell you, is quite in order: for the workers are always in-laws and 'joking relations' of the deceased (daughters-in-law or the wives of younger brothers), and are hence exempt from mourning.

On the eighth day or some time during the first week each guest makes a small gift of food to the family head, which is meant to be used in the funeral meal and represents the guests' 'greeting' or 'salute'. That day starts with a beer sacrifice, performed by the family head outside the sleeping hut of the deceased. The congregation consists of his (or her) male relations, the old men forming the usual inner ring while the youths, including the sons of the deceased, sit on the outside, looking forlorn and dejected, and being generally ignored. The family head addresses God (or sometimes the *kuci*), saying:

'We make mourning for so-and-so, who died. God, cause all people to have health. We offer you water (i.e. beer) because of the death. God, grant health to everyone; may no one die from now on.'

The beer is then drunk by the old men, which act concludes the ceremonial. Let me add that during this brief sacrifice, though it conforms so closely to the general formula of rituals, the men wear their ordinary clothes, only the bared head indicating the sacred occasion.

Soon afterwards the general meal begins. And now the house loses all appearance of mourning. It is crowded with visitors, there is constant coming and going, children get in one's way at every step, and everyone is busy preparing food, handing it round, or consuming it. The women laugh and joke while they work, the men no longer endeavour to behave severely, and even the chief mourners have turned into ordinary hosts or guests. If it is the funeral of an old man or woman, drummers and musicians will have been engaged, and soon the younger folk will sing and dance, men and girls apart, each group keeping to its own songs and dances. These are in no way peculiar to the occasion, but correspond in style and expression to any ordinary form of 'merrymaking'. Ample supplies of beer keep up the spirits of the gathering until nightfall, when the feast comes to an end, the visitors departing and the hosts retiring to their huts.

The period following the Eight Days' ceremony involves few prohibitions. Widows must continue to wear the simple dress of mourning and must not wash or do their hair; nor must they leave the compound, though they are now free to pursue their daily tasks. As regards the men, the brothers (or the husband) of the deceased should refrain from shaving until the Forty Days' ceremony, though this custom has now fallen into disuse. The men go about freely but will try to be at home at night. Guests will still occasionally visit the house, but now these visits are free from the restraint and show of grief that marked the earlier occasion. Forty days after the death and burial, the family head repeats the beer sacrifice, and another big feast takes place, which lasts two days but otherwise duplicates the celebration of the Eight Days.

The widows may now leave the compound and go into the town, though they may do so only at dark, when they cannot be recognized. The prohibition to wash or to change their clothes remains in force for another four months, and not until then may the widows begin to think about re-marriage. The final funerary rite is once more a copy of the previous feasts, save that all present will now wear their best and most festive clothes. The widows especially, if they are still young, will stain their hands and feet with henna and their eyes with antimony, prospective brides even in appearance. For if the question of re-marriage arises, the feast of the Hundred-Twenty Days also serves as an occasion for the family council at which this prospect is discussed and decided. Four months after a man's death, the Nupe argue, a pregnancy for which he was responsible must be noticeable. If so, the widow may not re-marry until the child is born and old enough to be left; the child, called *dzangi*, 'parting-gift child', would then belong to the father's family and stay with it. If the widow is not pregnant at the time (noticeably so, that is), she is free to re-marry, and even if she does not, any child she may subsequently give birth to will be disclaimed by the late husband's family.

It now remains to compare the traditional ceremonial with the modern Mohammedan version. The *goro* grave-diggers, as we know, are replaced by mallams, whose work and religious ministrations are surrounded by no secrecy. Nor are these restricted to the death of old people. They now consist in brief prayers, spoken or read in the presence of all the men of the house (women being excluded), both before the body is interred and again before the grave is closed. When the mallams later join the mourners they will continue to murmur prayers, rosary in hand. At the death of an important man, when the grave hut cannot hold all the mourners, the main prayers are said in the roomy entrance hut, and the body will be brought there for the service before being interred. On such occasions mallams of highest standing will officiate, the *Alkali* or *Liman* leading the prayers, and these are interspersed with passages of impromptu praise and eulogy. On such occasions, too, the men among the guests will wear, not the simple dress of mourning, but rich gowns meant to display their rank and position. The mallams are offered food and given a sum of money, only part of which is a payment for their services; the rest is intended as a pious offering, for distribution among all the mallams of the town. It is extremely shameful to give too little, and families will borrow money or pawn their belongings rather than risk dismissing the mallams with a gift that might be considered shabby; so that the pious aims are again made a vehicle for ostentation. The gifts of condolence are once more in money and are made, not once only, but two or three times, every guest being expected to give in accordance with wealth and status. Equally, the gifts have changed their name, being now known as *sadaka*, 'pious alms', although like the pagan 'greeting' gifts they are intended as contributions towards the funeral expenditure. The subsequent ceremonials become further occasions for alms giving, now on the part of the hosts; for a portion of the food prepared at these feasts is sent out to the mallams of the town or distributed among the poor.

The three funerary feasts are in fact described as *sadaka*, 'alms', or as *walima*, 'sacred feast'. The latter name seems hardly appropriate, since in the Mohammedan version these rites are almost entirely devoid of sacred or religious features. The sacrifice of beer and the private invocation of the deity have, naturally, disappeared; yet the mallams' prayer, which might have taken their place, is not repeated after the burial service. In other words, there is nothing in the funerary ceremonies that would show them to be 'ceremonies', sacred and not secular events, save the pious distribution of alms. But perhaps there is also less chance of confusing the sacred with a worldly occasion; for the Mohammedan version of the Eight Days and Forty Days does not admit singing and dancing and thus maintains the outward appearance of mourning. Only the last ceremonial includes 'merry-making' and finally discards the show of grief.

The Mohammedan funeral ceremonial clearly represents something like a compromise between traditional Nupe practice and the orthodox requirements of Islam; and like most compromises it led to unintended results. To begin with, the contrast between youth and old age has been minimized; for while traditionally only the old were buried with special religious offices (the *goro* sacrifice) and mourned in the early stages with singing and dancing, the former (in the form of the mallam's prayer) are now generally applied, and the latter are altogether omitted. Moreover, there has been a certain loss of mystic appeal and of emotional weight; for the secrecy which traditionally surrounds the burial has been allowed to disappear; and in the subsequent ceremonials the religious appeal is sustained, no longer by an esoteric sacrifice and invocation, but merely by the exercise of charity. If I considered both results to be unintentional and accidental I did so for these reasons. If we took the first result to be a planful adjustment to changed conditions, then we should have to assume that the distinction between youth and old age has been made less sharp because it ceased to be important; yet it has lost none of its relevance in Nupe social life.[1] And we should have to assume further, to account for the loss of mystic appeal, that Islam has radically altered the Nupe view of life and death; which, as we shall see, is once more untrue.

5. SOLEMNIZATIONS AND SOCIAL STRUCTURE

There is no need to point to the close affinity of the ceremonials surrounding birth, marriage, and death, with the rituals of more general religious bearing. Both operate with the same elements—private (or esoteric) invocations, libations, communal meals, and public 'merry-making' in the concluding phase. Both, too, conspicuously involve numerical calculations defining the occasion and sequence of rites. The congregations, of course, differ, though there is some overlap; for certain *kuti*, like the solemnizations, mobilize the kin group only, while at the funerary rites of men of standing all the dignitaries of the community will be represented. Like the *kuti*, finally, the ceremonials surrounding the crises of life have their implicit as well as their professed aims. The latter could not be 'professed' more clearly. The *suna* is there to name the infant in solemn fashion, and hence to assign to it its future place in the society while at the same time invoking divine protection; the wedding ceremonial sanctifies the union of man and wife and holds out the promise of progeny; and the funeral ceremonial disposes of the dead while one prays that there may be no further deaths; it imposes mourning as well as cancels it, and thus repeats or dramatizes, in the ritual sequence, the endless cycle of human existence. We have, I think rightly, called these rituals solemnizations; for they hallow all these events through relating them with the supernatural. But they do more. Through the form they take, that is, through the manner in which the rituals mobilize their particular congregations, they also express the principles and values governing the structure of the society. Think of the rules assigned to the father and grandfather in the ceremonial of birth, the former being expected to collect the 'medicines' needed for an easy confinement and to consult the diviner, the latter to announce the new-born's name. Or think of the complicated exchange of gifts which concludes the marriage ceremonial, of the double sacrifice in the bride's and the bridegroom's house, and of the selection of the bridegroom's envoys and the bride's companions. The funerary rites throw into relief both the social distinctions that go with sex,

[1] I am here referring to status in the society at large, i.e. to the access to rank and office open only to older men and to the respect they generally command, not to the kinship authority of family heads; the latter has indeed been weakened (see pp. 83, 251.)

age, and status and the varying degrees of kinship; even so specific a feature as joking relationship is built into the ceremonial.

Now, with a few exceptions—the role of friends in the marriage ceremonial, of age grades in marriage or funerals, and of rank-holders in the funerary rites,—the relationships mobilized in these rituals are kinship relationships; and through being mobilized in a sacred context, they are in turn affirmed and sanctioned. That the implicit efficacy of these rituals should serve to sustain the group based on kinship seems to fit the nature of the events so solemnized, which themselves primarily concern the kinship group. But these events do not only 'concern' the kinship group as, say, rain or fertility concern the village community; they punctuate its life and in fact determine its existence, that is, they create and renew it, birth and marriage replenishing the group and death depleting and re-ordering it. So that the circle is complete, the ritual 'content' and 'form' sustaining one another and, in a sense, coinciding. For the solemnization of these crucial events employs (and hence affirms) the very relationships brought into being by the events; and the professed aims of the ceremonials bear on the perpetuation of the human aggregate which their procedures serve to hold together.

V

MEDICINE

1. RATIONAL AND MYSTICAL PROCEDURES

THE term 'medicine' has been adopted mainly because it is simple and convenient without distorting too much the meaning of the Nupe word *cigbe*. The English equivalent, however, does not quite render the implications of the vernacular concept; for though the latter includes typical remedies, that is, materials applied for a strictly therapeutic purpose (as the Nupe see it), it equally includes materials whose alleged efficacy goes far beyond the treatment of ailments. In this latter sense *cigbe* is a substance or object which exercises remote and miraculous effects upon the efficacy of other objects, for example, tools or weapons, upon the outcome of human efforts of all kinds, and upon human fate in general. The correct though clumsy translation, then, would be 'efficacious substance' or 'force-in-substance' (as *kuti* meant 'force-in-ritual').

Indeed, the important thing about *cigbe* is that it is always a substance, compounded of natural materials which anyone in possession of the recipe can collect and process by relatively simple procedures such as pulverizing, boiling, mixing, or charring. Most Nupe, incidentally, maintain that the essential ingredients of *cigbe* are always roots of trees.[1] It is tempting to conclude that here the empirical knowledge of the processes of plant growth has led to the assumption of some inherent but communicable force stored up in the roots of plants and trees. Which assumption would fit in well with the idea that all forms of illness connote a weakening of the life soul. But no one theorizes on these lines. Altogether, Nupe medicine shows little concern with theory, metaphysical or otherwise. As regards the alleged importance of roots, the various *cigbe* recipes show that herbs, grasses, the leaves of trees, or animal matter are employed as often. The power of *cigbe*, then, lies in materials of almost any sort if suitably processed and combined, and the knowledge of *cigbe* is precisely this skill of 'using ingredients'.[1]

---

[1] Two informants, in fact, assured me that the very word *cigbe* was a contraction of *cigbā gbere*, 'tree root'.

We must now ask—to what extent is this knowledge empirically sound and the skill rationally employed? It can obviously not be entirely so since the non-therapeutic version of *cigbe*, credited as it is with remote effects upon objects or human actions, reveals at first sight already its non-empirical, miraculous nature. Yet the twofold use of medicine, therapeutic as well as non-therapeutic, suggests the corresponding distinction between rational practices and others irrational or 'magical'. To some extent this will prove a valid distinction, though one far less clear-cut or consistent; and this in turn is partly due to the ambiguity of the concept of rationality when it is applied to the practices of a primitive people. For they may act with rational intent but insufficient or faulty knowledge, so that their would-be empirical practices will conflict with our scientific knowledge, and hence strike us as irrational or 'magical'; while in a sense the converse case may equally occur.

I spoke of this before and need here only state the four possibilities entailed in these considerations. First, a procedure 'subjectively' rational, involving for the people the application of ordinary learned skills, may also be 'objectively' rational, that is, appropriate to the ends for which it is employed. Secondly, a subjectively rational procedure may prove futile and incongruous when assessed by 'objective' standards. Thirdly, a procedure professedly supernatural or mystical may yet prove appropriate, concealing some valid empirical principle. Lastly, a professedly mystical procedure may be such also from our point of view, that is, empirically false and incapable of achieving the ends for which it is employed.

Before examining each possibility in turn we must restate our criteria for assessing the mystical as against the professedly rational intent behind *cigbe* practice. In a very general sense, every *cigbe* procedure implies both kinds of intent. For even though Nupe medicine is, by definition, 'knowledge', which is usually purely technical as well as transferable through tuition or purchase, it is also given a mythical pedigree and related to the remoteness of God.[1] But these mystical associations are left almost entirely unemphasized, furnishing only a vague and ineffectual background, and can thus be disregarded. If, then, we are to credit certain procedures with mystical intent, they must exhibit it in a more pronounced and specific fashion. In the most obvious case the manufacture or application of *cigbe* will involve invocations of the deity and sacrifices proper, that is, open appeals for supernatural intervention. Where these are absent, we may yet search for that other evidence, of awe, fear, and a sense of the extraordinary or miraculous, which would set the procedure apart from pursuits

[1] See above, p. 18.

and interests of a profane kind. The 'sense of the extraordinary' if it is not vouchsafed by verbal expressions, is clearly the most difficult to identify. But it is at least likely to go together with uncommon procedures and with rigid rules, barring even minute departures from a given course of action, that is, with ritualization. In sum I would list these criteria of professedly mystical as against professedly rational intent: the degree of ritualization implied in the preparation or application of medicines; their secrecy or otherwise; their commercial or non-commercial, public or private character; the diverse ways in which the knowledge of *cigbe* is transmitted; and the different kinds of faith placed in it.

If previously we described 'ritual' behaviour as behaviour exhibiting a degree of rigidity not accounted for by its professed aim, we may now say, of the 'ritualized' procedure of *cigbe*, that its rigidity is not accounted for by the rational intent. For the Nupe, the latter lies in the application of material substances which as such possess a given efficacy. But often we find additional and incongruous rules such as these: certain medicines may only be prepared in certain months of the year; in certain treatments a particular procedure must be repeated three times; in the operation of setting a broken limb four splints (no more and no less) must be used. Here, then, the Nupe no longer rely on the empirical or pseudo-empirical knowledge of 'ingredients'; rather, they abandon their own 'scientific' principles, diluting them with rules of a different order—with ritual, and hence with 'mystic' observances.

Again, certain medicines, their preparation and disposal, are cloaked in rigorous secrecy, while others are not secret or no more secret than the skills or tricks of a particular trade. The latter kind is usually freely bought and sold, while the secret medicines can be given away only with special formalities or not at all, being accessible only to the relatives or perhaps friends of the 'owner'; so that some medicines are available to the public, like any commercial commodity, and others are unalterably 'private'. As we know, the knowledge of *cigbe* is mostly transmitted through ordinary teaching, and is such as any clever, observant, or widely-travelled person can acquire; but occasionally it is hereditary, the ultimate provenance of the knowledge remaining unexplained. Finally, while no one would assume that ordinary remedies, administered without ceremonial, are infallible, precisely this faith is put in the other, 'miraculous', medicines, even if they involve no explicit appeals to the deity.

These features, however, occur with varying degrees of definiteness; and, though they all hang together logically, they do not always appear together in practice. But considered singly, they offer only ambiguous criteria. Ritualization, for example, especially when it is slight, may represent only an item of 'knowledge', empirically futile and 'superstitious', but for all that entirely profane. And secrecy may attach to medicines, not because they are sacred or credited with miraculous efficacy, but because they are morally reprehensible. Our assessment of 'mystical' and 'rational' intent will therefore sometimes be uncertain and admit of borderline cases. Even so, it enables us to examine *cigbe* practice in the terms of the four 'possibilities' mentioned before.

(i) It is clear that this possibility can apply only to the therapeutic medicines. But only very few even of these satisfy our two conditions of rational intent and objective appropriateness. For several of the therapeutic medicines require the accompaniment of invocations or sacrifices, or otherwise exhibit at least an admixture of mystical intent; and those which do not, often fail on the second count. It is clear, however, that in this relatively backward society we must not assess the appropriateness or otherwise of remedies by too exacting a standard. Thus, if they do not conflict in principle with our scientific ideas and are such that their efficacy might at least conceivably be of the alleged kind, their actual worthlessness may be ignored; at least, it does not make them 'mystical', but only shows them to be crude, inadequate, or ill-chosen. This would be true of such remedies as herbal potions used for intestinal troubles, of salves or powders rubbed into snake-bites, or of certain simple surgical treatments. Few of these betray any true medical lore; the surgical operations are rarely applied and have little merit; most potions or salves prove on chemical analysis to have no positive value, though I found none that was actually harmful and a few that had a slight medicinal property, such as the absorptive or laxative effect of charred vegetable matter. Even so, these practices are at least of the right kind or resemble the right kind of treatment, and will for this reason be included in our first category.

Many more treatments are without even this semblance of appropriateness, suggesting merely blundering attempts, unguided even by faulty knowledge. Lunacy, for example, is treated by means of inhalations; smallpox is prevented by burning herbs in the entrance hut; pregnancy, by the wearing of a 'magic' belt; and for rheumatic pains one has this abstruse cure: the patient stands inside a hut, pressing the aching part of his body against the wall; the doctor stands outside and holds the 'medicine' with his foot against the wall, opposite the place where, on the inside, the patient's body touches the wall; the doctor then slowly drags the medicine to the ground, thus 'drawing the pain from the body'. Though this treatment seems to imply some crude reasoning from analogy, it clearly belongs, with all the other treatments just mentioned, to our second category, of practices utterly incongruous and not even conceivably capable of the alleged effects.

We must add, further, that a great many therapeutic remedies are ascribed so multifarious an efficacy that their 'rational' application to one kind of ailment is belied by the other, extravagant claims. The same substance will serve as an antidote for snakebite, as a cure for headaches, and as a potion applied in ordeals; and a herbal concoction for intestinal troubles will also be used to cure rheumatic pains in the fantastic manner just described. Thus the borderline between rational and pseudo-rational treatments is once more blurred, and the province of the former narrowed further. And here we may note that in a sense the Nupe wish to keep it narrow. For the one version of medicine which comes nearest to satisfying our two conditions of rational intent and empirical (if crude) appropriateness, that practised by the barber-doctors, is also criticized for this very reason. The barber-doctors are entirely profane practitioners, whose skill is a matter of cleverness and learning, involves no secrecy, and is at the disposal of all who can pay for their services. But their practice is largely restricted to the capital and the more sophisticated large villages, and little known or little thought of elsewhere. Indeed, the country people simply laugh when you suggest that the barbers have a knowledge of *cigbe*; 'barbers', I was always told, 'know no *cigbe*; all they can do is to cure headache'. Now some of my informants certainly knew that this was incorrect; furthermore, several village *cigbe* of the secret and mystical kind were also supposed to cope with headache. It was therefore not the efficacy of the remedies which the people held in ridicule but their purely profane character; and in denying that the barbers possessed any worthwhile knowledge of medicine, they really denied that their knowledge deserved the name of medicine. We note, then, a bias towards excluding from the genus *cigbe* those remedies which combine all the characteristics of a rational practice. The true *cigbe*, the people seem to feel, must at least in some respects bear the mark of the extraordinary or 'magical'. But this is no more than a bias since even in the villages where the art of the barber-doctors was so derided there exist purely profane, would-be rational remedies.[1] Their number, however, is strikingly small; so that in the peasant culture of Nupe, unlike the urban culture of the capital, the non-mystical or non-'magical' *cigbe* represents an exception from the rule.

[1] Also, this 'bias' is being obliterated by the modern usage of the word *cigbe* for all European drugs and medical appliances, in which the Nupe see nothing transcendental or magical, but the application of 'knowledge' proper.

(ii) We have already mentioned the therapeutic medicines which fall in this category in virtue of their fantastic nature or of the extravagant claims made for them. We need only add that there are no non-therapeutic *cigbe*, that is, medicines at first sight already 'miraculous' and irrational, which are handled in a would-be rational manner; all also imply at least some expression of mystical intent.

(iii) Strictly speaking, this possibility of professedly mystical but unwittingly appropriate practices does not apply to Nupe medicine. Trance possession attributed to spirits, magic dances meant to cure mental disorders, and similar treatments which might conceal a psycho-therapeutic efficacy under the mystical trappings are altogether absent. But the combination of invocations and sacrifices with remedies which are 'of the right kind' constitutes a borderline case since the people would attribute the success of the remedy (such as it is) as much to supernatural intervention as to the inherent properties of the ingredients employed. In a sense even the most absurd therapeutic remedies have a share of such a concealed empirical efficacy. In calling them absurd and worthless we were considering only their intrinsic inappropriateness to the effects ascribed to them; we cannot deny that the patient's trust in the efficacy of the medicine or the repute of the doctor may well produce at least an apparent relief. Which means, further, that the practitioner's medical notions will repeatedly receive some empirical support, whose spuriousness he is unable to judge.

(iv) Our last category comprises all the non-therapeutic medicines and a considerable number of therapeutic ones. Their objective irrationality cannot be mistaken. When a potion is said to make a person invisible, a salve to secure invulnerability, a herbal concoction kept in the village to keep away smallpox, or a powder applied to a hoe to double the farm output, there can clearly be no question but that only a miracle could make these 'medicines' effective. Nor is the mystical intent any less certain, being visible in the prescribed invocations, sacrifices, forms of ritualism, and so forth. It is interesting to note that several of these practices are based upon the principle 'like causes like'; by itself, this spurious theory would not establish the mystical intent since for the people it represents only one more item of would-be scientific knowledge. The same principle, in fact, also underlies a few therapeutic and strictly profane cures. But it seems significant that it is employed on a large scale only in the fully irrational practices, that is, in situations where success is vouchsafed also by mystical procedures. In other words, false knowledge tends to go together with transcendental guarantees (though more sound knowledge does not necessarily discard them).

Let me summarize. By our criteria of rational and mystical intent the whole range of non-therapeutic *cigbe* together with a good portion of the therapeutic ones would fall in the category of transcendental practices (religious or 'magical'); while only the rest of the cures proper, good, bad, and indifferent, would belong on the side of reason or near-reason. And since a great many of the cures in the former category are 'objectively' as futile or absurd as the non-therapeutic variety, it may be said that the Nupe tend to treat as 'magical' what is, by all standards, magical and to aim at miraculous effects by means openly designed for miracles.

2. PHARMACOPOEIA NUPEANA

It seems convenient to insert here a fuller description of Nupe medicines and medical (or pseudo-medical) treatments. Their therapeutic or non-therapeutic character will become clear from the description, as will also the share of 'irrational' or mystical observances. We must, however, anticipate the various classes of medicine experts and briefly state their respective specialities. First, we have the guild of barber doctors, who are all Mohammedans and whose craft is entirely therapeutic and would-be empirical; a few minor instances of 'ritualization' do not contradict the generally rational intent. Secondly, there is the corresponding and predominantly pagan order of *cigbeciži* or *bociži* ('medicine-men'), whose practice, both therapeutic and non-therapeutic, invariably betrays mystical intent. Thirdly, there are a few individual experts who belong to neither organization and may employ any kind of *cigbe*. Lastly, we shall meet with the owners of hereditary medicines, vested in the lineage or (in Nupe parlance) 'house'; these are both therapeutic and non-therapeutic, and always conspicuously mystical. In one isolated case a conspicuously 'mystical' medicine is owned by a whole community. Let me also recall that some medical practitioners are diviners at the same time, though there is no firmer link between the two professions.

These are some of the remedies known to the barber-doctors of Bida. Stomach trouble is treated by means of various potions: one consists of the infusion of a certain swamp plant; another, of the infusion of the charred bark of the oil-palm, sheanut tree or locust-bean tree, mixed with natron;[1] a third, of the pounded roots of a certain tree, mixed with powdered eggshell, dried in the sun and then taken with water. Light headache is cured by burning a certain common plant and making the patient inhale the fumes,

[1] The 'natron' is natural carbonate of soda from Lake Chad which is on sale in all Nupe markets.

or by preparing a potion from bits of earth extracted from a termite mound. For severe headache one applies an ointment to the eyes, compounded of the dried kernels of a fruit tree, the bark from the roots of another, cloves, and powdered antimony. Sometimes headache is treated quasi-surgically, by a species of bleeding; the barber makes a number of fine incisions into the patient's forehead and then rubs a paste of dried locust-beans and natron into the cuts. The counter-irritation thus induced may well offer a temporary relief, though the bleeding itself is probably too slight to have any effect; the cure, however, has an odd conclusion, the patient's head being knocked gently three times against the wall.

Ulcers and wounds are treated with powdered bark or roots, used either dry or damp, and left on the wound for two to three days. Broken limbs are first massaged with a salve made of palm-oil and the dried and powdered leaves of a certain tree (another remedy including dirt from a hen house and charred earth from a termite mound), after which one applies a ligature of rope, using four sticks as splints. The ligature is removed after three days, but the massage with the ointment is continued. If the fracture does not heal, this treatment is followed up with a 'stronger' one, to wit, a massage with snake poison. For smallpox one gives a potion made of the pods of a certain vine growing in the bush. There is also a 'prophylactic' treatment, applied when an epidemic is threatening; it consists either in drinking an infusion of the bark of the locust-bean tree, boiled together with some grains of sorghum or millet, or in fumigating the house, at night, by burning certain herbs. Pounded hibiscus seeds, taken like snuff, are given to patients suffering from asthma. For fever accompanied by rigor (malaria?) one drinks the boiled juice of the pawpaw mixed with natron; a more 'magical' cure consists in inhalations of the fumes from three ingredients burned together in an old, broken pot (never a new one)—a powdered herb, the swamp plant mentioned before, and twigs taken from a vulture's nest. We shall meet again with this predilection for old pots when discussing the medicines of the *cigbeci* experts; the vulture plays a part also in another remedy of the barber-doctors, applied to sore eyes: they are bathed in ash-water mixed with a pulverized vulture's leg. Other herbal concoctions are used in the treatment of gonorrhœa (called *tswashi*), syphilis (called *tunjeri*), and sleeping sickness; these remedies are similar in that the first two are said to increase the typical secretion until 'the whole disease leaves the body', while the last brings on diarrhœa, the germs of the disease being passed with the stool. Lunacy of a non-violent nature may be treated by means of inhalations, repeated several times day and night, or by means of a potion. For the inhalation one uses leaf-tips of the oil-palm, hair of a she-goat, and the pulverized genitals of a he-goat, all burned together in a pot; the potion is made of the sap of a certain 'male' shrub (that is, the fruitless variety, called *darabagi*, 'male *dara*'), the charred bark of another, mixed with natron. The patient, having been treated in this fashion, is said to calm down and eventually to recover, though the cure can never be certain. For violent and dangerous attacks there is no agreed cure. The barber-doctors, in fact, do not treat this form of insanity at all, but other people sometimes know a treatment, though it is always said to be difficult and uncertain. Thus one informant suggested that the patients must be made to fast until they calm down; and another recommended flogging (a treatment apparently widely applied in Yoruba country).[1]

A final group of medicines bears on conception and virility. Dried cocoyam, the charred bark of the *savi* tree, and onions, pounded and taken in water, are said to constitute a powerful aphrodisiac. Fertility of women is ensured by a potion, drunk the morning before cohabitation, made of an infusion of leaves of the tamarind tree mixed with natron. Delivery is facilitated by rubbing the womb with three herbs after they have been soaked in water for a night. There are also two 'contraceptive' medicines, one having a temporary effect only, the other believed to cause permanent barrenness. The former consists of two powdered herbs, mixed with bits of grass from a termite mound, and taken with water; the latter, of the charred stalk and leaves of a young cassava plant, mixed with henna root and natron, boiled in water, and drunk. The knowledge, incidentally, of the permanent 'contraceptive' is claimed to be purely platonic; the Bida practitioner at least has no chance of applying it in practice, not because he is reluctant to do so or because the Bida women avoid these shameful practices, but because they would not risk their reputation by thus openly consulting a 'doctor' in the town. Instead, my informants assured me, they go to 'medicine-men' in the villages, where they are unknown and their secret will be safe. A secret in fact it is; and here we meet with a first, though fairly mild, instance of reprehensible medicines, employed for immoral ends.

This list is far from complete, omitting, especially, the many variants of the same kind of cure.[2] The barber-doctors do not believe in specifics in the strict sense of the word; rather, there are several treatments for each ailment, and different practitioners

---

[1] The informant in question came, in fact, from Shari, a village on the border of Nupe and Yoruba.

[2] I recorded altogether thirty-four remedies known to barber-doctors, which number is probably fairly exhaustive.

will often know and apply different ones. Also, some specialize in potions or in poultices and lotions; others prefer treatment by means of inhalations, which the Nupe call *turare* (a Hausa word, meaning 'scent' or 'fumigation'). Certain more versatile experts know several remedies for the same illness, which they would try out one after the other. The position is summed up in this statement of a famous Bida 'doctor': 'Sometimes one medicine proves sufficient; but there is only one way of discovering the right one—to experiment and trust in God.' Certain barber-doctors, too, are specialists in particular diseases and are known as such. Thus only two men in Bida knew how to treat lunacy and only one Bida barber (whom I met in Ibadan, where he was staying at the time) knew how to treat sleeping sickness; similarly, there were specialists for venereal diseases, for eye complaints, and so forth. For certain ailments there are no treatments; their list includes blindness, idiocy, leprosy, elephantiasis, deafness, 'incurable syphilis', and, oddly enough, the common cold; my informants made it quite clear that the last was too trifling a complaint to deserve the attention of 'doctors'.

As we have seen, surgical treatments are almost entirely absent, and the use of splints in fractures is considered no more important than the application of some 'strong' salve or ointment. The barbers, in fact, herbalists at heart, deprecate the 'use of the knife' and emphatically deny its value. Said the head of the barbers' guild: 'The knife begets pain; how could it cure?' Though the same few herbs or plants appear in the majority of remedies, this does not mean that they alone have curative properties. On the contrary, it is considered that all plants contain some medicine, even if its nature or extraction are not known. It is considered equally certain that this medical knowledge, far from being static, is growing all the time, so that the barbers today possess medicines unknown even a short time ago. Once more, this is a question of experimenting 'with the help of God', and there are certain rough rules how to proceed. One tries first the bark of a plant or tree not hitherto used; if this proves worthless, one tries the roots, and finally the leaves or fruits. As to why certain parts of plants should contain *cigbe* and others not, there is no answer; or rather the usual answer is *'cigbe u de 'tsu a'*, 'medicines have no king' (that is, follow no proclaimed law): God has made them so, and men can only hope to learn by trial and error or by accepting the wisdom of others.

A strikingly large number of remedies employ plant parasites (called *etú*), and their special medicinal properties are strongly emphasized. If the alien growth of the parasites once suggested to the people some affinity with the nature of diseases and hence a possible application of the principle 'like cures like', no one today is aware of this notion. Nor are there any 'theories' as regards such abstruse ingredients as eggshells, the excreta of fowls, twigs from the nest of vultures, or grass from inside an ant-heap. Yet it is also difficult to see how the precept, 'experiment with the help of God', can have led to these peculiar discoveries. If they are 'superstitions', they are not, like other superstitions, the degraded offspring of more elaborate mystic or cosmological speculations. The treatment of lunacy, with its 'male' and 'female' ingredients, seems to suggest something of the kind; but there is no clear link between this cure and that other idea, that lunacy is a residue of 'male' sleeping sickness.[1] And in all the other fantastic remedies their intellectual antecedents are simply not traceable, not even to legends or folk-tales. Perhaps the remedies have been adopted, more or less blindly, from other groups and countries, on some of those informative travels of which the barber-doctors boast. As they stand, they are merely crude and absurd attempts at 'empirical' treatment, instances of that 'blundering' I spoke of before.

Any of the medicines just described might equally be the product of the *cigbeciži*, and a number are in fact identical. But unlike the barber-doctors, the *cigbeciži* also employ the fully irrational, non-therapeutic version of *cigbe*, and even their remedies proper, salves, potions, and the like, are much more often based on recipes of an incongruous and abstruse kind.[2] Thus a 'strong' potion taken for intestinal troubles includes the fluid extracted from the gallbladder of snakes, a potion alleged to cure smallpox contains a boiled lizard tail, and an ointment for rheumatic pains is composed, among other things, of powdered potsherds which must be obtained from old pots found lying about with the broken side up, any other position rendering the remedy worthless.

While these recipes seem as random and arbitrary as the more abstruse examples of the barber-doctors' art, others betray some underlying 'theory', some vague and often uncertain reasoning from analogy or from the principle 'like cures like'. Thus one expert had a cure for impotence consisting of a potion whose ingredients included, besides various roots and two kinds of pepper, also the powdered genitals of a he-goat.[3] A contraceptive credited with lasting effect is concocted from the roots of the

---

[1] See above, p. 37.

[2] Of the twenty-two *cigbeci* medicines I recorded fifteen belonged to that category, while the corresponding proportion in the case of the barbers' remedies was six in thirty-four.

[3] I have this incongruous evidence for the efficacy of the treatment. My servant, who was with me when I visited the expert, at once bought and drunk the potion to increase his virility. The next day I had to doctor him for severe indigestion.

tamarind tree, leaves of baobab, sorghum stalks, and the skin of a fish said to 'die at once when you hold it in your hand', the last ingredient being the most important. Another, temporary, contraceptive is prepared with grass taken from an ant-heap which must have three round mounds and must be broken open with the heel. The magic belt mentioned before, said to prevent pregnancy, is made of leather into which these two ingredients are sewn—hair from the tail of a mule and seeds from locust-beans 'forgotten' (i.e. overlooked) at the harvest. The reasoning from analogy is fairly obvious in the recipe for impotence and in the last appliance. In the lasting contraceptive the underlying 'theory' seems to rest upon this argument: since a freshly caught fish stands for fertility (in dream interpretation), a fish that 'dies at once' might plausibly be identified with its destruction. And of ants, which figure in the temporary contraceptive, it is said that 'one does not know their father and mother'; so that a medicine derived from ants would seem to promise precisely what its users desire. The former 'theory' is my own inference, while the latter, as we shall see, is explicitly mentioned. But it is incomplete apart from being abstruse; for it fails to account for the three mounds that are required and for the peculiar method of opening the ant-heap; nor yet does it state why grass taken from an ant-heap should, in other remedies, serve quite a different purpose.

The moral attitude of the *cigbeciži* towards such dubious practices as facilitating contraception and sterility differs considerably from that of the barber-doctors. While the latter simply claim that they have no chance of dispensing these remedies and shift the blame on their pagan colleagues, these both admit dealing in them and try to justify their actions. They maintain that they dispense these medicines only rarely and in deserving cases. At least, this is true of the medicine alleged to procure permanent sterility; the expert in question assured me that he had given it only once, out of pity, to a woman whose husband was forcing her to sleep with him while her first-born had not yet been weaned. In the case of the temporary expedients the conscience of the *cigbeciži* is more easily satisfied; they merely put up the price for frivolous clients, that is, for 'rich people who do not want children'. As a corrollary, the medicine for impotence is similarly expensive (costing as much as ten shillings), not only because it is difficult to prepare, but because it is something of a luxury; for the expert argued that since this remedy did not 'save people from death' but afforded them 'enjoyment' it was worth paying for. He was fairminded enough to add that he would lower the price in the case of poor clients.

As regards the non-therapeutic medicines, they are credited

with widely varying but uniformly fantastic properties. Thus a certain potion is said to make you invisible and invulnerable to guns; a similar protection is afforded by a powder carried in a leather bag which must be of two colours, red and black. Another powder, which may either be drunk in water or rubbed on the gun, assures success in big-game hunting. Two potions protect the drinker from all evil-wishers, who would in one case be struck with lunacy or sleeping sickness and in the other with blindness. It is interesting to note that while one of these medicines, called *zabadi*, can be used by both sexes, the other, called *imi-ya-ga* (both undecipherable words) is designed for women only. Conversely, there is a 'male' medicine called *eshe*; its composition is extremely complicated, numbering fifteen ingredients, and it can be rubbed on the body or on a hoe, or buried in farmland: its effect is to divert the fertility of all adjacent fields to the one farmed by the owner of the *cigbe*. Finally, there are two medicines associated with witchcraft; the first is the 'female' medicine *imi-ya-ga*, which, used as a potion or as an ointment or simply kept in the house, protects you from witches as well as spirits; the other is a potion called *waka*, which must be taken by the performers in the anti-witchcraft cult *ndakó gboyá* but is deadly to the uninitiated. Most of these medicines serve more than one function. Thus a snake-bite antidote called *dabwalé* can also be used as ordeal or kept in the house to guard it against thieves (who would be bitten by a snake), and the anti-witchcraft remedy *waka* similarly protects the house where it is kept, the thief being punished with blindness.

As has already been mentioned, the *cigbeciži* always employ professedly mystical procedures. To some extent these are visible already in the conspicuous ritualization attaching to certain of their remedies. More importantly, the practice of the *cigbeciži* also involves ritual invocations and rigid rules of secrecy, though the latter refer only to the recipe itself and do not otherwise restrict the use or disposal of the medicines. The invocation consists of the proper name for the medicine and of its particular *emisa* or 'greeting'. The names themselves do not necessarily distinguish this species of *cigbe* from the other, profane, variety; for several of the barbers' remedies similarly have names, which serve as labels and abbreviated references to the composition or efficacy of the medicine. Some of the names given to the *cigbeci* medicines, however, are more mystically obscure and as inexplicable as the names of most *kuti* or those that occur in divining. The *emisa* are fully ritual formulæ: they must be uttered, without the slightest deviation and in a respectful and humble manner, at various stages in the preparation of the *cigbe* and whenever it is dispensed. They play much the same part as the 'greetings' used in divining and are, like the latter, composed of sayings more or less trivial or apposite. A medicine alleged to facilitate childbirth, for example, is called *lamá*, from *lá má 'gi*, 'causing childbirth', and has a meaningless 'greeting'; the antidote for snake-bite *dabwalé* (an undecipherable word) commands the following 'greeting'—'The thing for washing, when a snake bites a person, (this) thing drives the illness away'. The 'contraceptive' made of grass taken from special ant-heaps, is called *botáfi*, a word derived from *botá*, the name for a species of grass and *fi*, 'to drink'; when the grass is removed from the ant-heap one repeats three times: 'One does not know the father of ants; one does not know the mother of ants'; of which crude allusion to the users of this remedy we have already spoken. The 'greeting' of another contraceptive remedy similarly plays upon an analogy—'A person without speech cannot tell', which means, a woman without fertility cannot bear children. The miraculous medicine alleged to make a person invisible and invulnerable has a name and 'greeting' which are highly suggestive; it is called *akpára*, the Nupe word for 'rifle', and is addressed thus— 'The night brings darkness. The eye sees in daylight, the eye does not see at night. There is nothing inside the earth save God' (that is, save things God alone can see, as he alone can see a person who has applied this medicine).

Perhaps the term 'invocations' will seem inappropriate in the case of these nondescript addresses or 'greetings'. But let me leave this point for the moment and only mention that invocations proper also have their place in *cigbe* practice. The *cigbeci*, like the barber-doctor, may add some new medicine to those already known; at least, this is true of the head of the order of 'medicine-men'. And whenever he discovers or invents a new remedy, he must perform a sacrifice composed of beer, a fowl, and a small portion of the new *cigbe*, speaking thus—'God, the medicine that has been prepared, here it is. May the medicine be successful. I am sacrificing to Kpara, I am sacrificing to Tswasha Malu, I am sacrificing to Tswako Dzana.' The names mentioned are those of ancestors of the head of the *cigbeci* guild; and the sacrifice is performed over the vessel in which the new medicine will henceforth be kept. As we shall see, both the invocation of ancestors and the treatment of the medicine vessel almost as a sacred shrine are features typical also of the hereditary medicines, which even more conspicuously reveal their irrational or mystical intent.

To turn to the medicines known to individuals. We may mention first that certain simple treatments are familiar to nearly everyone, being applied in the manner of household remedies or as a kind of 'first aid'; only when this fails or seems inadequate does one turn to 'professional' medicines. And even then one often asks friends and neighbours first before consulting the accredited experts. One does not pay in money for this kind of assistance but only offers a small return gift of kolanuts or food. The household remedies are mainly laxatives, or cures for toothache, headache, and slight wounds or bruises, though they include also certain crude treatments to induce abortion or prevent pregnancy—by sucking frogs or drinking the blood from the afterbirth. Normally, one uses infusions of common plants, ash-water or natron (both known as laxatives), ointments made of palm-oil or sheanut-butter, or damp earth (applied to cuts and the like); the more complex herbal concoctions and the use of bark and roots, which make up the *cigbe* proper, are entirely absent.

Certain individuals, are known to possess this more 'professional' knowledge as well. Like the barbers, they apply therapeutic treatments in a profane and would-be rational manner, and like the *cigbeci*, practise the non-therapeutic variety with more or less conspicuous mystical intent. Their skill extends to remedies alleged to increase virility and facilitate pregnancy, though contraceptives are outside the scope of the individual practitioner. 'Fantastic' treatments, however, are not. We already mentioned one such cure meant to remove rheumatic pains through 'drawing them from the body'. Two further treatments are of special interest, one because it is empirically sound, the other because it is surgical as well as daring and involves a clear apprehension of the symptoms of a relatively obscure disease. The first example concerns the use of the severely toxic *datura stramonium*. Many Nupe are aware of the effect of the seeds or powdered leaves which produce stupor and insensitiveness, and the experts prescribe small doses, taken in water, as a cure for pains; with less justification, they also recommend the external application of the leaves, soaked in ash-water and mixed with sheanut butter, for aching limbs. The second example is an alleged cure for sleeping sickness, which must be applied in the early stages of the disease, recognized by the swelling of the neck glands. I only met one expert who knew of this treatment, a man from Mokwa, whose repute had spread far and wide. The surgical treatment involves a deep incision in the skin above the glands, charred leaves of a bean variety being rubbed into the wound; the leaves are said to have a caustic effect so that, when the treatment is repeated twice daily for a week, the glands themselves can be removed. As an after-treatment the patient is given an infusion of bark and roots to drink, and a coarse grass and fish to eat. The expert did not claim that his cure was always effective: it would still depend on 'God's will'; but he showed me a man, bearing the scars of the operation, who, he claimed, had completely recovered.

Among the non-therapeutic medicines we meet again with the substance which makes invisible, and with another which enables you to see witches and also protects you from them. The latter consists of various rare roots and four cowrie shells, sewn into a leather bag dyed black and red, which you must keep under your pillow while asleep. Before handing the charm to the customer it is buried for one night together with a live chameleon, which contact communicates to the charm the peculiar powers of the animal (which is said to 'see in the dark'). The invisibility potion is concocted from the head, blood, and claws of a completely black fowl, a creeper torn off a tree while one's eyes are covered by a black cloth, and a mudfish. The emphasis on black accords with this notion of a substance whose effect resembles that of darkness and which is in fact known as *badúfu*, a mixed Nupe–Hausa word meaning 'dark place'.[1] The symbolism of covering your eyes is obvious, as is that of the mudfish, which buries itself in the riverbed. The same substance, in powder form, may also be carried in a black leather bag on the body, though in this case a piece of human skin must be added.[2]

There are several other non-therapeutic *cigbe* of less gruesome nature. The following examples all come from the same source, old Ndakotsu of Bida, a descendant of the old Beni chiefs and a noted diviner and 'wise man'. His medicines were as secret as they were fantastic; yet though they were not for sale, they were freely given to friends and acquaintances or to the young men over whose age grades Ndakotsu presided. Neither the application nor the preparation of these medicines involves invocations, sacrifices and the like; but their professedly mystical character is usually clear from the peculiar nature of their efficacy, which is attributed to the power of *fifingi* of animals or plants and hence presupposes explicitly religious conceptions. All medicines also imply, more or less clearly, the principle 'like causes like'. One example, mentioned before, is the powder applied to hoes which causes them to 'double' their output; its effect rests on one particular ingredient, leaves from a palm-tree split in two by lightning, the 'doubling' of the tree being responsible for the doubled efficiency of the tool. Another farming 'medicine', meant to secure a rich yam harvest, is made up of the head and left leg of a bush rodent and some grass torn out by the roots, and must be buried annually in the farmland in a new, covered pot; the explanation is that the *fifingi* of the rodent, which is known to feed on yams, will 'steal' all the yams

---

[1] For a different meaning of this term see below, p. 159.
[2] I was offered this useful *cigbe*, but the deal broke down since I was unable to supply the human skin, to the great surprise of the expert, who thought that I could easily obtain it from the local hospital.

(that is, their *fifíngi*) from the surrounding farmlands and carry them to yours. A rich grain harvest can be obtained by taking the head of an ass or donkey, its saddle cloth, and the excreta of a person who dies of smallpox, tying the three 'ingredients' into a bundle hung from a palm-tree on the farm: the grain will then grow as high as a person, since the *fifíngi* of the donkey, used to carrying loads on its back, will endeavour to 'pull up' the grain 'like a load'. Farmers can finally prepare a potent drink made of a black monkey's left leg, some leaves driven into a heap by a whirlwind, and beer: they will then work 'as fast as the whirlwind' and as 'tirelessly as a monkey'. Ndakotsu's father is reported to have owned also one of those protective *cigbe* which punish evil-wishers; it is said to have been particularly vicious, inflicting body-ache on any person who so much as stared at you. Nothing further, however, is known about this medicine, which has since been lost.

The picture changes again when we turn to the medicines hereditary in families or 'houses' or belonging to communities. Let me quote these examples. In Jebba Island I recorded an hereditary *cigbe* called *fúnagba*, which cures headache, pains in the body, and barrenness, and can either be drunk or used externally. Its composition is complicated, including seven ingredients, six of which are roots of specific trees and the seventh the root of any tree growing across a footpath (such roots being particularly 'strong'); these ingredients must be mixed with beer, blood of fowl (that is, the common materials for sacrifices), and some Niger water fetched by a young girl. Apart from its therapeutic effect, this medicine also protects the house from thieves and evil-minded intruders. In another village on the Niger I found a medicine called *atafá*, which has only the latter effect; it could, in fact, never be renewed if it were actually dispensed since its composition is unknown. In several villages I met with a medicine called *wasa* or *gába*, compounded of ten ingredients, one of which is the boiled head of a poisonous snake, severed before it released the poison; this medicine operates as an antidote against snake-bite, as a cure for stomach-ache, and sometimes also as a potion applied in ordeals; while its presence in the house affords protection from thieves and evil-doers. A medicine called *égbo*, from Shari, is used to treat headache and stomach-ache, and is also taken by the devotees of the *ndakó gboyá* before they put on the masks that go with the cult. Then there is the Jebba medicine *zumácikã*, which belongs to the village and is believed to protect the community from smallpox; as we remember, its composition is unknown and it acts through merely being present.[1]

[1] See above, p. 91.

MEDICINE 149

Most of these medicines, then, are 'multifarious', combining a therapeutic with a mystical or 'magical' efficacy. The latter may even be paramount and take an extreme form, as in the medicines efficacious by their mere presence and of unknown composition. Equally, these medicines are treated as 'magical'. They may only be prepared in certain months and not in others, unlike all other medicines; and while the latter are kept in the usual household containers, gourds or ordinary pots, the hereditary medicines are preserved in special earthen vessels, placed apart and decorated in the manner of sacred objects, with a strip of white cloth, a ring of palm-fronds or a crown of white chicken feathers. They all have mystically obscure names and more or less elaborate *emisa*, and some also involve regular sacrifices, either when the *cigbe* is newly prepared or on the occasion of the usual kinship rites and invocations of ancestral *kuci*. Finally, all these medicines are extremely secret and never sold for money, if indeed they are disposed of at all; if so, they may be given away only to close relations or perhaps friends, as a free gift 'for the sake of God'. Nor is their recipe (even if it is known) ever taught to others.

The special position of the hereditary *cigbe* is reflected in the nomenclature, for these medicines alone merit the epithet 'great', while all other medicines are called 'little'. Let us note that the verbal distinction refers, not so much to the miraculous effects with which the *cigbe* is credited, as to the procedure it sets in motion; for even a 'great' medicine may only cure headache or stomach trouble, at least with part of its efficacy. But the 'great' medicine alone involves proper acts of worship; and as it is bound up with the identity of kin groups through being hereditary, so it serves as a focus of kinship life, affording its supernatural aid primarily or even exclusively to the group to which it belongs and mobilizing it in the fashion of kinship rituals. The 'greatness' of the *cigbe*, then, lies in its social implications rather than in its concrete efficacy. Let us note also that its very 'ownership' is far from concrete. For the *cigbe* whose composition is unknown is also never examined, being renewed only from the beer and blood of the sacrifice. What is truly 'owned', is not any tangible, physical substance but only the vessel in which it is supposed to exist; so that this becomes a shrine for religious ministrations indistinguisable from ritual proper.

3. THE FAITH IN MEDICINE

The distinction between 'great' and 'little' medicines is drawn only by the practitioners and 'owners' of *cigbe*. The bulk of the people know little about these implications, and so grade the medicines differently. For them, medicines are simply either easily procured or not, available to the 'public' or monopolized, by families or perhaps communities. And they conclude, equally simply, that the more secret and private a medicine, the more powerful it must be. Experts and public, we may say, speak different languages. And here certain other discrepancies also arise. There are a great many stories current about extremely powerful (and extremely secret) medicines 'owned' and rarely if ever disposed of by certain villages, families or occupational groups (blacksmiths, hunters). When you know the 'owners' you will usually discover either that they credit the medicine with far less impressive powers or that it is by no means as secret as the public believes, or even that the medicine in question does not exist. Again, the people generally are convinced that certain very 'private' and miraculous medicines can yet be acquired at exorbitant prices: in reality, the medicines so described may not be for sale or, once more, may not exist. The public is also impressed or swayed by certain clever tricks which the experts perform with the ingredients of medicine in order to astonish the layman and advertise their skill but which they never regard as a true part of their craft. Thus a certain medicine for headache and stomach pains can be shown to extinguish flames or, more wonderful still, to make hands and feet insensible to burns; a piece of ironwood used in a very secret anti-witchcraft medicine can be shown miraculously to sink in water. But the Nupe expert rarely resorts to this method of self-advertisement; rather, he strongly insists on the difference between *cigbe* and *enya mã*, mere 'conjuring tricks', such as the Hausa charm peddlers and 'magicians' are fond of performing. Nor does he ever offer 'fakes', of this or any other kind, for the 'real thing' or show any cynicism regarding the value of his products. He believes in them as much as do his clients; and if their trust shows in the eagerness and awe with which they approach the expert, his seriousness and scrupulous attention to detail leave no doubt as to his good faith.

The question arises, what concrete proof the believers can have of the efficacy of the more fantastic and 'magical' medicines. In the case of the therapeutic remedies there exists, as I suggested, at least the possibility of some apparent if spurious empirical support; also their efficacy is understood to be in some measure uncertain and subject to the will of God. But no amount of belief in those medicines which turn a man into a miraculously successful farmer or make him invulnerable and invisible can conjure up the desired proof. The confidence inspired by their possession may indeed make the owner a keener farmer or a more courageous soldier and hunter; but though fortune may favour the brave it falls lamentably short of the absolute assurance the Nupe place in these *cigbe*.

The answer to our question can only lie in the rigid secrecy which surrounds these magic medicines. No one using them will talk about it; indeed if he did, the efficacy of the magic would be gone. Thus, though I might use the wonderful farming *cigbe*, my neighbours may, for all I know, also use it, or even a stronger version; and though I could make myself invulnerable, my enemies might have *cigbe* to make their guns infallible. If in these instances the belief in *cigbe* is such that it protects itself from being disproved, this is even more so in the case of the *cigbe* protecting you from witchcraft. For this is clearly itself an imaginary threat whose defeat by an imaginary weapon is altogether outside empirical considerations. To some extent the efficacy of the medicines said to procure invisibility equally belongs to the realm of imaginary happenings. Two of the many informants with whom I discussed this point supplied the clue. The first, who himself owned this medicine and maintained that I too could use it with the desired effect, added this odd instruction: the medicine must be taken at night, before going to sleep. He meant by this that the medicine affected, not the physical body of a person awake, but the *fifingi*, the disembodied shadow soul, of persons asleep. The second informant was even more explicit. He explained that the person drinking the medicine was able, in *fifingi* shape, to wander about at night when all were asleep, to enter their houses unseen, to touch the bodies of the other sleepers, give them nightmares, and even to kill them if they struggled or hit out: to which extreme, however, no 'good' man would resort, save perhaps against enemies.

If we should consider invisibility achieved under such conditions to be hardly worth the trouble, let alone to prove the wonderful powers of the medicine, this is not so for the Nupe. For them, the medicine does two things one cannot 'normally' do; it enables you to control the movements of your *fifingi*, which otherwise wanders about at will, in the random fashion exemplified by dreams; and it causes the *fifingi* to be hidden from the people it visits, while ordinarily it would appear to them in their dreams. Furthermore, precisely such willed and hidden nightly visits are thought to be peculiar to witches, so that the *cigbe* makes you their equal. I must add, however, that the rest of my informants did not describe the efficacy of the invisibility *cigbe* in such mystic terms. They spoke of it as being concretely effective and hiding your body from the eyes of others when you meet them, say, in the street. But they would emphasize, as in the case of the other miraculous *cigbe* mentioned before, that this medicine must be used in utter secrecy lest it lose its power. And here, it seems to me, we have the required loophole; for 'utter secrecy' I take to mean that the medicine may only be used at night, when you cannot be seen, or among strangers, when at least you cannot be recognized, that is, in situations when no one can prove anything. My informants refused to commit themselves on this point. But exactly this kind of argument was brought up in connection with another, similar, medicine not previously mentioned, namely, a *cigbe* said to enable a man to feign death and to arise from the grave unharmed and invisible; thus magically equipped he can disappear from his village unbeknown to all, to reappear, now in visible shape, in foreign parts. This seems to be the only advantage offered by this *cigbe*. Now this advantage, my informants assured me, was past, thanks to railways and motor-cars of all things; for nowadays the person using the *cigbe* could reach the strange place no more quickly than would others, using the modern means of transport. But it is not merely the utility of the *cigbe* which has disappeared, but its virtue. Since other people, travelling non-magically, might well arrive together with and run into the person who did so magically, the secrecy of the proceedings has been lost, and with it the efficacy of a *cigbe*. If this argument seems less compelling to us than to the Nupe, it yet confirms the point made before, that this notion of miraculous medicines protects itself from proof or disproof.

Let us return to the *emisa* which accompany various *cigbe* procedures. Clearly, they must have some share in fostering or confirming the faith which the people put in their mystical medicines. I have so far treated these formulæ mainly as evidence for 'mystical intent'; but they would seem to define a particular species of this intent and one particularly reassuring. For the *emisa* comes closest to a magic spell, having the same rigidity and being similarly indispensable for the desired effects; if so, it would turn the whole *cigbe* practice into a strictly magical procedure, that is, a procedure resting on the mechanical manipulation of substances and words rather than on appeals to some transcendental intelligence.

Neither conclusion, however, is quite correct. The names and addresses of *cigbe*, the Nupe insist, carry no power in themselves; this lies in the 'ingredients' alone. If the *emisa* is indispensable it is so only in the sense in which the titles and formal greetings of men of rank are indispensable, being meant to acknowledge or indicate the power that lies in the rank but adding nothing to it. Furthermore, the *emisa* of medicines is meant to acknowledge also the ultimate source of their power, that is, the presence and will of God. If the wording of the *cigbe* greetings hardly reveals that exalted function, the Nupe would point out that other, ordinary 'greetings' are similarly nondescript and uninformative. We recall, further, that on certain occasions the practice of *cigbe* also includes sacrifices and invocations proper, addressed to God or *kuci*.

We may conclude, then, that even the mechanical manipulations of *cigbe* carry some of that awareness of a transcendental intelligence which turns an otherwise 'magical' act into a religious appeal; and though the faith in this manipulation of 'ingredients' is partly a belief in their mechanical efficacy, this is yet understood to reflect, however indirectly, divine intervention. The *emisa* itself is neither fully a spell nor yet fully a prayer; it is an expression, couched in a conventionalized code, for the varieties of power mobilized in the *cigbe* procedure. Those who know the appropriate expressions also know the entities to which they refer and hence can manipulate them: for in the Nupe way of thinking as in ours there is no true and workable knowledge of anything unless that thing can also be named. Thus, though the *emisa* has no share in the powers it identifies and names, the very fact that it does so makes it an integral part of the mystically powerful operation. Finally, since these 'code' expressions are respectful ones, they stand, not for a simple command, but for a command tinged with submission, for a mastery which is half supplication, in brief, for 'invocations'.

4. THE PERSONNEL

The organization of the Nupe barber-doctors has been described elsewhere, and I need here summarize only the main facts.[1] The barbers are grouped in three guilds, centred in Bida, one in each of the three sectors into which the town is divided. They travel a good deal; a number have also settled in the larger villages in the country, and quite a few in towns outside Nupe. Each guild has its own titled head, elected by the guild and confirmed by the *Etsu* Nupe, who is also the most experienced and most highly reputed member of the profession; which standing is measured, simply, by the number of treatments known to him. In all my discussions with barber-doctors it was always the guild head who proved the best informed and to whom all others turned when in doubt or at a loss. The profession is loosely hereditary, some usually following in their fathers' footsteps; but men of other families may join the profession through being apprenticed to an established barber-doctor for about five years, during which period they pay for the tuition by surrendering the larger part of their earnings.

[1] See *A Black Byzantium*, pp. 289–301.

This, then, is a purely profane craft organization. Side by side with it exists that other, more secret and 'mystical' order, of the *cigbeci* practitioners. 'Side by side' is not quite the correct phrase; for the latter are active predominantly in the rural areas, though a few *cigbeciži* reside in small hamlets quite close to Bida, as does the present Master of the order. Theirs is quite clearly the older organization, which, in the modern capital, has given way to the Mohammedan barber guilds. Nor does the *cigbeci* organization today enjoy the official sanction of the Nupe State or any affiliation with the ruling dynasty. Yet it did so formerly, even in the Fulani régime, where its Masters were appointed and invested with a special hereditary rank by the sovereign of the country. Indeed, the *cigbeciži* trace the growth of their order back to the *fons et origo* of all things politic and traditional in Nupe country, the first kingdom of Tsoede. The somewhat fantastic pedigree of the *cigbeciži* betrays the mystic nature of the craft; for the third Master was no other than that Kpara who, as we have heard, went up to the sky and brought back the wisdom of 'ingredients'.[1]

This pedigree comprises eight ancestors, the son of the last being the present Master (and my informant), one Sheshi Benu. The first ancestor, said to have lived in the days of Tsoede, came of the sub-tribe Cekpã, from across the Niger, which even today is regarded by all Nupe as deeply versed in all kinds of secret knowledge. It was not he, however, who was the first *cigbeci*, but his son Malu, who acquired that knowledge by unknown means and was granted the title *Tswasha* still by Tsoede. He and his successors always lived in the capital of the kingdom, wherever it happened to be, as the king's official experts. The father of the present Master of the order, Mina Gunu, is said to have lived first in Rabah, the then capital, and to have come to Bida when the centre of the kingdom moved there. His son is a 'Master' only to the members of the order, bearing no longer an official rank, and not very well known to the general public.

I have called the *cigbeci* organization an 'order' rather than a 'guild' to do justice both to its dispersal through the country and to its secrecy which yet allows for the admission of new members. The organization is also extremely loose, involving little actual co-operation beyond occasional ceremonial gatherings and a few 'refresher courses' for the specially keen. But it has a common centre and source, constituted by the Master and his 'house'. Thus all known medicines have been discovered by one or the other Master of the *cigbeciži* and were handed on to the other members of the order. My informant claimed that he himself had discovered

[1] See above, p. 18.

certain new *cigbe*, and that on such occasions he had called together all his disciples, so that they might be present at the ceremonial preparation of the new medicine and learn its properties. Before him, his ancestors had similarly taught their knowledge to pupils, who in turn handed it on both to their offspring and to others, until the order spread through the whole country and even beyond Nupe. Yet all 'great' *cigbeciži* received their training at the source, from the present Master or his predecessors, and he mentioned five of his disciples to me, two of whom I also knew and from whom I obtained confirmation of this account.

During the period of tuition the pupil lives with his teacher, paying in gifts for the instruction. The secret of the more complicated medicines, known to the Master alone, the pupil must buy for money; which course is also open to any other *cigbe* practitioner even if he never underwent tuition proper. The period varies with the ambition of the pupil; those who wish to become really great experts must study continuously for three to four years, while those with lesser ambition can become proficient by intermittent tuition, for a month or so at a time, during a period of five to six years.[1] No one is refused; anyone who wishes to learn can do so if he has the required intelligence, and the time and funds. No *cigbeci*, however, can live merely on his professional earnings; even the Master practises, at least today, farmwork besides.

The individual *cigbe* experts are once more part-time practitioners, even if, occasionally, they own hereditary medicines at the same time. Nor do they confuse the two kinds of expert knowledge, one possessed by them as individuals, the other vested in the lineage or 'house' to which they belong. The former is often said to have been acquired, more or less fortuitously, on travels, especially to foreign parts; sometimes it is inherited, though only in the fortuitous way in which sons may (or may not) follow their fathers' interests or professions. One owner of *cigbe* thought that his grandfather, from whom he had inherited the skill, had learned it from the *cigbeciži*; but all other informants denied any such connection. The medicines differ greatly in secrecy according to whether they are therapeutic or not. The former are readily disposed of, against payment or return gifts, while the more miraculous medicines are given only to persons one knows well, or with some formality and ostensible hesitation. Let me quote this

---

[1] My informant drew a terminological distinction between the 'greater' and 'lesser' practitioners; the former alone, he claimed, were legitimately called *cigbeci*, while the proper name for the latter was *boci*. No one else, however, made this distinction, which seems to reflect only the familiar predilection of the Nupe 'intellectual' for neat linguistic categories. *Boci* is in fact only the Nupe-ized version of the Hausa word *boka*, 'native doctor'.

description of the procedure by an expert of great repute; it is interesting also since it illustrates the Nupe bent for neatly schematic and enumerative arrangements. When the expert is approached by a would-be customer he will at first deny all knowledge of the *cigbe* in question and maintain this attitude on three successive occasions; the fourth time, if the client still insists and so shows his eagerness or anxiety, the expert will at last relent and promise to prepare the *cigbe*.[1] He will not, incidentally, communicate the recipe itself; for the individual expert does not teach his craft, save to his own offspring or, perhaps, to a great friend.

We turn to the hereditary medicines proper, hereditary not only incidentally like the individually owned *cigbe*, but as it were *ex hypothesi*, being bound up with the identity of lineages or 'houses' and descending from family head to family head. We already discussed most of the features which set this species of medicine apart from others or, as the Nupe would say, make it 'great' where all others are 'little'. It now remains to examine the role of the sacrifices involved in this possession of *cigbe*.

The sacrifices are of two kinds. A first variety is still concerned with the practice of *cigbe* only. The owner of the 'great' medicine *fúnagba*, for example, who knew numerous other *cigbe* besides, performed a sacrifice of fowl and beer at the *fúnagba* shrine whenever he brewed any of the other, 'little', medicines. Sometimes he added a small quantity of the 'great' medicine in order to make the others more potent, thus using the former as a 'master medicine', unspecific and almost pure force or power. He would accompany the sacrifice with a brief invocation in which the *emisa* is followed by a proper prayer addressed to God and *cigbe*, thus:

'*Fúnagba!* The carpenter who uses the *nunci* tree (i.e. the wrong kind of wood) will fail to build a canoe. *Fúnagba* that now drinketh, Lord God, cause (that it) give us health.'

We note the close similarity between this invocation and those usually addressed to *kuti* or ancestors. The second variety of *cigbe* sacrifice in fact serves the latter purpose; more precisely, it overrules and replaces the normal kinship rites and sacrifices to ancestors. For while ordinary people perform such sacrifices (at birth, marriage, death, and so forth) over a grave or perhaps at a twin shrine, the owner of a 'great' *cigbe* does so over the vessel containing the medicine. In other words, the more rare and more specific instrument of supernatural appeal overrules the more common kind. It seems logical that the owners of such *cigbe*, who are usually well known even though everything else about it will

---

[1] My own experience bears out the necessity for repeated approaches, though not of the rule 'fourth time lucky'.

be secret, should be considered more fortunate than the ordinary run of people. Yet why this should be so, why some families should have this special standing *in rebus sacris* and others not, is not a question in which the people show any interest. 'There is no fixed number of medicines,' they say, and hence no rule governing or accounting for their distribution.

We need not speak again of the community medicine *zumácikã*, which represents an isolated instance.¹ But we may note certain transitional forms, in which ownership by lineages shades over into ownership by the community. For certain of the hereditary medicines are vested in 'houses' which equally hold hereditary ranks and offices, so that the two possessions go together. When the family head succeeds to the rank, he also assumes charge of the *cigbe*; and the people in fact say of this kind of medicine that it is 'owned' by such-and-such a rank (not person). Now as the rank represents a privileged position ultimately derived from the community and entails duties on its behalf, so the possession of the medicine assumes the aspect of a privilege and duty delegated, by the community, to the particular lineage and its head: these are not so much 'owners' as trustees or guardians, much as the hereditary village priests are appointed guardians of a community *kuti*. Usually the analogy remains on this abstract level; but in one instance it becomes more tangible, when the properties of the hereditary *cigbe* include efficacy as an ordeal: here, then, the possession of *cigbe* ceases to be private, and its application turns fully into a right or duty executed for the well-being of the community.

5. CIGBE AND MORALITY

Excepting the isolated community medicine, no class of *cigbe* is unequivocally good, or for that matter unequivocally evil. But particular medicines may be morally reprehensible, so that all the various groups of *cigbe* experts must in varying degree face the responsibility of practising a craft not above blame or suspicion.

The contraceptive remedies of the barber-doctors and *cigbecizi* represent the mildest case; for though their immorality is a matter of common agreement, almost everybody ignores it in practice, and the *cigbe* practitioners could easily claim the neutrality of experts catering for a public demand. This is indeed the attitude of the barber-doctors. The *cigbecizi*, whose craft is bound up with mystic rules and sacred knowledge, are also more fully aware of the moral conflict; their attempts to justify the dubious practices

¹ There may of course be others, in parts of Nupe which I did not visit. But it is certain that their number is very small.

thus reveals the underlying conviction that their skill should be morally blameless.

Yet it is precisely the adepts of the more mystical or sacred craft who must face this moral conflict in much graver form. For *cigbeciži*, individual practitioners, and the 'owners' of hereditary medicines alike also have knowledge of medicines not only morally dubious but straightforward evil and in fact called *cigbe benágŭ*, 'evil medicines'. Now this means, for the Nupe, several things. It means that the use of the medicine 'harms innocent people', as does the farming *cigbe* which increases your crops at the expense of your neighbours, or that the medicine 'kills people', as do those vindictively 'protective' medicines which punish thieves, evil-wishers, or personal enemies. Again, a medicine is evil if it is apt to be abused by evil-minded persons, which is true of the invisibility *cigbe* and perhaps also of the 'protective' variety, though my informants could not say precisely what kind of abuse there might be. Finally, the efficacy of the medicine might be mistaken for witchcraft, and is for this reason adjudged 'evil'.

The last reason seems to be the crucial one. To begin with, it applies in every case and also reinforces all the other reasons. Thus the person made unexpectedly prosperous with the help of the farming *cigbe* might easily be taken for a witch by his neighbours; much the same might happen in the case of the vicious 'protective' *cigbe*; while the medicine which makes you invisible or enables you to feign death endows you with precisely the gifts with which witches are credited. Furthermore, where some of the other reasons appear inconclusive, the resemblance to witchcraft is decisive. It is clearly inconsistent to condemn the 'protective medicine', meant to attack only evil-doers or evil-wishers, while accepting without qualms the efficacy of deadly ordeals, which do precisely the same. Admittedly, there is a difference; while in ordeals and the like it is the law of the country that takes its course, the *cigbe* places the power of life and death within the reach of individuals, and this power works, though not at random, yet blindly, not measuring punishment against offence. In a society like Nupe, where the self-help of blood revenge is unknown, this is logically adjudged immoral and evil. Yet in argument the Nupe do not reason this way; rather do they fall back on the stand-by explanation, that this 'punishment' and 'killing' may be confused with witchcraft.

Undoubtedly, the medicines which bring harm or death upon people (innocent or otherwise) are as such condemned. 'There is nothing nice about these medicines,' said the Master of the *cigbeciži*, with some understatement. Yet they are evil also because they meddle in something that has the appearance of evil. And when the Nupe are reluctant to talk about these medicines, the reason is, again, their resemblance to witchcraft, with which subject no one wishes to seem conversant. I know of no case where accusations of witchcraft were later withdrawn and admitted to have been caused by some such mistake; and there can of course be no other proof to show that these mistakes are in fact apt to happen. But linguistic usage proves how tenuous is this distinction between witchcraft and things that look like witchcraft. I mentioned before the generic name for the medicines alleged to make invisible—*badúfu*, 'dark place'; now the same word is also used for the medicines which, in popular opinion, are employed by witches, and hence by the adepts in an art itself called 'black' or 'dark'. Again, the 'male' farming *cigbe* called *eshe* shares its name with the male variety of witchcraft. The experts among my informants insisted that the linguistic connection was entirely fortuitous; and it is true that the two names are identical only in Beni country while in the riverain area, for example, one denotes male witchcraft differently. But the ordinary man in Beni country is convinced that the efficacy of this *cigbe* and witchcraft are one and the same thing. Whether these medicines have merely been unhappily named, so that their names came to suggest the identity with witchcraft, I cannot decide: as they are now used they clearly stand for such a judgment (or confusion) of identity.

Let me anticipate one further point concerning witchcraft beliefs. Since so many *cigbe* look like witchcraft it is pertinent to ask if some do not also serve (or are believed to serve) witchcraft. In Nupe popular opinion witches do use particular *cigbe* to make themselves invisible and, generally, to equip themselves for their nefarious activities. And if persons do not become witches merely through having the required medicine, the latter yet helps, or may even be indispensable since the witch can by no other means defeat the other, protective, medicines which their victims might possess.[1] Witchcraft and anti-witchcraft, in that view, is a battle of *cigbe*. Among the experts, opinions varied. All were agreed on the existence and efficacy of the protective *cigbe*; but while some thought that 'real witchcraft needs no *cigbe*', others considered it at least likely that witches possessed a particular medicine which lent them their sinister powers. None of the experts admitted to possessing or preparing this utterly evil kind of *cigbe*, but a few suggested that certain of their colleagues—always living in other parts of the country—did so and were lying when they disclaimed such knowledge. And here the question must rest.

The fact remains that the medicine experts, though they may deny the knowledge of this most evil *cigbe*, yet admit knowledge

[1] This view is documented in the statement on witchcraft quoted on p. 165.

of medicines almost as unequivocally evil. The same men, let us note, will also administer helpful, beneficial, 'good' medicine. On the whole, the latter are more numerous, and are considered more important when it comes to discussions or arguments. As for the others, the experts would claim that they take due precautions, giving the medicine away only to 'good people' and 'for the sake of God', not for ordinary gain. But these personal qualms do not explain away the confusion of moral standards and do not answer the question why practices contemptible by common agreement should yet be accepted and actively pursued. The answer seems to lie in the amoral character of the Nupe universe. There it is, composed of good things and bad, the handiwork of a deity which unconcernedly sets good beside evil. Man, it would seem, has no call to improve upon creation. The qualms of the *cigbeciži* are a concession to social conscience not to religious scruples; in the last resort they are concerned only with appearances—that their craft should not look like witchcraft. As regards the evil potentialities of 'medicine', they are accepted with the same optimistic cynicism with which the Nupe view the very world in which they live.

6. MODERN INFLUENCES

Islam has on the whole brought little change. It bans the hereditary medicines, since they approximate to the pagan worship of *kuci* and *kuti*, and may well have caused some of them to disappear. But the craft of the barber-doctors enjoys the respectability of a truly Mohammedan profession; while the medicines of individuals and the craft of the *cigbeciži* flourish among Mohammedans no less than among the pagans. Indeed many of these experts would regard themselves as good Moslems. Even the Master of the *cigbeciži* dresses like a Moslem, goes to the mosque, observes the fast and other rules of Islam, and boasts of his descent from men who served the Mohammedan Emirs of Nupe.

Nor do specifically Moslem practices compete seriously with the traditional craft. A great many mallams administer cures and sell charms or amulets, both prepared in strict accordance with the Moslem creed as they understand it. The cures all take the same form: the attributes of Allah or certain verses of the Qoran are written in ink on a wooden slate which is then washed clean, the inky water being drunk by the patient. The amulets, called *laya* (a Hausa word), consist of pieces of paper similarly covered with sacred writing, which are sewn into small leather cases and worn on the body. But Nupe religious conscience is accommodating: pagans wear the Mohammedan charms as often as Mohammedans consult a pagan (or semi-pagan) *cigbeci*. That the powers of *cigbe* are greater as well as more varied few will doubt; nor do the mallams themselves deny that many of the cures and other effects of *cigbe* are beyond their ken. It was, for example, a Moslem scholar of high repute who put me in touch with the *cigbecizi*, being himself a firm believer in the excellence of their art.

Modern medicine, as practised in hospitals and dispensaries, is a more serious rival. Nupe men and women who for the first time face this novel version of *cigbe* may be suspicious or openly afraid; often they will discontinue the visits to the doctor or dispenser, or leave unused the drugs they are given. A steadily increasing number, however, now have fair confidence in doctors and drugs and would be prepared to admit that our cures are on the whole better than theirs. This is true especially of minor surgical treatments and of injections of all kinds, that is, of treatments utterly unlike the indigenous practices and often 'miraculous' in their effect. This may seem a lukewarm statement; but I do not think that it can be put more positively or optimistically, at least as regards the average Nupe. Administration officials, teachers, and others who have been in close contact with Europeans are exceptions (though only to some extent).[1] Certainly, the Nupe are turning to European medicine much more slowly and waveringly than other African groups I know.

Now these other groups are also more primitive than the Nupe or without a similar, highly organized and would-be rational therapeutic skill. The diverse reaction is thus no accident. Fear and suspicion there would be in either case. But in the more primitive groups organized medicine, as a purely profane skill or knowledge, is entirely novel and unprecedented; it may have to fight religious prejudice, but not its own kind: while in Nupe precisely this is true. Other Africans might feel that European medicine clashes with their religious notions, or identify it with evil magic or witchcraft. The more sophisticated Nupe merely mistrusts the knife which, as everyone knows, 'cannot heal', or cynically suspects the doctors of poisoning patients who fail to recover. At best, he regards the European remedy as one of several possibilities, which he is wont to try out one after the other. And here the odds are not all in favour of the former.

[1] To wit, the following extract from an English composition on *The Hospital*, written in 1936 by a Nupe secondary school boy and corrected by his teacher. 'The disadvantage (of hospitals) is that when a man is taken there to be cured and if the nurses see that they cannot cure him, or perhaps he is given any kind of drugs and he still is exactly opposite as he was brought in, they give him a kind of medicine which makes he will die away.' The teacher found that only the last sentence needed correction, thus— 'they give him a poison and he will die'.

Many cases are already hopeless when they reach the doctors and hospitals, with the result that their remedies will appear to be no better than those of barbers or *cigbeciži*; above all, the European doctor does not profess to cure impotence or sterility, or to procure sterility; so that the most widely sought treatments are also an admitted gap in this new knowledge of 'medicine'.

VI

WITCHCRAFT AND ANTI-WITCHCRAFT[1]

I. THE KNOWLEDGE OF WITCHCRAFT

WHEN I first came to Nupe, early in 1934, the topic of witchcraft was one to be avoided. Three years before, the acquittal by the Chief *Alkali* of three alleged witches, a mother and her two daughters, had led to mob violence and to the stoning of the accused in the streets of Bida. Political passion, never quite dormant in the Nupe capital, at once flared up, the town was thrown into violent disorders, and troops had to be called out to quell the riots. Eventually an uneasy peace was restored, severe punishments having been imposed upon the main culprits; but for some years afterwards the relations between Government and the people remained strained and clouded by mutual distrust. The political repercussions of the witchcraft trial do not concern us here.[2] What is important is the strong and deeply rooted belief in witchcraft which the events revealed. And what was important to me at the time was the aftermath of suspicion and fear which the events had left.

When I started work in Nupe no one wanted to talk about these unhappy matters or indeed about witchcraft in general. For the people were not sure that the law had run its course; many feared that it would strike again should new facts come to light. Nor did the people quite know what to make of that law. They well knew that the White Man did not believe in witchcraft, as they also remembered that, not so long ago, the Government had banned the secret society which had the aim of combating witchcraft; but they did not know what were the Government's intentions concerning the victims of witchcraft. Were they to be left unprotected while the witches went free? Or would the White Man's odd manner of justice perhaps recoil on the complainants? The following story will, I think, illustrate this general bewilderment. In the

---

[1] A preliminary account of Nupe witchcraft, written after my first expedition, was published in *Africa*, vol. VIII, 1935. The present account, apart from being more complete, also corrects certain errors contained in the earlier one. [2] See op. cit., p. 423, and *A Black Byzantium*, pp. 126–7.

small riverain village of Kpatsuwa the nephew of the chief had suddenly disappeared and the people suspected a certain woman of having bewitched the young man. When the chief decided to report the matter to the District Officer, he was given this advice by his more knowledgeable friends in Jebba: 'Just tell him that your nephew has disappeared and no more; the White Man does not like to hear about witchcraft.'

In due course I could overcome the suspicion of the people and their reluctance to discuss witchcraft with a 'white man'. But there remained another, more deeply ingrained, reluctance, which is bound up with the very conception of Nupe witchcraft. Witchcraft is an evil thing, and thus an unpleasant matter to discuss. And witchcraft is also an intangible, mysterious thing, shrouded in secrecy for all but the initiates; and since only witches can really know about witchcraft, no one will wish to betray too much knowledge. It was no accident, then, that those informants who, eventually, gave me the fullest account were by others regarded as witches or at least as the helpers of witches. They themselves denied this; nor was their knowledge as positive and comprehensive as others assumed it to be. Often they admitted that certain aspects of witchcraft were beyond their definite knowledge, and food for speculation only. Let me make it clear that this did not mean that they too were insufficiently informed; it meant that this information did not exist, and could not exist by its very nature. As we shall see, it is this residue of intangible and unknowable things which keeps the belief in witchcraft alive.

There are, then, degrees in the knowledge of witchcraft. To begin with, there is the knowledge of the 'man in the street' as against that possessed by men whose profession bears on matters religious and mystic—the priests of certain cults; diviners who might be consulted when witchcraft is suspected; *cigbecizi* who traffic in medicines which 'look like witchcraft'; and Mohammedan scholars who take a general (and far from contemptuous) interest in the subject. But even the 'experts' are agreed only on the essentials of witchcraft belief, on the doctrinal points as it were; on other issues opinions differ widely and are only stated as such, as personal views, put forth tentatively or speculatively.

As an introduction to the 'doctrine' I propose to quote an account of witchcraft, translated literally, which was dictated to me by a Bida mallam and schoolteacher. The author's somewhat aloof standpoint is reflected in his use of such phrases as 'the people say' or 'the Nupe believe'; but what he says is on the whole what everybody believes, though we shall have to add one or two further facts which are equally matters of general knowledge.

'The women are those who have witchcraft. The *Lelu* is the one who is the elder (i.e. head) of the witches. If a woman should wish to practise witchcraft, she would go and visit the *Lelu*, saying she desired witchcraft-doing. The witches are wont to forgather at night under a tree; they would hold council as to the place they would be going to that day. The people say that the witches eat the body (*nakã*) of human beings. But it is one by one that they kill a person, the person whose turn it would be that day. The witches would go and look for someone to kill, they would then bring along the body, they divide and eat it. If the witches have no (other) person to kill, they will kill one of their own people, divide the body and eat it. One witch would do thus—kill her son or brother or grandchild, she would bring the body along, they would divide it and eat. But if the witches want money, they would take the man (the victim) to another country and go and sell him (to the witches there).—The Nupe believe that witches have medicine which makes them fly. They would be flying for example from this town to the place where the Hausa live, inside the night, they would return at daybreak. If they intend to kill a person they keep on looking for a person who is not healthy. Then, people say, they have a medicine which eats the life (*rayi*) little by little. They keep him so that he may be eaten, but if they find a person who is not sick, they would seize the shadow (*fifingi*) of the person who is healthy. Then he would begin to be ill, then they keep on eating his life (*rayi*), little by little, until he is dead. But if they find a person who has a medicine against witches, it would help him, he would recover, he would not happen to die.'

Let me add these comments. The word for witchcraft is *ega*, and for witch *gaci* (pl. *gaciži*), the suffix *-ci* indicating the actor or owner;[1] used by itself, *gaci* always denotes females. As the first sentences show, one can 'have' witchcraft, or 'do' and 'practise' it, much as one 'has' or 'practises' a faculty or skill. It is not hereditary; many examples are quoted of witches whose children 'have' no witchcraft or of girls who became witches in a family not otherwise contaminated by witchcraft. But a mother who is a witch may make her child one also, by feeding it on witchcraft *cigbe* or in some other fashion initiating it into the secrets of witchcraft. The method of acquiring witchcraft described in the text, by an approach to the head of the witches, is not the only one; a woman desirous of becoming a witch may also approach another woman who is known to be one and through her gain entry into the circle of witches; or she may buy one of those

---

[1] Cp. *lati*, farm, and *latici*, farmer; or *cigbe*, medicine, and *cigbeci*, medicine-man.

mysterious witchcraft medicines we spoke of before. As regards the role of *cigbe* in witchcraft, the text faithfully reflects popular opinion; and if it does not take account of the doubts of the 'experts', it yet makes clear a fundamental point in Nupe doctrine, namely, that witches must *want* to be witches (the infant who is inducted into witchcraft by her mother being an exception). Their evil actions are thus willed, and it makes no sense to speak of a witch who does not know that she is one or acts as such against her will.

The description of how the witches seize the victim's shadow and 'eat' his body or life is ambiguous and less precise than popular opinion on this point. When the witch attacks a person at night in his sleep, it is always his *rayi* or *anima* she feeds on, thus causing the body (*nakā*) to fall ill and waste away. But when the witch takes her victim to the gathering place, where all other witches will feast on him, it is only his shadow soul or *fifíngi* that is brought along and devoured, not the person in the flesh, who remains asleep in his house. Only in rare cases would the witches spirit away the body itself (as in the Kpatsuwa case mentioned before). Normally their handiwork is visible only in the sudden onset of an illness which no ordinary *cigbe* can heal. Often, there is further evidence; the person attacked by witches will have nightmares, see the witch in his dream and cry out her name.

The realism in the mallam's description is again misleading. That witches meet at night in the open, that they hold council, go out on their errands and later share in a communal meal, all this is part of Nupe belief. But no one believes that the witches do these things in the flesh, that is, with their whole and real body. It is only their *fifíngi* which go on these nightly excursions, their bodies, like those of the victims, remaining asleep in their homes. Thus, ultimately, it is a shadow which feeds on shadows, a shadow (of the dreamer) which sees a shadow (the witch), and it is invisible beings who meet at night, when no one is abroad, to commit invisible crimes. In this piling-on of intangible facts lies the unassailability of the Nupe belief in witchcraft: like an imaginary language it cannot be proved to be gibberish.

Though everything about witchcraft happens in an imaginary realm, this comes to earth as it were at two points. First, the accusations of witchcraft are made against real persons, not against shadows or invisible beings, and refer to victims equally real; and secondly, the alleged head of the witches, the *Lelu* mentioned in the text, is again a concrete person. As regards the first point, we shall later discuss the grounds upon which the accusations are founded. But we may at once ask—Does any woman really believe that she has joined the 'society of witches'? And, since witchcraft is something you consciously will and have, does any woman in fact entertain such intentions and put them into practice (whatever this may mean)? I cannot answer these questions directly. None of the alleged witches I met confessed to being one, which is hardly surprising; such confessions as might have been obtained in the past under the threats of punishment prove of course nothing. But I see no reason to doubt at least the possibility of individuals believing themselves to be or intending to become witches. The 'medicines' which make you 'like a witch' exist and can be obtained; the wish to avenge oneself on some other person by magic means undoubtedly also occurs, and is again catered for more or less openly by the various protective *cigbe*. Indeed, the Nupe would argue that a woman revengeful in everyday life is likely to entertain also the more sinister desires which make the witch. For my part, I would argue that in the case of neurotic or near-pathological individuals ordinary vindictiveness may turn into the desire to destroy and kill at random, which is precisely the desire witchcraft fantasies would satisfy. Whether such persons employ a 'medicine' or trust the power of their wish alone, does not really matter; in either case its fulfilment is imaginary: so that they cannot *know* if their intentions have been realized. But by the same token they cannot know that this is not the case; for as the imaginary nature of Nupe witchcraft precludes any disproof of its existence, so it precludes the possibility of proving (to oneself or others) that one is not a witch.

To turn to our second point, the acceptance of a real, live head of the witches. Let me admit that this notion puzzled me not a little. Yet there is no ambiguity about it. The head of the witches, the people maintain, is identical with the titled head of the women, who in every Nupe town or village is elected by the women traders and confirmed by the village chief or, in Bida, the *Etsu*. Her normal office is concerned with market affairs and the control of the commercial activities of women. The actual title *Lelu* is said to have been abandoned in Fulani times, having been replaced by two other titles now in use, in Bida by the title *Sonya* (the Nupe-ized version of the Hausa title *Sarauniya*, 'queen' or 'chieftainess'), and in the villages by the title *Sagi* (of unknown derivation). It is difficult to argue about matters of this kind, but the explanation does not sound convincing; I feel tempted to assume, rather, that *Sagi* has always been the woman's official rank, quoted in connection with her secular duties, while *Lelu* was the name for her mystic office, used only in that context. At least, this is the position today. In ordinary conversation the people always refer to the woman in question as *Sagi*, and you ask for her when you wish to meet the head-woman of a village; but when the talk is about witchcraft the same woman is referred to as *Lelu*. Whenever, in various villages, I asked to meet the *Lelu*, the question caused neither surprise nor confusion; I was usually quite readily taken to a woman who was introduced to me as the *Sagi* so-and-so.

Now, the *Lelu-Sagi* is said to be elected by the rest of the women because she is known to be a witch, and to be confirmed by the chief on the same grounds. But she is held to be a 'good' witch, who would employ her secret knowledge for the good of the community. Whether she had 'reformed' before being entrusted with the responsibilities of her office, or whether these caused her moral reform, is not a question the Nupe ask themselves or care to answer. The *Lelu* is certainly not a witch who has previously wrought harm (so far as ordinary people can tell); but equally certainly she must 'have' witchcraft to fill her office. For this consists, on the mystic plane, in controlling her colleagues, restraining their nefarious activities, warning the chief of the presence of alien witches, and generally acting as his trusted agent in these matters. Thus, though the *Lelu* is believed to admit new members to the 'society of witches', she is also believed to refuse admission to those whom she considers too dangerous or headstrong. But the *Lelu* is not expected to eliminate witchcraft altogether: she only keeps it within reasonable bounds. To quote a typical information: 'If there is much witchcraft in a village, many people dying of illness, the chief would summon the *Lelu* and order her to restrain the witches, so that the troubles may diminish.' When in a conversation I suggested that the *Lelu* was something like a 'policeman of the witches', my informants agreed that this was an admirable way of putting it.

The principle behind the conception of the *Lelu* thus seems to be that you must set a thief to catch a thief. The question still remains how one knows that one has really got hold of a 'thief' (or a suitable one). I got to know five *Sagis*, one of whom had recently 'discovered' and accused a witch. None admitted that she 'had' witchcraft; but two claimed that they could tell a witch because they had the required *cigbe*. They would not produce it; but since I myself owned this wonderful medicine I was not in a position to argue. As for the other people in these villages, they either knew nothing about the *Sagi's* possession of the *cigbe* or considered it to be further proof that she was indeed a witch; while the women who disclaimed all knowledge of witchcraft were simply thought to be lying. I can only conclude that the *Sagi* is elected and appointed because she is in a strictly concrete sense qualified for the position of a female 'elder', being of a suitable age, the most respected among the women traders, and the ablest in this or other female professions; all these things I found in fact to be true of the *Sagis* I met. And I would conclude further, that the position of leadership among the women who practise a trade or profession is apt to be identified with power of witchcraft, as the whole market organization of the women is in a sense identified with the fantasy organization of witches. So that the economic independence of women, which is so largely a moral independence as well, seems to furnish the logical basis for the ascription of witchcraft. Let me break off at this point, which we shall reach again by a different route.

2. MALE AND FEMALE WITCHES

The Nupe text from which we started requires a final correction. Its summary assumption that only women are witches is somewhat inexact. Women alone are *evil* witches, who would desire to do all the things that witches are supposed to do; but there exist also male witches, who are in some measure their partners in crime. They are odd partners: they do not work evil themselves; they do not go out on the nightly search for human victims; on the contrary, the male witches are said to be 'good' people, who would curb the evil desires of the women. Yet precisely the most sinister effect of witchcraft, the killing of the victim (as against merely weakening his health), is thought to depend on the co-operation of both sexes.

We note the exact parallel to the two fatal 'diseases of God', leprosy and sleeping sickness. There, too, the two sexes appear as the two components of the supernatural threat, which is less grave if one alone is involved, and deadly only when the two are combined; and there, too, the female agent plays the decisive part. In the sphere of witchcraft, that part stands for the active evil will; while the role of the male agent is merely permissive or perhaps negative, that is, consists in *not* willing that the evil intentions be frustrated.

Thus far all Nupe are agreed. But on all other details concerning the alleged partnership of men and women opinions are once more divided. Only in Beni country and around Kutigi are the male witches called by a special name, *eshe*; elsewhere one uses *gaci*, and specifies the sex if necessary. If this is not done, the word is taken to refer to women. Most people hold that the male witches are much fewer in number than the female ones; thus it is thought that all the witches in a village, or seven, or three, share one male helper. They would visit him at night to solicit his help; but while some think that it is only the *fifingi* of man and woman who meet in this fashion, others are certain that it is the real persons who do so. In the former view the man's share lies merely in giving his consent; in the latter, he supplies the woman with witchcraft *cigbe* and perhaps divines for her a 'lucky' day and the most helpful procedure. In the latter view, too, the male partner in witchcraft is not really a witch but a *cigbeci* or diviner, though one who made a compact with witches. It is interesting to note that this was the opinion of informants who were themselves *cigbecizi* or diviners and claimed to have 'heard' of others (all now dead) who had done this sort of thing. Other informants, who believed in the existence of male witches proper, supplied all manner of details. The male witch, like the female one, must acquire the appropriate *cigbe*, which is prepared by the hunters from grass they pulled out of the mouth of a grazing buffalo. The neophyte must drink an infusion of this grass and wash himself with it for five days, during which period he must refrain from sexual intercourse: afterwards he possesses all the powers of witchcraft so far as they are attainable to men. But he must never eat porridge out of a cracked gourd, lest his powers desert him. Also, the male witch keeps his *cigbe* in an iron bell hidden in the roof of his house, while women carry theirs in a belt or in their hair.

There are no attempts to explain why the true or the more dangerous witches should always be women; and though no one assumes that every evil woman becomes a witch, the question, why some women are only 'bad' in the ordinary sense of the word, and others so evil that they turn to witchcraft, is never raised. In either case 'God made it so', that is, he implanted in certain women that stronger will of evil. Nor can the ordinary person at once tell when evilness is of the less and when of the more harmful kind. The tree is known by its fruits: when a mysterious sickness or sudden death appears in the community, one is clearly in the presence of the greater evil. There are certain procedures, to be discussed presently, whereby the crime can be traced back to the culprit. But more basic than these procedures is the conviction that the person guilty of witchcraft must be a 'bad' person. It is thus that suspicion starts, which the various methods of proof may then confirm (or not). And the suspicion fastens upon the most visible clues of 'badness', the character and everyday behaviour of a person. All informants agree, stating their views in much the same phrases, that a witch is always a woman 'who does not laugh', who never 'plays', who dislikes and resents jokes, who gets angry over trifles, who is always morose and forbidding and never cheerful, who talks little and has no friendly words for anyone. 'Our witchcraft is in the mouth', the Nupe say, that is, is shown by the absence of smiles and pleasant speech; while among the Hausa, for example, 'witchcraft can be seen in the eyes of a woman'. Certain of these clues will be borne out by the biographical sketches which I shall later quote. But let me emphasize that they represent merely a 'theory', firmly held though it may be. When I visited a noted witch with one of my informants (who had strongly stressed the morose and stern aspect of witches) I found her to be a pleasant-spoken young woman, whom I could easily make laugh by some small joke. When, later, I pointed out this apparent anomaly, my informant retorted that the woman had merely put on an act to throw off my suspicions; towards her own people she would still be morose and unfriendly.

But even if these clues are mere theory, they help us to understand the ascription of witchcraft to particular persons. If I tried to sum up briefly the Nupe character as it appears to the observer, I should say that the average person is always friendly, pleasant-spoken and polite, very fond of jokes, chatty, and given to ready laughter. To some extent such behaviour is consciously cultivated. To be unfriendly or unpleasant in intercourse is definitely 'bad form'; polite etiquette has been developed to a fine art; and in the routine of social life joking and playing have their appointed place. Whether the rules of etiquette do not sometimes serve to repress fiercer and less placid leanings, we may for the moment disregard: the point is that politeness and pleasantness constitute the accepted ideals of behaviour, the sort of morale the Nupe believe in. And this morale is valid more fully for the women than for the men, since the women stand outside the two provinces of social life where placidity and friendliness are, on occasion, out of place, namely, esoteric ritual and political struggle.

It is, then, the absence of the accepted morale which makes the Nupe suspect witchcraft. The woman who behaves as the Nupe think witches do is one whose character belies the common precepts and ideals of conduct; she is ill-conditioned, eccentric, 'atypical'—what Margaret Mead would call a 'deviant personality'. In other words, the suspicion of witchcraft fastens upon 'abnormality'; not the physical abnormality, say, of cripples, hunchbacks, or strikingly ugly people, which is merely a matter of ill-luck; nor the mental abnormality of lunatics, which is the handiwork of spirits: but the abnormality of social and moral deviants.

Yet ill-conditioned and eccentric individuals, morose and quarrelsome characters, are as frequent among the men and as openly disapproved. The question therefore remains, why this argument should apply to women only. And unless we are prepared to consider this concentration upon female witchcraft to be sheer accident, we must assume that it is in some fashion symptomatic of the life of the society which created the belief. I shall in fact make such an assumption, more precisely, I shall assume that the fear of female witches is causally related to certain threats and tensions pervading the social life of the people, being a 'symptom' of these disturbances. Like any psychopathological symptom, too, the witchcraft beliefs contain an indication of the causes from which they spring. As we shall see, the symptoms are easy to read; for the Nupe witchcraft beliefs express the social threats and tensions from which they spring with little disguise. These become visible, in particular, in three sets of facts: first, in the explicit reference, mentioned before, to the market organization of the women; secondly, in the concrete accusations levied against alleged witches; and thirdly, in the existing legends about witchcraft. The first kind of evidence belongs to the formulated statements on witchcraft, and hence to the 'doctrine' proper; the other two, however, to some extent conflict with the doctrine, emphasizing traits of witchcraft which are disregarded or passed over in direct statements and discussions. This fact seems itself important; for it suggests that the traits in question betray fears or desires too vital and too disturbing to be openly admitted. Which assumption, too, will be borne out in the further discussion.

3. SEX ANTAGONISM

Let me first quote the witchcraft legends, though this means anticipating a little; for they are concerned less with witchcraft as such than with the origin of the anti-witchcraft cult *ndakó gboyá*, which will occupy us later. In fact, the legends do not even mention the words 'witch' or 'witchcraft'; but the implication is clear since they describe how the evil doings of certain women could only be suppressed by a 'secret' which everybody knows is employed against witches only. There are two such legends, one esoteric, being known only to the adepts of the *ndakó gboyá* cult, the other widely known and quoted.

The first legend tells about a 'certain king of Nupe' whose mother was an interfering woman, constantly meddling in his affairs. Whatever the king did his mother would frustrate, so that 'she caused the *Etsu* to be powerless'. At last he consulted a diviner and asked for his help. The diviner instructed the king to procure ten lengths of cloth. The diviner then sewed the pieces together, in the form of a tall, hollow tube, and used a 'secret' on it. The cloth rose up, flew through the air, and dropped upon the king's mother, covering her. It carried her up into the sky, and she was never seen again. From this day on the 'secret' remained a *kuti* of the kings. Whenever a woman is guilty of witchcraft, the king will employ the *kuti*, which is the *ndakó gboyá*.

The second legend, apart from being more widely known, is also more precise in its 'historical' allusions, naming the Nupe king in whose reign the critical events are said to have occurred; he is the same *Etsu* Shago whose reign saw the discovery of *cigbe*.[1] At the time, the people lived a lawless life, behaving insolently and 'refusing to listen to the Great Men'. Men would steal each other's wives and commit adultery without shame. The older women, especially, caused much trouble; they quarrelled among themselves and 'gave no peace'. The more law-abiding among the men grew angry and spoke harshly to the women; but these 'replied with insolence'. To continue *verbatim*: Now there was a young man, who had great strength. He set out and went into the bush. He then covered his head with cloth, like this (here the informant veiled his head with his gown, holding its end above his head, imitating the cloth mask of the *ndakó gboyá*). He reached the place where the women were causing a disturbance and yelled thus— '*Yi-i-i-i*' (the cry of the *ndakó gboyá*). When the women heard him they fled in fear. But one old woman did not run away. The old men also came, they waited for the woman to give way until they were tired: but she did not run away. The younger ones had all fled and left her alone. Thereupon the old men said to her—'*ezo, ezo*' (the ritual salute of the *ndakó gboyá*).[2] Thus they caught the woman. At last they killed her with an iron rod (*sāyi*). The men said: 'Even though she saw the *kuti* she did not run away; thus she was killed.'

We note two things: in the legend the evilness of the women implies striking at men or at least at their authority; also, the truly evil woman is pictured as old and as older than her victim or the man helpless against her (the king in the first legend and the young man in the second). On both points the legends side with the practice rather than with the theory of witchcraft, that is, with the concrete accusations, not with the formulated belief. According to the latter, the witch attacks human life at large, not only men, and she can be young or old, married or unmarried. The concrete case histories, however, show that the majority of victims are males, and usually younger men who have fallen under the influence of an older woman, who is then readily identified as the witch; while the alleged witch is always married, and often middle-aged or old. There is a further cleavage between 'theory' and 'practice'. As will be remembered, our text suggested that witches attack their own kin only exceptionally. This notion is

---

[1] See above, p. 17.
[2] This is not strictly correct. '*Ezo*' is the salute of the *gunnu* priest, but it is here used as though it belonged to the *ndakó gboyá* cult. These and other references to the cult will become clear later (see below, pp. 190 *et seq.*).

further elaborated in popular belief; for it is generally held that a witch who would attack her own flesh and blood cannot do so alone but must enlist the help of other witches, not related to the victim. Kinship, then, in some measure deflects and frustrates the evil designs of witches. It is in fact true that witches are only rarely accused of harming their own blood relations; I recorded only two cases of this kind, both referring to the witch's own children. But the victims are not necessarily strangers; as often they are affinal relations of the woman witch (her son-in-law, her husband, his brother or the brother's children, or the husband's children by another wife).

From this varied evidence the following picture of the witch emerges: she is the enemy of men and of male authority; she seeks to dominate men; her evilness is somehow bound up with married state and occasionally with old age, that is, age beyond childbearing; and her evilness is often directed against a husband and his kin. Now all these traits fall into place against the background of that other belief which links witchcraft with the economic position of the women; for seen against this background, and allowing for the fantasy disguise, the witch is accused of doing mystically precisely what the women, in virtue of their economic power, are accused of doing in real life. So that the witchcraft beliefs and fears paraphrase a true state of affairs and the anxieties and frustrations arising from it. Consider, then, for a moment that 'true state of affairs'.

To begin with, a great many Nupe men, peasants as well as craftsmen or members of the 'free professions' in the town, are heavily in debt to their trader-wives, on whom they often have to rely for money for tools, for some unforeseen heavy expenditure, and even for such items as the brideprice of a son or funeral expenses, which it is the man's duty to defray. If this dependence on the wife must detract from the man's proper status as the 'breadwinner', his authority is seriously diminished also by another factor. In the Nupe kinship organization most rights and obligations descend in the paternal line; and as sons (to a lesser extent, daughters) derive their kin group membership (membership of a particular 'house') from their fathers, have a place in their father's home and labour team, and inherit his property, land or profession, so they normally look to him or his male kin for economic support. But where the mother is the richer, the inheritance she will leave will be at least as important, and even while she is still alive her sons or daughters will turn to her for financial help. Frequently, in fact, the mother will pay directly, and not only through loans made to her husband, for a son's marriage, buy him clothes or luxuries, or shoulder the cost of a more expensive education. Let me make it clear that the mother is always expected to do the best for her children, and to pamper them in small matters, by giving them sweets, tasty tit-bits, and occasional presents. Nor is her more consequential economic help strictly unexpected and against the rule: but it is a rule of *faute de mieux*, whose coming into play inevitably connotes the failure of the more basic rule, that it is the father's role to meet the economic requirements of the household. Here, as in the instance mentioned before, the economic independence of the women connotes the inadequacy of the men.

There is a further point, already touched upon in a previous context. In Nupe, the women traders are proverbially 'bad' wives and 'bad' women, that is, women of loose and immoral character. Going on long journeys as they regularly do, they neglect their household duties and, while away from home, live the life of prostitutes. This is true even of the many women who only visit the market in the town, the Bida night market being a recognized place of assignation. All this is bad enough in the case of childless women; but in their case such immoral conduct is condoned, if with a shrug of the shoulders. As proverbial, however, as the moral laxity of the women traders is their desire to avoid having children. It is they who are the most regular customers of the various dealers in 'contraceptives'. They thus pile one iniquity upon another, having chosen not only unchastity but that utterly unnatural and despicable thing, voluntary barrenness.

Whether the woman exceeds the proper role of a wife and mother or rejects it, in part or entirely, she has successfully set aside a believed-in social norm. Now, this is no longer an instance of social abnormality, rather the opposite, if by 'normality' we mean all that is common, usual, expected: but it is a normality one hates and regrets, and contrasts with a desired state of affairs unhappily uncommon. This is borne out in every conversation; in the many quarrels between husbands and wives; in the many divorces and separations (and equally in the resigned attitude of husbands); in the comments of the medicine experts which we quoted before; in nostalgic talks of the men about a happier past when 'women knew their place'; and in the exclusion of unchaste and childless women from religious ceremonials.

This, then, is a clash between ideal and reality. But it is in no sense seen as fortuitous or transitory, as the result of some unfortunate maladjustment which could have been avoided and can conceivably be set right if one only made the effort. The harking-back to 'the good old days' is merely an escape from a reality which one is helpless to alter. For no one speaks about a future when everything should be better than it is now; and though the impact of alien influences and the vast increase in trade and traffic in the last few decades may well have aggravated the situation, all the available evidence (of genealogies and life histories) proves that the morals of women and the fate of marriages were, for the last four or five generations at least, much what they are today. Nor is this harking-back more than half-hearted; no one would claim that there was a time when all women were chaste and submissive, when they did not trade and earn money, and when contraceptive practices were unknown. Indeed such a claim, were it ever made, would be belied by the character of the *gunnu* ritual and by various legends and stories. Briefly, for the people the ideal was always out of step with the reality; so that we must judge this conflict to be inherent in the make-up of the society, whose economic system (which has certain moral consequences) is as unquestioned as are its ethical conceptions (which condemn these consequences).

This is important: for it is the inescapable nature of the conflict which finds expression in the belief in women witches. Nupe society, forced into an ambivalent attitude towards the role of women, which it cannot but accept and cannot but hate and call evil, also ascribes to them the powers of witchcraft. The coincidence as such is a matter of observed fact. But we can go further, and interpolate the psychological mechanism which turns the coincidence into a causal nexus, and hence enables us to call one thing the 'cause' and the other the 'symptom'. The mechanism is familiar: it lies in the projection of internal conflicts and of the frustrations so caused upon an external agent, real or imaginary. In our case, the awareness of an ideal state disturbed fastens upon the successful disturber; the helplessness in the face of a threatening situation turns into the positive fear of persons; and while one is incapable of dealing with the situation, one can at least deal with concrete individuals, whom one can accuse, persecute, and punish. So that in being made the witches of the society, the women are made to carry its fault or failure.

It is clear that this explanation holds good only on the assumption that the beliefs in witchcraft have been fashioned by men; for on almost every point we argued from a male standpoint. The legitimacy of this assumption need hardly be defended. The assertion of mundane morality, through legal institutions, falls to the men exclusively; above all, Nupe religion, its practices and doctrine, are fundamentally a male concern; and as it is the men who know and speculate about religion and have charge of the transmission of religious knowledge, so the notions of witchcraft must have been their creation. Situations of this kind are of course common; a great many societies are in this sense men-made and men-run; and if, like Nupe, they also afford considerable initiative and importance to women, they often, once more like Nupe, take back with one hand what they give with the other, that is, punish the permitted presumption by producing some belief in female witchery (whether taken literally or not).

But the male standpoint does not hold throughout; for the Nupe condemnation of voluntary sterility represents the women's judgment as much as the men's. From earliest youth the women accept child-bearing as the mission of their sex. If later in life they deny it, they deny what they know to be 'human nature': hence their furtive dealings with the medicine-man abortionist and the admitted shamefulness of this traffic. Let me stress that this means more than an attempt to evade the moral judgments of others. The Nupe woman has her lovers openly, and as openly flaunts her wealth and independence, the adverse moral judgments of the men notwithstanding. So that, in hiding the shame of not wanting children she hides a shame of which she is aware and a guilt which she accepts. This guilt is probably shared much more widely; for every woman who takes concrete steps to avoid child-bearing there must be another who at least harbours the secret desire. However this may be, like the frustration of the men, the guilt of the women, open or secret, is projected into the picture of the female witch. For the women equally accept this picture. Though they may not have created the witchcraft beliefs, they yet have a hand in transmitting them and keeping them alive; at least, they share in gossip of this kind, if less openly than the men, and fabricate such stories. Whenever they do, they speak as accusers, vehemently denying that the role of the witch could apply to them. Even so, they accuse their own sex and, circuitously, themselves.[1]

The men, then, in the witchcraft fantasies, condemn an antagonist; the women, in the same vicarious fashion, condemn their own guilt. In the concrete punishment, however, which witches are expected to suffer the male standpoint once more emerges paramount. It is the men alone who battle with witches, defeat and chastise them, through the male society of *ndakó gboyá*, as it is also the men who, in the legends about witchcraft, are credited with the discovery of this weapon; and this, as we shall see, is employed, not only to trace and punish the culprits, but also to threaten and to subdue the womenfolk at large.

There is a certain twist to this picture of male vengeance. In the legends the men, in the person of the diviner and the 'old man', are straightforward destroyers of witches. But general

[1] Margaret Mead has drawn attention to the nexus between witchcraft beliefs and willed female sterility (see *Male and Female*, 1949, pp. 232–3). Her views, stated in a broader context, bear out much of what I have tried to say.

belief assigns to them a more ambiguous role, holding that some —the diviners, medicine-men, and 'male witches'—also assist the female witch and hence become her partners in crime. This may still seem to be only a fantasy paraphrase or 'projection' of real life, where the man's role is similarly ambiguous; for he will both claim domestic authority and surrender it, thus so-to-speak aiding and abetting the female ambitions. In a more subtle sense, however, the witchcraft fantasies stand for the triumph of the male. Consider that the woman witch, to be successful, must make a compact with men—diviners, *cigbeciži* or male witches. Her fullest, that is, deadly powers depend on male aid, so that the men can curb her activities and frustrate her designs. Indeed one firmly clings to the belief that this is nearly always so, and that the male witch is 'good' and the female alone 'evil'. If a few men, whom no one can name, are willing to 'aid and abet' women witches, they have as it were betrayed their own sex; even so, their help has to be begged by the female witch. In brief, the men, victims of female ascendancy in real life and victims of female witchcraft in fantasy, are on the same fantasy plane also the masters of the women; and if in one sense female evilness may prevail, in another it exists on sufferance, subject to male permission and, ultimately, revenge.

So understood, the fantasy picture of witchcraft conjures up a relationship between the sexes which reverses reality, putting power for helplessness and dominance for submission. The projection of the conflict between reality and ideal thus merges with its resolution in terms of a wish-fulfilment. We conclude that Nupe witchcraft beliefs afford a double relief: the frustrations caused by a hated 'normality' are not only externalized so that they can be vented on concrete victims, but also spirited away and compensated in fantasy.

Both the projective mechanism and this other mechanism of 'compensation', which we interpolated between 'cause' and 'symptom', between certain conflicts and frustrations and the belief in female witchcraft, operate unconsciously, though the conflicts and frustrations themselves are fully conscious. But it might be asked if the 'causes', too, are not likely to reach down into the unconscious and to a level deeper than that represented by conflicts over authority, kinship position, or morality. These are all motives entailed in a particular social organization. And since the belief in female witchcraft is widespread throughout human society it would seem legitimate to search also for a cause of a more fundamental order, over and above those peculiar to this one type of society. The Nupe witchcraft beliefs, with their dichotomy of 'good' male and 'evil' female witches, indeed seem to point in that direction, towards some basic antagonism of the sexes.

To substantiate this hypothesis I may be allowed to digress a little. It is, I think, true to say that man surrenders to woman his virility in the sex-act and his independence and self-containedness in the love relationship; the fulfilment of his desires is thus bought with the sacrifice of Ego-completeness. If we take this sacrifice to be unconsciously hateful, as I think we must, and accept this ambivalence of love-hatred as the source of an inescapable antagonism having no normal or legitimate outlet, then the belief in female witches (of the Nupe or any other people) represents a 'displacement' and licensed expression of the repressed hatred. The phrase 'having no normal outlet' requires some comment. Different cultures fashion the normal social relationship between the sexes in widely diverse ways, as has been amply demonstrated in the work of Margaret Mead. But few societies can by this means fully resolve the conflict of sex antagonism. If the society makes the men the socially dominant sex, it is able to compensate for the surrender of virility but fails to express the importance of the woman as sexual partner and procreatrix, and hence invites male fears of female revenge; and if the social dominance of men is reduced, either by design (as in some societies) or in consequence of uncontrollable social processes (as in Nupe), this produces the kind of situation we have been discussing. There is some evidence that a carefully balanced relationship between the sexes can avoid this impasse.[1] But where it does not, the psychological mechanism of projection, with its offer of vicarious or fantasy hatreds, comes into play.

Now this is only a bare formula, couched in terms of universal validity. Let me fill it in with details from Nupe society. To begin with, the 'surrender' and loss of 'completeness' on the part of the men may be felt more strongly in some societies than in others, that is, reach consciousness to a different degree. The Nupe men, certainly, make much of the physically weakening effects of sexual intercourse, and teach the younger generation to husband their strength; they also, as we know, readily employ aphrodisiacs and so betray their fear of the loss of potency. At the same time, they will comment on the sexual voraciousness of the women, who never seem to have enough lovers. The Nupe, incidentally, do not conceive of erotic relationships that could avoid this threat to their virility: homosexuality among the men does not seem to occur and is thought absurd as well as repulsive. Yet again, homosexuality does occur among the women, which fact is well known to the men.[2] For the Nupe, then, the woman is more 'complete'

[1] See my chapter on 'Dual Descent in the Nuba Hills', in *African Systems of Kinship and Marriage*, ed. A. R. Radcliffe-Brown, 1950, pp. 354 ff.
[2] See *A Black Byzantium*, p. 152.

in herself than the man and her sex less vulnerable; above all, her satisfaction, more insatiable than the man's, threatens his virility. So that everything we said before, in general terms, about male 'surrender' and 'incompleteness' is sharply accentuated in Nupe culture.

Everything, too, reappears, appropriately rephrased, in the witchcraft fantasies: witches feed on the life and strength of a man as women do on his virility; and his anxieties are allayed or compensated in a wish-fulfilment which sees the female witch incomplete, possessed only of half her power without a help she must beg of men.[1]

Admittedly, the witchcraft legends fail to corroborate this view, containing nothing that could be construed into a reference to the sexual dominance of women. Rather on the contrary: in the first legend the witch is a 'mother' dominating her son; and though the second legend enlarges upon the licentiousness and sexual greed of the young women, the really dangerous 'witch' is pictured as an old hag against whom younger men are helpless. But the aspect of female dominance is there; and if it is removed from the sphere of sex it is brought closer to the overt anxieties and frustrations of the Nupe men. They face precisely this threat, from 'mothers' who assume an illegitimate power in the family, and from overbearing women who abandon their role of partners in marriage. Perhaps the 'old woman' too fits into the picture; for being 'old' means being beyond child-bearing; so that the figure of a woman who has left child-bearing behind would seem to stand for all the women who reject it. If then, the legends fail to express the antagonism between the sexes in its basic and universal form, they express instead the immediate, concrete conflicts of the society. In other words, of two possible motivations the legends embody one.

This leads me to my final point. This new explanation, in terms of a basic sex antagonism, neither overrules nor clashes with those previously suggested, in terms of other motivations. Rather, they are all valid, relating to different aspects or elements of that total phenomenon, the Nupe witchcraft beliefs. It is indeed a fundamental feature of social phenomena, if they are of any complexity, that they tend to embody a plurality of motives, belonging to varying levels of human concern, impulse, and consciousness. Our several explanations reflect this plurality of motives; more pre-

[1] I am aware that psycho-analysts may read the facts differently and relate the fantasy picture of female witches to a love-hatred of women which has its roots in the man's mother-imago, or in the conflict between 'tenderness' and 'sexuality' in love, or perhaps in the sadistic components of the sex act. I will only say, briefly, that my analysis of Nupe society does not bear out these alternative explanations.

cisely, there had to be three explanations, corresponding to different levels of motivation, which are levels of generality as well. The first was concerned with the ascription of witchcraft to concrete individuals: this we related to the overt value judgments of the people, that is, to the conscious assessment of socially desirable conduct and character traits. The second explanation was concerned with the ascription of witchcraft to the female sex: here the processes creative of the belief were unconscious though set in motion by judgments on socially desirable behaviour and by the conscious conflict between ideal and reality. The third explanation, once more concerned with the ascription of witchcraft to women, was in terms of unconscious impulses springing from an unconscious conflict: and this we took to be determined, no longer by particular social circumstances, but by events on that 'deeper level' on which sex antagonism, in man everywhere, has its play. There is perhaps a further, most general level of enquiry; for we may clearly ask why there should be witchcraft at all? why people should believe in such a deadly evil inexorably vested in some of their kind? This question must for the moment be postponed.

4. SYMPTOMATOLOGY: CASE HISTORIES

As has been said, only a witch, or a person possessing the appropriate *cigbe*, is able to tell a witch; others can only suspect the presence of witchcraft, however reliable the indications. The clues employed in this work of detection are similarly divided, into esoteric signs visible only to the fellow witch or sorcerer, and the crude indications which everyone can read. The former are, needless to say, entirely intangible and mystical. Thus at night you may see witches breathe fire (if you are yourself a witch); if a lesser witch meets a more powerful one, tears will spring to the eyes of the former; witches, finally, see one another in their dreams. Persons possessing a *cigbe* which makes them like witches should also be able to see or recognize them, and such medicines, as I have said, are in fact produced; but a few sceptics dismiss these claims as so much idle talk. It is a highly qualified scepticism, casting no doubts on the witchcraft beliefs as such. The Master of the *cigbeciži* summed it up most clearly, in this analogy: 'We see the lightning; we say *Sokó* causes it: but has anyone seen him do it? So we see what witches do, but who says he has seen a witch is lying.' The mystery which surrounds the manner of beholding witches extends also to their appearance; for the Nupe have no clear picture of what a witch looks like save that she looks horrid and fearful.

Though ordinary persons cannot see witches, dogs and cats can, and will give sound when witches are about (one of the case histories to be quoted presently, mentions a 'clue' of this kind). Ordinary mortals find their clues only in the tangible effects of witchcraft. Some of these sound rather childish. If, for example, you walk on the road and pass a person, and you suddenly fall into a hole which you feel quite sure 'has not been there before', then the person you passed was a witch; or if you watch two persons fight, one strong and powerful and the other thin and weak, and the former has it all his own way until, without apparent reason, he suddenly collapses and feels pain, then his opponent is obviously a witch. These two 'clues' refer both to male witches and female ones, and so do not necessarily indicate the truly evil and dangerous power of witchcraft. A more serious sign is mentioned in a number of stories. They are about men who had some quarrel, however slight, with a woman and immediately afterwards suffered from severe pains in the head and eyes, the eyes becoming inflamed and the sight affected, which proved the woman in the case to have been a witch. We note the quarrel which preceded the illness: the specific 'clue', then, implies that more general belief that witches are always vindictive women, who cannot stand opposition and are ready to punish the slightest injury.

The case histories supply few further criteria. The witch may be pretty or ugly, a local woman or a stranger, old or young (though more often the former), married, divorced, or widowed, childless or a mother. Oddly enough, the suspicion of witchcraft against a widow or divorcee does not always discourage suitors, nor does the charge of witchcraft always cause the husband to seek divorce. Yet the husband faces an unpleasant future (the chances of being 'bewitched' apart), since he will be as friendless and disliked as his wife. This is no heroic indifference, but the indifference of men resigned to their wives' misdemeanours, real or mystical.

Let me, in conclusion, quote four case histories, selected both for their variety and their intrinsic interest.

(1) The women in the case are the three accused in the Bida witchcraft trial, the husband of one of them being my informant. Her name was Wusa, and my informant her second husband. She was first married to a farmer in a hamlet outside Bida, but there was a quarrel and the marriage broke up. After her divorce Wusa returned to her home in the town, both her parents being still alive. There she met my informant, who fell in love with her and married her. The couple lived happily for ten years or so, having no children. Wusa had a younger sister, Aramatu, also married in Bida. That marriage was an unhappy one; husband and wife often quarrelled, and the husband used to beat his wife. On one such

occasion the mother of the two sisters was present, and spoke harshly to the husband, who shortly afterwards fell ill and died. It was then that people began to suspect Wusa and her family of witchcraft; there was plenty of gossip, and when Aramatu later married her late husband's younger brother, in the usual Nupe levirate, people called him a 'witch's man' and avoided his company. The couple were living on the farm but frequently came to town to stay with Aramatu's mother; this gave rise to new gossip, for it is very unusual for a Nupe man to pay such visits to his mother-in-law, and the people concluded that Aramatu's second husband had come completely under the influence of the two women.

The matter was brought to a head a few years later, by an event that happened in Wusa's household. She was then about thirty-five or forty, and had a guest, a Hausa employed as Muezzin in a Bida mosque, staying in the house. One day he complained about the food Wusa gave him to eat; she resented his remarks and the two quarrelled. Shortly afterwards they had another quarrel, over a trivial matter, the Hausa flying in a rage and striking Wusa in the face so that her nose bled. Wusa's mother happened to visit her that day, found her crying, and was told the reason; apparently nothing further happened then, though my informant was away at the time and found his mother-in-law gone when he returned. He comforted his wife, who was still crying as well as furious, and thought no more about it, until, a fortnight later, the Hausa fell ill, suffering from severe headache and inflammation of the eyes, and suddenly died. Now everyone, the husband included, was convinced that Wusa as well as her mother and sister were all dangerous witches. The three women were formally charged with the crime, with the results described before.

(2) The events here described happened shortly before my second visit to Jebba Island, in the up-river village of Kpatsuwa. The story, much fuller of mystery and miraculous features, was well known in all the riverain villages, and it is interesting to quote two versions, one from Kpatsuwa itself, where I learned it from the people most closely concerned, and the other from Jebba, where it was told me by a man who knew about the events from hearsay only. The two versions, as we shall see, differ not a little, the hearsay version representing clearly something like an incipient myth. To begin with the local account.

The brother's son and prospective heir of the old chief of Kpatsuwa, a young man called Braima, was married to a pleasant young woman, but was also friendly with a much older woman, called Ketswamasa, who was the wife of a friend of his, a local drummer. The relationship between Ketswamasa and Braima was of the kind known as *nnákata* (lit. 'mother-of-the-house'), which is best described as that of a patroness and her protégé. Influential and wealthy older women frequently patronize younger men in this fashion, occasionally sending them gifts of food and drink, inviting them to their houses, and helping them in various ways. Ketswamasa, who was the best potter of the village and a rich and clever woman, was in a position to offer this patronage, and probably cultivated the friendship of the young chief-to-be for a particular reason; for it was generally assumed that she hoped to become *Sagi* when Braima succeeded to the chieftainship. There was no suspicion at the time that Ketswamasa was a witch.

Late one evening in November 1935 Braima was drinking beer in his uncle's house with Ketswamasa's husband. After the latter had left, Braima's wife saw her own husband walk out of the house in the direction of the nearby river, presumably, she thought, to relieve nature. From this walk in the dark Braima never returned but simply disappeared, none of the neighbours having seen him. The wife grew terribly excited, wept and screamed, and accused Ketswamasa of having bewitched her husband. She was not at once believed, though the people were certain that Braima had not fallen into the river or met with some other accident. The chief, greatly worried, went for advice and help, first to the missionary at Mokwa, then to the *Alkali* of Mokwa, and finally travelled to Bida to tell the *Etsu* about the mysterious disappearance of his nephew. The *Etsu* apparently only expressed the pious wish 'May God help' and advised the chief to be patient. So the old man returned to his village, waited for three months, and finally performed the usual burial service for people whose bodies cannot be found. By then everyone was convinced, especially the women, led by Braima's widow and the then *Sagi*, that Braima had been bewitched and that Ketswamasa was the culprit. Her husband drove her out, without formal divorce, and she went to live with her brother's family. There she was living when I visited Kpatsuwa, friendless and so feared that my informants refused to take me to her house in the dark (though they did so willingly in daytime).

The Jebba informant had the names all wrong, calling the witch Zena and her victim Jiya. I discovered later that these were the names of persons involved in a different witchcraft case, said to have happened several years ago in some other riverain village; quite probably other details of that story have equally merged with the report on the Kpatsuwa happenings, which would be a familiar feature of myth-making. According to the Jebba version Braima (to call him by his true name) suddenly disappeared in the middle of day, while his wife was busy cooking; she saw him go out to relieve nature, called out to him, heard him say that he was coming, but never saw him again. The house where all this happened stood far away from the water, so that Braima could not have fallen in the river. The people knew at once that this was witchcraft, and the *Sagi* (my informant said, 'the *Lelu*') denounced Ketswamasa to the chief; for she claimed that she had seen Ketswamasa hide the young man's body in a baobab tree. Also, the day after the disappearance, Braima's dog started barking at the tree, keeping on for three whole days, which seemed to confirm the *Lelu's* story. The chief was too afraid to take action at once; eventually, he summoned Ketswamasa and ordered her to surrender to him her witchcraft 'medicine', which he in fact obtained, though he never mentioned the fact when the police began investigations. The people of Kpatsuwa, however, were still worried, and sent a deputation to the missionary in Mokwa, to the *Alkali*, and to Bida. The deputation returned, having failed to obtain any promise of help against the witch. Ketswamasa, the informant admitted, had never previously done any wrong, but was sure to 'do more now'. He concluded by advising me, on my forthcoming trip to Kpatsuwa, to ask the chief straight out for the 'box' in which the witch had kept her *cigbe*. (I did so, but was told that there existed neither a *cigbe* nor a 'box'.)

The Jebba version, then, fills in certain miraculous details (the hiding of the body in the baobab tree), adds certain accepted *motifs* of witchcraft (the barking of the dog, the witch's 'medicine'), and so, in a sense, conventionalizes the story. It equally increases the mystery and precludes more firmly any conceivable rational explanation, for example, that Braima might have slipped in the dark and fallen in the river. This explanation is probably the true one; for the whole thing happened in November, when the river was high, and outside a house standing on a slippery buff overlooking the river. Perhaps, too, Braima, who had been drinking all evening, had not been too steady on his legs. Some time later, the body of a drowned man was in fact fished out of the river at Jebba. The police made enquiries, and though the face of the drowned man was too disfigured to permit complete identification, he wore a ring which Braima's wife identified as having belonged to her husband.

It is interesting to record the reactions of the interested parties when I taxed them with this fact. The Kpatsuwa people said doubtfully that the drowned man 'might have been' Braima, but added that, in any event, this was only his *nakā*, while the witch destroyed his *fifingi* and *rayi*; my informant in Jebba maintained that the body was definitely not Braima's, the ring being only proof of another witchery. As regards the alleged witch, I gathered from the comments of the Kpatsuwa *Sagi* and other women, that they all disliked Ketswamasa, whom they called unfriendly and overbearing, though they admitted that she was a clever and successful woman. But it is likely that the accusation of witchcraft was inspired, not only by this general and orthodox disapproval of an unpleasant personality, but by specific jealousies—on the part of the *Sagi*, who may have feared a future rival, and on the part of Braima's wife, who may have hated her husband's patroness.

(3) This case history contains a number of unusual features. It concerns a middle-aged woman from Jebba Island, called Adi, who seems to have led a blameless life until certain events in 1934. There was one thing, though: Adi had become a frequent visitor of the local mission, in spite of several attempts by her husband and family to stop her. Now, the Nupe attitude towards missionaries is not hostile or even unfriendly; but the missions gain their following and their converts only from among strangers or people without kin or friends, all 'decent' persons keeping aloof. Perhaps, then, Adi's intimacy with the missionaries made her unpopular; certainly, suspicion readily fastened upon a woman who was thus flouting her kin and disregarding the common rules of conduct. Thus, when a woman in the Kede camp on the island, whom Adi knew but slightly, died suddenly and mysteriously, it was generally believed that, before her death, she had cried out Adi's name; gossip at once called her a witch, and when, shortly afterwards, a child of Adi's husband by a co-wife died, everyone was convinced, the child's mother being the first openly to accuse Adi of witchcraft. Her husband drove her from the house, and she went to live with a daughter. Her daughter firmly maintained to me and others that her mother was not a witch; but about that time an attempt was made, probably by someone in her family, to poison Adi. She was saved by the missionaries, but continued to be regarded as a dangerous witch, so dangerous that her story was told me in utmost secrecy and on condition that I reveal it to no one in Jebba (an odd request this, considering that nearly everybody knew it).

(4) The last case history is the least circumstantial. I am quoting it for this very reason; for it shows how the suspicion of witchcraft can arise and grow without being helped either by precise 'clues' or by definite personal hostilities. This is the case of the young woman whom I visited and found so conspicuously different from the accepted notion of gloomy, severe, and unfriendly witches. She was a native of Doko, where she had first been married to a peasant, bearing him two children. Both died in short succession, and the husband shortly afterwards divorced her, though only on

the grounds that she had neglected her children and so caused them to fall ill and die. If anyone suspected her of witchcraft at the time, he did not say so openly. The young woman then married a trader in Bida, engaging in trade herself. The second marriage was childless and apparently happy, until, four or five years later, the husband's young sister, who lived in the same house, fell ill and died. Also, the husband's trade seems to have gone badly, while his wife's business prospered. It was then that the suspicion of witchcraft began to be voiced. When I was in Bida all the neighbours were convinced that the woman was a witch; so was her husband, who told me so himself in strict confidence. All the same, he continued to live with her. He admitted that 'he was afraid' as well as that his wife was unfaithful to him and had many lovers. But, he added, there was nothing he could do about either of these things. And this was the state of affairs when I left Bida.

I recorded five other case histories, which add little that is new. Let me then draw up a brief summary. In every case the accusation seized upon an unexplained sudden death or some rapid deadly illness. The latter was not always mysterious; in two cases it was a well-known disease, smallpox and dysentery: invariably, however, death was said to have come within a few days. In seven cases (out of nine) the victim was a male, and in five of these, a young man bewitched by an older woman; in the remaining two cases and one other the 'witch' attacked children (her own, her husband's brother's, or a co-wife's); only in one case was the victim another woman. The case histories make it clear that one does not invariably look for reasons to explain the witch's anger or vindictiveness against her victim; three of the instances quoted and one other are without motives of this kind. Rather, the suspicion fastens upon the woman's character as a whole, which always betrays the wish to dominate or oppose men, or at least to reject the submissiveness expected of women. Our first two case histories, where the 'witch' is a mother-in-law, an unpleasant hostess, and the ambitious patroness of a young man, are as it were textbook examples. But the crucial character traits are as plain in the case of the woman who runs off to the mission or in that of the wife who neglects her children, is unfaithful to her husband, and becomes his successful rival in trade. The case histories not quoted complete the picture: there the witch is a woman who cheats a young man of his pay (and bewitches him when he complains); who berates her husband's younger brother for contributing too little to the household budget; or lords it over a husband feeble in character and sick in body.

5. COUNTERMEASURES

Neither the evidence which should precede the countermeasures nor these themselves are uniform or rigidly laid down; rather, there are a number of alternative procedures, employed as chance and expediency may dictate. One can, to begin with, rely on the official 'witchfinder', the *Lelu* or *Sagi*. Then there is that incontrovertible 'proof', the naming of the witch by the victim in dream or delirium, which must occur five times to be truly conclusive; but this testimony is not always applicable nor does one always wait for it. Nor yet does proof by ordeal seem indispensable, although the Nupe know two such methods. The first consists in the application of the snake-bite medicine *wasa* mentioned before, which the accused is made to drink, the belief being that a true witch would be killed by a snake. The second ordeal is administered by the masked members of the *ndakó gboyá* society, who would take the suspect woman into the bush and make her scratch the ground with her finger-nails; if after a time (left to the discretion of the inquisitors) blood comes out from under her finger-nails, this proves her to be a witch. No informant could remember a concrete case when the first ordeal was applied; while the second disappeared with the official ban on the *ndakó gboyá*.

A witch convicted by one or the other method might be warned by the village chief, perhaps also fined, and if possible ordered to repair the harm she had done; an unrepentant witch was formerly flogged and driven from the village. Several informants maintained that a witch was never killed, since this would bring the revenge of all other witches upon the community; but according to others a dangerous witch was denounced to the *Etsu* Nupe, who would hand her over to his executioners. Above all, there are various magic means whereby witches are killed or at least frightened and subdued, though several of these have disappeared in most of Nupe country and are today known from hearsay only. One such method appears to have employed the bull-roarer (called *vúgu-vúgu*;[1] another consisted in a dance called *kútúkpa* (a word denoting the clanging noise made by a galloping horse), which is said to have afflicted witches watching it with a swollen throat, so that they could not swallow or eat and must die of hunger.[2] Only

---

[1] I met with an amusing 'secularized' version of the bull-roarer in Katcha, where the nightwatchman of the Niger Company used it to frighten off burglars.

[2] This method, too, has in a sense been secularized. For the steps and passes of the dance and the fantastic dress worn by the dancers have been preserved in another dance, called *sorogi* (a species of tortoise), which is meant for entertainment only and is frequently performed by groups of young men touring the country after the end of the farming season.

two deadly weapons against witches have survived. The first is private as well as casual, and consists in the anti-witchcraft *cigbe* which individuals can acquire; the second, public and ritualized, lies in the *ndakó gboyá* cult and in the activities of the society of that name. In Nupe eyes, it is the most powerful weapon of its kind, and since its inception, probably several generations ago, it seems to have overshadowed all other anti-witchcraft measures.

As we know, the cult has merged with the main ritual of Nupe, the *gunnu*, where the *ndakó gboyá* masks appear during the vigil in the bush, to frighten novices, warn the youths to obey their elders, and whip offenders.[1] If in this context the apparition of *ndakó gboyá* is suggestively called 'the policeman of the *gunnu*'; the 'police' duties extend to witchcraft also; for the masks reappear later, during the public phase of the ceremonial, to frighten all women, to discourage would-be witches, and to weaken, by their very presence, the evil powers of witchcraft. If the *ndakó gboyá* is thus thought of as a deterrent and preventive, it may also assume the character of punishment proper; for the masks are expected to drag the suspects into the bush, subject them to the ordeal described before, and kill the 'proved' witch—unless she pays a heavy ransom, which loophole, as we shall see, has far-reaching consequences.

But this is only the combination of two distinct cults. It is well understood that the peculiar powers of the *gunnu* do not depend on this addition to its ceremonial, customary though it had become. And as each cult has its own specific aims, so it can, at least on occasion, be performed independently. Nor have the officiants of the *ndakó gboyá* anything to do with the officiants or the priest of the *gunnu*. Normally, in fact, the former are strangers in the village where they perform, being members of a 'secret' society represented only in a few localities and called in specially for the occasion. Furthermore, in the north and east of Nupe, where this society never established its influence, the combination of the two cults is unknown. It is true, however, that in the rest of the country popular opinion, unaware of the esoteric organization of the *ndakó gboyá*, often confuses the two.[2] It is possible that this view was encouraged by the society itself since it kept that organization in the dark. A line in the *gunnu* songs, for example, seems cleverly designed to obscure by its ambiguous meaning the relationship between the two cults. It reads—'*gunnukó u yi Gboyá*', which may mean either 'the *gunnu* priest calls the *Gboyá*'

[1] See above, p. 83.
[2] This applies especially to foreigners. Thus the Yoruba neighbours of the Nupe call the *ndakó gboyá* cult *igunnu*.

(a correct statement of the fact that the secret society is called in by the *gunnu* priest), or 'the Great *gunnu* is the *Gboyá*'.

The full name of the cult means 'Grandfather' or 'Ancestor *Gboyá*'; the latter word is neither a personal name nor a word that has any other meaning, though it contains the recognizable root *gbo* 'to be large' (in a physical sense). The expression 'Grandfather' in this connection has no ancestral connotation but merely indicates a show of respect. The masked apparitions also command a special address or salute, namely, *nyentso sagba*, 'One who puts to flight'. The name *ndakó gboyá* is employed for the ritual performance as such, for the masks appearing in it, and for the 'spirit' the masks are thought to represent; the cult members are simply referred to as *ndakó gboyáži*, 'the *Ndakó gboyá*-ones', and their organization is called the 'society' of *ndakó gboyá*.

The masks of the *ndakó gboyá* are unlike any other masks used in the cults of Nigerian peoples. They bear no similarity to human or animal features; each mask consists of a long tube made of white cotton cloth, just wide enough for a man to stand inside, which is suspended from a wheel-shaped bamboo frame fixed to the top of a tall pole, about twelve feet in length. The man representing the spirit stands inside the cloth tube which comes down to the ground, holding the pole in his hands. He will move about with varying speed, occasionally jumping and running, and lift and lower the pole or incline it this way or that, making the cloth tube swing and sway: which motions make up the 'dance' of the *ndakó gboyá*. There are two small slits at eye-height in the cloth; but the dancer can see little through them, and depends on the help of assistants (two or four in number and known as the 'servants' or 'interpreters' of the *ndakó gboyá*), who lead him along and clear the way for him, carrying sticks to drive back the onlookers. In large ceremonials up to ten masks may be employed, though normally there will be two or three, or even one only.

It is always a strictly kept secret who is inside the mask. Even when you know every member of a local *ndakó gboyá* society (as I did) and therefore know that one of them must be the dancer in the mask, the people will refuse to answer such questions. Nor will they agree to an informal rehearsal merely to show you the technique of the thing; for to step inside the mask is already a magic or mystic action, which requires the appropriate setting and preparations. The performer must first drink and wash himself with the *cigbe* which alone gives him the 'strength' to represent the *ndakó gboyá* and, before this, must sacrifice beer and fowl over the *cigbe* shrine and the cloth masks. Nor does the profane phrase 'to represent the *ndakó gboyá*', do justice to the situation. To begin with, the 'medicine' used by the performer is the *badúfu* kind which makes you 'like a witch'; once more, then, the rule holds that it needs Beelzebub to drive out Satan. Furthermore, once the performer is inside the mask he is inseparable from the thing he 'represents'; he *is* the *ndakó gboyá*, the people insist, and no longer so-and-so, whom you know and have talked to. Once during the ceremonial I offered food and drink to the 'man in the mask', suggesting that he must be in need of refreshments after his exhausting performance. My offer was ridiculed and I was told (as I had expected) that 'spirits do not eat'. Any person who has not been initiated into the *ndakó gboyá* society or has omitted the preparatory rites would be killed by the mask as soon as he entered it. The mask, of course, is just cloth, and must be cut and tailored; many masks also show patches and signs of repair. But again, once the sacrifice has been performed over them, they are no longer merely a material object, but the thing itself which they signify.

It is not easy to say what that 'thing' is. I have called the *ndakó gboyá* a spirit, partly for the sake of convenience and partly because this is the popular interpretation. But its nature is more indefinite. It is not one of the numerous *aljenúži* which people the world: it is only 'like an *aljénu*', that is, non-human, powerful in a mystical sense, normally invisible (unless embodied in the dancing mask), endowed with the same kind of voice spirits have—an inarticulate, whining falsetto, sounding 'like the wind'—and a creature of *Sokó*. Now understood like this, the *ndakó gboyá* stands apart from the whole body of Nupe belief. But to say it again, this is only the cruder, popular view. There is another, esoteric explanation, which links the *ndakó gboyá* belief more closely with the conceptual framework of Nupe religion. It is rarely offered in so many words. It was given me by the Master of the *ndakó gboyá* society when he said that the *ndakó gboyá* was not a spirit, but *asiri gboká*—a 'strong secret', that is, a knowledge or skill of a mystical and powerful kind. We remember that the same interpretation is expressed in the two legends about the origin of the *ndakó gboyá*. They do not describe it as a 'spirit', but merely as a 'secret', as something implying 'great strength', and as the knowledge of some mysterious, supernatural way of acting. They equate the *ndakó gboyá* with that principle of a mystical force, capable of being invoked and manipulated by man, which is embodied in the Nupe concept of *kuti*; indeed, in the concluding phrases of the legends it is referred to by that name.

The legends also illustrate certain other features of the *ndakó gboyá*, such as the voice of the apparition and the salute due to it. The iron rod (*sàyi*) mentioned in the second story is one of the paraphernalia of the cult; and the description of the cult in the first story as a '*kuti* of kings' bears on the important link between the secret society and Nupe kingship. The legends, however, are silent both about the society itself and the beginnings of its organization, dealing only with the origin of the 'great secret', not with the machinery devised to exploit it. For an account of the latter we must turn to the more prosaic and rational traditions preserved in the family of the Masters of the cult. Oddly enough, in this quarter the legends are unknown; the present Master was unacquainted even with the esoteric version which, according to my informants, was taught to their forefathers when they were initiated into the society. I can only conclude that, with the growth of the purely secular (that is, political) machinery of the secret society, the men at the centre lost interest in these, to them, recondite stories. The present Master did not call them untrue; he thought that they might well be true, referring to events in other parts of the country of which he no longer had any knowledge. This was also the way he thought of the *ndakó gboyá*, as a 'secret' somehow discovered, and later put to organized use by his society: it was this 'later' phase of which he was eager to speak. I must add, finally, that in certain places on the south bank of the Niger the legends are entirely unknown. There the people hold that the *ndakó gboyá* had been among the various magic secrets which Tsoede brought to Nupe. They thus regard the anti-witchcraft cult not only as a 'cult of kings' but as bound up with the very origin of kingship.

The headship of the *ndakó gboyá* society is held in a lineage whose remembered pedigree goes back only four generations, to one Mamako Gana, a hunter of Dibo extraction.[1] He is said to have already possessed the magic of *ndakó gboyá*, to have practised it against witches, and to have taught it to others. His son, Sara Jiya, was a great traveller, and finally settled at Kusogi Danci, a small village on the river. When Masaba, the younger brother of the first Fulani Emir of Nupe, rebelled against his elder brother and founded his rival kingdom south of the Niger (1838), he met Sara Jiya and, so it is said, was greatly impressed by his magic powers. Recognizing the importance and value of the *ndakó gboyá* cult, Masaba made its master his servant and gave him the most appropriate title *Majĩ Dodo*, 'Master of the Terrible'. After Sara Jiya's death, when Masaba had become *Etsu* Nupe in Bida, he made one of Sara Jiya's pupils the new *Majĩ Dodo*, a certain Ndasaba, a Bida man and a diviner and barber-doctor by trade. After the latter's death the title reverted to Sara Jiya's sons, whom Masaba called to the capital; four of the six sons obeyed the

---

[1] The Dibo sub-tribe of Nupe occupies the easternmost district of the country. The descendants of Mamako Gana still wear the facial marks of the Dibo sub-tribe.

summons and settled in a hamlet near Bida, which they called Kusogi, in memory of their old home. When the then *Majī Dodo* died, the eldest of the four brothers succeeded to the office, receiving his title at the hands of *Etsu* Abubakari. He was in turn succeeded by his son, Yizufu, the present *Majī Dodo* (and my informant), who was appointed by *Etsu* Bello (d. 1926).[1]

The society itself appears to be only some eighty years old. It was only during Masaba's reign in Bida (1860–73) that the Masters began to accept novices and to train initiates from outside their lineage, thus transforming a kinship-bound observance into a cult society. The membership spread indirectly as well, each man initiated by the Master in turn initiating his own kinsmen and sometimes also strangers from other villages. Each of the groups so founded acts in a body on all ritual occasions, thus forming a local cell or 'lodge' of the society. I listed eight lodges north of the Niger, all founded by men initiated in Kusogi; they are widely dispersed through the country, being found, for example, in Sakpe and Shebe in the centre of Nupe Emirate, in Epa in the extreme west, and in Esã in the north; many more are strung along the south bank of the river. The founders and heads of lodges are lesser Masters, being called the *nũsaži* ('elders') of the society while the men whom they have initiated are their *bara* (dependents or servants).

Neither the headship of lodges nor ordinary membership are simply hereditary; the sons or younger brothers of deceased members (the usual heirs) must be specially initiated by the head of the lodge, while his prospective successors must be formally accepted by the Master. Ordinary members, whose initiation was second-hand, are not permitted to make further proselytes. Nor could they do so since the indispensable cult paraphernalia are in the possession only of the Elders, who received them at their own initiation. The distinction between the two grades is somewhat blurred by the factor of kinship; for the sons or brothers of the Elder, who share his house (which contains the paraphernalia) and will one day succeed him, are by these facts placed on a slightly different footing from ordinary initiates, who cannot claim such privileged intimacy. For the Master of the society, however, this

[1] There is a separate branch, under its own Master, at the original Kusogi. It was called into being by the first *Etsu* of Patigi, the small Emirate on the south bank of the Niger which the British Government granted to the dispossessed original Nupe dynasty. The *Etsu* felt that he needed a *Majī Dodo* of his own and appointed one of the two sons of Sara Jiya who had stayed behind when their brothers emigrated to Bida. The male line becoming extinct, the office later went to a sister's son, who had, however, to be initiated by the Bida Master. The latter is, in all other respects as well, regarded as the superior and true head of the cult.

distinction does not exist; for him, every member of the cult alike is his 'child' or his 'father's child'.

The procedure of initiation was described to me as follows. The candidate presents himself to the Master or Elder, bringing with him a gift of beer and fowls, intended for the sacrifice which will conclude his initiation. He stays for ten days, having 'lessons' every day. He is taught the procedure of the ceremonial, the ways of manipulating the mask, the special dance steps and drum rhythms, and the legend of the *ndakó gboyá*.[1] He also learns a number of ritual rules: that he must not eat snakes, lest his children will 'never walk'; that he must refrain from sexual intercourse for a week before performing the *ndakó gboyá*; and how to use the medicine which is to give him 'strength' for the performance. If the novice is to become an Elder or the founder of a new lodge, he will also be taught the manner of sacrificing beer and fowl over the cult objects and the prayer formula—'Iron rod, do not permit anyone to do evil things. Tsoede, may he give us children. The children we have, and our wives, God may give them health.' The novice is repeatedly examined, and beaten with a twig if he makes mistakes. Should he prove incapable of learning his 'lessons' after ten days, he would be dismissed as a hopeless case. Normally, the period of tuition proper will now be at an end, and the final sacrifice will be performed jointly by master and pupil. For three years afterwards the novice will frequently visit his master, now merely to 'salute' him, bringing a gift of five kolanuts each time. During this period the novice will join in every performance of the *ndakó gboyá* arranged by his master, being lent a mask for the occasion. When the three years are over, the novice becomes a fully fledged member of the society; upon a final payment he receives a mask of his own, and will henceforth be able to perform the *ndakó gboyá* independently, though he would still need the help of his master, who alone owns the required *cigbe*. Only if the novice becomes the founder of a new lodge, will he receive the 'medicine' itself, in its usual decorated earthen vessel, together with two other cult objects, a number of iron rods with small bells on the top (called *sãyi*) and a small iron chain, described as a piece of the 'Chain of Tsoede'. We note this use of the royal emblem; it fittingly appears in a cult protected by royalty, including an invocation of the ancestor king in its ritual, and called a '*kuti* of kings' in the legends describing its origin. Initiation into the society is expensive, especially for the prospective founders of lodges. The grandfather of one of my informants, for example, paid the equivalent of £20 (or twice the customary

[1] In the branches of the society unfamiliar with the legend, this is replaced (quite consistently) by the story of Tsoede (see above, p. 192).

brideprice). Since few can afford the high fee, the membership, at least in the higher grade, is perforce restricted.

As will have been seen, the organization of the *ndakó gboyá* society shares certain features with that other 'closed society', the order of the *cigbeciži*. I knew of no case, incidentally, in which the same individual belonged to both. But there are certain relevant differences. The *ndakó gboyá* society rests upon a network of lodges and centres of ritual collaboration, not upon a number of scattered individuals; it is much more highly centralized as well as closely knit; and its growth is restricted not only by the high initiation fees but also by the rule, unknown among the medicine-men, that not every member can recruit new ones. It is interesting that no new initiations have taken place in the lifetime of the present generation. My informants could offer no explanation for this. The spread of Islam is certainly not responsible: the various Masters received their rank from Moslem Emirs, and the present incumbents, at least, consider themselves good Mohammedans.[1] Also, the increasing wealth of the country should have made entry into the *ndakó gboyá* easier, not more difficult. I suspect that the Masters of the society, or perhaps their royal protectors, stopped further recruitment precisely in order to prevent the society from growing too large and unwieldy; for as we shall see, its very power, its efficiency under centralized control no less than its financial success, would seem to depend on the smallness of the group which shares in the secret activities.

These activities fall into three groups. The first, of more personal character, concerns only the heads of lodges and follows the familiar pattern of ritual observances entailed in the 'ownership' of 'Great *cigbe*' or of a *kuti* priestship. Thus the head of the lodge will perform all his ancestral sacrifices over the *cigbe* vessel and the other cult objects, which are always kept together in a special hut. He performs a similar sacrifice also as a fixed annual rite (in the 7th or 12th month), now on behalf of the local community, to ensure its well-being and the fertility of the womenfolk. On such occasions one mask will also appear and dance in the village, which performance has no bearing on witchcraft or the punishment of witches. The funerary rites for the Elder of the lodge again include this sacrifice and masked dance.

The second group of activities consists in the performance of the masked dance upon request, that is, when the society is called in by some village in the area, either because it is celebrating the annual *gunnu* or because it feels itself threatened by witches. It is on such occasions that the masks will cleanse the village of witchcraft by 'frightening' the women or bringing an individual witch

[1] The tiny hamlet of Kusogi, for example, includes a small mosque.

to justice. Let me here say a few words about the secrecy of the proceedings. I have called the *ndakó gboyá* organization a 'secret society'. It is clear, however, that the existence of the society is no secret; everyone knows about it, and everyone has at one time or other seen it in action. Nor is there any mystery about the localities which harbour the lodges. But certain weighty secrets remain: the rules and observances of the *ndakó gboyá*; the training of the adepts; the very source of their power; and, above all, the identity of the masked actors. When a village chief or *gunnu* priest summons the members of a lodge he addresses himself only to the head, and does not know whom the latter will choose for the masked dance; the rest of the people may not even know the master of the lodge, and would certainly not know his helpers or 'servants'. This mystery becomes both deeper and more formidable when the masks appear uninvited and unannounced: this is the final group of activities of the cult members, which makes them a 'secret society' in the full sense of the word.

For it seems that the members of a lodge also made a habit of touring all the neighbouring districts, unexpectedly appearing in the various villages, on the pretext that these had to be 'cleansed of witchcraft'. They would scare the women and threaten 'witches', demanding a heavy ransom before they let them go, and a heavier ransom still (up to £100) before they would leave the village. Often, the villagers had to appeal to the *Etsu*, so that he might finally order the *Majī Dodo* to recall his 'children'. No one doubted that both the Master of the society and its royal protector connived in these extortions; equally, they shared in the proceeds, two-thirds of which went to the society and its Master, and one-third to the *Etsu*. Sometimes, too, the *Majī Dodo* would take the initiative, requesting the *Etsu's* authority (never refused) to send his agents to a 'witchcraft infested' district. Or the *Etsu* himself might mobilize this *kuti* of kings, ordering a 'great' *ndakó gboyá*, staged by all the lodges of the country together, with very similar results. Traditionally, it is claimed, these performances by royal request never took place in Bida; nor was there any pretext for it since the *Lelu* or *Sagi* of the city amply protected its people from the threats of witchcraft. Whether this rule was meant to uphold the 'king's peace' in the capital or to protect its wealthy citizens from the greed of the secret society, we cannot decide. However this may be, the rule certainly no longer applied under *Etsu* Bello, under whom the abuses of the *ndakó gboyá* remained altogether unchecked.

My information on this point is supported, not only by official reports, but also by the testimony of the present *Majī Dodo*, who held office then and frankly admitted the whole story, naïvely adding that 'the *ndakó gboyá* people were doing beautifully'. When, in the peace celebrations of 1918, the Nigerian Government encouraged the people throughout the territory to perform their tribal ceremonials and festivities, *Etsu* Bello ordered a 'great' *ndakó gboyá*, with twenty masks, to be staged in Bida. Afterwards, the cult society went 'on tour' through the districts, in the customary way. According to the *Majī Dodo*, every village asked for a visit, a great fear of witchcraft suddenly sweeping the country. Invited or not, the *ndakó gboyá* people continued their tour for a whole year, sucking the country dry and collecting vast sums. A final performance, again ordered by *Etsu* Bello, took place in Bida in 1921; it lasted for a whole day and ended once more in a prolonged and profitable 'tour' of the country. This time the effects were even more disastrous; complaints began to reach the Administration, many villages were unable to pay their tax, while some even emigrated to other parts. At last Government stepped in and banned all further performances.

The proscription of the *ndakó gboyá* only applies to Bida Emirate, not to the Nupe districts south of the Niger which lie in a different Province. There the *ndakó gboyá* society is still active, though it seems to have reformed its character, and a memorable performance, vividly remembered, took place in Ilorin in the Jubilee year 1935. It is remembered especially because it demonstrated the power of the *ndakó gboyá*; a Yoruba man who scoffed at the masks and refused to take off his cap (as all onlookers must do) is said to have at once been 'struck down' and killed. Nor is the prohibition taken literally in the smaller, out-of-the-way villages, where the masked dance is still performed, if without its witch-hunting aspects. Let me here insert the description of such a performance.

6. A NDAKÓ GBOYÁ CEREMONIAL

I saw it in October 1934 (the 7th month in Nupe counting) at Kutigi, where it was staged by men from Shebe, a *ndakó gboyá* lodge a few miles away. The performance represented the annual ceremonial of the Shebe lodge, repeated in Kutigi (where I had been staying) in my honour: or so it was claimed.[1] I need not describe the preparatory sacrifice and the other ritual preparations which took place in Shebe, in the house of the Elder. The public

[1] I later found that this was not quite correct. My presence in Kutigi was regarded merely as a convenient pretext (and protection) for the resumption of the customary 'tours' of the *ndakó gboyá* people. Apart from a perfunctory 'salute' at the beginning of the ceremonial, neither the dancers nor the public took much notice of me, which I for one was glad to observe.

performance began at dawn, when one of the masks suddenly appeared in the streets of Kutigi, making its presence known by its shrill falsetto scream. There were only two masks in this performance; but they were never seen together, one disappearing in the bush before the other appeared from some unexpected quarter, so that this impression of a Nupe onlooker was not so far off the mark—'the masks are numberless: they spring from the ground and are swallowed by the ground'. Later in the morning, people began to appear in the streets and two drummers took their position on the market place. Soon the market place was crowded with men, women, and children. The drummers were drumming and singing, and the mask began to dance, now and again rushing at the crowd, which would disperse with shrieks of fear and sometimes with laughter; but the laughter was forced and nervous, and certainly did not stop the people from running away. The younger women, especially, would escape to the nearest house, to hide in the doorway. The masked dancer always appeared accompanied by two 'servants', who were guiding his steps, made room for him with the help of big sticks they carried, and also acted as his 'interpreters' when, later on, the chief and other notables joined the crowd; the 'servants' would 'translate' the respectful salutes of the newcomers to the 'spirit', and the latter's shrieks and weird noises to the audience. These spirit messages were always the same and pretty nondescript; they assured the people that God would give health to the community and children to the women, and would keep evil from the village.

An hour or two later the gathering assumed a more definite shape, having until then moved this way and that in an irregular and amorphous fashion. Also, more firmly arranged in distinct groups and made to take an active part, the crowd was losing its earlier nervousness and fear. Old men were playing the part of organizers and ushers, forming the onlookers into a large circle, men on one side, women and children on the other, the mask and the drummers in the centre. The younger women were clapping hands, hesitatingly at first, an old woman here and there indicating the rhythm with her hands high in the air. Finally, both men and women started to sing. A number of old women from Shebe formed a prominent group, leading in the singing and shaking gourd rattles in rhythm. Suddenly an old woman, the *Sagi* of Kutigi, stepped into the middle of the circle, and began to dance opposite the mask. She was followed by two of the Shebe women, who were shaking their rattles, singing as though addressing the mask, and occasionally breaking into a long-drawn, high-pitched shriek. The mask continued to dance inside the circle, with varying speed, now calmly, now excitedly. From time to time the servants, as though listening to the mask and translating its wishes, would order the drummers to change the rhythm; or the mask, silent until then, would stop and talk some gibberish in a falsetto voice, which meant another 'message' or salute, duly translated by the interpreters. Or finally, the mask would set out on a sudden excursion, breaking through the circle, run down a side-street and temporarily disappear.

The mood of the gathering grew more and more excited until, about noon, just when it seemed that the excitement would reach fever pitch, there was a sudden hush. The drumming paused, as did the dancing and singing. The mask stood still, flanked by the 'servants', and a number of old women walked up to it and, on their knees, with bent head, saluted the mask. They handed small gifts of money to the 'servants', which were meant to buy the 'protection of the *ndakó gboyá*'. (This, I was told, was only a token payment: formerly heavy sums were paid in the same fashion.) Soon afterwards the mask disappeared, now without returning, and the pause turned into a midday break, when everyone went home. At about 3 o'clock the mask reappeared on the market place, which soon filled with people, and the proceedings of the morning were resumed. The drumming and dancing went on into the night, to the light of torches and hurricane lamps, uninterrupted even by a gathering thunderstorm. At about 9 o'clock the mask danced out of the circle and disappeared in the dark, not to return. 'You see', a bystander pointed out, 'how it is swallowed up by the ground'.

The crowd of onlookers included not only every soul in Kutigi, among them all the local notables and the Fulani District Head (a 'royal prince' from Bida), the contingent from Shebe, but also many strangers who had learned of the forthcoming performance. The attitude of the crowd was an odd mixture of enjoyment and fear. Of the former there could be no doubt; for a long time afterwards people were talking about the 'nice' and 'beautiful' performance as though they were commenting on an ordinary festivity, and the 'servants' of the mask several times pressed me to say whether the '*ndakó gboyá* had pleased me'. But there was no question either of the fear. It was clearly voiced already in the women's songs; for unlike many ceremonial songs of Nupe, those sung at the *ndakó gboyá* are far from nondescript or ambiguous.

(1)

One does not call him friend
When he comes to stay in the bush:
A friend (he) is when he leaves.

(2)

We are saying—'A stranger has come (in the night)'
He is greater than the chief.
We are saying—'being greater than the chief,
May he go away when day comes.'

(3)

We are desiring the cloth (mask)
Which covers the Great One.
God is in front,
He is in the back (i.e. being everywhere and all-powerful, God will protect us).

The attitude towards the *ndakó gboyá* could not be better expressed: he is a 'friend' only when he leaves, a powerful 'stranger' whom one wishes to see gone; and while one must invoke the secret of the 'cloth', it is yet so terrifying that the thought of God alone gives comfort. But let me stress that this is not merely the unthinking expression of conventional sentiments; the fear and awe referred to in the songs were clearly visible even in this ceremonial, devoid though it was of the more sinister implications of witch-hunting and punishment. When the old women presented their gifts of a few pennies to the mask, they were acting genuinely and in all humbleness; and any person whom the mask approached, man or woman, was as genuinely terrified. Men whom I knew to be sophisticated and 'enlightened', such as the local dispenser and one of my servants, ran and hid behind a hedge when the mask suddenly towered over them.

Nor can there be any doubt but that the people believe in the magic effects of the ceremonial. Even after the mild version I happened to see I heard the remark that the village was now clear of witchcraft. This attitude does not really conflict with the well-known extortions practised by the *ndakó gboyá* society; the admission of the abuses is one thing, and the belief in the anti-witchcraft cult quite another. Thus the Government's ban of the *ndakó gboyá* was thought regrettable if indeed not disastrous; everywhere the people spoke with envy of their cousins in Patigi who had kept their *ndakó gboyá* and hence preserved 'the only sure protection against witchcraft'. Often have I been told that in the rest of Nupe there was now no means of fighting witches, and no protection 'save God', who, as we know, is inscrutable, idle, 'far away'.

To be sure, even the *ndakó gboyá* is not a full protection. Though it may frighten witches and temporarily 'cleanse' a community, it cannot exterminate witchcraft. For not only must the ceremonial be repeated, at least year by year, but each performance does no more than restrain the evil machination of witches. When I asked if the *ndakó gboyá* society, given its former power, could suppress witchcraft altogether, the answer was invariably the same: '*u jĭ táimako*', 'it would help'. As in the belief in the *Lelu*, the Nupe expect their anti-witchcraft magic only to keep down witchcraft, 'so that it would not be too bad'. If the Nupe knew our saying about poverty they would no doubt say that witchcraft, like the poor, will always be with us; all man can hope to do is to keep it within reasonable bounds.

7. ON THE MEANING OF WITCHCRAFT

The discussion has led us back to a question previously raised—Why should there be this stubborn belief in witchcraft? I am not now referring to the ascription of witchcraft to women or to particular individuals and personalities, but to the notion of witchcraft as such which underlies these specific ascriptions, that is, to the basic premiss that some mystic power of evil is simply given and ultimately ineradicable. As regards the specific ascription of witchcraft in Nupe thought, we explained it as a projection or displacement of hatreds and aggressive desires from the sphere of rational social life into one mystically sanctioned. We may now add that, through such projection and displacement, the doctrine of witchcraft both permits anxieties to become articulate (if in fantasy language) and shows them an outlet, or scapegoat. Other scholars have viewed witchcraft beliefs in much the same light.[1] And they would agree also with this calculation of the 'gain and cost of witchcraft' (to quote Kluckhohn's suggestive phrase). The individual gains inasmuch as he is shown a legitimate outlet for his frustrations and tensions, legitimate since the society has licensed the aggressive talk and action through which the frustration and tension are relieved or 'ab-reacted' (as psychiatrists would say). And society gains inasmuch as the 'ab-reaction' is not random but canalized; indeed, society utilizes the very mode of ab-reaction in turning it into an attack upon behaviour and character traits held undesirable.

None of these explanations, however, touches upon that premiss of 'witchcraft as such'. The former concern, essentially, the social canalization of anxieties, frustrations, tensions, hatreds, into variants of the belief in witchcraft. And these will depend on the make-up of the given society or culture: while in Nupe certain features of the social structure seem to be the determinants, in

[1] See C. Kluckhohn and D. Leighton, *The Navaho*, 1946, pp. 172–81.

other societies, differently organized, different factors might prove relevant (for example, among the Navaho, the smallness of the group, envy of wealth, and irregular, autocratic leadership).[1] But might it not be that the whole belief in witchcraft (of any kind) is similarly a variant, one of several possibilities of canalizing anxieties and tensions, which would once more depend upon something in the make-up of cultures? It must be so, since there exist societies (if few in number) which are without this kind of belief even though they are not without conflicts or tensions. And it must be so also for another reason.

Granted that suppressed hatreds, unresolved conflicts, and the like occur in most (or all) societies, they could surely be offered adequate relief by means other than beliefs in witchcraft. The hatreds and the persecution of aliens; licensed occasional outbursts of hectic excitement; or the licensed aggression of war or of sectional combats, are familiar instances; all three also occur in Nupe. It may of course be that they offer insufficient relief, or themselves add further anxieties or tensions. But there is no way of measuring the potential of these different chances of relief; we cannot compare them and say 'each can only do so much', as we might say of the lack of vitamins in one kind of food that it must be made good by their presence in another. If the incidence of neuroses and other psychopathological derangements is an index of unrelieved mental tensions, then the reliefs just mentioned are indeed 'not enough' in Nupe; but they are not enough even combined with witchcraft beliefs. However this may be, witchcraft beliefs exist *although* there are these other possibilities of relieving tensions; which is true not only of Nupe but of most societies in the world. We must conclude that they have a *raison d'être* of their own, apart from that implied in the psychological mechanism of projection, displacement, and the rest: which *raison d'être*, as I have suggested, must lie in 'something in the make-up of cultures' (of most cultures).

In a paper written many years ago I attempted to formulate that reason. As I now know, I was wrong; my attempt was vitiated, above all, by the fact that I had considered Nupe witchcraft in isolation from the rest of the religious system. But since my error too is instructive I may be allowed to repeat here the main argument.[2] I argued that religious faith, if it clings naïvely to the promises of religion—of guidance as to how to act; of supernatural or divine protection if that guidance is followed; and of some ultimately just and benevolent order of things—must on occasion face failure. For only too often are these promises belied, by

[1] Op. cit., pp. 174, 177, 178–9.
[2] See *Africa*, vol. VIII, pp. 444–5.

disease, sudden death, misfortune, injustice, that is, by the evil things in the world. Thus in all religions there are attempts to justify or resolve, or to dismiss as merely apparent, this contradiction of promise and fulfilment. The attempts vary in philosophical refinement. The religious doctrine may, in the vein of stoic philosophy, explain the presence of evil as a foil for the visibility of the good; or it can make the evil things, like the sufferings of Job, a touchstone of faith; or it may lay their cause into the imperfection of man, so that his sins (willed or not, actual or intended) are behind the apparent failures of divine providence. Or finally, and more crudely, the religion may contain a loophole within itself, admitting a province where evil is simply allowed to reign. The devil of naïve belief is one embodiment of this loophole-idea; the witch another.

It is true that the belief in the evil actions of witches bears only upon a narrow variety of that abstract 'evil in the world' meant by philosophers or theologians. Even so, the 'loophole' remains. Let us remember also that the belief in witches safeguards itself from being 'found out' and proved or refuted by empirical means; in embracing this incontrovertible belief, then, religious faith itself is safeguarded from being found illusory and refuted by reality. Speaking practically, the acceptance of witchcraft (or of the devil) saves the believer from false hopes or disillusion; speaking philosophically, the acceptance of an ultimate X within the divinely ordered universe saves that order. Admitting that there is a province where the believed-in guidance and protection do not fully reach, we save the belief in laws to guide us and in that promise of protection. Witchcraft, in brief, is a chapter in apologetics, albeit crudely written.

So far my original conclusions (somewhat paraphrased). Now though they are, I believe, correct for other systems of religious belief, they do not seem to apply to Nupe religion. Granting that beliefs in witchcraft can save faith in a divine order of the universe, in Nupe religion, there is nothing of the kind to save; if in other societies or cultures there must be the admission of that ultimate X to account for, or explain away, the failure of religious guidance and promise of protection, in Nupe, this guidance and promise have never been offered. Nupe religion, as we know, admits accidents at every step; it promises only fallible guidance and protection; the observances or ethical rules it upholds are not meant to be counted upon against the many evils which are also in the world—malevolent spirits, diseases, uncontrollable misfortune. Indeed, the deity himself has put them in the world and suffers them to exist, being unconcerned with the fate of his creation. Why, then, should there be this further, special assumption of the evil of witchcraft? The problem which it might serve to solve simply does not exist.

Yet there remains another problem, requiring a kindred solution. With the admission of accident, with the conception of an unpredictable and amoral universe, the problem of the presence of evil is solved intellectually or, at least, argued away on the intellectual plane. But this solution leaves an emotional gap. For I hold that there is a deeply seated desire for certainty, which demands satisfaction of an essentially emotional kind, that is, the awareness that the world is not only certain, but concerned with *you*—your fate, your happiness. And where this demand is refused (as in Nupe) anxieties and frustrations must again arise and press for some ab-reaction and solution. But now those other outlets which might relieve the pent-up tension, through random acts of aggression or some explosive catharsis, would prove inadequate; they would take care of the symptoms but not of the conflicts from which these spring. Nor can the disturbance of the longed-for certainty be overcome save by discovering the disturber; the vague dissatisfaction with an abstract state of affairs must be capable of crystallizing into the accusations of concrete agents. Above all, there must be the chance of practical action, so that the people aware of the threat also have the satisfaction of dealing with it. In other words, precisely because you know that the world around you holds out no promise of certainty nor any supreme design, you conjure up an arch-enemy with whom at least you can reckon, on whom you can vent fears and hatreds, and over whom you may hope to triumph, be it Satan or the witch.

The witch is, perhaps, less of an arch-enemy, since only some of the evils of the world can be laid at her doorstep. Yet the conjured-up picture of human beings who are unaccountably evil and unaccountably cause death and disease does take care of a portion of the uncertainty in the world. Now, we previously said that the admission of a province of life where the benevolent design of the universe does not reach saves the faith in that universe: this clearly does not apply. We must now say—the admission of a province of life where malevolent forces can be defined (and attacked), makes it possible to bear a universe devoid of such design. To be sure, this is no longer our 'loophole' theory; but it is as it were its photographic negative, or the same mathematical formula with all pluses changed into minus signs. Crudely speaking, you may have a God of Justice and Mercy, naïvely conceived, and devils or witches in the background; or you may have an Idle God, remotely in the background, but at least devils or witches to grapple with.

That the notion of witchcraft may arise from such opposed conceptions is, I think, borne out by the history of witchcraft beliefs in our own civilization. For these flourished both when faith was naïve and when it was weakened by the first scientific revolution. Science, of course, did not attack certainty at large; rather, it opened the vista of new laws and a new order governing the universe. But it destroyed the subjective certainty, that emotionally satisfying awareness of a universe concerned with man. So that this sudden loss revived the search for some arch-enemy.[1] Among the Nupe, it was not a question of a sudden loss; they had misconstrued their universe from the first.

One final comment. The preceding discussion may seem to imply that the belief in witchcraft serves to maintain or 'save' a state of affairs worth maintaining and saving; previously too, we argued that witchcraft beliefs and practices 'attack undesirable behaviour', 'resolve conflicts', and 'relieve tensions and anxieties'. One might conclude that societies can do no better than foster beliefs in witchcraft, and that our balance sheet of their 'gains and cost' must show a heavy credit side. Such views are sometimes expressed; it has been pointed out, for example, that witchcraft beliefs provide a 'harmless outlet in imagination for impulses forbidden in real life;' that they direct aggressiveness 'into socially non-disruptive channels' and so resolve 'the problem that every society faces: how to satisfy hate and still keep the core of society solid'.[2]

Let me stress that I presumed no such absolute utility of witchcraft beliefs. I suggested that they resolve certain conflicts or problems: but I did not say that this is a 'good' solution or a final one. The aggression invited by witchcraft beliefs is as harmful as anything a society can produce in the way of 'disruptive' practices; the relief offered by witch-hunting and witch-punishing is no more than temporary and their capacity to allay anxieties no more than illusory: for if witchcraft beliefs resolve certain fears and tensions, they also produce others. Nor is there anything unique in this. If witchcraft beliefs represent a very imperfect 'solution', cultures are full of similarly shortsighted reliefs and spurious correctives. In a sense, the remedies are always better than the complaints; for they enable individuals to go on living and societies to go on functioning without having to face the task, often impossible of achievement, of completely re-fashioning the social system. But they are the kind of remedy which both becomes

---

[1] Cf. this passage from H. Butterfield: 'It would appear to be the case that astrology, like witch-burning, was considerably on the increase in the sixteenth and seventeenth centuries, in spite of what we say about the beginning of modern times' (*The Origin of Modern Science*, 1949, p. 21).

[2] C. Kluçkhohn and D. Leighton, op. cit., pp. 173, 177.

a drug and poisons the system. Or, to change the metaphor, we may liken witchcraft beliefs to a safety valve: but let us be clear that the engine which needs it has been badly constructed; nor is the safety valve itself safe.

VII

STRANGE GODS

IN this chapter I propose to discuss the adoption, by the Nupe, of originally alien beliefs and practices. We shall not be concerned with the pure mechanics of 'borrowing' or 'diffusion'; at least, we shall be concerned only with the motives behind these processes. For we cannot but assume that the adoption of novel or alien elements into any religious system, far from being haphazard, does follow from intelligible motives, which must in turn relevantly bear on the character of the religion and, ultimately, of the whole culture of which it is a part. So that the information so gained will either confirm our interpretation of that character or correct it, bringing to light hitherto unperceived aspects.

This may only be a heuristic assumption to begin with; and other, more specific ones, could at once be added—that the novel features must bear some affinity to the traditional pattern; or that they serve to redress some pre-existing inadequacy; or that they offer a chance of expression to some new trend, say, a changed outlook of the people, which the traditional beliefs and practices failed to satisfy. It must be admitted that in the anthropological field the prerequisite evidence is not easy to procure and that even the first step, the mere discovery of the alien elements, may be difficult or uncertain. Fairly recent additions are usually readily traced; but in the absence of historical records originally alien features long since absorbed may remain unidentifiable. Which proviso holds fully in the case of Nupe religion. Furthermore, the inferences we might draw from our study of 'adoptions' must be corroborated by the appropriate negative evidence, that is, by instances of 'rejection'. But though here we are likely to meet with further technical difficulties, mainly because there might be no record of the rejected chances, the situation in Nupe does afford relevant evidence of this kind. It lies in the religious observances practised by close neighbours of the Nupe or by immigrant groups in their midst, with which the Nupe people are fully familiar, yet which they did not choose to adopt or imitate. Finally, the adoption of alien features, or indeed of a whole alien creed, may conceivably have taken place under pressure; in which case none of our assumptions would apply, or would apply without considerable qualifications. Again, the situation is simplified in Nupe; for only in the case of Islam was the adoption of the alien creed backed by social and political pressure; all other adoptions (or rejections) were spontaneous and voluntary. Let us make this aspect our starting point and begin with a brief outline of the chances of this nature that were offering to the Nupe.

I. ADOPTIONS AND REJECTIONS

The southern neighbours of the Nupe, the Yoruba, possess a religious system which contains many features diametrically opposed to those characterizing Nupe religion. Yoruba religion is based upon a pantheon of deities, all anthropomorphously conceived, who severally govern the universe. Each deity has his (or her) definite sphere—the sky, thunder, rain, land, sea, forests, animals, fishes, crops, special diseases, special skills, divination, and so forth; so that the universe is as it were split up and departmentalized in detailed fashion. The deities are served by a number of specialized orders of priesthood; they are represented, with beautiful realism, in bronze, wood, terracotta, and stone; and masked dances and ritual drama, employing again realistic likenesses, play a prominent part in all Yoruba cults. As has been mentioned, the average Nupe is familiar with the main features of Yoruba religion. Not only has he encountered them on his many travels, but in the area west and south of the Niger Nupe and Yoruba settlements are interspersed, and in certain cases even joined together in twin villages (as in Shari or Shonga). Above all, since 1860 or thereabouts colonies of Yoruba known as *Konú* have been settled in numerous villages of Nupe country, where they form well-defined sections and specialize in their traditional crafts of weaving and indigo dyeing. Though today wholly 'Nupe-ized' in language and mode of life, they still publicly perform one of their masked ceremonies, the *eguŋguŋ*, known as *gugu* to the Nupe, which serves both as a funeral rite and as an annual ritual safeguarding fertility and well-being. The northern and north-eastern districts of Nupe are conquered territory, inhabited by people of Gwari extraction, who came under Nupe domination in the last hundred years and are still referred to as 'Gwari slaves'. Their traditional culture must have closely resembled that of Nupe, while an effective process of Nupe-ization has obliterated most of the differences that did exist. But a few sections of the Gwari-Nupe have preserved a cult alien to Nupe practice; it is called *sogba* and is concerned with childbirth and the cure of barrenness, with the conviction and punishment of criminals, and with the special burial rites for people killed by lightning. Again, there is a large and influential colony of Hausa in the capital Bida. These immigrants too have kept alive one of their typical cults, the *bori*, which they stage publicly in the streets and squares of the town. Another group of immigrants settled around Kutigi, in the centre of Nupe country, towards the end of the eighteenth century; they were Mohammedans hailing from Bornu and brought with them one of their traditional ceremonials, the *gani*, which contains several features strikingly 'un-Nupe' in character.

All these, then, were potential models for the Nupe to follow; as we shall see, the Nupe reaction towards them was neither uniform nor, at first sight at least, consistent.

(i) *The Hausa Bori*

To begin with a clear case of 'rejection'. It is represented in the *bori* cult, which can at once be described as utterly uncongenial to Nupe religious conceptions. It is based upon the shamanistic idea of spirit possession, revealed in hysterical or cataleptic fits and in trance states, when the person so affected is believed to speak with the voice of a spirit and to behave like one. These states may occur spontaneously or may be artificially induced, especially by the use of music, which is again distinctly foreign to Nupe, employing the monotonous, arhythmic playing of a single-string fiddle. When spontaneous, the fits or trance states are regarded as spirit-caused mental disorders, while the induced states are regarded both as therapeutic measures and as means of spirit control in general. The 'theory' behind the cult is briefly this. There exists a wide variety of spirits (*aljannu*), some benevolent, others evil, each bearing a special name and character, and revealing itself in the particular gestures, gait and voice exhibited by the possessed person. Each spirit also has a tune and dance step peculiar to it, and one believes that the playing of the tune and the performance of the dance both evoke the spirit in normal individuals and placate and control it in those 'possessed'. Any person exhibiting the spirit-caused disorders is therefore placed under the observation of a cult member, who is expected to identify the spirit, and to placate and exorcise it. The latter act does not mean the final departure of the spirit; the aim is, rather, to bring the spirit 'visits' under control, so that they materialize only when evoked in the *bori* dances but do not otherwise threaten the human host. Each person so cured becomes a member of the *bori* cult; but many others will try to join it without this particular qualification, seeking the occasional trance induced in the *bori* dances. The *bori* cult thus has its own society, which is loosely organized (though it has a number of officials of varying rank) and is constantly enlarged through the inclusion of 'cured' patients and of those 'normal' individuals who have been successful in soliciting the 'spirit possession'.

There is no secrecy about the cult and its dance performances; they are staged at frequent intervals, both in private houses and in public, and are always watched by interested Nupe crowds. But no Nupe will join in the dances or has ever entered the society. Note that the cult thus rejected revolves upon a 'treatment' of mental derangements, of diseases, that is, for which Nupe therapeutic art admits to have no reliable remedy. Yet, though always ready to experiment with new cures, neither the Nupe public nor the medicine experts have been persuaded by the *bori*. Admittedly, the *bori* is not simply another cure or remedy: it involves the wholly strange experience of auto-suggestion and hysterical abandonment or ecstasis. It equally involves, on the intellectual plane, the acceptance of new premises (the detailed spirit universe). But as we shall see from our next example, a somewhat similar intellectual readjustment did in fact occur in the case of another alien cult and 'cure'.

(ii) *The Sogba Cult*

This cult occurs among a section of the Gwari who call themselves Gwari-Basa and live near Wushishi, to the north of Nupe, and also in a number of villages belonging to the conquered, Nupeized parts of Gwari country. Its name, *sogba*, means 'lightning', both in Gwari and Nupe. The cult is widely known also in other parts of Nupe country, and is everywhere regarded as alien, in spite of certain obvious 'Nupeisms'.[1] The name for the hereditary priest, for example, is *Žigi*, while the Gwari priests bear different names, and the whole cult is called a *kuti*, which is once more not Gwari nomenclature. In its more elaborate form the *sogba* cult culminates in an annual communal ceremony, fixed for the 2nd or 7th month, at which the men sacrifice a dog in great secrecy and the women sing and dance, carrying iron rods with bells closely resembling the *sãyi* of the *ndakó gboyá*.[2] The cult further includes a small-scale ritual of the movable type, performed by the priest at the request of clients, both fellow villagers and strangers.

These *ad hoc* ministrations are invoked for one of two reasons,

[1] It is not certain that the cult is in fact of Gwari origin; according to some informants it came originally from Yagba (a southern section of the Yoruba), and has been brought to Gwari and Nupe by immigrants from that country.

[2] This annual ritual was absent in the place I visited, Wushishi, its sketchy description being derived from verbal information only. The account that follows, however, is based on direct observation.

either to procure the fertility of childless women or to bring about the punishment of offenders, especially of thieves, whose identity is unknown. In either event a small payment in kolanuts and money is made to the priest. The ritual involves the use of a special cult object unknown in the rest of Nupe; it consists of a forked wooden post, cut from a certain tree in such a manner that it resembles a 'tree cut in two by lightning' and planted in the ground in the priest's house, either inside a hut or in the open. Around the foot of the post there are a number of flat, black, polished stones which are described as 'thunderbolts' (*sogba* or *sokógba*). Nothing is known about the origin of the stones save that some had been collected by the grandfather of the present priest and others inherited from more distant ancestors. The priest also owns a few of the bell-rods mentioned before and a *cigbe* shrine containing a nameless 'medicine'.

The client is made to sit in a hut away from the scene of the actual rite, which is executed by the priest and two assistants (his sons or brothers). The priest crouches in front of the forked post, his assistants standing on his right and left, each gripping one of the branches of the fork. The priest pours a little beer on the 'thunderbolts' and on the ground, and briefly and informally invokes the *kuti*, explaining the nature of the request. The operative phrase is—'*Sogba*, may the woman bear a child', or—'*Sogba*, may the evil person (for example, the thief) be killed'. If the aim of the rite is to procure childbirth, the priest afterwards goes to the woman, touches her with one of the bell-rods and gives her a little of the *cigbe*, which she must drink daily for four days. The barren woman will then hope to bear a child; and the person who had suffered injury at the hands of an unknown culprit will be assured that the latter will be killed by lightning—not at once or within a definite period, but surely some time in the future. The latter notion bears on a final duty of the *sogba* priest, which is to bury all persons killed by lightning and to perform the appropriate rites for these victims of divine punishment.

The children born after the intercession of the *kuti sogba* are tied to the cult for life. Immediately after the birth of the child the *Žigí* must be informed, so that he may in turn 'inform the *kuti*' by means of another sacrifice. Afterwards the *Žigí* presents the infant with a special charm in the form of a tiny dagger, which the child (and later the grown person) must always wear around the neck. Invariably, the child is given the name *Sogba*, and is generally referred to as *egi sogba*, 'child of *Sogba*'. If such a child falls ill, his parents will seek help, not from some other *kuti* or from professional medicine-men, but again from the *Žigí*, who does not charge for this further assistance: the child thus remains the responsibility of the *sogba* cult. Also, when such children grow up and marry they will as a matter of course invoke the *sogba* sacrifice, so that their union might be similarly blessed. The same idea, of the special protection enjoyed by *sogba* children, is expressed in this at first glance incongruous fashion: *sogba* children, even as adults, may help themselves with impunity to food and things of small value from any trader on the market. If we call this practice a 'licensed theft', we can see an oblique logical connection between this impunity and that other function of the cult, the punishment of thieves.

So much for the observances in the Gwari (or Nupe-Gwari) communities. The Nupe attitude towards the cult as such and towards the annual ceremonial is one of mild curiosity or indifference: they are, for the Nupe, merely the peculiar customs of 'foreigners'. Nor has the use of the *sogba* ritual for the purpose of inflicting supernatural punishment spread to the rest of the country. This may seem puzzling; for though the Nupe have their own ordeals to bring to justice criminals who deny their guilt, this method can only be applied when suspicion has already fastened upon a person; and though the Nupe possess their deadly *cigbe* against burglars and evil-wishers, these act merely as means of protection which must be acquired beforehand. As for the magic punishment of unknown offenders after the event, the supernatural armoury of Nupe appears to lack such means. Even so, this aspect of the *sogba* cult has not been utilized. I can suggest only this reason: such punishments after the event, placed within the power of the wronged person, come very close to personal vengeance; which is utterly foreign to the legal conceptions of the Nupe. As their elaborate judicial machinery precludes all secular self-help, so it would seem to preclude also this option of supernatural vengeance.

At the same time the Nupe in the neighbourhood of villages possessing the *sogba* cult claim that they now call in the *sogba* priest to bury persons killed by lightning. Since this obviously happens only rarely, the practice can have no great weight in the religious life of the people; nor can I be certain that it is followed regularly. Yet several Nupe sections, and not only those which have adopted this special burial custom, also share, if more vaguely, the Gwari belief that death by lightning may be a punishment for theft.[1] The Nupe who adopted the burial custom, then, have seized upon a religious practice which seemed to fit conveniently their own mystic ideas or fears.

The most thorough adoption concerns the use of the *sogba* ritual as a remedy for barrenness. Numerous Nupe women, from

[1] See above, p. 33.

communities all over the country, have made the pilgrimage to the nearest shrine and priest, and numerous persons, both young and old, bear the tell-tale name *Sogba*. The degree to which the alien cult has taken root is best seen from a text on the practices surrounding childbirth which I recorded in Bida long before I knew anything about the *sogba* cult, and which contains this straightforward statement:

'If a woman has no child and she is a pagan, she would go and visit the place of *sogba*, she would go and pray for a child. The pagans have a hut with a *kuti* inside. The priest will translate (talk to the *kuti*) on behalf of the woman or man who come to visit the *sogba*. The priest receives money from the person who comes. If God agrees and that person has a child, it will be named *Sogba*. It will wear a charm round his neck, everybody seeing that person will know that he is a child of *sogba*.'

The traditional religious or quasi-religious practices of Nupe certainly do not lack 'cures' of sterility. If here a further magic treatment has been added to the numerous existing ones, this would seem to bear out the ever-visible desire for children. Nor do the religious conceptions of the people, which so readily allow for alternative practices and several trials, conflict with the desire behind this addition. But let us note this. Though the Nupe make use only of one particular feature or benefit of the alien cult and disregard its wider context (of which, in fact, they are mostly ignorant), this piecemeal adoption yet commits them to a radically changed outlook. For they accept, with the miraculous powers of *sogba*, also the tie forged between these powers and the beneficiary. And this whole idea, that an ordinary person can for life be dedicated to a *kuti* and stand under its protection, has no parallel in Nupe religion. The practical consequences of this dedication are neither burdensome nor very important; even so, they clash with the conventional way of looking at 'medicines' or *ad hoc* rituals as at so many expedients, solicited when one needs them, paid for, and then forgotten.

(iii) *Yoruba Influences*

Yoruba religion, the third on our list, has hardly touched Nupe. The elaborate cosmology of the Yoruba, their pantheon, and their effigies or idols had no influence upon the beliefs and practices of the Nupe. Nor has the *gugu* cult of the Yoruba settlers in Nupe found any response other than detached or amused interest.

There seem to be two exceptions. The first is exemplified in the bronze figures on Jebba Island which have been accepted as sacred effigies and cult objects.[1] It is unlikely, incidentally, that these figures are Yoruba in origin; but they are of the same kind as the effigies of deities worshipped by the Yoruba. Now, the Nupe do not regard their figures as representations of deities; indeed the whole question, what or whom they represent, evokes no great interest. For the Nupe, the figures are merely 'likenesses' of a man and a woman (who is sometimes called the man's mother) and, more importantly, relics of Tsoede. Their possession is understood to be exceptional and indeed unique; and even though they figure prominently in one of the Jebba rituals, they do not add anything relevant to the purely religious conceptions. The images are simply the unusual objects of an unusual, 'royal' cult, but not more magically effective or possessed of special meaning because they happen to be shaped in human likeness.

The second exception is more important. In Mokwa and one or two villages in the river valley, we meet with a masked dance called *elo* (a meaningless word in Nupe), which is quite unlike any Nupe dance or ritual.[2] It does, however, somewhat resemble the Yoruba *gugu*, which equally occurs in Mokwa, not only in its paraphernalia but also in certain gestures and motions of the dancers. The *elo* dancers wear long-sleeved hoods of coloured cloth cut like those worn in the *gugu* and cover their faces with coloured wooden masks, carved in grotesquely human features and surmounted by horns. The masks resemble those of the *gugu* only in that both are meant to represent a human face; but in the *gugu* the design is produced by cowrie shells sewn on to the cloth, while the *elo* type is reminiscent rather of the masks used by the southernmost sections of the Yoruba, or by the Ibo and other tribes in Southern Nigeria. The people who perform the *elo* know little about the origin of the masks or, indeed, of the whole ceremonial. It is said that Tsoede brought it from the south and established it in certain villages of his small river kingdom 'because he liked the dance so much that he wanted to see it again and again'. The masks now used are the work of the wood-carvers of Shonga (a mixed Yoruba-Nupe village on the Niger), though this particular skill has since disappeared; one or two masks are quite recent, having been made by a craftsman at Rabah who has preserved the old art. The hoods of cloth, on the other hand, are an innovation; in the youth of one

---

[1] As has been mentioned, similar figures, though both smaller and cruder, are found in Tada, another riverain village. What is said here about the Jebba figures equally applies to the Tada 'idols'.

[2] I recorded the *elo* in Mokwa, in Rabah (a few miles away on the river) and in Gbajibo, north of Jebba. In addition, smaller villages and hamlets in the neighbourhood, which do not themselves possess the *elo* masks, perform the dance annually with masks borrowed from Mokwa.

of my Mokwa informants, a man of about sixty, the *elo* dancers used to wear skirts and cloaks made of dried grass, probably like those worn in the *mamma* ritual of Jebba; it was only later that the cloth hoods were adopted, 'because they looked nicer'. I have no doubt that they were modelled on the almost identical dress of the *gugu* dancers, with which the Mokwa people at least are so thoroughly familiar. They themselves disclaim any such connection, which is admittedly not borne out by any other features of the two cults.

Granting the alien origin of the *elo*, we must add that it has been fairly thoroughly Nupe-ized. To begin with, it has taken its place among the 'fixed' ceremonials, being performed annually in the 9th month (in Mokwa and Rabah) or 6th month (in Gbajibo). Like the other Nupe ceremonials, the *elo* is in the charge of one of the titled elders, whose office includes the responsibility for the annual performance and the tuition of the dancers. The most important mask, called *elokó* ('Great *elo*'), is also stored in his house, while the other masks and dresses are kept in the houses of other rankholders. When the masks appear in the dance they are addressed, in Nupe fashion, by a special salute, *eluló* ('Bird of *elo*'); the songs are in Nupe, the style of the music and most dance steps are typically Nupe, as are also the drums which are played throughout the dance.[1] But the dance performance itself has retained its uncommon character. All the dancers are men; but among them are three, wearing highly ornamented masks with curved twin horns, who are said to represent 'female' figures, the mask of the 'Great *elo*' belonging to this category. Two other dancers, wearing hoods pulled over their faces and head-dresses of feathers, are described as 'male'. Two more figures, wearing simple masks surmounted by one straight horn, are called *gara* (lit. 'robber'). These last figures are perhaps the most unusual; for while the 'male' and 'female' masks stalk about, or jump and dance much as do ordinary dancers or the masks in the *ndakó gboyá* and *mamma*, the *gara* plays the part of a bogey-man who frightens the children, and of a clown whose pranks delight old and young; which double role is otherwise unknown in Nupe dance ceremonial. The behaviour of the 'male' and 'female' masks, incidentally, is in no way suggestive of this ascription of sex. In addition, there are two unmasked young men who join in the dancing and clowning and wear fringed skirts made of leopard skin, their bare legs being painted with white spots ('like the spots of leopards')—another conspicuously non-Nupe feature.

The most incongruous aspect of the *elo* lies in its purpose, or

[1] The *elo* includes only one musical instrument uncommon in Nupe, an iron double-bell, beaten with a stick.

rather in its absence of purpose. Although it has a definite date like other rituals and although the masks must dress in secrecy, there is nothing sacred about the performance. No sacrifice or ritual preparations precede or accompany it; and the *elo* is positively stated to be nothing like a *kuti*, but merely *dzodzo*, 'play'. The dance seems to contain the remnants of some plot or dramatic theme; the various roles of 'male' and 'female' figures and of 'clowns' or 'robbers' can suggest nothing else. But again, the people deny that there is such a plot or that these 'roles' have any meaning. The *elo* songs, certainly, betray none. Here are a few of them, each consisting of a brief line which is endlessly repeated throughout the corresponding phase of the dance.

> *Zwákule, zwákule* (meaningless).
> I am calling Kolo (a name, here applied to *elo*),
> he is coming slowly.
> The *elo* matures every year.
> They are calling Kolo, he swings his leg,
> *ebi du, ebi du* (meaningless).
> Every year we are making *elo*.
> The *gara* appears, there is his face.

In a sense, the *elo* is a mixture of ritual and entertainment. But unlike the usual Nupe ceremonial, in which the ritual part precedes the 'play', the *elo* involves ritual only as it were in its administration (in the fixed date, the secret dressing-up of the actors, the formal apportionment of relevant duties); the rest is pure entertainment. Perhaps, in its original form, the *elo* was more fully a ceremonial, with some religious purpose as well as a plot. But even this the Nupe would deny; for although they sanctify the practice by ascribing it, in familiar manner, to the ancestor king, they impute to him no reasons other than (we might say) aesthetic ones. Nor have these reasons quite ceased to work. At the Bida *salla* in 1936 I saw a dancer with an unusual headdress which I had never seen before, neither at the previous *salla* nor on other occasions. The dancer himself was one of the *sorogi* dancers mentioned in a previous context;[1] but on his head he wore a brass cap with two horns. Subsequent enquiries elicited the fact that the headdress had been made by a Bida brass-smith to the specifications of the dancer: and the latter had meant to copy the horns of the *elo* masks which he had seen and admired in Mokwa.

(iv) *The Gani of Kutigi*

I have elsewhere described this cult and the manner in which it took root in Kutigi and the adjacent communities, so that I need

[1] See above, p. 188.

only summarize the salient facts.[1] Unlike the *elo*, the *gani* can clearly be traced to its alien origin, and its importation into Nupe, by Moslem immigrants from the north, can even be dated with fair accuracy (having occurred probably about 1760–70). The Moslem character of the ceremonial is visible, above all, in the esoteric part, which takes the form of a symbolic burial in the Mohammedan manner; it is further emphasized by the often voiced claim that the whole ceremonial represents an observance of Islam, namely, the celebration of the birthday of the Prophet—a claim which has little validity.[2] Even so, the *gani* has been firmly adopted also by the pagan population and, what is more important, has been adopted as a ritual or at least as a ceremonial of serious and sacred import. Yet in calling the *gani* a ritual or ceremonial I am stating my own conclusions, couched in our conventional terminology. The Nupe have no suitable name for this performance which has many aspects of a ritual act without conforming to a 'ritual' as the pagans understand it. They all emphasize that it is not a *kuti*; but neither do they call it *dzodzo*, mere 'play', in spite of the great scope given to mummery, display, crude pranks, and merry-making generally. They either use the non-committal term *nya'nya*, 'dancing', or simply argue that 'the *gani* is the *gani*', that is, unlike any other tribal festivity. Linguistic usage, it seems, has not quite caught up with this novel and ambiguous species of ceremonial.

The *gani* ceremonial has for its main theme the periodical reconstitution of the village age-grade associations, that is, the acceptance of novices into the first grade and the promotion of older boys and youths to higher grades. These corporate promotions go hand in hand with a reshuffling of the various ranks held in each age-grade association, and hence with an upgrading or downgrading of its members. If the age grades thus appear dominated by competition and the notions of rank and career, they merely mirror as well as anticipate interests paramount in Nupe political life. As I phrased it elsewhere, age-grade life serves as an 'education for citizenship';[3] and this aspect too is given expression in the *gani* ceremonial, together with other ideas of more general import, bearing on growth and maturity.

In the ceremonial each age grade is assigned a specific role, acting under its leader, who bears the title *Ndakotsu*—'Grandfather of

[1] See 'The Gani Ritual of Nupe', *Africa*, vol. XIX, 1949.
[2] This is clearly shown by the discrepancy in the dates. The Birth of the Prophet (*Ma'ulid*) falls on the twelfth day of the first lunar month of the Mohammedan calendar (in 1934 the 29th March), while the *gani* celebrabrations start on the tenth day of the 4th month in Nupe reckoning (in 1934, the 25th June).
[3] See *A Black Byzantium*, pp. 383 *et seq.*

the king'. Thus led, the age grades walk in procession through the village to salute the chief and all the other notables of the community, join in the dancing, engage in wrestling matches, and meet one another in a realistic 'battle', to be described presently. The esoteric rite of the *gani*, the 'burial service' mentioned before, is performed by the leaders alone, in a secret place away from the scene of the public festivities. The younger boys are all dressed up as girls and imitate, in exaggerated and ridiculous fashion, the walk and dance steps of the women. This masquerade, though highly elaborate and considered a most relevant aspect of the celebration, is not further explained; but the context makes it clear that it carries the same meaning of a change of roles which underlies the similar mummery of the *gunnu*.[1] For this meaning is again expressed, now by means of a conspicuous symbolism which everyone understands, in certain other episodes of the *gani*, meant to dramatize the admission of the novices and the various promotions from grade to grade. There is the 'death and burial', loudly mourned by the crowd, of a 'little girl', indicating the abandonment of infancy by the young boys about to enter the first grade. In a preceding phase a 'little boy' is similarly buried and mourned, that is, shown to abandon boyhood for adolescence. Lastly, the youths of the most senior grade appear dressed up as 'warriors' and 'horsemen', meeting their juniors in a mock battle which seems to symbolize the final stage of adolescence, when youth must hold its own against adults, compete and struggle with them, and break into their ranks. All these things actually happen in the 'battle', whose very realism seems symbolic of the severe competition for position and power which characterizes Nupe life. In brief, the *gani* ceremonial is a typical *rite de passage*, dramatizing the crucial phases of male adolescence and adoption into manhood. Seen against this background, an unusual feature of the *gani*, too, falls into place. Obscene sexual jokes and allusions, normally never used, appear in the *gani* songs and are freely bandied about during the festivities, both by old and young: we may conclude that they serve to throw into relief a final aspect of adolescence, sexual maturity.

The ceremonial lasts three days, and each day concludes with a hectic dance in which the sexes meet in utterly unrestrained fashion. Nor does this unrestraint end with the dance; for during the three nights all the normal rules of sex morality are in abeyance. This temporary abandonment of moral restraint, which applies to every person in the community, implies, of course, more than merely a symbolic reference to adolescence and sexual maturity. It represents one of those periodical concessions to moral

[1] See above, p. 113.

or sexual licence which are familiar from many societies, primitive and advanced. We know that they occur also in the traditional annual celebration of the *gunnu*. And here it seems significant that the people of Kutigi and the other communities now performing the *gani* have abandoned the *gunnu* in this fixed, annual form.[1] Whatever other reasons have contributed to the abandonment of the annual *gunnu*, the fact that it shared with the *gani* this one feature may well have been decisive; for it would seem to be in the very nature of this concession to unrestraint that it must not be duplicated.

There is evidence to show that the sexual licence belonged to the *gani* already in its original form in which it reached Nupe country. This original *gani* equally included some connection, apparently broad and unspecific, with age-grade life and male adolescence.[2] To some extent, then, the Nupe found in the *gani* a cult fortuitously congenial to their own interests and ideas. But let us note that the *gani* expresses them with unaccustomed sharpness: the masquerade of boys as girls, sketchily treated in the *gunnu*, is fully exploited in the *gani*; and nowhere else is age-grade life dramatized with such effect.

Other 'Nupeisms' in the *gani* are clearly the result of adaptation and remodelling. Thus, though the ceremonial retained its original name, its songs and prayers are in Nupe; the latter, spoken at the secret 'burial service', conclude with the typical Nupe formula— 'May the whole town have health'; the musical instruments, the music itself, the dance steps, and the whole design of the ceremonial, with an esoteric part preceding the public 'merry-making' —all these are taken from the traditional practice. Yet equally, the *gani* contains conspicuously novel and 'un-Nupe' features. The very notion of a ceremonial having a proper plot and being staged as a drama with consecutive scenes has no parallel in Nupe. The same is true of the precise symbolism of the *gani* and of the masquerade of warriors and horsemen; the latter, incidentally, appear as riders of hobby-horses, which mummery is equally unknown in the rest of Nupe. So are the standards with which the age grades parade during the ceremonial, some of which are combined with crude symbols of the sexes. The open eroticism of the *gani*, finally, contrasts strikingly with the normal mood of Nupe ceremonials.

[1] See above, p. 83. It will be remembered that the performance of the *gunnu* as a movable rite (which is still practised in Kutigi) does not include the 'mixed' dance and the period of erotic licence.

[2] The evidence in question is based on accounts of the *gani* celebrations in its country of origin and among the nomadic Fulani. See *Africa*, vol. XIX, 1949, p. 177, n. 2.

Let me stress that the 'congenial' aspects of the *gani* did not cause it to be simply accepted into the ceremonial repertoire of Nupe; nor do its 'uncongenial' features represent merely unassimilated remnants. In a sense both such a straightforward acceptance and complete assimilation were precluded by the circuitous manner in which the *gani* was adopted and which was meant to preserve rather than to obliterate its alien character. Here I must explain that the community where the *gani* took root represents, on a small scale, a composite or 'plural' society. It is composed of three distinct sections—the Bornu immigrants (called *Benu*); a group of hereditary hunters (*ndaceži*); and a group claiming the status of aboriginal inhabitants and calling themselves 'Owners of the Land' (*kintsoži*). In this heterogeneous community the alien provenance of the *gani* ceremonial remained intact; its esoteric rites are performed only by members of the immigrant group, and the whole *gani* is still, for the people of Kutigi, an observance unequivocally 'belonging to' or 'owned' by that section, even though all others join in the public celebrations. They in turn remained the owners' of their own traditional cults, the *žikinta* (performed by the group of hunters) and the *gunnu* (performed, as a movable rite, by the *kintsoži*). But in performing its proper ceremonial each congregation acts on behalf of the whole composite community; and all three ceremonials are considered indispensable, in a supernatural sense and in their diverse ways, for the well-being of that wider group. The *gani*, therefore, came to be adopted, not through simply diffusing to the other sections, but through being acknowledged by them as a vital contribution which its 'owners' can make to the common weal. The sectional 'ownership', in other words, was transformed into a sectional 'task', and the divided congregation, into a religious division of labour.[1]

It is clear that this manner of adoption is adjusted to the particular problems of a 'plural society', helping to maintain or buttress its precarious, divided unity. And other societies, facing the same problems, have evolved much the same solution. Yet though the religious division of labour has this very wide application, it may be pointed out that, in Nupe, it remains 'congenial' to the character of the religious system; for it only develops further the ideas underlying Nupe priestship and the Nupe form of ritual, 'owned' by kin groups but operating for the 'common weal'.

[1] Let me note briefly that the same conception reappears, somewhat modified, in the attitude of the Nupe people at large towards the *gani*, which they regard as the 'possession' of the people of Kutigi. This aspect, which has been fully treated in the article mentioned above, is not relevant to the present discussion.

2. ON MOTIVES

We turn to our crucial problem, the motives underlying these adoptions and rejections of alien observances. Since in our examples both responses were voluntary, not imposed by extraneous pressure or constraint, we may legitimately argue that the acceptance must have rested upon some appeal, some kind of pull, which the novel practice exercised upon the recipients-to-be, and the rejection upon the lack of such an appeal or perhaps its opposite. This 'appeal' or 'pull' is clearly a complex thing. First and foremost, it is a pull of interest; in other words, we may search for some specific interest or 'need' pre-existing in the recipient culture, which the novel practice seems capable (or incapable) of satisfying.[1] The relevant factor, however, is not the pre-existing interest or need as such, but a residual interest or need; what we must show is not so much that the society is deeply concerned over such-and-such issues (for example, the fecundity of women) but that this concern is unsatisfied even where it is met by pre-existing institutions. The *gugu* ceremonial, for example, answers interests strongly pronounced in Nupe life in the fixed rituals promising communal well-being, and in the ritualization of death; but since a series of traditional ceremonials profess the same aims, the residual interest must be small, if it is felt at all. The concern over childbirth, on the other hand, is by its nature such that it would always remain active and press for additional promises or safeguards.

The concern or aim of the alien observance may obviously be expressed in a form more or less novel and unprecedented; and the degree of novelty must clearly itself affect the ease of adoption. But this effect is difficult to assess. Often, we shall no doubt argue that, the more novel a practice, the more uncongenial must it be to people still thinking in terms of traditional ways of acting; so that the novelty would act as a brake upon the free play of interests, as a counter-pull as it were. Yet we cannot exclude the possibility that the novelty of the practice will help rather than hinder the adoption; for its 'uncongenial' form may itself correspond to some pre-existing interest, that is, to a diffuse desire for unusual and unprecedented experiences. Now all the alien religious practices which the Nupe have adopted contain some 'uncongenial' or unprecedented features. Shall we then say that the latter must have exercised a certain appeal in their own right? Perhaps—though

[1] The term 'pre-existing' is here used in a somewhat loose sense, without the implication of precise chronological evidence. It implies, however, that the interest or need in question can be established independently, that is, can be shown to obtain apart from the adopted (or rejected) practice.

the same lack of congeniality also characterizes the practices which have been rejected. Or shall we assume that, for the adoption to occur, the pre-existing interest must have outweighed the uncongenial character, while in the case of rejected practices the balance was the other way? There is evidence for this. The *gani*, with all its alien elements, clearly answers powerful pre-existing interests, and indeed improves upon the respective traditional institutions; the *gugu*, conversely, has nothing of the kind to offer: it is only another fixed ritual, duplicating the aims of the traditional rites, so that, apart from being uncongenial in form, it also appears redundant in content. The *bori* could answer at least a weak pre-existing need, since it offers a cure for lunacy of which the Nupe are deficient; yet it also clashes utterly with their religious beliefs and, above all, with the psychological tenor of their religious life. The *sogba* cult seems to exemplify this balance between interest and congeniality even more clearly. For the Nupe adopted only that aspect of it which corresponds to a strongly pronounced and in a sense inexhaustible interest (in fecundity), while rejecting both the annual ceremonial, whose aims seem redundant, and the *sogba* ordeal, which was altogether alien to the pre-existing aims or interests. Much the same is true of the bronze figures of Tsoede, which were embodied in Nupe ritual only as emblems of kingship, without any of the features normally implicit in the worship of 'idols'.

Let us be clear that this assessment of a balance between interests and congeniality holds only with two provisos. First, it is largely based on *ex post facto* arguments. The *gani*, for example, fits a 'pre-existing need' only in the form in which it exists today. If we judge this affinity of interest to be sufficiently great to have outweighed the uncongenial features we do so because in the event the latter proved no insuperable obstacle; but we cannot be certain how much remodelling, of content and purpose as well as of form, has gone into the acceptance. Nor can we say that the *bori* or *gugu* would have proved incapable of such remodelling. All we can really say is that no such attempts have been made. Have they not been made because there was no sufficiently strong interest to make the effort worthwhile? Again we can only answer—perhaps; for the *elo* would seem to contradict this argument. There, an uncongenial practice has been fitted into Nupe life for no apparent 'need' at all, unless we are prepared to consider the addition of a pleasurable (and novel) occasion a felt 'need'. And if we do so, the mummery of the *gugu* and the unusual dance of the *bori* would seem similarly acceptable.

Secondly, our arguments hold only if other factors in the situation can safely be neglected; and of one of these, the relationship between the potential donors and recipients, this cannot be assumed *ab initio*. Rather, this factor must be added as a likely third determinant of adoption or rejection. Surveying our data from this new angle we meet with a wide variety of situations. The *elo*, the Tsoede 'idols', and the *sogba* cult were adopted strictly from outside, without any corresponding fusion or integration of the 'owners' with the recipient groups. But here a further distinction must be drawn: while the Tsoede idols and the *elo* were taken over from fully distinct and in fact unknown donors, the *sogba* was found among neighbours and was 'taken over' only in the sense in which people turn to some promising, if otherwise unfamiliar, place of pilgrimage. Furthermore, the 'owners' of the *sogba* cult, viewed with Nupe eyes, occupied the inferior position of a conquered 'slave' population. Perhaps, then, the barrier of status was readily overcome only in the case of the fertility ritual, with its strong affinity of interest, while in the case of the other aspects of the cult it added to the 'counter-pulls' which made for their rejection.

The *gani*, *gugu*, and *bori* represent observances adopted or rejected in circumstances which involved the fusion or integration of donor and recipient groups. But again, the conditions differ in relevant respects. The Bornu and Yoruba immigrants arrived *en bloc*, maintained themselves as compact groups, and were thus integrated, as segments, in the host communities; the Hausa colony in the cosmopolitan city grew haphazardly, as the result of the irregular immigration of individuals of all classes and occupations, and never achieved internal cohesion; it only fused amorphously with the host community, but was not integrated in it. The kind of adoption, therefore, which turned the *gani* into a 'sectional task' was neither feasible nor called for in the case of the *bori*. It might, on the other hand, conceivably have worked in the case of the Yoruba ritual, even though this cult answers no 'residual' need. But here we must consider that the Yoruba came to Nupe, not as immigrants claiming equal status (as did the Benu), nor yet as free immigrants, but as prisoners of war freed and settled by royal command. Whatever the effect of the other 'pulls' in this rank-conscious society, the barrier of status must have weighed heavily on the side of rejection. Admittedly, it did so effectively only as regards the cult as such; minor features, such as the dress of the dancers which reappears in the *elo*, were adopted across the barrier, for their aesthetic attraction and novelty. Yet the barrier has at least prevented this 'borrowing' being acknowledged.

In brief, the acceptance or rejection of the alien observances involves the efficacy of several conditions and results from their varying combination and interplay. I have tried to tabulate the relevant data in the form of a synoptic chart capable of exhibiting the multiple correlations. The features listed are those discussed above, plus and minus signs indicating their presence and absence respectively. I also attempted to grade the interests satisfied by the various cults by doubling the plus signs in the appropriate cases; a similar grading of 'congeniality' seemed irrelevant in the light of the final result.

	(I) Integration of donors and recipients	(SD) Status distinction operating against donors	(C) Congeniality of form	(SI) Satisfaction of interest	Outcome
bori	−	±	−	+ (as therapeutic measure)	Rejection
gugu	+	+	−	+? (pleasurable novelty)	Rejection
gani	+	−	−	++	Adoption
sogba (fertility cult)	−	+	−	++	Adoption
(general cult)	−	+	−	−	Rejection
elo	−	−	−	+? (pleasurable novelty)	Adoption
Tsoede idols	−	−	−	++	Adoption

In other words, adoption (of a voluntary kind) occurred when

$$I^{\pm} \ldots SD^{\pm} \ldots C^{-} \ldots SI^{++}$$

and when

$$I^{-} \ldots SD^{-} \ldots C^{-} \ldots SI^{+}.$$

That a strong interest should outweigh the absence of congeniality and render the factor of integration irrelevant is hardly surprising; but it is puzzling that this should be true also where the interest appears to be small and even uncertain (as in the *elo*). Perhaps, then, we have underrated the residual 'need'? If so, it must have sprung from some inadequacy in the pleasures and excitements afforded in the pre-existing situation. Although this assumption cannot, for obvious reasons be fully substantiated, it is not altogether unwarranted. Mokwa and the other communities practising the *elo* are in fact poor in ceremonials offering, apart from occasions for worship, also the purely pleasurable stimulations of dancing, singing, and conviviality; for while most Nupe communities have two or three ceremonials of this kind, Mokwa has only one apart from the *elo*—the *gunnu*,—the remaining rituals being sober esoteric sacrifices, unaccompanied by music, dancing, and public 'merry-making'.[1] We mentioned in a previous context that the number of fixed ceremonials is fairly uniform throughout Nupe;[2] we may now add that the proportion of ceremonials of such combined appeal is similarly uniform. This I take to indicate that the Nupe need for regular pleasurable stimulations has as it were found its own level. Which would mean, further, that Mokwa and the other communities were only balancing a psychological deficit when they adopted the *elo*. Certainly, several of the communities which exhibit the normal Nupe level of ceremonial-*cum*-pleasurable occasions had an equal chance of embracing the *elo* or of copying the similar *gugu*, but have not done so. So that the adoption, by a few groups, of the alien ceremonial for no motive other than that of adding another festivity did yet answer an unsatisfied 'need'.

But let us note a final source of error. We have spoken of the 'pre-existing' interests or needs as though they were bound to be constant, the measure of their satisfaction alone being variable. It is conceivable that this assumption is unwarranted, and that the adoption of the new observance reflects, not a pre-existing interest unsatisfied, but an interest strengthened owing to some change in social conditions. As regards the *elo* and *sogba*, there is no evidence to support this alternative hypothesis. It is, however, borne out in the case of the *gani*. This ceremonial, as I put it before, improves upon the traditional Nupe institutions which ritualize adolescence and age-grade life; it dramatizes these events in a specific and detailed manner where the equivalent traditional ceremonial, the *gunnu*, merely deals summarily with the transition from youth to adulthood, embodying it as one aspect among others in its design. Now, though the age grades have undoubtedly always served to mirror the dominant interests of Nupe life, in rank and in promotion in status, the interests themselves must have gained in

---

[1] The same is true of Rabah, though there Mohammedan influence has today obliterated the *gunnu*. Gbajibo, the third community practising the *elo*, has two other ceremonials which combine religious with generally pleasurable stimulations, the *gunnu* and the *mamma*; but the latter is celebrated in secrecy, by the men alone, and only as a movable ritual.

[2] See above, p. 70.

importance with the growth of the Fulani Emirate. As the latter gave greater impetus to desires for a political career and imparted greater severity to the competition for rank and status, so the age grades assumed a novel, and more weighty, significance. With this, the fuller and more specific ritual elaboration of adolescence seems entirely consistent. It was not so that the pre-existing desire to give ritual elaboration to important things had been inadequately expressed; rather, things became important in a new way: so that, when the Nupe adopted the *gani* ceremonial, they were seizing upon a chance to express a changed outlook and a desire reoriented.

As we shall see, the more far-reaching conversion to Islam similarly involves such changing interests and newly emerged trends. Are then, perhaps, any trends visible in Nupe today which may in future lead to further adoptions of alien practices? I will hazard this prediction. The pressure of competition and the obsession with promotion in status, grown strongest in the capital, are visibly leading to anxieties and frustrations, and to mental instability. The incidence of neurotic disorders seems to bear out this tendency, though inadequate records forbid a more definite statement.[1] The mass hysteria of the witchcraft trial mentioned before offers clearer evidence. Such increased tensions may well seek relief in some form of self-abandonment: the *bori* possession cult seems to offer precisely this chance, which might one day be seized upon, its 'uncongenial' appeal notwithstanding.

3. THE CHARACTER OF TRIBAL RELIGION

The preceding discussion referred only to the adoption of isolated practices and items of belief but made no mention of individuals or communities wholly converted to an alien pagan creed. Nor is this unexpected. The religions of pre-literate peoples are not normally of a proselytizing kind. They promise no particular reward to the converted, nor do they place any premium on the conversion of others. Indeed, it seems true to say that this issue never arises, for, as we anticipated, primitive religion is essentially a tribal or national religion, conceived of as inseparable from the particular identity of the group professing it. Expressed differently, primitive religion does not constitute a 'church' which exists in its own right and can be entered (or left) solely by reason of its creed and of the transcendental benefits promised to the believers.[2]

---

[1] See *A Black Byzantium*, p. 402.

[2] Durkheim's famous identification of 'religion' (of any form) with a 'church' seems to me to rest on an arbitrary use of the latter term; for whatever else may be meant by a 'church', it must mean 'a community organized

No machinery therefore exists to deal with such contingencies—no provision for tuition of the converts-to-be, and no formal procedure of admission or perhaps excommunication. To say it again, that sum-total of beliefs and practices we call Nupe, Yoruba, or Gwari religion, is simply the religion of the people who, on other grounds also, call themselves Nupe, Yoruba, or Gwari; and though it is possible for single observances or even items of belief (such as the belief in the significance of death by lightning) to be adopted or 'borrowed', the notion that the religion as a whole can be exported or changed for another is inconceivable.

This self-sufficiency of the Nupe faith goes together with a marked detachment and tolerance towards other creeds. The Nupe, as we know, are greatly interested in discussing the religions of others; but they do so dispassionately, and indeed think it possible that the radically different beliefs of their neighbours are justifiable and, in a vague sense, as 'right' as their own. The co-existence of widely varying practices in Nupe itself must have helped in fostering this tolerance towards alien beliefs; certainly, any person showing such tolerance is not for that reason considered an apostate or even a doubter. The Nupe creed simply lays little claim to any exclusive possession of spiritual truth. Yet it is not for that reason less securely held. If the Nupe do not argue that their creed is the best of all possible creeds, neither do they question that, for them, it is simply given, as is their language and all the other features that go with 'being a Nupe'. Their detached tolerance thus seems only the obverse of this self-sufficiency of 'tribal' religions.

The fact that alien observances are sometimes adopted for their apparent utility or some other attraction is not felt to be inconsistent with this notion of a 'given' tribal religion; at least, the inconsistency is corrected by tacitly granting that alien practices could yet 'become Nupe', that is, could be added to those which, at that stage, were indicative of the social identity. The accomplished fact, then, re-establishes the *status quo*; the new religious practice, now regularly executed by a population which by numerous other criteria regards itself as one, as 'the Nupe', becomes itself 'of Nupe'; so that the people can again detachedly view 'alien' observances or beliefs. Let me restate this in more general terms. The conscious identity of Nupe, as of any society, comes from the awareness of a large stable array of modes of behaviour understood to be typical of the society; any single

by officials into an institution which bestows gifts of grace' (on all who seek it), which makes 'the sacred generally 'accessible', and under whose authority members can be 'enrolled' (see Max Weber, 'The Social Psychology of the World Religions', *Essays in Sociology*, p. 288).

change in this array does not alter the continued consciousness of identity, but is subsumed in it.

This is, of course, a familiar situation, which ultimately accounts for the continuity (or continued self-awareness) of societies even when their cultural possessions, or for that matter their populations, change. Much will depend on the gradualness and restricted scope of the change; a sudden change in which new modes of behaviour greatly outweigh the 'array' of pre-existing ones may disrupt the continued identity. But it need not always do so. For the process just outlined may also be reversed: the society facing such far-reaching changes may yet fasten on to some particular cultural possession which remained unchanged, and consider it sufficiently relevant to furnish a criterion or symbol of the continued identity. Often, as we know, a creed or some religious observance preserved amidst the changes will prove to have this relevance.

This process, too, can be observed among the Nupe, among the colony of emigrants in Lagos, who have lost nearly every feature of culture, including language, which would normally sustain that awareness of 'being Nupe' or 'still being Nupe'. But they have preserved one traditional cult, the *gunnu*; and they still regard themselves as Nupe (calling themselves either Nupe or, more often, Takpa or Tapa, by the Yoruba name). The two things go together; in discussions, when the people wish to emphasize their tribal identity, they at once mention the possession of this cult which, to them, seems decisive.

Let me say a few words about the Nupe colony in Lagos. It numbers perhaps 5,000 people, both scattered over the outlying hamlets and villages and occupying a special quarter in the city of Lagos.[1] The Nupe settlement is claimed to be of considerable antiquity, going back to the Portuguese era, and to have attained its present important and honoured position towards the end of the last century, when the self-made head of the Lagos Nupe, a certain Gana and a 'noted warrior', was elevated to high rank by the Yoruba town king. This Gana, who incidentally was taken to England to be presented to Queen Victoria, was the grandfather of the present chief of the Lagos Nupe, a man of about seventy. Gana's rank, *Osode*, is still held by his descendants, and with the rank goes the priestship of the *gunnu*, which Gana had somehow assumed. The Lagos *gunnu* is a combination of three rites all subsumed under the same name, the *gunnu* itself, the *ndakó gboyá*, and the ritual of the Chain of Tsoede, the paraphernalia of the three

[1] The Nupe quarter in Lagos is known to everyone; its main thoroughfares are called *Tapa Street* and *Osode Street*, the latter deriving its name from the title held by the head of the Nupe colony (see below).

rites being stored in the 'House of Osode'. Here, too, the crucial ceremonials take place. For though each Nupe hamlet or village in Lagos Colony performs its own rites and several of them possess their own paraphernalia, the ceremonial in the 'House of Osode' comes first and gives the signal for the other performances. Thus the scattered groups of immigrants are held together through being mobilized in the common religious activity, while the Nupe in Lagos Town form a single congregation in the strict sense of the word. The religious rites thus preserved are therefore more than merely a symbol of tribal identity: they also make this identity concretely effective, that is, turn a group aware of itself into one effectively co-operating, if only on one, crucial and impressive occasion.

As regards the rites themselves, they are full of distortions and unorthodox innovations, due partly to the adaptation of the cult to the urban conditions and partly to genuine misunderstandings, linguistic and otherwise.[1] Yoruba influence, too, is visible, in certain anthropomorphisms which have crept into the interpretation of the *ndakó gboyá*. Altogether, the latter has come to overshadow completely the *gunnu* rites proper: the masks, of which there are seven, are now of two kinds, tall ones representing 'fathers', and smaller ones representing 'sons'; while the *ndakó gboyá* as such, far from being understood as an impersonal force, is positively stated to be a male spirit, and is even given a 'wife', symbolized by an upturned pot half-buried in the ground.

But not all the innovations represent merely errors or distortions of a fortuitous and unwitting kind. Three in particular express the new significance attaching to this ceremonial of a group in exile. First, the cult society of the *ndakó gboyá* has been remodelled into a secret society in the strict sense of the word, rigidly organized, and having its lodges in every Nupe village on the coast. Its head is the *Osode*; its members must be Nupe by paternal descent; and initiation is both difficult and expensive, though once it is achieved it remains hereditary. For the people, the *ndakó gboyá* society is unequivocally, and impressively, a piece of 'Nupedom'. If it is difficult to enter the society, this only means that it has come to represent something like an inner ring or élite among those who can call themselves Nupe; and if the *ndakó gboyá* society is now so planned that it includes every Nupe settlement and perpetuates itself by hereditary succession, this makes it another support of tribal identity.

[1] Thus the dance of the young men is called *gunnu ba*, which really means 'place of the *gunnu*', and the courtyard where the esoteric part of the rite takes place is called *kuso*, 'bush'.

We must note, secondly, that all the Lagos Nupe, without exception, are today Moslems. Oddly enough, they claim to be good Moslems, even though they openly and proudly 'own' the *gunnu* and the other pagan rites. Yet the people see no conflict between the faith they now profess and their adherence to the pagan cults. The two are kept in separate compartments: the Moslem faith belongs to the present; the pagan observances are a token of a past one wishes to continue: they simply go with remaining a Nupe. And if the pagan observances are also supernaturally effective, this seems almost incidental to that other, more relevant, import, of offering occasions to act as Nupe.

Finally, when the Lagos Nupe perform the public episodes of their cults, they do so in the same circumstances in which the alien enclaves in Nupe country stage their religious observances. The *gunnu* and *ndakó gboyá* are watched with keen interest by the whole native population of Lagos; above all, the Nupe 'owners' of the ceremonials are expected to perform them for the well-being of 'the whole town', including the Yoruba, and occasionally at the request of the Yoruba town chief, if some calamity (for example, witchcraft) threatens the population. Here, then, we meet with the exact counterpart of that 'religious division of labour' which turned a cult alien in Nupe into a contribution to the common weal. But the conception of the 'common weal' has been significantly widened; for the prayer formula of the Lagos ceremonials contains a new phrase—'May the whole of Nupe country prosper'. This is clearly a further expression of that 'awareness of social identity', kept alive by a tribe in exile; indeed, no more convincing expression can be conceived than this concern with the welfare of the distant mother country.

4. CONCLUSIONS

The absence, in Nupe, of complete conversions to an alien creed has a notable exception in the steady expansion of Islam. Paradoxically, though the Nupe in strange parts preserve their traditional religion because it is so much the symbol of tribal identity, in Nupe country itself that religion is disappearing. And unlike the Lagos Moslems, who keep Islam and the traditional observances apart, the Nupe in their own country have accepted 'conversion' in all its implications, including the rejection of the earlier creed. Perhaps this is no paradox. For while the emigrants have only their religion to fall back on if they wish to prove to themselves that they are still Nupe, in their own country this issue does not arise. There, Nupe social identity is still sustained by that wider 'stable array' of social facts—unbroken occupation of the same territory; political autonomy; and numerous norms of behaviour and types of relationship.

With all this the next chapter will deal. Let me here only explain an apparent omission; if this discussion made no mention of that other religion demanding complete conversion, Christianity, the reason is, simply, the unimportance of Christianity in Nupe life. The number of converts is extremely small and the progress of Christianity insignificant. The Nupe generally are not hostile to those who have become Christians; they do not subject them to special disabilities; nor do they despise them; only mallams will sometimes call Christians, contemptuously, *káfiri*, 'unbelievers'. Here, too, the general attitude is one of tolerance, though it is more pronounced among pagans than among Moslems. The former (including nominal Moslems) quite often send their children to mission schools, and most Nupe keep on friendly terms with missionaries or African evangelists. But this tolerance always goes with the conviction that Christian missionizing will remain ineffectual; friendliness with Christians is unobjectionable only because it is of no consequence. Nor do the Nupe ever commit themselves by their association with Christians. They do not intermarry with Christian converts; they do not ask them to their family feasts; and the converts never come from solid, stable families, but from among unattached individuals—old people without relations, young orphans, or the children of strangers. Even among these, I was told, apostasy often occurs in later life. And here it is not the pagan religion which is the greatest rival of Christianity, but the steadily encroaching Islam.

VIII

ISLAM IN NUPE

1. THE CONVERSION TO ISLAM

IF the pagan religions surrounding Nupe lack the features essential to complete conversion, Islam has them all. It is a proselytizing and super-national creed; it is embodied in a church; it provides for the requisite tuition and for special procedures of admission; also, the conversion to the new, non-tribal, religion went together with a significant restructuring of the society so converted.

The historical background of the Islamization of Nupe is fairly clear. According to Nupe tradition, the fifteenth king after the mythical Tsoede, Jibiri, who reigned about 1770, was the first to adopt Islam. But the names of even earlier rulers seem to indicate Mohammedan influence (Abdu Waliyi, 1679–1700, Ibrahim, 1713–17, Abubakari Kolo, 1742–6). Towards the end of the eighteenth century, under Etsu Ma'azū, the impact of Islam had gained both in strength and purpose. It was then that Mallam Dendo came to Nupe as an emissary of the Fulani Emir of Gwando, entrusted with the double task of spreading Islam and of paving the way for the Fulani conquest, which was itself a phase in the Holy War that had been raised in the north of Nigeria. Even before Mallam Dendo's arrival, apparently, it had become customary to include mallams among the court officials of the Nupe kings, as diviners, chaplains, and advisers on matters spiritual and secular. Dendo filled this role with great efficiency, so great that he soon became the actual ruler of the kingdom. Aided by other mallams and agents of the new regime, and by a mercenary army officered by Mohammedans, he effected the overthrow of the old dynasty and turned Nupe kingdom into a vassal state of the Fulani Empire whose supreme head, the Emir of Sokoto, styled himself *Sarkin Muslmi*—'King of the Moslems'. From then onwards, Islam became the official religion, not only of royalty, but of the state, spreading through all the channels of bureaucracy, to the craft guilds and merchants, and along the main trade routes of the country. Though its firmest hold is still upon the capital it has reached also the peasantry in the districts and some of the riverain population.

From the beginning, then, Islamization in Nupe was bound up with political interests and represented a change 'from above'. During the long-drawn internal wars which accompanied the Fulani rise to power acceptance of Islam meant identifying oneself with the new regime. Even today Islam stands for some such identification, with the powers that be, with the social élite, and implicitly with the culture that grew up in the capital where that power is centred and the élite resides. Islam thus added to the unification of the conquest-state, extending the area of a common culture over a population otherwise unified only by political means. More precisely, it transformed a mere holding-together, ultimately by coercion, into a belonging-together—the conscious belonging-together that goes with a shared creed.

This twin machinery of unification, political and religious, was not an entirely new thing. When the Fulani established their rule over Nupe they did so over a society itself held together essentially by political means. For though the older Nupe kingdom had grown from within the Nupe tribe and largely coincided with it, it did not rest on 'tribal' solidarity or unity alone. Rather, the political unity of the kingdom was superimposed upon heterogeneous tribal sections, autonomous communities, and a population bound to widely diverse religious practices. So that on this level already the state had to create its own religious supports. The emblems of the ancestor king Tsoede and the myths and rituals associated with his person stand in this sense for the kingdom and its overriding unity; much as the 'state church' of Islam stands for Fulani rule. But there are these differences. Islam, of course, is a religion in its own right, and one open to any country or regime; while the religious observances surrounding Nupe kingship derived their sacred import only from this association and have no meaning outside the political or national setting. The 'royal cults' and myths, therefore, specifically buttressed sovereignty and tied the population to the institution of kingship; Islam does so only incidentally and indirectly, through being the faith of sovereign and ruling class. Finally, the royal cults were merely added to the series of rituals peculiar to the various communities and tribal sections; their diverse religious life was left intact, being only made to include some observance expressive of the new 'belonging-together'. Islam supersedes all the diverse beliefs and practices; it makes proselytes, not scattered cult members, and involves complete identification, not merely the acceptance of tokens of identity.

These contrasts reflect both the different potentialities of Islam and of the pagan cults, and the different conditions in which the religious unification occurred, here following upon an alien domination, and there buttressing an indigenous kingdom still 'tribal' in many respects. It is difficult to draw any general conclusion from this fortuitous combination of two sets of factors. It may seem suggestive that the alien conquest and the indigenous state employed religion in radically different ways. But then, the particular employment of religion in support of the alien conquest also accorded with the potentialities of the religion professed by the conquerors. In other words, the alien ruling group happened to carry with it a creed which, being proselytizing and non-tribal, seems to have offered precisely the support their regime demanded; and this being so, it is futile to speculate on the kind of situation that would have arisen had the conquerors not professed such a suitable creed. Indeed, without the impetus of Islam the whole conquest would probably not have taken place or taken that particular form. We may point out two things, however.

The Islamization of the country is far from complete, both in that it reached only a portion of the population and in that it often remained superficial. Thus Islam, far from superseding the indigenous ceremonials, often merely furnished new, additional ones. The new ceremonials stand for a common cult, no more; and this in turn stands for a new unity, of the Mohammedan regime and the conquest-state: but it stands for it only as another 'token of identity'. So that the regime based on conquest is still employing the same religious support which characterized the indigenous kingdom. If this means that the potentialities of Islam have not (or not yet) been fully utilized, in other respects they required correction. For Islam points beyond the state which may adopt it for its church; for the Nupe, it means conversion to a creed uniting a vast population in Nigeria and West Africa (though few Nupe would think of Islam as a world religion). Also, as we have said, this creed of a ruling class lacks the explicit reference to sovereignty which the pagan 'royal cults' possessed. Thus, to serve as a buttress of 'State and Throne', the broad conception of Islam needed some narrowing down and its practice some remodelling. As we shall see, this has indeed been achieved.

Let me first say a few words about the motives which induced individuals and whole communities in Nupe to embrace the new faith. The Fulani did not resort to mass conversions imposed by force. But the prestige value implicit in this creed of a ruling class was only one of its inducements. It offered, besides, two more specific material advantages. First, conversion to Islam promised safety from slavery; secondly, the patronage of nobility, which peasants and craftsmen would seek for economic reasons as well as to secure legal protection, involved accepting the religion of the rulers.[1] The rough and ready conversions which were the result cannot have involved any elaborate rules of spiritual preparation. Indeed, during the early Fulani regime, there were no such rules, though there was a set procedure. A man declaring to his chosen patron, not to any member of the clergy, that he wished to become a Mohammedan, and the gift, in return, of a turban and sword, sealed at once the conversion and the grant of patronage. Today, the procedure is, at least in theory, a little more elaborate and less worldly. The would-be convert is supposed to turn to a mallam for the necessary tuition, which is brief and superficial, consisting only in memorizing a few *surat* of the Qoran. In due course, he will make the declaration of faith (that is, speak the first *surah*) during the service in the mosque, after which he can don a turban, the visible sign of the accomplished conversion. A few older men I met had in fact undergone this procedure. But nowadays most adults as it were slip into Islam; they simply decide to attend the mosque (however irregularly), to perform the prescribed observances (however perfunctorily), and to exchange the indigenous phrygian caps for turbans. They may, however, seek tuition afterwards, many mallams having such 'self-made' Mohammedans among their pupils. The younger people professing Islam have mostly grown up in that faith; many received tuition in a Qoran school in their youth; others merely had parents who, in spite of their own pagan beliefs, arranged for their children a birth and naming ceremony in Mohammedan style.

The observances followed by the Nupe Mohammedans are as simple and liberal as is the procedure of conversion. The five basic duties of Islam—bearing witness to the One God; reciting the five daily prayers (*salât*); giving alms; observing the Fast (Ramadhan); and making the pilgrimage to Mecca—are, for most Nupe, reduced to two. When you ask a Nupe what makes a Mohammedan, the answer is invariably this—*jĩ salla* (i.e., saying the daily prayers) and keeping the Fast. The declaration of faith in One God has slipped into the background of things taken for granted. This is not unnatural; since the traditional belief of the Nupe knows one deity only, as abstract and remote as the God of Islam, the testimony to His uniqueness strikes no one as a point of great importance. Nor are the Nupe greatly exercised over the finer theological distinctions between *Sokó* and *Allah*; mostly they regard them as two names for the same being. The giving of alms (*sádaka*) is, as we know, embodied in numerous institutional occasions; but it is regarded merely as a desirable thing, not as an obligation in its own right, deserving to be listed among the

[1] See *A Black Byzantium*, pp. 142–3.

'foundations' of the faith. The pilgrimage to Mecca does not even fall under the heading of desirables; at least, it is desirable only in a very abstract and remote sense, the whole notion being, for most Nupe, utterly unreal and impracticable.[1]

The duties just discussed are only as it were minimum obligations, referring to the explicit practical tasks incumbent upon Moslems. In addition, there is the whole body of learning, theological and more general, that goes with this creed the very first steps of which concern scholarship, reading, writing, and knowledge of the 'book'. Furthermore, Islam is a way of life—*sunna*—no less than a doctrine; as such, it bears on kinship rules, the position of women, ethics, and law; on art and forms of recreation; and on the attitude towards other creeds.

2. DAILY WORSHIP

Yet even the basic, 'minimum', duties represent a mode of worship, and hence a 'way of life', utterly novel to people reared in traditional Nupe culture. The prayers in an alien tongue, which must be memorized and repeated in word-perfect fashion, have nothing in common with the variable and informal addresses of the deity typical of the Nupe ceremonials. This is true equally of the whole notion of daily prayers, that is, of a routine of worship pervading workaday life and not restricted to rare festive occasions or times of need and anxiety. The worship inside buildings is similarly unprecedented; and so is the idea of individual worship in the place of group ceremonial. Even the gatherings at the mosque on Fridays or festive days represent only the massed worship of so-and-so many separate individuals, not a collective act, resting on collaboration and a division of tasks, such as the Nupe know. It is true that most Islamic countries possess orders or sects (*tariqa*) whose rules of worship aim at overcoming this separateness of individual devotions. These are turned into a collective response in which inter-stimulation has full play and which may reach a state of frenzy through the endless repetition in unison of prayer formulæ, through prescribed movements of the body, or with the help of music and dancing. But the self-abandonment of these practices (*zikr*) and their aim of achieving a mystic union of worshipper and deity seem alike alien to the mood of Nupe religious ceremonial. Certainly, neither the religious orders nor their collective acts of devotion have influenced Moslem worship in Nupe.

[1] Significantly, among the many hundreds of Nigerians I encountered in the Sudan and on the Red Sea coast, at varying stages of their pilgrimage, I met only two Nupe men. And in the whole of Nupe country, there were, during my stay, only three returned pilgrims, two of whom were of Fulani extraction.

Finally, the character of the Moslem priesthood has no counterpart in Nupe. Strictly speaking, Islam has no priesthood; any person of sufficient scholarly standing can hold services or administer the religious rites, though it is common for selected individuals to become the officiants (*Imam*, *Liman* in Nupe) in particular mosques and for the head of the clergy to be appointed or confirmed by the sovereign of the country. Often, too, these appointments stay in the same family, if only incidentally. But normally, there is no trace in Mohammedan priestship of rigidly hereditary tenure, nor of a 'miraculous birth' or similar mystical qualifications. Again, in other Islamic countries the widespread cults of holy men, or holy families, descended from saints or from the kin of the Prophet, have superseded the more prosaic, ordinary priestship. These ideas are once more absent in Nupe, though there is one significant exception. For around the historical and political figure of Mallam Dendo something like saint worship has sprung up. A mosque erected over his grave has become almost a place of pilgrimage, at least for the Fulani aristocracy; and stories of a legendary character about his life and exploits are current throughout the country. The Arabic name for such holy leaders, *sayyid*, is unknown to the Nupe; but they have coined a new word for their one saint—*Mankó*, 'Great Mallam'.

These various divergences have to some extent been resolved by Nupe-izing the orthodox Moslem practices. A minor instance are the open-air mosques found in many smaller or half-pagan villages. They consist of a ring of stones laid out in the open usually under a shady tree. This simple arrangement does not reflect only the simple needs of a small congregation, or its rational desire to economize; even a small congregation could build a mud-hut of the usual type and call it a mosque. Rather, the arrangement seems to indicate also some perseverance in the old manner of worship, which disappears only when Islam is more firmly rooted. The mosques, of whatever kind, introduced a novel social feature also in separating the worshippers from different neighbourhoods; for any fair-sized village will contain several mosques, scattered over the locality, so that each *efu* or ward has its own building. In other words, the coincidence of the actual congregation and the community at large, typical of the pagan ceremonials, no longer holds. It is reintroduced, however, on special occasions. In addition to these local mosques, where the daily prayers are said, any populous Nupe village also possesses a large, central mosque for the service on Friday and on feast days, that is, for the worship of a congregation made coextensive with the community.[1]

[1] This does not apply to Bida town, whose tripartite division is reflected in the three main mosques of the town (see *A Black Byzantium*, pp. 43, 89).

The daily prayers (*salla*) spoken in Arabic (which few understand) and the weekly service in the mosque (*aduwa*) have become fully part of Nupe life, and if they lack the stimulus of pressing needs or the thrill that goes with rare occasions, this is not felt or ever commented upon. But the Moslem observances have also been remodelled, partly in a revolutionary fashion. As they exist today, they afford expression to the same pressing anxieties which animate the pagan rites, and do so with the same persuasiveness of a direct, articulate appeal to the deity. Over and above the stereotyped prayers, the Nupe have others which ask for special benefits and are meant to take care of such contingencies as a drought or the threat of an epidemic. These prayers may be said both privately, by any family head for his household, and publicly, in the mosque, by the *Liman* on behalf of the whole community. The special prayers are always said after the regular ones and, most important of all, are spoken in Nupe, not in Arabic. In addition, any household or kin group which faces some deep anxiety or threat will arrange a *walima*, that is, a ceremonial meal at which a fowl is killed and a mallam, specially invited, utters a brief prayer; again, an invocation in Nupe follows the Arabic formula, so that this observance differs only in minor details from the communal meal of the pagan ceremonial.[1]

Let me here quote four Nupe-Mohammedan prayers, concerned with harvest and rain. They have been recorded in two different places, Bida and Lemu, and show the familiar looseness and variability of phrasing, which no orthodox Moslem prayer ever permits; above all, they invoke *Sokó*, not *Allah*, and thus wholly recapture the content and style of the pagan invocations.

Prayer at Harvest time (Bida).

Lord God (*Tsoci*), protect the house from the dangers of the harvest season, such as fire, such as falling ill with fever, such as drought. Give us health, *Amin*.

The same (Lemu).

The harvest is cleared: *Sokó*, protect us from fire; *Sokó*, protect us from smallpox; *Sokó* protect us from the heat that dries up everything.

Prayer at the Beginning of the Rains (Bida).

Sokó, may he give rain in plenty. May he give food that thrives beautifully. The grain, may it thrive beautifully. *Sokó*, send us

---

[1] The Nupe would in fact say that *walima* is only the 'Mohammedan name' for the ceremonial which the 'pagans' know as *biki*. (See above, p. 110.)

water which falls down upon man. And the man who is in a canoe on the water, and the water in the bush, protect them also for all of us.

The same (Lemu).

Lord God, protect us from the danger which is in the rain, and the storms, and also the lightning. Protect the house from it. Give us health, *Amin.*

3. CEREMONIALS

We turn to the big religious feasts of Islam which, in their annual recurrence at least, should come closest to, or rival most fully, the fixed pagan ceremonials. Of the seven orthodox Moslem festivals, the Nupe celebrate only three: the Mohammedan New Year, *Muharram*, and the two feasts known in Arabic countries as *Id el Fitr* and *Id el Azha*, the former concluding the month of *Ramadhan*, the latter falling in the 'month of pilgrimage', at the end of the Mohammedan year.[1] The Nupe call the Moslem New Year's feast *navũ* or 'Torches', and name the first month of the year after it; the month of *Ramadhan* is called *etswa azũ*, 'Month of the Fast', and the feast which succeeds it *sallagi* or 'Little Feast' (lit. 'prayer'); the *Id el Azha*, also known in Arabic as *Id el Kibir*, Great Feast, is called *sallakó*, which has the same meaning. The months in which these two feasts fall, the 10th and 12th, respectively, are known by their names.[2] Let us note that in embracing only three of the festivities of Islam the Nupe have retained that 'normal level' of regular ceremonials which we could discern in their traditional religious life.[3]

In all Moslem countries the purely festive aspects of the *Id* tend to outshine the strictly religious ones. These are represented in a religious service held in the open, attended by vast crowds and led by the *Imam*; in the generous giving of alms; and (on the 'Great Feast') in the sacrifice of an 'unblemished animal ... to commemorate the name of God over the brute beasts which He has

---

[1] A third, the Birthday of the Prophet, is identified by the Nupe with the *gani* ceremonial, as we have seen, on very little evidence. (See above, p. 217).

[2] These dates correspond to general Moslem practice. But the correspondence is purely nominal since the Nupe calendar operates with the intercalation of a 13th month while the Moslem calendar keeps strictly to the lunar year. In consequence the Nupe feasts always fall roughly in the same season while the orthodox Moslem celebrations correspond in no way to a seasonal calendar.

[3] See pp. 70, 225. This applies only to communities fully Islamized; in a first phase, one of the Mohammedan feasts, the *navũ*, may simply be added to the pagan cycle of rites (see below, p. 244).

provided' (Qoran, *Surah* XXII). All three features occur in Nupe, the animal being always a fattened ram, killed and eaten in every household that can afford the expense on the third day of the feast. Few Nupe, however, know anything about the meaning of the sacrifice save that it is ordered by the Prophet as a 'sacred occasion'. Much more important is the holiday atmosphere which pervades the three days of the feast. Everybody dresses in his best clothes and visits friends and relations or pays his respects to a noble patron. In Bida, the people throng the streets and gather in the public places to watch the *Etsu* and the 'great ones' of the country ride in resplendent procession from the service to the royal palace. There, outside the palace, a vast crowd is entertained, at the *Etsu's* order and expense, with food for body and eyes; there are equestrian displays, and the performances of professional dancers and musicians, clowns and jugglers.[1]

We note that the two-phase pattern of the pagan ceremonials, in which esoteric and sacred activities always precede the public merry-making, no longer applies: there is nothing esoteric about the religious service, 'merry-making' pervades the whole feast, and one of the 'sacred' activities, the sacrifice of the ram, does not open but concludes the ritual proceedings. Indeed, the *salla* is a spectacle rather than a ritual, at all stages open to all—to men and women, to townsfolk and strangers, and to people of every age. Its main significance lies precisely in this: the *salla* brings together nearly the whole Moslem community, not only symbolically, through being a common observance (or a 'token of identity'), but concretely and physically. At least, it does so potentially. The *salla* is also performed outside Bida, though on a lesser scale, all the larger villages having their own celebrations, when the local District Head, that is, the Emir's representative, plays the part which, in the capital, falls to the sovereign. But the Bida *salla* remains the centre and always attracts visitors from the country, so that at one time or other every Nupe Moslem will attend the celebrations in the capital.

If the *salla* lacks the thrill of secret preparation and esoteric observances, it yet provides others—the thrill of a splendid spectacle and, above all, that of being brought close to the powers that be. Altogether, the emphasis of the *salla* is as much political as religious. It serves as a display of kingship and hence as a buttress of sovereignty no less than as a sacred occasion. In mobilizing the religious community it mobilizes also the population of the Moslem state; so that the religious appeal blends with the confirmation of political allegiance. It is in this fashion, then,

[1] For a fuller description of the 'Great *salla*' in Bida, see *A Black Byzantium*, pp. 143–4.

ISLAM IN NUPE

that the all-too-broad unity of Islam is (as I put it before) narrowed down to the scope of a national church.

The *navũ* is to some extent a smaller replica of the *salla*, including, again, the state procession to the mosque, with all its display of royal splendour and evoking the same festive mood of a large city bent on enjoyment. But the royal display occupies only a brief phase, on the morning of New Year's Day; and the enjoyment has a new emphasis, on youth, and on moral licence.

On the eve of New Year, at nightfall, the young people of Bida, both youths and girls, forgather at the three streams that cross the town. The girls come in little groups, while the boys and young men are formed into companies, each composed of an age-grade association under its leader. They sing and dance on the way, and the youths all carry torches, which they swing or throw high up in the air, and sometimes brandish at one another in playful attacks. Arrived at the river the youths remove their gowns and the girls their upper garments, and thus stripped to the waist wade into the water. They splash about, with much shrieking and laughing, try dance steps, jumps and somersaults, and the boys engage in brief wrestling bouts, invariably terminated by a ducking. Now and again this clowning gives way to a mock battle, when the boys will thrust and throw the torches at one another, age-group fighting age-group, not seriously, but keenly and with marked excitement. It needs skill to catch the wildly flying firebrands or to parry those aimed at you. Nor are narrow escapes uncommon, and first-aid treatments for burns are a regular aftermath of the *navũ*. The excitement of the fight, moreover, is matched by the openly erotic excitement provoked by the occasion. This is indeed unique; at no other time will Nupe girls disrobe in the presence of men or show themselves with bare breasts. The girls will keep to the dark side of the river; but the youths throw torches in their direction to surprise a girl while she is undressing or bathing. There is cruder horseplay, too, the boys trying to seize the girls or to bump into them as though unwittingly; while in the shadows and under the bridge couples pursue their amorous play unseen. But though there is plenty of teasing and joking, the language is never obscene. About midnight the bathing breaks up and the young people return to their homes.

This prelude to the *navũ* was not always so tame. Until fairly recently the mock battle of torches was meant quite seriously.[1] The three different bathing places are chosen in accordance with the threefold dynastic division of the city, and are visited by the age-grade associations in the respective local division. The diverse

[1] The word 'battle' has been chosen advisedly. All informants describing the usage emphasized that it was 'like a war'.

loyalties which govern the town hold their sway over youth as well as adults; and on the occasion of the *navũ* the factional jealousies, never fully submerged, were allowed to come into the open. Thus the torch processions invariably led to organized and heated fights between the three groups; on the way back from the river, especially, one would ambush the other or try to invade the rival territory. The battle is said to have lasted the whole night, being fought with torches, sticks, stones, and any handy weapons. Injuries (some say, even death) inflicted in the course of the *navũ* went unpunished; for on this one night the law of the land was suspended. Eventually, in 1920 or thereabouts, the excesses of this all-too realistic play forced the Government to intervene and to forbid this phase of the *navũ*.

In spite of its realism, however, the mock battle not only legitimized factional hostility but also diverted it into relatively harmless channels. For though the boys and youths would give vent to sentiments commonly felt, they themselves were still outside serious politics and not yet genuinely caught up in factional strife. They would still be play-acting, however realistically, much as their whole age-grade life, with its imitation of adult ranks and ambitions, is play-acting and a make-believe copy of 'real life'. For the population of the city, whose sons and brothers took part in the 'battle of youth', this was in the nature of a vicarious and controlled catharsis of tensions grown over the year; for the young fighters, it was the climax of age-grade life and a seal set to this 'education for citizenship'. Needless to say, the practice is still vividly remembered. And it is not only the older people who talk nostalgically about their more exciting youth; the young people today have preserved at least the idea of the thing. Small boys with whom I talked before the *navũ* explained to me with great glee all that they and their age mates were going to do to their 'enemies'. In the end, of course, they did nothing; so that today the 'battle of youth' has moved a further stage towards mere make-believe.[1]

The licensed aggression of the torch festival reappears on the next day in a new context, that of kinship. For the *navũ* is also an occasion for *ma dzo*, for 'joking', that is, for the licensed liberties commonly referred to as 'joking relationship'. Though much less formalized than in other African societies, the institution of joking relationship plays a clearly defined part in Nupe social life. The individuals standing in this relationship are called *dzomanci*, 'playmates', the relationship itself being derived mainly from kinship position. Thus the joking relationship obtains between grandparents and grandchildren of the opposite sex; between cross

[1] See also *A Black Byzantium*, pp. 396–7.

cousins; between a man and his elder brothers' wives; between a man and his mother's brother's wives; between a man and his wife's *dzomanci*; and between a woman and her father-in-law and her mother-in-law's sister's sons. The relevance of this arrangement for Nupe kinship organization does not concern us here; nor need we consider the joking relationship as it affects everyday life. Let me only stress that the active partners in this relationship, that is, the individuals entitled to take the liberties, are always young people; older persons cease to engage in the joking relationship or become engaged in it only as passive partners, as the victims exposed to the liberties. In practice, then, the joking relationship is asymmetrical, amounting to liberties taken by children or youths with their elders and, in the majority of cases, by one sex with the other.[1] The liberties themselves take this form. Whenever an 'active' partner in the relationship meets his playmate he would lightly beat him or her with a stick until the victim appeases the assailant with a small gift of money. Or boys and young men would visit the home of a playmate, tie his (her) hands and feet with a grass rope, until once more a small ransom is handed over. Throughout the *navũ* this play goes on. Everywhere you see boys armed with sticks or carrying grass ropes handy; and whole bands of them will swagger along the streets looking for their 'playmates' among the girls and women, shouting at them, brandishing their sticks, and trying to seize them, with unequal success. For the 'passive' partner is allowed to evade the punishment, to retaliate, and even to cheat. Quite a few of the older men when they are caught by their young assailants do not pay the required ransom, but merely press their fingers into their playmates' hands as though handing over a coin, and escape by this ruse. And the women and girls on the market sit behind their wares with a stick or grass rope ready in case a 'playmate' tried his extortions on them. There is no serious note in all this: it is fun, and nothing else, taken in good part by everyone. Throughout this play another *motif* is also visible. The *dzomanci* will often be aided by his friends, and during *navũ* you will everywhere see youths walking in pairs and holding hands, two friends facing together the adventures of the day. Thus the *navũ* becomes a multiple occasion for mobilizing and demonstrating the main social relationships governing Nupe life—age-grade solidarity; political allegiance; kinship bonds; and friendship.

It is difficult to define precisely the Islamic kernel in the Nupe celebrations of the *Muharram*, mainly because the character of

[1] Joking relationship also occurs outside the kindred, between certain Nupe sections and other tribes, or within Nupe communities between occupational groups. As these relationships play no part in the *navũ*, they are here disregarded.

the feast varies widely in Moslem countries. The bathing in the river is a common feature of the *Muharram*; but it does not concern the young particularly. Now in Nupe, the older people, too, perform the prescribed New Year's ablutions; but they do so at home, in water fetched by the women from the river; the bathing in the river, then, with its erotic suggestiveness, is an instance of Nupe-ization. Again, the play with fire, in the form of bonfires or torches, is fairly common; and in Shiite countries especially, the celebrations also include mock violence and battles. But these have a specific religious emphasis, being a commemoration of the last battle and martyrdom of Husain: of which association no Nupe is aware. Indeed, no Nupe knows or has any theory about the meaning of the 'torches'. Whatever the origin of the feature, the fact that it has come to serve political motives and the organization of adolescence, is plain evidence of its remodelling by Nupe hands.

The *navũ* has spread widely through Nupe Emirate, and today occurs even in villages almost entirely pagan, such as Doko, Sakpe, and Jebba Island, where it is simply added to the cycle of traditional rituals. The public service in the mosque, of course, disappears, as does also the realistic 'battle', that is, the political emphasis peculiar to the situation in the city. Each locality performs the ceremonial independently, and no one thinks of visiting the capital to watch or join in the celebrations there. Yet though there are these numerous independent congregations, the *navũ* is understood to be an identical ceremonial and one which each community shares with the capital and royalty. Its specifically Moslem character is entirely obscured; but no Nupe links the origin of the *navũ* to pre-Mohammedan or pre-Fulani times. Rather it is always thought of as a new ceremonial, bound up with the new regime and as such added to the diverse observances of the country. Thus, though it has become part and parcel of the separate life of villages, it is also identified with the kingdom that embraces them all. So that a rite of Islam is again 'narrowed down' to the concerns of the state and employed in the manner of the older 'royal cults', as a mere 'token of identity'.

4. THE MOSLEM WAY OF LIFE

Our attempt to assess the influence of Islam on the Nupe way of life is rendered difficult by the fact that we do not know precisely in what shape or form the new creed reached Nupe country. Indeed, even in 'typical' Moslem countries the observances of Islam vary extremely widely. And though this difficulty is somewhat less serious in the case of the strictly religious aspects, since these are, at least in their fundamentals, embodied in a written doctrine and uniformly transmitted through the teaching of the Qoran, even this teaching can vary within wide limits; above all, it can be reinforced or belied by the models of practical conduct exhibited by the teachers. Thus we shall presently speak of the confused notions of the Nupe on Moslem cosmology and hagiology, and of their lack of interest in the historical background of Islam. But how far this attitude reflects the Nupe reaction towards the new creed or merely their faithful acceptance of a creed loosely and confusedly taught, it is obviously difficult to say. Quite probably the latter is the true picture; for there is no reason to assume that the first emissaries of Islam were more erudite or theologically-minded than the majority of mallams today. According to some accounts, in fact, the famous Mallam Dendo was little better than a peddler of Mohammedan charms. However this may be, when it comes to the general moral precepts or codes of conduct that go with Islam, we are more uncertain still. Islam reached Nupe through many hands and by many stages, and in a form probably considerably affected by the modes of life of the Sudanese and West African societies where it first took root. Furthermore, many of these are closely akin to Nupe. If then, we find Moslem practices more or less closely attuned to Nupe traditional culture, this may only represent some previous 'remodelling' and, from Nupe point of view, a fortuitous correspondence, not any effort on their part to render the new creed more 'congenial'.

Let me illustrate this by one example, the position of women in Moslem-Nupe society. In orthodox Islam the woman is man's inferior by the will of God, and made to obey him (*Surah* IV). Though women may be as true believers, they are permitted no share in religious activities and rarely given the chance of religious tuition. Legally and socially they are subjected to various disabilities; women (not men) must 'observe continence and not display their ornaments' (that is, must be veiled before strangers—*Surah* XXV, 31); and Mohammedans marrying 'infidel' women must not let 'them go back to the infidels', being responsible for their spiritual welfare (*Surah* LX, 10). None of these tenets applies to Nupe Islam. Women are as free as men and legally as fully qualified; the veiling of the women is unknown; and though the Nupe do not admit women to the mosque or other religious observances, girls of the upper classes are often taught the Qoran. Is this, then, an adjustment of Islam to traditional Nupe notions? Hardly that, for this contrast is true only in comparison with Moslem practices, say in India or the urban society of Arabia and the Eastern Sudan. It disappears when we compare Nupe with the nomadic Moslem tribes in the Sudan or with the Mohammedan Emirates in the north of Nigeria. The Fulani invaders of Nupe, who started the great wave of Islamization, were probably as liberal or unorthodox in their attitude to women. So that the Nupe would have received their new creed already remodelled by the donors, and the true contrast would be, not between orthodox Islam and the Nupe version, but between the former and African Islam.

To turn to the other aspects of the Moslem 'way of life', first, to the high value placed on scholarship. Even the most humble follower of Islam is aware of it. Tuition in the creed and *jĩ katũ* (reading, book-knowledge in general) are to him almost one and the same thing; and greater religious perfection coincides with wider learning. The title mallam, 'scholar', freely accorded to the pious, already indicates the trend of thought. One mallam friend of mine expressed it aptly when he spoke of the *ciŋwa katũ*, the 'greatness of learning', which makes any Mohammedan scholar equal to the other great ones in the country—rankholders, noblemen, or wealthy landowners. Not that the mallam is necessarily poor or a commoner; many mallams are wealthy, and many members of the titled aristocracy pride themselves on being scholars as well. But the professional scholar does not require the badge or rank nor the backing of wealth to be granted the privileges of high status. His learning makes him the companion of the 'great ones'; his ministration at naming ceremonies, weddings or burials opens him their houses; and even a poor mallam can marry into rich or noble families if his scholarly repute is high; for in this case the bride's father will defray the costs of the brideprice, counting this expenditure as a pious gift of alms.[1]

There are, of course, degrees of learning, and hence distinctions in the status of mallams. In largely pagan villages anyone who has learned to recite a few *surat* of the Qoran and performs his daily prayers is called a mallam; in the Mohammedan capital the name is reserved for those who also teach the Qoran, though the adepts in the art of sand-divining and the sellers of charms are equally included in that class. Mostly a further distinction is drawn between the simple, humble mallam, who knows only the Qoran (or, more often, only small portions of it) and the true scholar, who must have studied *litafi* (books) or *kpikpe* (knowledge) as well. Men of the latter class read eagerly and widely, and acquire books where they can or copy out rare manuscripts. Ignoring, however, the few mallams who practice as judges and have studied the various relevant legal digests and commentaries, the reading of these 'learned men' tends to be indiscriminate and their 'know-

[1] The social position of the mallams and the whole question of Moslem learning and tuition has been fully discussed in *A Black Byzantium*; see especially pp. 102, 378–83.

ledge' a miscellany of incongruous items. Often the 'books' they get hold of are merely odd assortments of bits of literature, the same volume perhaps containing an extract on marriage law, a page or two on astrology, a treatise on the human body, and a fragment of some Hausa chronicle. Nor does the specific knowledge of Moslem theology fare any better. Again it is a medley of incongruous bits of information and in no way approaches the orthodox teaching of Islam.

The further down you pass in the scale of Nupe Mohammedan scholarship, the more confused and fragmentary becomes this knowledge. Take this summary account of creation and the powers of God which was given to me by one of the 'simple' mallams: 'Mohammed was the first man on earth; the devil (*Sheitan*) sends illness and misfortunes; after death, the good people become kindly spirits (*aljénu*), while evil persons are turned into dust'. Which last statement was the only reference to the ethical sanctions of Islam I encountered in Nupe; for hell or heaven or the last judgment are never mentioned. The notion, incidentally, that Mohammed was the first man is widespread; but otherwise the ideas about creation and the universe are far from uniform. Here is a different and fuller account, recorded from another mallam of this class: Formerly, when all the people lived together in the same place, there existed 'little gods' (*sokó tetengi*), whom God (*Allah*) sent down to earth to take away the souls (*rayi*) of the persons whose life was nearing its end. But the people grew frightened at this mysterious and unannounced demise and tried to evade it by scattering over the earth. So God introduced a new kind of death, heralded by illness, or overcoming man suddenly, through lightning or other natural disasters. These 'little gods' are the *malaika* (the Arabic *mal'ak*, 'angels'). In addition to the messengers of death there exist also *malaika* who bring rain, cause the crops to grow, and watch over man; the chief one amongst them is Jibelelu (Gabriel); others are Mikailu, Ismailu, Ibrahimu, though my informant did not pretend to know them all.

The knowledge possessed by the 'true' mallam is hardly less unorthodox, even though it is fuller and more ambitious. The following text was dictated to me by a gifted pupil of the most famous mallam of Bida and fully conformed to the master's teaching.

'In the beginning there were Adama and Mother Adā. They had three daughters, Mureamu [Miriam, Mary], Fatima [daughter of Mohammed], and Barkisa [Bilkis, the Queen of Sheba], and numerous sons. These were all prophets. God then divided the world into pagans and Moslems. The greatest king of the pagans was Firauna [Firaun, Arabic for Pharaoh], who conquered the whole earth and had immense wealth. He had seven houses, in each of which a fire was eternally burning; criminals were thrown into these houses, to be burned to death. He also had seven houses filled with wonderful things and a hundred beautiful women in each. Good people were rewarded by being admitted to these houses and being made free of the things they contained. Once there happened to be a great drought and famine; but Firauna prayed to God, and rain fell. Thereupon Firauna said to the people: "Have I not sent rain? I am your God." Thus he claimed that he himself was God, and all who denied him, the Mohammedans among them, were fettered and left lying in the sun until they perished. Firauna decided to make war on God in the sky. He called all his men together and made them build a huge tower. This lasted sixty years. When the tower reached up to the sky, Firauna ordered his soldiers to shoot at the sky with bows and arrows, for two years. But God destroyed the tower and innumerable people perished. Then God called his prophet Musa [Moses] and ordered him to rise against Firauna. Thus Musa called together an army; but it was much weaker than Firauna's, so that the true believers, led by Musa, were turned to flight. Pursued by Firauna they reached a river as wide as the Niger; God caused the water to dry up so that they could cross, but when Firauna's army followed, it was swallowed up by the river. Now Musa ruled over the world and established the reign of God. When he died, he was succeeded by the other prophets, Abraham, Yisa, Haruna, Idirisu, and finally Mohammed.'

There is no need to point out the motley nature of this account. Yet the people uncritically accept these crude narratives as evidence of 'learning' as they similarly accept the lists of 'angels' and the string of names with which diviners bolster up their 'astrology'.[1] Since the traditional Nupe beliefs possess little or nothing of this kind, it might be thought that Mohammedan lore fills some pre-existing lacunae. But this is not really so. The average Nupe Moslem is no more interested in the pseudo-Mohammedan cosmology or hagiology than is the pagan Nupe in myths of this kind.[2] But the former remains 'book-knowledge', which goes with the new religion and is expected of its teachers; so that a great many topics

[1] See above, p. 59n.
[2] The experiences of Christian evangelists offer interesting corroboration. The theological cosmology of Christian teaching evokes no interest among the Nupe. An evangelist told me about his abortive attempts in this direction, when his converts-to-be frankly admitted that they 'knew nothing' about the creation of the world but could not be convinced of the value of knowing more.

with which indigenous sacred knowledge was never concerned are now tacitly assumed to be within the ken of mallams. Whenever you ask the 'man in the street' about the origin of the world, about the sun, moon, and stars, or about the rules of the calendar, he will refer you to the mallams—'these are things the mallams know'. More often than not, this trust is sadly misplaced. But as the Nupe lack of interest in mythology admits of one exception, namely, myths or legends about the genesis of Nupe kingdom, so the growth of the Moslem Emirate has become the theme of numerous stories and quasi-mythical traditions.[1] To be sure, they are not Moslem traditions in the strict sense of the word; but they are traditions about the crucial events of Islam as seen through Nupe eyes. In this sense they add to the religious supports which the Fulani Emirate has come to command, much as the pagan kingdom drew some of its strength from the cycle of myths devoted to Tsoede and his miraculous deeds. And in this sense, too, they may be said to 'fill lacunae', that is, to replace a mythology outdated by events.

Among the other features of the Moslem 'way of life' several fit remarkably (and fortuitously) into the pattern of Nupe culture. This is true, for example, of the attitude to representative art, which is absent in Nupe and discouraged by Islam; of certain general rules of marriage, such as the payment of a 'brideprice', the ease of divorce, and the preference for marriage within the kindred;[2] of the custom of circumcision and one of the dietary rules of Islam, the prohibition of eating pig.[3] The ease with which Moslem kinship rites or the Islamic method of divination found a niche in Nupe life has already been discussed.

There are a few exceptions, however. The Nupe preference for *yawó dengi*, marriage within the kindred, refers only to cross-cousin marriage and excludes the marriage of parallel cousins, which Islamic practice permits and recommends; similarly the sororate, common in Moslem countries, is forbidden by traditional Nupe custom; conversely, the Nupe preferential marriage, between a young man and his mother's brother's widow, is unknown to

[1] Some of these have been quoted in *A Black Byzantium*, pp. 78–9.

[2] The Nupe 'brideprice'—*ewó yawó* ('money of marriage')—corresponds to the 'dower' (*Mahr* or *sadaq*) of Islamic law. The ready acceptance of their equivalence is seen in the linguistic usage, the Arabic word *sadeiki* having become almost a synonym for *ewó yawó*.

[3] Strictly speaking, traditional Nupe culture does not taboo the eating of pigs; but there exists a general idiosyncrasy of this kind, and the Nupe do not keep pigs (unlike their Yoruba neighbours). Another dietary rule of Islam, the prohibition of intoxicants, clashes with the great liking of the Nupe for sorghum beer and with the prominent part this drink plays in all sacrifices. The Nupe Moslem have, in fact, abandoned beer for palmwine, which many consider to be exempt from the Qoranic prohibition.

Islam. In all these cases the result has been an odd compromise. In Bida, the Moslem type of marriage is now more frequent than the traditional type; while among the Mohammedans outside the former is absent and the latter still fully in force. The observance of the levirate is somewhat puzzling. Islam permits the marriage with a brother's widow whether the brother is senior or junior to the deceased; in pagan Nupe, marriage with an elder brother's widow is forbidden, but marriage with a younger brother's widow greatly encouraged. Now, in the villages these rules still obtain; in Bida, however, the first kind of marriage is practised, though not very frequently, while the second never occurs. It seems, then, that in the type of marriage which Islam permits but the indigenous custom disallows, the hold of the latter is still sufficiently strong to prevent any widespread adoption of the novel practice; while the type of marriage both permitted by Islam and strongly pressed by local custom has been abandoned by the more 'orthodox' Moslems. This instance contradicts our previous argument as to the fortuitous fit and hence ready acceptance of certain Moslem customs. Rather, we must admit that such a given fit may, paradoxically, entail the rejection of the custom in question. Has it been rejected so as to prevent any blurring of the division between Moslems and non-Moslems, and thus to emphasize the new, different 'way of life'? It would seem to be so; but since this is the only instance of the kind I can only suggest the possibility. The strong hold of the indigenous practice is finally shown in a type of marriage as definitely forbidden by Islam as it is encouraged by Nupe custom, namely, the nominal marriage of a boy with his paternal grandfather's widow. This *yawó suna* ('marriage in name') is practised both in Mohammedan Bida and in the pagan districts. It is clearly bound up with the idea of reincarnation and with the corresponding practice of naming a grandson after his father's father: identical in name and 'soul', the grandson also assumes the nominal status of his *alter ego*. And as the traditional belief remained unassailed by Moslem doctrine, so the practice rooted in it withstood the impact of the new usages.

The most serious divergence between indigenous custom and Moslem ideas occurs in inheritance. The Moslem law of inheritance implies, briefly, the division of a man's property among all his offspring (both male and female) as well as his wives, their respective shares varying in amount.[1] Nupe custom, on the other hand,

---

[1] The inheritance of women's property can be disregarded. Women in Nupe own only personal belongings and money, and can dispose of them more or less as they like—to sons, daughters, or their husband. Though the Nupe practice is more fluid than the Mohammedan usage, the two do not clash; nor has the former changed under Moslem influence.

makes a younger brother or, in the absence of surviving brothers, the eldest brother's son the main heir, excluding wives and daughters. It must be borne in mind that the main property in rural Nupe is land, worked co-operatively by a 'house', that is, by the male members of the extended family—a man, his younger brothers, and his and their sons.[1] The traditional rules of inheritance thus prevent the fragmentation of land and keep intact the large labour team bound to it; for the land descends together with the headship of the family group, and thus with the command over the 'house' and labour team.[2] The acceptance of the Islamic rules of inheritance would change all this: the land would be progressively fragmented, the labour team broken up, and the headship of large families would disappear. But the Nupe have not turned to the new system in summary fashion; they still exclude wives and daughters from inheritance and largely kept intact the succession to the titular headship of the 'house'. But that most critical innovation, the division of landed property among sons, has steadily been gaining ground. It is important to note, however, that this is not simply a result of the pressure of Islam. I have shown elsewhere how the political and economic changes which began with the Fulani conquest and continue to the present day encouraged individual as against family enterprise and deprived the productive organization of the large family group of its former economic advantages.[3] My point now is that the 'individualistic' type of inheritance exemplified in Islam was also the type the new situation demanded, so that the changed outlook which happened to coincide with the impact of Islam provided additional motives for its acceptance, or for the acceptance of the way of life it represents.

In a wider sense the mere presence of the new religion in such circumstances answered the 'demand of the situation'. The political and economic events which were disrupting family co-operation also assailed the whole authority of family heads and their hold over the younger generation. In consequence the latter, sons or younger brothers of men still pagan, were turning away from the traditional cults (and are doing so even today), not for any particular benefits they were expecting of Islam, but because there was logic in the mere 'turning-away'; for this meant abandoning religious practices which, more or less openly, stood for the *status quo*, for parental authority and an outmoded family structure. The great appeal of the *navŭ*, which concedes greater freedom to

[1] See *A Black Byzantium*, chap. III.
[2] This situation is somewhat modified among the craftsmen in the town (see op. cit., chap. XIV). The conclusions drawn further on, however, apply to the labour teams of craftsmen as much as of peasants.
[3] Op. cit., pp. 124, 374–6.

youth, or of the *salla*, which is silent on issues of family authority, is the obverse of this picture.

Here I am repeating facts mentioned previously, though the emphasis is now not on the 'vulnerability' of the older cults in the face of change, but on their dislodgment by the new religion in the country.[1] Islam, as we have seen, proved the stronger mainly because these other changes had prepared the ground; it was a beneficiary of the social upheaval as much as a cause contributing to it. Differently expressed, Islam acted in the manner of a new model, inviting to be followed since it happened to appear at a critical moment, when older norms were breaking down. To be sure, it was a model doubly inviting; it both typified upper-class behaviour and offered alternatives for usages no longer satisfactory, and hence placed a premium on non-conformism. Without it, the dissatisfactions might not have crystallized so easily and the process of change would have been more erratic. As it happened, they found a ready focus or 'model'.

We turn to the final aspect of the Moslem 'way of life', the attitude of the believer towards other creeds. I have called Nupe religion tolerant. Islam, as we know it from other parts of the world, is the exact opposite. It has all the self-righteousness and intransigence of a fervently proselytizing creed; and it lays claim not only to the exclusive possession of spiritual truth but also to an ultimate ascendancy over all other religions—to the 'inheritance of the earth', promised to the believers and meant to be secured by secular domination and 'victory in the field'.[2] In Africa, where Islam now faces pagan peoples as it did in its early history, this claim to supremacy must stand in a literal sense, meaning the superiority of believers over utter unbelievers, of people who have seen the light over mere barbarians, and of Lords and Masters over some lower species of humanity. In the Sudan, for example, this attitude is well marked. But in Nupe there is, by and large, little trace of it.

Undoubtedly, all Moslems pride themselves on being true believers and many, more or less contemptuously, look down upon the pagans. But as I mentioned before, scholarly mallams will yet frankly admit their interest in the pagan cults; few would consider it incongruous or invidious to discuss, in a purely academic spirit, the beliefs and practices of the 'unbelievers'; and the average Nupe Moslem views them as tolerantly. Nor would a Mohammedan bar all social intimacy with pagans (as I have seen it done in half-Mohammedanized parts of the Sudan) or decline to visit them in their houses or receive their visits in his. Even friendship occurs

[1] See above, pp. 97–114.
[2] See D. S. Margulies, *Mohammed*, 1939, pp. 67–8.

across the barrier of religion. The following comments by the chief of Pichi illustrate perhaps the extreme of Nupe tolerance, 'There are three benefits', he said, 'Islam, Christianity, and the *kuti*. Some of us have chosen one, others the other. One may be stronger than the rest: but this we do not know.' To be sure, this tolerance cuts both ways; and indeed, this Nupe version of Lessing's Nathan saw nothing strange in 'making *salla*' and attending the *gunnu* as well. But then, he was only a self-professed Moslem, whom others considered a pagan at heart.

Yet, though his attitude may not be typical of the Nupe Moslems, it is typical of the outlook of the people among whom Islam finds its converts. The final step of conversion changes it but little; indeed, it can hardly be otherwise since conversion is so loose an affair and not a real 'step' at all. But in so far as the outlook of the confirmed Moslem is changed, carrying with it that pride and awareness of superiority, the pride and superiority are social rather than specifically religious. What counts is, first and foremost, the assimilation to upper-class culture, and only secondarily the deliverance from unbelief.

5. CONTACT AND INTEGRATION

In this chapter we were dealing with instances of a much-discussed social process, 'culture contact' or 'acculturation'. The wider theoretical issues involved are beyond our present scope; but no discussion of this kind can avoid touching upon one such general problem, namely, the relationship between the cultures brought into 'contact' and the 'resultant' culture emerging from it. Now, this is a question of end-states, of the final outcome of these processes of change and contact; and logically, we should start with their analysis.

The physical model of 'contact', of a 'clash of cultures', or of their 'impact' upon one another, is more misleading than helpful when picturing these processes. We revert, therefore, to our paradigm, a group possessed of given modes of behaviour, habit patterns if you like, which comes to face new models of behaviour of such-and-such pull or attractiveness. That the reactions are likely to be complex and intricate no one will deny; more importantly, they are progressive, that is, take the form of chain reactions. It is clearly not so that the new models are simply accepted, rejected, or exchanged for the habitual ways of acting as it were once and for all, after which no further readjustment will occur. The religious conversion of a people certainly is not a simple all-or-none affair, but a process of many stages in which an initial acceptance may spread further, be deepened or changed in some other way, and an initial rejection might similarly be modified. My point is that this is not a coherent process moving towards completion, in which a given goal exercises an unvarying 'pull' and steadily gains over the counter-pull of traditional norms; rather, the process is piecemeal, determined by pulls and strains that emerge stage by stage and only operate from one stage to the next.

It might be argued that the Nupe do have before them the 'given goal', namely, the complete observances of Islam as they are taught by its missionaries and practised by the confirmed Moslems. But as we know, the Nupe often resort to half-measures and compromises. Let us not dismiss these as preliminary steps or instances of 'cultural lag'. They clearly represent attempts at reconciling, at a particular stage, the pulls and counter-pulls of customary and novel observances. But no ideal or permanent balance is calculable in advance, partly because the social strains set up by any change in the customary observances will not at once be visible, and partly because the 'pull' of the new models does not remain constant.

The people who accept one or the other new model of behaviour cannot at once assess all the implications of acceptance. They may understand roughly (though even this need not be true) that, say, worship of *Allah* and the observances of *kuti* are mutually exclusive, so that accepting the former must mean abandoning the latter; but they cannot anticipate certain more remote consequences entailed, for example, in the lack of emphasis, in Moslem ceremonial, on paternal authority, in the absence of specific assurances on the productivity of the land, or in the character of the new congregation which no longer coincides with the village community. Yet these consequences will eventually be felt, as strains of one kind or other and as problems requiring solution. The solution can only be achieved by further changes, either through readjusting the pre-existing modes of behaviour or through turning once more to the new model. Stated somewhat crudely, cultural change, once it makes the first breach, is carried on by its own momentum. But we must note that the 'pull' of the new model is itself altered in the process; for any previous response to it, entailing as it does strains and instability, also alters the way in which the people will now view the model, as a solution for hitherto non-existing difficulties, or as itself requiring remodelling. Thus adoption of Moslem inheritance follows logically when Moslem ceremonial (among other things) fails to sustain paternal authority; and Moslem worship is at some stage remodelled to recover the direct appeal to the deity for rain and fertility.

But these processes cannot really be reduced to a precise chronological sequence, the multiplicity of motives effective at any stage forbidding such a reconstruction. Nor can we isolate any first step, forced upon the people, from others that followed spontaneously. What was forced upon the people was essentially a total situation, at once political, economic, and religious; any step may be the first, nor need the others follow immediately.[1] Only theoretically can we conclude that they all hang together, though occasionally we can trace the nexus more firmly, even into the future, towards adjustments yet to come.

Let me illustrate this on an example bearing on the widest efficacy of Islam, its very success in proselityzing the Nupe. Coming as it did as a religion of conquerors and ruling class, it both endorsed the social barrier and provoked attempts at overcoming it. In keeping conversion loose and easy, and in utilizing the emphasis on learning, which, on an elementary level, was widely accessible, the Nupe turned Islam into a means of social mobility. But the result, a religious division cutting irregularly across the society, even across single communities, clearly presented new problems; and their solution took the form of a 'remodelling of the model'. The ('unorthodox') tolerance of Nupe Moslems towards pagans is one such reaction to a cleavage which, if it were allowed to retain its sharpness, would break up every community. Another, though it occurs in one case only, lies in that 'religious division of labour' between Moslems and pagans which we recorded from Kutigi. But consider also that the spreading of Islam must tend to obscure the class barrier which it formerly sustained and on which Nupe society is still based; and if one day Islam sweeps the whole country, that problem will arise with even greater acuteness. To some extent the commonly accepted distinction between grades of mallams tends to preserve or re-establish the class barrier; for the 'knowledge' which makes the 'true' mallam is more readily accessible to the leisured and wealthy than to the craftsman or peasant. However, the full consequences of this conflict are not yet visible. Indeed, we cannot predict if the conflict itself will stay; for extraneous changes (political or economic) may well weaken or remove the class barrier. Yet if it remains, the model of Islam might again show the solution, its sectarianism offering the possibility of diverse and even opposed religious alignments.

So much for the processes of change and 'contact'. As regards that end-state, it has become almost a dogma of many anthropologists that it always represents a unique cultural situation, something in the nature of a *'tertium quid'* which has no precise

---

[1] This should be taken literally. I found communities still observing the *gunnu*, where the economic co-operation of the large family group had disappeared (e.g. Doko or Mokwa); while in others, which had abandoned the *gunnu*, the old system of inheritance was only beginning to break down (e.g. Lemu).

antecedents in the 'parent cultures' and invariably amounts to more than a mere 'fusion or mixing'. Rather, 'the clash and interplay of two cultures produce new things'.[1] In cultural changes 'old elements are abandoned and new ones developed in close and constant relation to the existing configuration'.[2] To quote Herskovits' summing up of this school of thought: these scholars hold that 'the arithmetic of culture contact is never a process of addition. . . . A culture of multiple origins is different from any bodies of tradition that have contributed to it. The dynamics of acculturation . . . are creative.'[3] In the terms of our subject matter we should have to admit that Nupe-Islam is not so-and-so much Nupe religion plus so-and-so much Islam but a fundamentally novel phenomenon, unprecedented, integrated, self-contained.

Now the processes we outlined, devious, piecemeal, involving partial adjustments and often unstable compromise, make it clear that their end-result is indeed a 'new thing'. Yet equally they suggest that it is not, at any stage, fully integrated or self-contained. Whichever way we understand 'integration', or for that matter its antithesis, the mere 'fusion or mixing', no summary judgment of this kind is possible.

Taken at its most concrete meaning, the integration of a cultural item in a new setting would imply that the respective modes of behaviour are performed regularly and in predictable situations. But clearly there are degrees of this regularity. The Moslem *salla* or the pseudo-Moslem *navũ* represent fully regular, predictable modes of behaviour; so do the Fast of Ramadhan, the daily prayers, and the observance of alms-giving. But Moslem-style divination or medical practices, the Moslem solemnization of kinship events, and the Moslem rules of preferential marriage, are much less regular and predictable. They represent ways of acting which people may or may not choose, having become established only as cultural 'alternatives', to borrow Linton's phrase.[4] The visits to the mosque are even more irregularly observed, while the concern with Islamic mythology or theology is purely sporadic if not exceptional.

Nor is the picture more uniform when we understand 'integration' to mean, more abstractly, a firm fit between the originally alien elements of culture and their new setting. This fit can only be of three kinds: it may be one of purpose, the alien elements exhibiting some rationally intelligible utility or appropriateness in the new setting; or it may be visible in the logical consistency

---

[1] B. Malinowski, *The Dynamics of Culture Change*, 1945, pp. 21, 25.
[2] R. Linton, *The Study of Man*, 1936, p. 360.
[3] M. J. Herskovits, *Man and his Work*, 1948, p. 534.
[4] Op. cit., p. 273.

obtaining between the two; or the 'fit' may be psychological, in that the old and new modes of behaviour exhibit the same emotional 'tone' or 'ethos'.[1]

Undoubtedly, there is evidence for the nexus of utility or appropriateness, even though its character varies widely. The great ceremonials of Islam conspicuously serve political interests and the regulation of adolescence; equally they have been fitted into the cycle of routine and recreation. The daily prayers, the fast, and alms-giving have no such momentous part to play; yet precisely because they are inconsequential and depend on private decisions alone, they have come to exemplify adherence to the new creed in a manner both conspicuous and easy to assume. In other words, they serve as distinguishing marks, as badges of Islam, much as do the turban or other suggestive items of dress. Yet worship in the mosque rather than in the open, a flexible system of priestship rather than one based on inheritance or supernatural vocation, or the Moslem variants of marriage in the kindred have no particular utility. Indeed, worship in the village mosque tends to weaken the solidarity of the community which all other features of the social organization aim to uphold; while the inadequacy of the Moslem rules of widow marriage had to be corrected by a remodelling of the funeral customs.[2] Again, the Moslem funeral ceremonial fails to express the important social distinction between old age and youth.[3] And the muddled pseudo-Islamic mythology is surely nothing but an incongruous, valueless 'addition'. All we can say about the appropriateness of these novel practices is that they conform to the rules of Islam; which is only repeating that Islam has in fact been adopted, with all these features, whether they have an ulterior purposefulness or not.

Logical consistency, even the interest in simulating it, is widely absent: think of the employment, by the Mohammedan sovereigns, of the *ndakó gboyá* cult; of the *navũ* performed without any notion of or, for that matter, curiosity about the meaning of this ritual of fire; or of the preservation of the pagan marriages between grandmother and grandson by people otherwise consciously committed to Moslem practice.

Only on the plane of psychological effects is there a close and indeed convincing 'fit', the result, quite clearly, of selection and remodelling. Thus the mystic and ecstatic observances of Islam are absent; and the hectic, sexually excited mood of the *gani* or *navũ* merely duplicates the mood formerly evoked in the *gunnu*. Integration, then, is complete only where it bears on the ethos of

[1] For the theoretical basis of this argument see my *Foundations of Social Anthropology*, 1951, pp. 384–5 *et seq.*
[2] See above, p. 122.   [3] See above, pp. 129–30.

Nupe religion; but integration here means persistence, so that in the one instance in which the adoption of the new creed is truly not a mere 'addition' it also ceases to be a 'new thing'.

It is hardly surprising that this 'fit' should apply to the emotional 'tone' of religion and should prove the tenacity of predispositions so deeply rooted in the personality. Even so, there can be no finality about it; this is only the picture as we see it today, and it is possible that further developments, or strains only slowly gathering weight, will bring a change here also. In a previous chapter I ventured a prediction of this kind.[1] Let me now add that traces of such a change are already visible. For the *navũ* is more violent than the *gunnu* or any traditional rite used to be, and focuses its violence more sharply. Also, it was left to the new ceremonial to embody the 'licensed liberties' of joking relationship, which are otherwise played out privately and sporadically. As we remember, they are enacted mainly between the sexes and between boys and older men, and hence set aside respect, relationships and rules of etiquette normally scrupulously observed. Thus publicly staged, the 'licensed liberties' clearly provide a gratification sharper and more consciously aggressive than traditional usage could have afforded. Here, then, the greater political tensions in the city and the greater strain set up by changing moral standards seem to demand this more explosive relief: certainly, the older 'ethos' would not have condoned it.

[1] See above, p. 226.

IX

CONCLUSIONS

1. ON TYPES OF RELIGION

WE possess no systematic typology of religion, either of the great world religions or of the forms typical of 'primitive' societies. Perhaps indeed, as Max Weber suggests, the 'historical individualities' and the 'highly complex nature' of most religions preclude any truly comprehensive conspectus; so that we could aim only at partial typologies, concerned with one or the other aspect of religion, such as its effect upon the 'economic ethics' of societies, which was Weber's own theme.[1] However this may be, we cannot hold Nupe religion *in toto* against a given and agreed series of religious types, comparing it with them or identifying it among them. We cannot summarily say—'Nupe religion conforms to such-and-such a type of religion': which is clearly the sort of thing one would wish to say in a chapter on 'Conclusions'.

Yet we have a wide (if unsystematic) knowledge of diverse religious systems with which that of Nupe would bear comparison. At least, it can be so compared if we consider separately the various kinds of efficacy which we generally ascribe to any one religion. Let me here speak of 'competences' of religion; for what I mean is, crudely speaking, the things religions 'do' for individuals or societies; the effects they have upon their lives and actions or, if you like, the 'needs' they are capable of satisfying. There is no need to refine our terminology further. We are all agreed that religion 'does' certain things, has particular effects, and satisfies particular desires, needs, or purposes. We can, I suggest, distinguish four main 'competences' of religion, though the division between them is probably never very sharp: (1) The capacity of religion 'to furnish certain supplements to (the) view of the world of experience' which 'our intelligence is driven to demand';[2] (2) its capacity to announce and maintain moral values or, more generally, an

---

[1] Max Weber, 'The Social Psychology of the World Religions', *Essays in Sociology*, ed. by H. H. Gerth and C. W. Mills, 1947, p. 292.
[2] Herman Lotze, *Outlines of a Philosophy of Religion*, 1892, p. 7.

'economic ethic', that is, its competence to guide 'the practical impulses for action;[1] (3) its competence to hold together societies and sustain their structure; and (4) its competence to furnish individuals with specific experiences and stimulations.

The first three instances refer to the nexus between religion and other, autonomous, spheres of interest—the understanding of the universe; morality; maintenance of the given society. The last 'competence' refers to an interest intrinsic to religion, which, however, merges with all the others and imparts to them their peculiarly 'religious' character. Clearly, without that added interest the desire to understand the universe would belong to science; the efforts at maintaining society in a given form would represent civic or political aims; and the ethical tenets would be just that and no more. In other words, we should not be speaking of religion but of something else.

It may therefore seem impossible to define this 'intrinsic' interest of religion save in circular fashion, as a 'religious need' or a need for 'religious experiences'. But we can at least analyse 'religious experience' further and describe it more explicitly. For it always contains two things—something in the nature of an emotional state or a psycho-physical stimulation, and a more or less articulate assurance. William James means the former when he speaks of the 'organic thrill' which 'comes over us' with 'the thought of supernatural relations';[2] and Max Weber refers to the latter when he speaks of the 'annunciations and promises' that go with every religion.[3]

The circle reappears, however, between these two components of religious experience. For since the 'organic thrill' is religious (and not, say, aesthetic, or purely organic, as in fear) only when it goes with the awareness of 'supernatural relations', it presupposes some prior, more basic assurance or belief that there *is* a supernatural that can be experienced or a divinity in some manner knowable. Yet equally, that assurance and belief (if they are 'religious') are not in the nature of assurances given once and for all or of beliefs learned and held in a detached, theoretical manner. Rather, they depend on the repeated, vivid acts of experiencing the 'supernatural', which strengthen the belief and give substance to the assurance. Religion, as it were, both announces that there is the realm of the transcendental or divine and provides occasions for experiencing and hence proving it. Mystics will hold that there is no such division and therefore no circle either, but that there exist experiences simply creative of belief and revealing that basic

---

[1] Max Weber, op. cit., p. 267.
[2] *The Varieties of Religious Experience*, 1928, p. 27.
[3] Op cit., p. 270.

assurance. Rationalists may, with Bishop Berkeley, argue that belief is inescapable but 'for want of attention' and a 'wilful shutting of the eyes'.[1] And philosophers have been trying to break the circle by adducing logical proofs for the existence of God and divine providence: so that these might be shown of necessity to exist, while the religious experience only enables man to behold them.

We need not concern ourselves further with this circle. The people we study are neither theologians nor philosphers who must save religious faith from doubts and criticisms. Theirs is a simple belief and, as we know, an unambitious one. As for ourselves, we take that basic assurance to be simply the crucial assertion of all religious doctrines and the premiss of all religious experiences and actions.

To return to our four 'competences'. It is, I suggest, in that light that we usually compare diverse forms of religion and make statements about their character or 'type'. Thus we should point to the greater or lesser interest of religions in cosmological speculations and the construction of a *Weltbild*, and to their varying concern with morality and pragmatic norms of action. Again, we should compare tribal or national religions with universal ones; 'churches' differently organized; and the diverse emphases of religions, here on the solid mass of worshippers, and there on exceptional individual efforts, on what Weber calls 'virtuoso' as against 'mass religiosity'.[2] Finally, we should distinguish between religions cultivating the peculiar 'thrills' of mystic experience and other, more prosaic ones, between orgiastic and dispassionate, ritualistic and non-ritualistic observances, or between religions exploiting particular aesthetic stimuli and others disregarding this additional appeal. In this connection, too, we might refer to the relative weight of 'magical' and specifically 'religious' features, meaning in the former case, briefly, an assurance resting on the manipulation and enforcement of supernatural benefits, and in the latter the assurance that comes from the appeal and submission to a divine intelligence.

These examples are neither exhaustive nor exhaustively analysed. In each case distinctions of degree will occur side by side with distinctions of kind. More importantly, in each case we should find on closer analysis that the particular 'competence' of any religion derives unequally from the different elements in its make-up. For the complex of beliefs and practices we call a religion is made up of three things or 'elements'—a doctrine formulating the content of ideas; a congregation, that is, an organized collectivity of believers and officiants; and a set of observances, that is,

[1] *Principles of Human Knowledge*, Sec. cliv.
[2] Op cit., p. 287.

actions more or less ritualized. Needless to say, the three elements are inseparable: for ritual actions require the warrant of doctrine and execution by a congregation; while the doctrine finds practical expression in rituals and has validity only for the group of believers.[1] Now, there is a certain correspondence between the different competences and the different elements of religion. The *Weltbild* and the ethical tenets are clearly conveyed primarily by the formulated doctrine; the bearing of religion upon group structure, though it may be implicit also in the doctrine, derives primarily from the character and constitution of the congregation. But in the case of the specifically 'religious' experiences on one side and ritual action on the other, this correspondence no longer holds.

It is true that behaviour ritualized in some manner and perhaps enlisting the aid of poetry, music and the visual arts, acts directly as a psycho-physical stimulus, evoking particular excitements or emotional states. But so does, through cognitive channels, the idea content of religion, both by the very way it pictures the transcendental world (as serene or familiar, and as fearful or mysterious) and by the language it employs (clear or elusive, simple or weighted with stirring metaphors). To some extent such stimulations also come from the element we termed the congregation; for this term includes two kinds of groups, the collectivity for which the particular religious tenets are valid, that is, the community of believers; and the collectivity of individuals who meet together in the acts of worship. In the religious practices peculiar to small groups, say, village communities, the two may in fact coincide; in the religion of a tribe or nation, they will diverge. However this may be, the community of believers has only the one competence of maintaining the given society. The congregation-in-worship, while sharing in this competence inasmuch as it mobilizes particular human aggregates within the society, through its varying scale also brings into play definite psychological stimuli: think only of the two extremes, worship in crowds or in solitude.

We must consider, finally, that ritual action is effective, not only directly, in the manner of sensory stimuli provoking psychological effects, but also symbolically, through pointing to other facts or to ideas about facts in the manner in which signs point to the things signified or a drama demonstrates a moral or message. That rituals may be fully 'dramas' need not be especially emphasized. Whether they are or not, the 'message' carried by sym-

---

[1] The term 'elements' was chosen only for the sake of simplicity. We should speak, more correctly, of the three *dimensions* to which religion, like any social fact, belongs, viz.—the dimension of physical action (through its rituals), of grouping (through its congregation), and of idea-systems (through its doctrine). See my *Foundations*, pp. 79–80, 83, 85.

bolic behaviour may concern all the other competences of religion —explanation of the universe; ethical tenets; and support for a given form of society.

This complicated interplay, with all its various possibilities, is illustrated in the diagram below. In practice, of course, only certain of these interrelations will be utilized or emphasized in any religious system, and will thus establish its particular construction or type. Yet in trying to define Nupe religion in this sense we are also doing more than merely placing it within such a theoretical typological schema. For since this is constructed on the basis of the 'competences' of religion and upon the premiss that religion 'does' something for people, it clearly bears on why's and wherefore's and permits us to explain why a particular religion is what it is. It is clear, further, that this explanation will be in terms of some intelligible nexus between the religion we wish to understand and the society where it happens to occur and achieves or proves its competence.

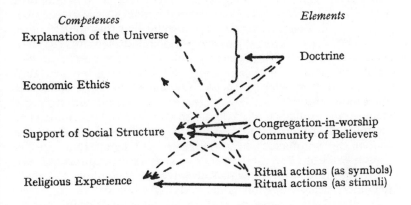

Now, in the case of the first three competences the position is simple. Since they refer to interests or purposes existing in their own right, the competences already indicate the nature of the nexus, which will be one of subservience, on the part of religion, to the given interests or purposes; in more general terms, the nexus will be one of purpose and means-to-end relations, religion contributing means for the attainment of the other ends. Only this must be added. In speaking of religion as having this or that competence we are referring only to the nature of its capacities: we are predicating nothing about the completeness or success with which they are realized. This can only be discovered through examining concrete instances, when we may well find that the employment of religion falls short of its potentialities or leads to conflicts rather than to success.

In the case of the 'intrinsically' religious interests, however, this viewpoint is inapplicable. We cannot now measure what religion 'does' or is capable of 'doing' against given things outside that 'need doing'. Indeed, we conclude that the things in question need doing, that particular mental states and assurances need to be provided, only because religion, which provides them, in fact exists. Yet the competence of religion to offer occasions for such experiences is not for that reason self-contained and irreducible save to a postulated desire for this kind of occasion. Clearly, even this desire does not exist in isolation, forbidding all further search for some explanatory nexus with the circumstances of human and social existence. But the nexus is now of a different kind, namely, a causal one. We no longer view the various interests or purposes that exist in social life as ends towards which religion contributes such-and-such means, but as causes making the people living with such interests and purposes seek the experiences we call religious. So that we interpolate psychological mechanisms between the two. Religion still 'does' something for people; but this something is now a matter of mental states expressed and of pressures relieved. There will be little disagreement on this point; we must, however, guard against over-intellectualizing this efficacy of religion. William James, for example, saw in religion a 'solution' for a felt 'uneasiness', for the 'sense that there is something wrong about us as we naturally stand.' [1] The formulation is not perhaps very fortunate. More importantly, it is one-sided, referring only to the share of the 'annunciations and promises' of religion, that is, to its content of ideas. Yet the anxieties or stresses arising in social life ('as we naturally stand') are also resolved in religion by the sheer dynamics of its excitations and reliefs.

To these two viewpoints a third one must be added; for the nexus between religion and the other circumstances of social life may also take the form of logical consistency, when we can point to identical premisses or formal principles embodied in the religion and in the social facts surrounding it. This aspect has so far escaped us; for it does not constitute a special competence of religion; rather does it run (so far as it is visible at all) through any or all competences. But so far as it is visible it enables us again to state, or explain, why a particular religion 'is what it is'.

I will not pursue this general discussion further. The three categories of explanation here suggested—in terms of purpose, of psychological causality, and of logical consistency—underlie all attempts at understanding social facts; which thesis has been fully

[1] Op. cit., p. 508.

discussed elsewhere.[1] Let us, then, turn back to Nupe religion and summarize its character or 'type' on the lines of our list of competences.

2. *Weltbild*: MORALITY

Nupe religion offers practically no cosmological knowledge; what there is of it is conveyed only by the doctrine and not, symbolically, by ritual. There is no interest in any far-flung picture of the universe such as a detailed mythology might present, nor in any closely reasoned account, the 'supplements' of rational knowledge being restricted to positing a remote, vague creator and enumerating a few of his creations. And here speculation stops at the phenomena intimately affecting human life (health and disease, procreation and death, dreams, certain features of inanimate nature). The rest is simply tacitly accepted. Nor are there attempts to interpret the world in anthropomorphous terms and so bring it nearer to human comprehension. The only link between man and this featureless transcendental world, apart from the supernatural controls somehow placed at his command, is vouchsafed by the belief in reincarnation and in an eternally active life principle. The humanly appealing theme of an other-worldly life is left untouched.

The language in which all this is conveyed is the familiar language of everyday life, simple and intentionally clear. Where the vagueness of the subject precludes satisfactory precision, there is recourse either to a simple 'we don't know' or to attempts at exploring linguistic meanings. The former does not imply any suggestion of a relevant mystery behind the visible world, but merely the placid admission of things unknowable. The latter betrays the conviction that the knowledge about the world, such as it is, is meant to be clear and can be clarified if the workaday tool of language is only carefully examined. This aimed-at clarity is further suggested by the predilection for parables and analogies, for juxtaposition or opposition, and by the many enumerations by twos and fours which pervade the doctrine.

This schematicism is essentially abstract, involving no visual or similarly palpable aids, such as an alignment with colours or spatial orientations. Nor are these invested with symbolic meaning save in a few isolated instances (when black stands for secrecy and evilness, red for prosperity, and right and left for male and female respectively). Enumeration again serves only to order things schematically and clearly, the symbolic potentialities of numbers being ignored: thus there are no lucky or unlucky numbers, no numbers in any other way meaningful (save, in a crude form, in

[1] See my *Foundations*, pp. 256–7 *et seq.*

divination). The belief in lucky or unlucky days and months is not really an exception; for the numerical order underlying their selection is neither systematic nor valid apart from this one context.

It is important, however, that the tendency to enumeration and schematic juxtapositions does not characterize the formulated doctrine alone ('There are four things in the world'); it is as typical of the way in which individuals express their own speculative and occasionally unorthodox views, for example—'There are two gods, one in the sky, the other on earth'; 'The female spirits live in the water, male spirits on the land.' Thus there is some interest in speculation, which is often keen and readily engaged in. But it relates only to the given topics of religion, that is, to notions already formulated, and does not attempt to break new ground. In other words, the people are content with a bare and fragmentary *Weltbild*, but feel the desire, though not for wider knowledge, yet for greater clarity in the knowledge they possess. In either case the treatment is schematic rather than syllogistic, and nominalistic in that it leans on the intelligibility of words and on semantic exercises.

The religious knowledge so framed exhibits close consistency with other sectors of the culture. The non-anthropomorphous and abstract character of religion tallies with the non-realistic art of Nupe, and the emphasis on schematic arrangements in the former, with the geometrical-ornamental accent of the latter. Perhaps, too, there is a logical nexus between the unconcern with deities or humanized features of the universe and the absence of any drama proper (either in art or religion). The tendency to enumerations is visible also in Nupe folklore and in the Nupe calendar (where months are referred to by numbers). The same is true of status differences, political ranks, and age grades, which are always presented in schematic form and precisely numbered, even at the cost of inaccuracy; let me add that in a large number of communities the senior and politically important ranks number four. Nor are dichotomous arrangements less frequent; think only of the common juxtaposition of *Zitsú* ('town king') and *Žigi* ('town priest'). The dualism of the sexes, in particular, is carried to a considerable extent through Nupe language, which assigns a gender, expressed by adding the attribute 'male' or 'female', also to trees and plants. The interest, finally, in analogies and semantic exercises is amply exemplified: in Nupe literature, where whole stories are based on puns or on the ambiguity of words; in attempts at producing persuasive pedigrees for present customs by means of etymological speculations; and in ordinary conversation.

These are all preferred ways of handling and ordering material (of whatever kind); and since they are visible both within and without the sphere of religion we may say of the latter that it is an expression (among others) of the basic intellectual orientation of the people. There is one exception, however. In the secular sphere the Nupe are keen historians, always interested in tracing things back to their past. In their religious conceptions this interest is almost entirely absent; so far as it exists, it ceases to be religious, being satisfied with summary references to extraneous, political-historical events, such as the introduction of a cult by Tsoede or the origin of some religious practice in the reign of a particular king. At this point the attitudes towards things sacred and profane diverge; only the latter require a precise time perspective; the former are simply given, or adequately explained by that timeless *ultima causa*, the deity.

To return for a moment to the Nupe bias for dualistic conceptions. Though we have grouped it with the other 'intellectual orientations', with predilection for enumerations, parables, and so forth, it clearly betrays more than this kind of predisposition, serving also to articulate the sharply felt and emotionally weighted antagonism of the sexes, as in witchcraft fantasies and in the belief in the deadly female 'germ' of the 'diseases of God'. And since the awareness of this antagonism springs from unconscious sources, it would seem to be of a different and more fundamental order than the other expressions of the dualistic bias. Shall we, then, hold the two apart? Even so, there remains the uniformly dualistic *Weltbild*, whether it expresses the unconscious sexual anxieties of men or their dispassionate intellectual efforts to order the phenomena of the world. Or shall we assume some play of cause and effect between the two, taking the awareness of sex antagonism to be at the root of the intellectual bias, in the sense that it shaped a predisposition towards finding dichotomies also in all other areas of experience? Clearly, we might equally assume the opposite, that is, that the conception of sex antagonism in witchcraft and elsewhere would not have crystallized had it not been facilitated by a congenial intellectual predisposition. There is, I think, no answer to these questions. The dualistic viewpoint is simply one of the cardinal possibilities upon which the human intellect can seize in structuring the world of experience; and the antagonism of male and female represents once more one of very few possibilities available to societies, or to man in society, in their efforts to structure the universe of human relationships. All we can legitimately say is that the two emerged together, in mutual consistency.

The witchcraft belief simply that other dichotomy, of 'good' and 'evil', as does the belief in spirits and in the character of humans inscrutably fashioned by God. But this dichotomy is formulated only on this cosmic scale, referring to the 'things that are in the world', and has no narrower, pragmatic or ethical application. As for the realm of ethics, Nupe doctrine is altogether silent. It upholds no ideal man, nor condemns his antithesis. There is no eschatology, no mythology exemplifying rights and wrongs, crime and retribution, and no promise of reward to the law-abiding. Nor is the formulated doctrine concerned with norms of action of more common currency, the simple rights and wrongs of everyday morality. 'Economic ethics' has its place in ritual; since this turns upon such things as birth, marriage and adolescence, crops and the exigencies of the seasons, prosperity and wealth, that is, upon events and conditions involving practical decisions, the respective courses of action are implicitly upheld as desirable, worthwhile and 'right'. But they are not 'announced' or 'revealed', neither commanded nor yet conspicuously dramatized. Their significance is left to preliminary knowledge, the worshippers knowing at the outset what to expect of the ritual, both as regards its aim and the promises it vouchsafes. And these are again silent on ethical issues. The fortunes anticipated and the misfortunes that may befall you imply neither merit nor punishment: they simply happen, while religion means no more than an aid in attaining or evading them.

Only two explicit ethical commands occur in the whole range of Nupe rituals. They refer to filial obedience (enjoined in the *gunnu*) and to the blessedness of fecundity. But we remember that the relevant episode of the *gunnu* is also the first to fall victim to change, and that other religiously sanctioned aids, the services of the *cigbeci*, are dispensed in disregard of the moral condemnation of childlessness. On balance, then, Nupe religion is amoral. As we anticipated, the crucial issue in most religions, how to reconcile the discrepancy of religious merit and practical rewards, simply does not arise. Nupe religion takes life as it is, offering no 'annunciations and promises' that would redress its iniquities, and hardly even endorsing the equity that should govern it.

This equity is largely left to the care of secular agencies alone. Religion plays a part only indirectly, through sanctioning the persons—kings, chiefs, executioners—who act as guardians of the accepted good. The sanction lies essentially in ritual, that is, in the various ceremonials involved in the assumption of these offices or entrusted to their holders. But let us note that these men guard, not really morality, but only that part of it which has solidified in the form of politically enforced law. Differently expressed, Nupe society knows mainly crimes and few 'sins', and only lawful, not saintly behaviour. On occasion religion abandons even this indirect support for the conventions of morality; for certain rituals deny these conventions, as in the sexual licence of the *gunnu* and *gani* or in the condonation of violence in the *navũ*. At this point, then, the logical consistency between religion and the rest of social life ceases to be valid. Morally, the rituals in question have no message; or their message is a circuitous one, exemplifying the rule by the exception. Their 'competence' cannot therefore lie in this topsy-turvy picture of common morality: rather, as we already suggested, does it lie in the offer of explosive relief from normal constraints.

Let me say a little more on the amorality of the Nupe creed. Nupe religion, as we have seen, sanctions only the powers that be, the machinery of political control, and hence the claims of secular society to declare what is right and wrong. Religion by itself vouchsafes no direct and 'higher' assurance of this kind. It does not as it were speak for society, but only stands behind the appointed spokesmen. Needless to say, most religions go beyond this *carte blanche* for secular society. And in doing so they achieve two things: doubts and conflicts arising in mundane ethics can be resolved by the assurance that there are these other, 'higher' or 'eternal', values; and these can in turn serve as ideals which man is called upon to approach, however imperfectly. So that religion can both absorb the iniquities of human existence and give it an impetus towards making the world better than it is. Nupe religion can do neither. Thus conflicts over mundane ethics can be absorbed into religion only in the one province which itself proclaims the inevitability of conflicts, namely, in the hostile fantasies of witchcraft. And offering nothing 'higher' than an endorsement of mundane ethics, religion is emptied of its impetus towards world improvement: it is static, non-progressive, non-messianic, and once more content to take 'life as it is'.

3. RELIGION AND SOCIAL STRUCTURE

There is a certain overlap between this new nexus and the one just discussed. For since any group, of whatever structure, is such only in virtue of the norms of acting enjoined upon its members, the pronouncements of religion upon 'right' and 'wrong' conduct (say, 'thou shalt honour thy father and mother') already serve to uphold the group so constituted (the family, or the society based upon filial piety). Yet there is that special competence of religion to uphold group existence and structure as such, and not only such specific manners of acting as may form the subject of ethical commands. Nor can group existence and group structure be 'commanded': they can only be demonstrated or circuitously affirmed, though occasionally they are explicitly asserted, as in Judaism with its tenet of a 'chosen people', serving a tribal or national God.

Again, Nupe religion lacks such explicit assertions, as it lacks also that conspicuous focus of group existence, a tribal god. There is no conception that the deity is concerned with this one people only or that the Nupe people are the sole or chosen possessors of true religion. To be sure, there are the legends explaining how the Nupe acquired *cigbe*, the Chain of Tsoede, and particular rituals; but it is understood that other peoples also have medicines, rituals, and supernatural skills of various kinds. The Nupe tribe lays claim only to the possession of certain *particular* instances, not of the *genera* ritual or medicine. Even so qualified, this claim or title becomes an aspect of group identity and hence one of the supports of the tribe's existence as a group. A similar possession of particular observances and sacred skills also identifies the groups of diverse or lesser inclusiveness: the state (which possesses the 'royal cults'); the village community (which may possess a special *kuti*); and the kin group (which possesses hereditary *cigbe* and ancestral sacrifices.

This possession is adjusted even more finely, so that it comes to affirm, not only the corporate identity of this or that group, but also its internal structure. For as the administration of the village *kuti* is vested in single kin groups but serves the whole community, so it endorses the make-up of a group in all other respects similarly segmented yet co-operative; and as the administration of kinship rituals falls to the senior man in the lineage and descends in that line but is meant to benefit also wives, mothers, daughters- and sisters-in-law, so it endorses the basic kin group, the extended family or 'house'. All of which implications are contained in the Nupe conception of the 'ownership' of cults.

This ownership, though corporate, does not *make* the group in question; it pertains to groups already constituted as such by other criteria, whatever they may be—common language, territorial possession, citizenship, descent, cohabitation, and so forth. The possession of the religious observances is thus a feature of group identity only in combination with all the others and in fact presupposes them. This relationship is reversed only once, in the case of the Nupe emigrants whose title to 'Nupedom' rests solely on the retention of the traditional cults.

The Nupe congregation, in the wider or narrower sense, is such inevitably, mainly by descent, and not by individual choice, as is the case in a 'church' open to all comers. Fundamentally, this is a closed religion, bound up with membership of tribe, nation, village or kin group, and part of the 'estate' of these groups. In a few instances—most (not all) *cigbe*, divination, the unimportant sacrifices to spirits—the benefits of religion are accessible to individuals *qua* individuals, even to strangers from other tribes. In all other respects individuals share in the ministrations of religion only in virtue of their membership of the respective groups, and share in them on equal terms. For there are no qualifications which might make one unpredictably a vessel of divine grace, nor degrees of sacredness attainable by personal endeavour. The miraculous birth of the *gunnu* priest comes closest to the former conception; while the technical skills of *cigbe* and the *ndakó gboyá* society with its open recruitment at least enable individuals so inclined to become active agents of the supernatural. Even so, these are not qualifications for religious excellence nor calls for spiritual leadership. The Nupe congregation has equal access to grace and blessings; it knows no spiritual leaders or chosen vessels: it is a 'mass', not a 'virtuoso' religion.

But consider that secular life, with its ranks and status differences, is governed by precisely these notions of individual effort after excellence and of unequal access to existing benefits. In a sense, then, the ideals of secular and religious life are opposed to one another. Yet if they were not thus opposed, if effort after excellence held good in the religious congregation as much as it does in the mundane society, the diverse achievements might easily clash and lead to divided leadership. As it is, this cannot happen. One of the results is that Nupe religion, unlike other creeds, is incapable of compensating the failures of secular ambition with the promise of spiritual success or exaltation; another, that religion can achieve that other competence, of fully supporting 'mundane ethics'. It need not have been so. The egalitarianism of this 'mass religion' might have meant the promise, and hence that other 'compensation', of equality before God, as against the inequalities of which Nupe life is full. But this potentiality is left unexploited. In so far as Nupe religion deviates from the values governing secular life, it does so with insufficient emphasis to carry such a message of hope; indeed, the message it might have carried would be belied by too many other features of the creed and manner of worship.

We have so far considered the 'congregation' in the wider sense, as a community possessing such-and-such observances and means of communing with the supernatural. Understood as a collection of individuals worshipping together, the congregation again endorses or upholds the relevant groups existing within the society, now through mobilizing them in the act of worship. The tribe is not a congregation in this narrower sense, and the nation becomes one only intermittently and partially; but the presence of these inclusive groups is recalled in the prayer formulæ which mention the ancestor king Tsoede and on occasion call divine blessing upon 'the whole land of Nupe'. The village community is invariably a congregation-in-worship (and is mentioned in the prayer), as is also the kin group, in the different kinship ceremonials. As for individuals, they may by themselves solicit the more technical supernatural aids; but there is no true worship by individuals, only worship in groups or, in solitary sacrifices and the like, on behalf of groups.

The congregation-in-worship, over and above mobilizing a particular group, also mobilizes it in such manner that its internal structure is thrown into relief. We recall such features as the 'inner circle' of worshippers, composed of mature men; the roles of officiants, vested in titled elders or family heads; the precedence of rank, observed in the communal meal; the subordinate tasks assigned to adolescents, the obedience demanded of them, and the partial exclusion of women and strangers. The arrangement of the congregation, then, mirrors the status arrangements meant to be valid in mundane society, so that the latter is demonstrated so-so-speak, in model form, dramatized, and endorsed by the sacred context.

We note again that religion has no message of its own, transcending or reversing the secular norms: there is no preaching of, say, 'the first shall be last'. Even the festivals of youth, *gani* and *navũ*, though they grant to the adolescents a freedom and initiative not normally enjoyed, also exemplify in various ways respect for rank and loyalty to political leadership. Nor does religious practice cancel that paramount factor in secular society, wealth: we remember the cost of rituals (communal or kinship) and of supernatural aids privately solicited, which causes the former to vary in scale with available means and may make the latter inaccessible to the poor. This point is important since one feature of ritual procedure may seem to indicate a reversal of the secular ideal. I am referring to the uniform, simple dress obligatory in the pagan rites, which thus excludes the visible tokens of wealth from the circle of worshippers. It was left to the Moslem ceremonials with their chances for display to remove this egalitarian touch. But it is only a touch and no more, representing no effective symbolism; for the people do not derive any message or moral from it but regard it merely as a ritual rule among others, meant to draw the line between sacred and profane occasions.

Let us therefore call Nupe religion conservative, non-revolutionary, and again, non-messianic. Only in one respect does the congregation fail to 'mirror' social reality correctly, in that it upholds a subordinate position of the women which is not true in real life. For the men, religious practice thus expresses an ideal frustrated in every-day experience. But in this one sphere of conflict where religion no longer endorses 'life as it is', it is also incapable of contenting the believers, forcing them to resort to the fantasies

CONCLUSIONS 273

about female witches and to the vicarious satisfaction of witch-hunting. Nupe religion, we must conclude, cannot hold its own as a messenger of ideals.

4. ASSURANCE AND STIMULATION

We have already mentioned the circular efficacy linking these two components of religious experience. Yet they can be separated in analysis, as much (or as little) as the mere knowing and learning of religious truths can be held apart from the actual living through acts of devotion.

Concerning the assurances about the world and man's place in it which can be known and learned, there is little to say, and most that can be said is negative. Nupe doctrine does not teach that the universe is benevolent or that the deity is closely concerned with human fate. Though man has skills and ritual procedures to invoke supernatural aid, their outcome will often remain uncertain. Thus these skills and procedures contain only traces of the calculable forcefulness of 'magic'. The strictly technical manipulations of *cigbe* come closest to this conception; yet they, too, are subject to the will of God, or accident, and even the miraculous medicines in which one places absolute confidence involve 'invocations' (not 'spells') and hence an element of submission. In the last resort, man can only appeal and supplicate; if, on balance, Nupe religion is optimistic, this only means that it holds out hopes in the face of a world governed by accident, not that there is an assured or reassuring design behind it.

To turn to the 'stimulations'. We need not stress again that the self-abandonment of the mystic or visionary is utterly foreign to the Nupe. Never does the worshipper face his god in solitude, drawing only upon his inward experience or seeking private illumination. Nor is the mood he seeks in his worship entirely religious, that is, unattainable save through the 'thought of supernatural relations'; for in all the major rites at least, that mood emerges also from the added stimuli of music, dancing, crowd behaviour, and perhaps sexual excitement. Generally, the mood of Nupe worship is restrained and calm, leading to no extremes either of fear and stress or of exultation. The absence of elaborate ritualism precludes the tensions that go with rigidly prescribed gestures or speech; in avoiding nocturnal performances most rituals also avoid the sharp accents of fear and mystery; and the rules of ritual etiquette usually curb abandoned behaviour.

Above all, the mood of Nupe worship lacks development. The ritual prepares and holds a sense of the sacred in various, familiar ways—through rules marking off the ritual occasion from ordinary ones; through the subdued, solemn manner of applying oneself to the ritual task; and through the serious import of the supplication. But this mood is merely 'lived through'; it involves no mounting expectancy, pressing for some culminating experience or final fulfilment. In the act of worship proper, embodied in the esoteric phase of any rite, the prayer or the sacrificial meal might play that part. Intellectually, the prayer represents the crucial moment, when the whole purpose of the ritual is made clear and the appeal or hope articulately expressed. In the large-scale ceremonials, too, there is some emotional preparation for that moment, drumming and singing being abruptly silenced when the prayer is about to be uttered. Yet it is uttered too early in the proceedings and uttered too informally to come as a culminating stage. The sacrificial meal stands out in that it concludes the act of worship proper; but just then the solemn mood is also visibly fading.

The movable rites and minor observances, consisting as they do only of prayer and sacrifice, do not progress beyond that short-lived 'sensing of the sacred'. And if the great ceremonials offer further excitements and something akin to a final climax, these no longer grow out of the awareness of transcendental events, but are achieved through the massed stimuli of more common appeal —music, dancing, and so forth. As I suggested in an earlier context, some anticipation of the final stimulations must fuse with the mood of the worship proper; as the congregation in turn retains some sense of the sacred even in the phase of the 'merry-making', though in the absence of elaborate symbols acting as 'reminders' that sense is none too secure. What is important is that the worship as such does not work up to any final 'fulfilment'; rather, the emotional tensions remain diffuse and without climax. They only sensitize the congregation to the 'annunciations and promises' voiced in the ritual but do not prepare the worshippers for revelations.

The bush vigil in the *gunnu* may seem an exception since here certain pronouncements are made to a congregation previously exposed to fear and the thrills of mystery. But again, this is not a true climax of religious experience; this episode is only a prelude to the actual rite (and can in fact be omitted); while the pronouncement is concerned with nothing more momentous than an admonishment of adolescents. Indeed, the very mood of fear and mystery, which would seem so congenial to the expectancy of revelations, must be called exceptional. One other ritual, the *mamma*, is staged in a similar atmosphere; but it occurs only in a few communities and is performed with little excitement or awe; nor does it carry any message or 'annunciation'.

Another exception is more important. In each Nupe community the calm and restrained mood of worship is reversed once, in the

CONCLUSIONS

abandoned excitement of one or the other of the three ceremonials *gunnu, gani* and *navũ*. This break in the 'ethos' of Nupe religion carries its own explanation; for it is understood as a licence, setting aside normally valid and precisely named controls—of sex and of physical violence against political opponents. Here, then, impulses repressed in secular life are compensated, and tensions generated through the repression, offered explosive, or 'cathartic', release. Religion, in providing these outlets (on circumscribed occasions), anticipates as well as canalizes the working of psychological mechanisms, which might otherwise operate in random fashion or beyond the control of the society, in the 'private worlds' of neuroses and psychopathic fantasies.[1]

Probably no society is free from some such repressions. In Nupe, they are clearly traceable. The 'ethos' of Nupe life is again generally calm and restrained; but in some measure it is only meant to appear so. That it also conceals deep anxieties and tensions is shown by the witchcraft fantasies, which belie the acquiescence so often typical of the overt relationship between the sexes. And in one sphere of social life, in political ambition, passions and anxieties come to the surface. Consider, however, that this intense political rivalry is itself an instance of 'constraint', imposed as it is by the rigid class society. Indeed, it is doubly 'constrained'; for the passions here aroused are not permitted free play, as they might in some kind of jungle ethics, but are hemmed in by an intricate code of etiquette imposing semblance of gentility and acquiescence. We must conclude, then, that the uneven mood of Nupe religion indicates an 'ethos' kept calm and unexcited through those circumscribed chances of unrestraint. In other words, while certain facts of worship express the calmness meant to govern mundane life, others make it possible, through absorbing its disturbances into their own explosive mood. As we know, the balance is imperfect; there are the sudden outbursts of political passion when pent-up tensions find 'random' relief, as well as escapes into neurosis. Let us note a further point. One familiar 'compensation', in the form of fantasies about a golden age or a promised millennium, is entirely absent in Nupe religion. The Nupe attempt to resolve the 'uneasiness' of reality not in ideological fashion but, as I put it before, by the 'sheer dynamics' of repressions lifted and emotional tensions relieved.

Here we are already touching upon the fusion of 'assurance' and 'stimulation'. It occurs, briefly, when 'living through' the acts of worship leaves some lasting effect upon the individual's attitude towards the world around him: the cathartic relief of the few hectic rituals implies precisely this. Yet the effect is diffuse and in

[1] See my *Foundations*, p. 356.

a sense crude, containing no intellectual insight or gain; nor perhaps is the gain a lasting one. In a cruder form still, much the same change is entailed in any exciting or pleasurable interruption of workaday routine and in the consequent readiness for further work; which effect, too, must be ascribed to the Nupe ceremonials and festivities. But clearly, the fusion of 'stimulation' and 'assurance' can operate also on a higher, that is, more conscious, plane. It is in this sense that theologians think of the access of faith or fortitude entailed in acts of worship and William James speaks of the 'assurance of safety' and the 'new zest which adds itself like a gift to life'.[1]

Undoubtedly, this is true also of Nupe religion, even though its acts of worship are without precise revelations and merely voice hopes impressive only because they are reinforced by diffuse excitements. Yet if we grant this access of faith, we must grant also that it will have to prevail against difficulties, failures and disappointments. Acts of worship, therefore, both build up faith and draw upon it. Somewhat differently expressed, we have made this point in an earlier context; there, too, we suggested that only the fixed rituals, whose aims are fundamentally unspecific and whose design brings into play all the more stirring stimulations, can assume the former role; while the movable rites and all the other contingent observances, being prosaic and meant to be successful in specific needs, apply faith and draw upon it as much as, fortuitously, they may strengthen it.[2] Let me add this observation only. The fixed rituals, though they engender faith, are not meant to be repeated or changed for the sake of greater efficacy. They are prescribed occasions when man can commune with the deity and touch divine power, and through this alone a source of assurance. Also, their number is small, so that Nupe life is not punctuated with occasions creative of faith. Here, then, we meet with something like an economy of faith which seems to have found its own level.

In other religions this economy may work differently. Certainly, it seems to work in Nupe, where it goes together with an unambitious doctrine allowing for the failure of specific appeals and upholding no firm over-all assurance. For by and large, the tenor of Nupe life is optimistic; nor are there any instances of individuals turning cynics or being driven into unbelief by disappointed hopes. Does this mean that the zest and assurance evoked in the acts of worship (but tempered and hence protected by the cautious doctrine) are sufficient to endure and pervade all the efforts of practical life? or only that religious experience is not meant to be enduring and pervasive?

[1] Op cit., pp. 403-4.   [2] See above, pp. 105-6.

We cannot precisely measure this psychological aftermath of acts of worship. But we can assess it indirectly, from the concern with religious experiences visible in everyday life. And here it is quite clear that our second assumption is the correct one. For the acts of worship do not leave any vivid awareness of the achieved communion with the deity nor any lasting sense of the holy. There is nothing of 'religiosity' in the Nupe character. He knows, of course, at all times, that there is a God and a realm of the supernatural; but ordinarily this is tacit knowledge, of no practical relevance, neither permanently awe-inspiring nor permanently exhilarating. Crudely speaking, the Nupe are religious only on religious occasions; in between, life is an affair of secular values and rules-of-thumb. That even sacred places are 'sacred' only at certain times of the year is part of the same attitude; so is the absence of any conception of personal holiness. Even Islam, with its daily prayers, its Friday service, and its pious scholars, has hardly affected this attitude. For the daily prayers have become unthinking routine, without any touch of the mystic; being a mallam is a profession among others and often combined with them; and the Moslem cult of saints or 'holy men' found no response.

All this means that the spheres of religion and the profane remain clearly separable. Probably few religions merge completely with secular life so that every possible action bears some reference to transcendental notions. Nor, of course, can we conceive of religions which would at no point coincide with mundane interests. But the border zone between the two can be more or less wide and more or less sharply circumscribed. In Nupe, this zone is narrow and sharply outlined. Wherever the 'competences' of religion bear on mundane interests we can readily mark the point where the coincidence ceases. There is no 'carry-over' from one to the other. Thus religion sustains the offices of chiefs, kings, and other exponents of authority and law: but their person is not sacred, and criminals convicted by these holders of supernaturally sanctioned offices are not treated with any show of awe or sacred horror. Religion helps to bind together the kin group through the belief in reincarnation, through ancestral sacrifices, and through the solemnization of marriage and birth: but the Nupe do not, on normal occasions, speak the names of the ancestors with bated breath or constantly worry about placating their spirits. Marriage is in no sense sacred, and children are not holy; even children whose birth is ascribed to the efficacy of sacrifice are not treated in any special way.[1] Nor, finally, are the sick who recover with supernatural aid or the crops that thrive after some rite has been duly

---

[1] The only rules of this kind are entailed in the *sogba* cult, of alien origin.

performed subject to special taboos or other rules meant to recall the divine intervention.

Nupe religion, then, has a defined place in the scheme of things. It is not that scheme itself, embracing or giving meaning to all other things with which human life is concerned. If religion engenders assurance and optimism, human life yet relies equally on the assurance and confidence that go with rational skills and mundane experiences. This is hardly unexpected. A religion which provides no *Weltbild*; which keeps aloof from moral judgments; which upholds no messianic ideals; and which rejects the incalculable revelations of mystics, is also a religion content with its own province. That province still 'supplements' or completes all the others and 'transcends' whatever they offer in the way of rational understanding, practical measures, and exhilarating or reassuring experiences. But this careful fit of a province among others, even though it completes their series on a higher, transcendental plane, has something of the rational. It savours of some plan of giving unto religion only what is hers, by some right that can be reasoned out. Perhaps we should say that Nupe religion is as rational as religion can be.

But this is, in religion, not a golden mean. The Nupe case does not prove that a religion thus rationally tempered saves the believers from disturbing doubts or cosmic fears just because its claims and promises are so unambitious. Nupe religion may well aim to be a sort of Plutarchian creed, steering a middle course between unbelief and too much belief, where man neither 'directeth and opposeth all his plaints and lamentations against fortune and casuality', nor yet 'will think and say that every disease and infirmity of his body, all his losses . . . and his repulses and disgraces are so many plagues inflicted upon him by the ire of the gods and the very assaults of divine justice.' [1] But in thinking neither wholly one thing nor wholly the other, the Nupe yet invite one sharp repulse to their mood of optimism: for they know the deep fear of witchcraft. And this is not, in their case, a fear of the consequences of impiety or of 'divine justice'; rather is it born of the awareness that the universe is inadequately controlled, and hence that the province of religion is too narrow.

[1] Plutarch, 'Of Superstition'; *Moralia*, translated by Philemon Holland, 1911 edition, p. 380.

INDEX

Abnormality, physical, 115, 171
Abortion, 146
Accident, in creation, 37, 104, 203, 204, 273
Acculturation, 253, 256
Adolescence, v, 82, 83, 111, 112, 218, 219, 225, 226, 244, 252, 257, 268, 272
Aesthetic factors, 97, 106, 223, 260, 261
After-life, 24–5, 33, 121, 265
Age differences, 81, 101, 111, 123, 125, 129–30, 257; grades, 80, 83, 92, 111, 126, 217–19, 225, 241–2, 243, 266; old, 22, 83, 123, 174, 257
Aggression, Aggressive behaviour, 201, 204, 242, 250, 258, 268, 275
Aims of ritual, professed, 103, 111, 114, 130–1, 211; 'additional', 'implicit', 111, 114, 130–1
Alien cults, 16, 26, 207, chap. VII, 277n.; congeniality of, 221–2, 224, 245; integration of, 256; Nupeization of, 215, 219, 227; and social pressure, 208, 221, 251; utility of, 221–3, 256–7
aljénu, see Spirits
Allah, 235, 238, 254
Alms, 118, 129, 235, 246, 256, 257
Amusement, 9n., 29, 95, 120, 216, 225, 240
Analogies, *see* Parables; Analogy, principle of, in medicine, 136, 137, 142–3, 147
Ancestors, 6, 9, 23, 24, 25, 26, 32, 33, 34, 68, 74–5, 100, 109, 116, 119, 149, 156, 195, 270, 277; ancestor chief, 31, 71, 74, a. king, *see* Tsoede
Angels, 59n., 247
anima, 21, 23

Animals, mythical, sacred, 13, 16, 23, 27–9, 33; in dreams, 66; in decorations, 29; in sacrifice, 75, 108–9, 121
Anthropomorphous, 2, 11, 26, 208, 229, 265, 266
Anti-social, 20
Aphrodisiacs, 140
Apolegetics, 203
Aptitudes, 55
Arabia, 245; arabic, 26, 56, 59–60, 64, 78, 238
Art, 236, 249, 262; decorative, 29; realistic, 208, 266
Assurance, *see* Certainty
Astrology, 59, 247
Authority, kinship, 83, 112, 130n., 174, 251, 268; secular, 268, 271–2, 277

Barber-doctors, 62, 64, 136, 138–42, 143, 144, 146, 157, 192; organization of, 153; b.-surgeon, 118
Bathing, 82, 241, 244
Beni sub-tribe, 77, 78, 83, 97, 147, 169
Benu, *see* Bornu
Beer drinking, 24, 54, 109, 249n.
Bell-rods, magic, 194, 210–11
Berkeley, Bishop, 261
Bida, 38, 49, 51, 52, 54, 56, 83, 97, 117, 119, 120, 138, 140, 147, 154, 163, 175, 182–3, 193, 199, 209, 216, 240, 241–4, 250
Bidney, D., 4, 6
Biological processes, 21, 24
Birth, 21, 23, 25, 33, 49, 50, 52, 66, 88, 89, 94, 103, 211, 221, 268, 277; ceremonial, 115–16; facilitating b., 140, 145; b.-marks, 31n., 72, 73; text on, 213
Blessing, 104–5
Blood, 74, 76, 88, 91, 92, 95, 101, 109

N.R.—T

INDEX

Body, human, 23, 30, 33, 36, 165–6, 185
bori cult, 209–10, 222, 223, 226
Bornu, 209, 220, 223
'Borrowing', 207, 227
Brideprice, 119, 174, 246, 249
Bull-roarer, 188
Burial, 10, 22, 77, 78, 122, 123, 124–5, 209, 211, 212; symbolic, 22, 218, 219
Butterfield, H., 205n.

Calendar, 65, 70, 84, 104, 239n., 249, 266
Cataleptic fit, 209
Categories, basic, of Nupe religion, 8, 10 *et seq.*
Catharsis, 106, 110, 204, 242, 275–6
Cekpā sub-tribe, 154
Certainty, in religious belief, 37, 65, 104, 204–5, 260–1, 273, 277; desire for, 204
Chameleon, 40, 147
Character traits, 23, 25, 29, 258, 277; and suspicions of witchcraft, 170–1, 181, 182, 187, 201
Charms, magic, 21, 80n., 143, 147, 160, 211
Chiefs, Chieftainship, 25, 31, 52, 71–2, 81, 85, 88, 89, 96, 111, 188, 196, 218, 268, 277; appointment of, 72, 88; elected, hereditary, 70, 85, 89; and priestship, 72, 266
Childless women, attitude towards, 82, 112, 175, 177, 180, 182; cures for, 21, 89, 140, 145, 212–13; in ritual, 82, 112, 113; in medicine, 143, 162
Children, possession of, 52, 177, 180, 213, 277; posthumous, 122, 128
Christianity, 2, 186, 231, 248n., 253
Church, concept of, 226, 234, 261; official, national, 232, 241
cigbe, *see* Medicine
Circumcision, 118–19
Clowns, 215, 240
Coitus, 21; *interruptus*, 22n.
Commercial activities, 167, 172; *see also* Trade
Compensations, offered in religion, 112, 178, 271
'Competences' of religion, 259 *et seq.*, 277
Competition, 217, 218, 226

'Completion', concept of, 71, 77, 79, 103, 107
Community and ritual, 34, 100–1
Conception, 21, 115, 140, 176
Conflicts, social, *see* Tensions, social
Conjuring tricks, 150
Conquest, 232, 233–4, 251, 252
Consecration of divining apparatus, 54, 55
Contraceptives, 21, 140, 143, 145, 148
Congregation, 106, 109, 130, 237, 244, 254, 261–2, 270–1
Conversion, religious, 226, 230, 254; to Christianity, 231; to Islam, 230, 232–5, 253
Cosmology, 9, 11, 142, 261, 265; moslem, 245, 247–8, 249
Cosmopolitan, 97, 223
Creation, 11, 12–13, 17, 19, 21, 29, 32, 35–6, 104, 203, 247, 248n., 265, 267–8
Crises, of community life, 97; of individual life, 114, 115, 121
Crocodile, sacred, 27–8, 68
Crops, 71, 103, 108, 238, 247, 268, 277
Crowd behaviour, 262, 273
Culture change, and belief, 207, 228, 251, 252, 254–5, 258; and medicine, 160–2; and ritual, 73, 83–4, 96–8, 114, 219, 226, 268; predictions of, 226, 258
Culture contact, v, 253, 256

Dance, dancing, 77, 78, 81–2, 88, 93, 95, 101, 106, 117, 118, 119, 120, 214, 215, 217, 219, 225, 236, 273; at funerals, 123, 127; magic, 5, 188, 194, 195, 209, 216; men's, 120; women's, 95, 119; separation of sexes in d., 77, 82, 101, 110, 113, 127, 218
Days, of the week, 56–7; 'lucky', 53, 67, 266
Death, 10, 22, 24, 25, 33, 35, 37, 50, 66, 77, 121 *et seq.*, 204, 247, 265, 277; abnormal, 124; attitude towards, 121–2, 123, 125, 130, 221; feigning d., 152, 158; of chiefs, priests, 123; sudden, 184, 203; symbolic, 218; *see also* Lightning
Deities, 2, 12, 208, 214, 266; *see also* Gods, 'little'
Deity, supreme, *see* God

INDEX

Descent, 24, 102; paternal, 174; women's, 123
Deviants, 171
Devil, 12–3, 203, 204, 247
Dibo sub-tribe, 192n.
dibo saba ritual, 71, 74–5
Disease, 5, 12, 16, 20, 22, 25, 29, 30, 31, 32, 50, 74, 88, 89, 132, 203, 204, 238, 247, 265, 277; types of treatment, 135, 138–43; and witchcraft, 166, 182, 187
Divination, Diviners, 23, 24, 25, 37, 75, 80, 87, 88, 105, 115–16, 118, 130, 138, 164, 170, 192, 232, 266; 'sand'-d., 53, 55–64, 78, 249, 256; 'shell'-d., 38–55
Divine justice, 278; omnipotence, providence, 35, 36–7, 203; divinity, 260
Division of labour, religious, 220, 223, 230, 255
Divisions, religious, in Nupe, 1–2, 68, 70, 233, 255
Divorce, 182, 249
Doctrine, Dogma, 8–10, 17, 36, 37, 65, 99, 164, 176, 201, 203, 236, 245, 261–2, 265–6, 268, 276
Doko, 16, 40, 54, 70, 186–7, 255n.; rituals of, 71–84, 97
Drama, Dramatizing, 114, 208, 218, 219, 225, 262, 266, 272; dramatic mood, 38–9, 55
Dreams, 22, 30, 33, 151, 166, 181, 188, 265; interpretation of, 65–7
Drought, 16, 20, 25, 34, 74, 238
Drums, 80, 92, 94–5, 194, 274
Dualism, Dualistic conceptions, 11, 34, 35–6, 87, 121, 265, 266–7
Durkheim, E., 226n.
Duties, religious, delegation of, 102, 103, 157, 220; sectional, 220, 223
dzakó ritual, 84, 85–6, 89, 94–5, 96, 107, 108

Earth, 11, 17, 24, 25, 26, 35, 266
Economic factors, organization, v, 83, 97, 100, 169, 174, 176, 235, 251, 255; *see also* Commercial activities, Trade
Ecstatic worship, 3, 210, 226, 236, 257, 261
Effigies, 16–17, 68, 94, 208, 213–14, 222
Egalitarianism, 271, 272

Elders, 111, 215, 272; of *ndakó gboyá* society, 193–5
Elements, Four, 60
Elite, *see* Ruling class
elo ceremonial, 16, 68, 87, 107, 214–16, 223, 225
Emir of Nupe, 53, 72, 160, 232, 240
emisa, *see* Greeting
Emotional aspects, factors, 3, 6–7, 55, 81, 83, 106, 110, 111, 129, 133, 200, 204, 224, 260, 262, 274; e. 'tone', 257, 258, 273
Empirical evidence, knowledge, 3–5, 6–7, 21, 103, 133, 134, 135, 142, 166–7, 203, 259
Entertainment, *see* Amusement
Enumeration, tendency to, 156, 265, 266, 267
Esoteric, 6, 79, 86, 101, 107, 111, 129, 171, 218, 219, 225, 229n., 240, 274
Ethics, *see* Morality; 'economic', 259–60, 263, 268; mundane, 269, 271, 277; ethical tenets, 262, 263
Ethnic division, 1, 87
Ethos, 257–8, 275
Etiquette, 171, 258, 273, 275
Etsu Nupe, *see* King of Nupe
Evil-doers, -wishers, 94, 144, 148; e. influences, 94, 98; e. in the world, 12, 33, 36, 203–4; e. medicines, 151, 157–60; spirits, 13, 27, 29–30; *see also* Good and Evil
Excitement in worship, 82, 83, 110, 115, 273, 275, 276
Execution, Executioner, 89, 94, 124, 268

Failure, of medicine, 134; of ritual, 105; of supernatural appeals, 33
Faith, 4, 6, 37, 202–3, 227, 261; access of, 276; in medicines, 134, 150–3; in rituals, 103–7
Family, 20, 54, 86, 88, 100, 120, 238; 'breadwinner', 174; extended, 251 270; head, 86, 102, 123, 126, 127, 130n., 156, 157, 178, 251–2, 272
Famine, 87
fará, *see* Ghosts
Fast, 235, 256, 257
Father, authority of, 251, 254; role of, 116–18, 119–20, 130, 174–5
Fees, of barber-doctors, 117; of diviners, 53; of grave-diggers, 125; of mallams, 128

Fertility, 31, 33, 94, 96, 98, 208; of land, 16, 131, 144, 254; of women, 16, 83, 100, 102, 107, 108, 140, 145, 195, 211, 212–13, 222, 268
Festivities, inclusion of in ceremonial, 68, 76, 106, 225, 239
fifingi, see Soul, shadow
fitakŭ ritual, 71, 74
First-fruits, 71
Fish, in divining, 44; in dreams, 66; in medicines, 143; in sacrifice, 80, 108; fishing, 88
Flogging, 81, 82, 106, 107
Floods, 87–8, 89, 94, 98
Folklore, 5, 28, 142, 266
Food taboos, 194, 249
Force, in medicine, 132, 152, 156; in ritual, 13 *et seq.*, 73, 104, 105, 109, 191
Free will, 12, 19
Friends, role of, 119, 131, 240, 243, 252
Fulani, 9, 91n., 154, 167, 192, 199, 219n., 226, 232–3, 234, 235, 244, 245–6, 249; *see also* Conquest
Fumigation, 139, 141
Funerary rites, 85–6, 87, 98, 122–30, 257; of chiefs, elders, 85–6, 123, 195

gani ceremonial, 216–20, 223, 225–6, 257, 268, 272, 275
Gbajibo, 215, 225n.
Gbedegi sub-tribe, 87
Ghosts of the dead, 22, 23, 26, 125
God, 2, 9, 10 *et seq.*, 20, 21, 24, 25, 28–9, 34–6, 40, 50, 53–4, 56, 65, 77, 90, 100, 105, 109, 115, 127, 133, 145, 203, 235, 238, 254, 261, 277; aloofness of, 12–13, 15, 18, 32, 35, 105, 109, 133, 200, 204, 235; 'for the sake of', 15, 160, 267; 'of G.', 10–11, 36, 79, 141; 'with the help', 'by the will' of G., 13, 141, 142, 146, 152, 170, 273; 'little gods', 17, 235
Good and Evil, 12–13, 20–1, 22, 35, 36, 37, 105, 265, 267; witchcraft, 170, 178; *see also* Evil
Government intervention, 83, 96, 163, 197, 200, 242
Grandfather, role of, 116–7, 120, 130, 250
Grave, ancestral, 24, 75, 119; gravedigger, 122, 124, 125; types of, 124, 125

'Greeting', in divining, 44–6; of *elo*, 215; of medicines, 92, 144–5, 149, 152–3; of *ndakó gboyá*, 198; of rituals, 80, 107
Group existence, identity, 118, 227–8, 229, 230, 270; structure, 103, 111–12, 114
gugu ritual, 208, 213, 214–15, 221–2, 223, 225
gunnu ritual, 14, 15, 68, 71, 73, 77–84, 85–6, 87, 95–6, 97, 98, 101, 102, 105, 106, 107, 110, 112, 114, 123, 189, 195–6, 218, 219, 225, 228–30, 255n., 257, 258, 268, 271, 275
Guidance, supernatural, 37, 64–5, 67, 203
Gwari tribe, 16, 77, 78, 124, 208, 210–13

Harvest, *see* Crops
Hausa tribe, 26, 39n., 96, 150, 160, 170, 209–10, 223
Health, 20, 71, 84, 88, 89, 94, 96, 98, 100, 265
Hectic worship, *see* Ecstatic
Heredity, 23, 24
Herskovits, M. J., 256n.
Hierarchy of supernatural aids, 34, 100, 105
Hippopotamus, 39–40
History, interest in, 267; of Islam in Nupe, 232–3; and myth, 4, 8; of *ndakó gboyá* society, 192–3; of order of *cigbeciži*, 154
Hobbyhorses, 219
Homosexuality, 113, 179
Hospitals, 147n., 161
House, *see* Family; in divining, 39–43, 46, 50
Humorous episodes, 82, 95
Hunters, Hunting, 49, 64, 71–2, 75–6, 84, 94, 123, 220

Ideals, secular and religious, 268, 271, 272; social, 112, 175, 181
Idiocy, 29, 141
Idols, *see* Effigies
Illness, *see* Disease
Immigrants, 209, 217, 223
Impotence, 142, 143, 162
Incantations, *see* Invocations
Inhalations, 135, 139, 140, 141
India, 245
Inheritance, 174, 250–1, 254

INDEX

Initiation, 83
In-laws, 121, 174, 187
Invocations, 44–6, 100, 101, 106, 129, 130, 133, 137, 144–5, 153, 194, 273
Irrationality, of medicines, 133, 135–7; of religious beliefs, 99
Islam, v, 2, 9, 12, 13, 17, 26, 38, 53, 54, 66, 83, 114, 195, 208, 209, 217, 225n., 230, chap. VIII., 272, 277; basic duties of, 235–6, 256; and divination, 55–6, 59, 64; feasts of, 239–44, 257; and solemnizations, 117, 118, 119, 120, 122, 124, 160–1, 256; and medicine, 138; saints of, 237, 245, 277; scholarship in, 164, 232, 246–7, 252, 272; sects of, 236, 255; islamic dress, 235, 257

James, William, 260, 264, 267
Jebba Island, 16, 27, 40, 51, 52, 54, 68, 70, 84–7, 97, 98, 148, 186, 214
Joking, in ceremonials, 107, 126, 127, 171, 218, 241; -relations, 126, 131, 242–3, 258

Katcha, 16, 28
Kede sub-tribe, 87–8, 89
ketsá ritual, 68, 84, 87, 88, 89
King-maker, 85, 87
King of Nupe, 153, 188, 192–3, 195, 196–7; kingship, 31–2, 52, 192, 216, 222, 233, 267, 268, 277
Kin group, Kinship, 23, 34, 75, 100, 102, 131, 149, 242–3, 270, 272, 277; ceremonials, 131, 272; in *ndakó gboyá* society, 193, 149, 156; and witchcraft, 173–4, 178
Kluckhohn, C., 201, 205n.
Knowledge, Nupe conception of, 6, 19, 133; *see also* Empirical
Kolanut cultivation, 68
Konú immigrants, 208
Kpatsuwa, 183–6
kuci, see Soul, Kinship
kuti, see Ritual
Kutigi, 51, 52, 54, 83, 169, 197–9, 209, 216–20, 255
Kutiwengi, 68

labá, see Sacrifice, Libation
Labozhi, 68
Lagos, Nupe of, 228–30, 270
Language, use of, 11, 16, 54, 109, 262, 265; gender, in Nupe l., 266; obscurity of, 118, 218, 241; semantic aspect of, 265, 266
Law, 32, 77, 85, 163, 176, 212, 268, 277; of self-help, 158, 212; moslem, 235, 236, 246, 250–1; legalization of marriage, 119
Leadership, spiritual, 271
Legends, *see* Mythology
Lelu, 165, 166, 167–8, 185, 188, 196
Lemu, 238, 255n.
Leopard, 28–9, 215
Leprosy, 36–7, 77–8, 124, 141, 169
Levirate, 122, 250
Libation, 14, 54, 76, 81, 92, 101, 109, 125, 127, 130
Life principle, *see* Soul, life
Lightning, 33, 124, 209, 211–12, 247
Lineage, 86, 120, 155, 156, 270
Linguistic evidence, 6, 8, 109, 134, 159; *see also* Names
Linton, R., 256
Livelihood, *see* Subsistence
Lotze, H., 259n.
Lowie, R. H., 3
Lunacy, *see* Mental disorders

Magic, as against Religion, 1, 3, 21, 152–3, 261, 273; magical medicines, *see* Miraculous m.
Male-female, 37, 94, 95n., 142, 169, 265, 266, 267; in divining, 43, 44, 63, 95n.; masks, in *elo*, 215; medicines, 144; Tsoede figures, 214; witchcraft, 169–71, 173–8, 187
Malinowski, B., 256n.
Mallam, 56, 64, 66, 117, 119, 120, 124, 128, 232, 235, 238, 245, 246–7, 255; M. Dendo, 232, 237, 245
mamma ritual, 84, 90–4, 96, 98, 101, 104, 105, 112, 225n., 274
Market, *see* Commercial activities
Marriage, 25, 52, 66, 102, 174, 268; ceremonial, 119–21, 130–1, 277; of cousins, 249; of mallams, 246; rules, 249–50, 256, 257; of *sogba* children, 212; of widows, 122, 128, 250
Masks, 16, 68, 87, 208; of *elo*, 107, 214–15, 216; of *mamma*, 91–3, 96, 104, 215; of *ndakó gboyá*, 190–1, 194–5, 197
Mead, Margaret, 171, 177n., 179
Medicines, 2, 6, 9, 17–21, 25, 31, 34, 36, 78, 89, 100, 104, 116, 130,

chap. V, 270, 273; community m., 91, 148, 157; discovery of new m., 141, 154–5; European, 161–2; for farmwork, 137, 147–8; 'great', 100, 109, 119, 149–50, 156, 195; hereditary, 20, 134, 138, 148–9, 156, 158, 270; ingredients of, 132, 134, 137, 138–42, 146–8, 152; preparation of, 132, 133, 134, 145; purchase of, 20, 133, 134, 143, 149–50; 'protective', 144, 148, 158, 212; therapeutic and non-therapeutic, 133–8, 142, 146–7; shrines, 91, 92, 149, 211; vessels, 91, 92, 145, 149, 195

Medicine experts, individual, 146–8, 155–6, 158; 'm.-men', 138, 140, 142–5, 157–8, 161, 170, 211; organization of, 154–5

Menstruation, 66, 115

Mental disorders, 29, 30, 36, 37, 135, 137, 139, 142, 171, 209–10

'Merry-making', 82, 95, 101, 107, 120, 127, 129, 130, 217, 225, 240, 274

Message, religious, 262, 269, 271, 272

Messianic, 269, 272, 278

Metaphysics, 4, 7, 132

Millenium, 275

Miraculous, 5, 6, 8, 73, 77, 102, 185; medicines, 132–4, 135, 137, 144, 150, 151, 154, 273; qualification of priests, 72, 85, 102, 237, 271

Misfortunes, 29, 30, 33, 52, 171, 203, 268

Missionaries, 184, 186, 231

Mohammed, *see* Prophet

Mohammedan, *see* Islam

Moieties, religious, 86

Mokwa, 16, 27–8, 68, 83, 87, 91n., 107, 146, 214–16, 225, 255n.

Months, of rituals, 70–1, 84, 90–1; propitious, 67, 266

Morality, 12, 19, 20–1, 25, 29–30, 33, 82, 105, 176, 236, 260, 261, 268, 269; and medicine, 140, 143, 157–8, 268; moral standards, reflected in ritual, 111–14, 258; m. values, 259; morality of women, 175

Mosque, 160, 195n., 236, 237, 241, 244, 256, 257

Mother, position of, 174–5, 180

Music, Musical instruments, 80, 88, 94, 102, 106, 209, 215, 219, 236, 262, 273; musicians, professional, 119, 127, 240

Mystery, mysterious, 14, 23, 25, 181, 196, 262, 265, 273, 274

Mystic, 4, 5, 7, 8, 24, 31, 55, 99, 129, 261; mystics, 260, 278; in Islam, 236, 257; mystical medicines, *see* Miraculous m.

Myth, Mythology, v, 4, 6, 8, 9–10, 17–8, 20, 77–8, 233, 249, 256, 257, 265, 268, 270; incipient, 184, 249; of origin, 9, 247–8, 249; of rituals, 77–9, 87–8; of witchcraft, 172–3, 177, 180, 191–2, 194

Mythical charter, pedigree, 79, 133

Names, for religious concepts, 2, 7, 8–9, 11n., 76, 109, 115, 129, 217; in divining, 44–5, 61–2, 79, 134; of medicines, 144, 149, 152–3, 159; for witchcraft, 165, 169

Naming, of children, 23–4, 52, 211; ceremonial, 116–17, 130, 235, 250

National religion, *see* Tribal religion

Navaho, 201n., 202

navũ ceremonial, 241–4, 251, 256, 257, 268, 272, 275

ndáduma ritual, 84, 89–90, 94, 107

ndakó gboyá cult, 18n., 83, 96, 112, 144, 148, 172, 177, 188, 189–91, 229–30, 257; initiation into, 192, 193, 194–5; medicine, 190, 194; society, 190–7, 271

Ndakotsu (head of age grades), 80, 92, 217

Neighbourhood, 237

Neuroses, 99, 167, 202, 226, 275

New Year, 239, 241, 244

Niger river, 16, 27, 32, 68, 84, 87, 89–90, 97, 103, 107, 154, 192, 214, 233

Nigeria, 232, 234

Night, Nocturnal, 83, 91, 101, 152, 166, 181, 273

Nightmares, 29, 30, 66, 151, 166

Nobility, 48, 50, 51, 240, 246

Normality, in nature, 103, 104; in social life, 111, 171, 175, 178, 181

Novices, 80, 83

Numbers, lucky, 265–6; numbering, 115, 130

Nupe kingdom, state; 1, 17, 31–2, 34, 103, 107, 154, 232–4, 244, 249, 270; tribe, nation, 1, 2, 9, 14, 19, 31–2, 102, 271

INDEX

Objects, cult, 15, 16–17, 31, 211, 214
Optimism, 21, 51, 160, 273, 278
Ordeal,¹ 77, 89, 98, 136, 144, 148, 188, 222
Orientations, intellectual, 267
Ownership, of medicine, 20, 134, 138, 149–50; of rituals, 11n., 14, 19–20, 70, 87, 102, 195, 220, 230, 270

Parables, 265, 267
Patigi, 88, 193n.
Patronage, 235, 240; patroness, 184
Personality, see Character traits
Philosophy, 203, 261
Pichi, 16, 28, 40, 79n.
Pilgrimage, to Mecca, 235–6; places of, 87, 213, 237
Plants, 21, 132, 141; p. parasites, 141–2
Play, Pleasures, see Amusement, Merry-making
Plural society, 220
Plutarch, 278
Poetry, 262
Political factors, organization, v, 1, 32, 34, 49, 50, 70, 75, 83, 97, 171, 226, 231, 233, 240, 241–4, 255, 257, 258, 260, 267, 268, 272, 275
Prayer, moslem, 129, 236, 238–9, 256, 257, 277; pagan, 8, 13, 15, 18, 19, 20, 64, 74, 75, 76, 81, 90, 92, 95, 100, 101, 104–5, 107, 116, 125, 127, 156, 194, 219, 230, 271; significance of, 109, 236, 274
Pregnancy, 21, 66, 115, 128, 135, 143, 146
Priest, Priesthood, 7, 14, 52, 72–3, 78, 85, 87, 88, 102, 164, 189–90, 195, 208, 210, 211, 271; dress of, 73, 87, 108; moslem p., 237, 257
Private medicines, 134, 150, 157; rituals, 75, 76, 100, 272
Procreation, 21, 265
Projection, 176, 178, 201
Proliferation of religious thought, 31, 33, 34, 64
Pronouncements, religious, 106, 111, 144, 260, 274
Prophet (Mohammed), 217, 237, 239n., 240, 247, 248
Proselytizing, 226, 234,'252
Prosperity, 20, 75, 76, 100, 102, 108, 268
Prostitutes, 82, 112, 175

Proverbs, see Sayings
Psycho-analysis, 108, 180n.
Psychological 'deficit', 225; factors, mechanisms, 37, 176, 178, 201, 256, 260, 264, 275; relief, 201–2, 204, 226, 258, 264, 269, 275; 'tenor', 2, 222,
Psychopathology, 172, 201, 202, 275
Psycho-therapeutic, 5, 137
Puberty, 118
Punishment, supernatural, 25, 33, 82, 113, 124, 209, 211, 212, 268; by medicines, 144, 148, 158

Qoran, 56, 59n., 160, 235; quotations from, 239–40, 245–6; schools, 235

Rabah, 214, 215, 225n.
Radcliffe-Brown, A. R., 111
Rain, 28, 33, 50, 71, 74, 131, 238–9, 247, 254
Rank, and ownership of medicine, 157; and priestship, 72, 85–6, 94, 102, 157, 215; see also Status
Regalia, 32, 72, 74, 194
Reincarnation, 23–4, 35, 50, 116, 121, 250, 265, 277
Religion, Religious, definition of, 3 et seq., 99, 260; experience, 260, 261, 264, 273; and everyday life, 277; mass and virtuoso r., 261, 271; religiosity, 277
Remedies, see Medicines; household r., 145–6
Respect, for age, 83, 111, 112, 258; filial, 83, 112; for rank, 272
Retribution, divine, see Punishment, supernatural
Revelations, 274
Riddles, 16
Rites de passage, 114, 218
Ritual, concept of, 9, 13 et seq., 31, 33, 34, 35, 36, 50, 89, 100, 104, 115, 130, 149, 156, 217, 252, 254, 262, 270; definition of, 99; r. dress, 73, 80, 83, 101, 107, 111, 127, 272; 'fixed' r., 15n., 52, 65, 68, 73, 75–83, 84, 89, 90–6, 98, 100–1, 103, 105, 195, 210, 215, 221, 239, 276; funerary r., 85–6; local varieties of, 1, 2, 68–70, 98; 'movable' r., 68, 73–5, 84, 87–90, 98, 100–1, 104, 105, 210, 225n., 274, 276;

INDEX

r. procedure, 2, 6, 14, 19, 78, 80, 101, 104, 106; repertoire, schedule of, 69, 70–1, 84, 97, 239; request for, by individuals, 87, 88
Ritualization, 99, 108, 134, 135, 137, 144, 261, 262, 265, 273; of adolescence, 225, 226; of death, 121, 221
Riverain, *see* Niger river
Roots, in medicine, 133, 141, 147, 148
Royal cults, 32, 34, 191–2, 194, 214, 233–4, 244, 270
Ruling class, 233, 234, 252, 253, 255

Sacrament, 109
Sacred, 6, 7, 10, 55, 56, 106, 109, 110, 129, 131, 133–4, 136, 157–8, 216, 240, 272, 277–8; individuals, 73, 271, 277; localities, 16, 76, 79, 80, 96, 277; sense of the s., 273, 277
Sacrifice, 14, 16, 24, 25, 26, 27, 31, 34, 50, 67, 74, 76, 80–1, 88, 89, 90, 92, 94–5, 100, 107, 119, 127, 194, 197, 225, 270, 272; to medicines, 91, 133, 137, 145, 153, 156; moslem, 239–40; Nupe conception of, 109–10; sacrificial food, 109; s. meal, 101, 110, 238, 274
Sagi (head of women), 167–9, 184, 186, 188, 196, 198
sakó ritual, 71, 75–6
salla festival, 216, 239–41, 256
Salute to chiefs, elders, 44, 82, 93, 111, 152; *see also* Greeting
Sapir, E., 7n.
Satan, *see* Devil
Sayings, 8, 12, 13, 14, 45
Schematism, 265–6
Science, 3–4, 5, 8, 134, 135, 205, 260
Seasons, Seasonal events, 71, 103, 268
Secrecy, 14, 19, 20, 75–6, 81, 91, 172, 191, 210, 225n., 265; of medicines, 20, 134, 140, 144, 147, 149–50, 151–2, 155; *see also* Esoteric
Secret society, 83, 189, 196, 229
Semen, 21
Sensory satisfaction, 106
Sex, act, 179; antagonism, 94, 112, 176–81, 187, 267; differences, 126, 130; morality, 177, 218; open reference to, 113, 118, 218, 219;

polarity, 36–7, 79, 121; relationship, 275; and ritual, 82–3, 110, 112–13, 257; of spirits, 26–7, 266
Sexual excitement, 82, 273; licence, 83, 110, 113, 218–19, 241, 244, 268, 275; taboo, 82, 101, 110, 115, 194
Shamanistic ideas, 209
Shame, of bride, 120, 121; of childless women, 112–13, 177; of contraceptive practices, 140, 177
Shari, 140n., 148, 208
Shaving of head, of new-born, 117–18
Shebe, 193, 197–9
Shonga, 208, 214
Shrines, 14, 19, 26, 149
Sins, 203, 268
Skills, learned, in religion, 19, 20, 53, 54, 55–6, 273, 278; in medicine 133, 136, 271
Sky, 11, 21, 24, 35, 40, 248, 266
Slaves, 208, 234
Sleep, 22, 151, 166
Sleeping sickness, 36–7, 141, 142, 146, 169
Smallpox, 25, 74, 91, 98, 124, 135, 139
Smith, W. Robertson, 8n., 110
Social, functions, 111, 114; integration, 223; mobility, 255; solidarity, 205, 257; structure, organization, 111, 130–1, 251, 260, 262, 263, 269–73; s. structure and witchcraft, 178, 201; s. values and ritual, 111, 130; and witchcraft beliefs, 176, 181
sogba, sokógba, see 'Thunderbolts'; s. cult, 124, 208, 210–13, 222, 223, 277n.; children, 211–12.
Sokó, see God
sokokó ritual, 84, 96, 98
Songs, 8, 11, 12, 15, 93–4, 95, 101, 102, 119–20, 123, 127, 215, 225, 274; of *elo*, 216; of *ndakó gboyá*, 199–200
Soul, 7, 21 *et seq.*, 33; of the dead, 23–5, 125; kinship, personal s., 22, 23–6, 30, 31, 34, 35, 49, 77, 100, 109, 116, 119, 120, 153, 250; life s., 22, 23, 30, 33, 34, 35, 165–6, 185, 247, 265; shadow s., 22, 30, 35, 36, 65, 147, 151, 165–6, 169, 185
Speculations, etymological, 44, 76, 79, 132n., 266; religious, 55, 79, 265, 266

Spells, 19, 20, 104, 152-3, 273
Spirits, 2, 5, 6, 12, 13, 22, 26-31, 33, 34, 36, 54, 65, 171, 191, 203; animal, 27-8; s.-doubles, 29-30; offerings to, 27, 54, 66, 89, 100, 109; guardian, 24; s.-possession, 209-10, 226; nature s., 27, 34, 83
St. Croix, F. W., 9n.
Stars, 11, 33, 59, 64, 249
State church, religion, 32, 232
Status, 50, 51, 53, 85-6, 101, 111, 123, 125, 128, 129, 131, 225, 226, 266, 272; barrier, 223, 224, 246
Sterility, female, 20, 32, 143, 162, 175, 313; male, 21
Stimulation, 37, 106, 110, 224, 225, 236, 260, 262, 273-6
Stones, sacred, 16, 74, 109
Strangers, role of, 19, 53, 78, 81, 87, 88n., 90, 91, 107, 111, 182, 212, 276
Subsistence, 84, 108
Sudan, 236n., 245, 252
Supererogatory elements in Nupe religion, 30, 32-3, 104
Supernatural, 3 *et seq.*, 99, 103, 130, 260, 277; s. aids, alternative, 34, 65, 105; s. aids, social appropriateness of, 34; definition of, 3-4; 'supernaturalism', 3
Superstitions, 5, 8, 115, 135, 142
Supreme being, deity, *see* God
Surgery, 139, 141, 146, 161
Survival, 16
Swearing, 13
Symbols, 107, 110, 262, 265; symbolism, 17, 51, 110, 218, 219, 229, 265; of colour, 51, 107, 108, 144, 147, 159, 265; in dreams, 66, 108, 143; of left and right, 94, 108, 265; in medicines, 144, 147; uncomprehended, 108

Taboos, 272
Tada, 214n.
Tasks, religious, *see* Duties, religious
Teaching, of divining, 43, 53; of Islam, 233, 235, 245, 247; of medical knowledge, 20, 133-4, 153, 155; of religion, 8, 176, 215, 227
Temples, 16
Tensions, social, 172, 176, 181, 205, 226

Theology, 12, 32-3, 34, 36, 261, 276; Augustean, 36; moslem, 236, 247, 256
'Thrill' of religious experience, 106, 110, 260, 261, 274
'Thunderbolts', 16, 40, 211
tidzana ritual, 88, 89n.
Tolerance, 227, 252-3, 255
Torches, in ceremonial, 241, 244, 257
Tortoise, in divination, 38; in folklore, 28-9, 108; in ritual, 80, 81, 108
Town as against country, 49, 50, 53, 64, 122, 136, 226, 232-3, 240, 250, 251n., 258
Trade, traders, 50, 52, 53, 64, 97, 176; female, 168-9, 187
Trance, 137
Travel, 50, 52, 53, 64, 134, 142, 155; magic, 152
Trees, parts of, used in medicines, 132, 141; in ritual, 54, 74, 80, 102
Tribal god, 269, 270; marks, cutting of, 117; religion, 2, 98, 103, 226-30, 233, 234, 261, 262
Tsoede, 31-2, 34, 74, 87, 91, 97, 103, 107, 154, 192, 249, 267, 271; bronze figures, 94, 214-15, 222; chain of, 88-9, 94, 194, 228, 270; relics of, 32, 68, 72, 84, 94, 97, 223
turare, see Inhalations
Twins, 14, 26, 31, 34, 100, 119

Umbilical cord, 23
Underworld, 11
Unification, religious, 233-4
Universal religion, 103
Universe, benevolent, divinely ordered, 202, 203, 204; Nupe u., 32, 33, 34, 100, 104, 278; understanding of, 260, 263; Yoruba u., 208

Validity of ritual, 2, 103, 262
Values, Value judgments, 181, 269; *see also* Social values.
Vernacular, vi, 17, 132
Vigil in the bush, 83, 95, 112, 274
Village community, 2, 15, 16, 19, 25, 31, 49, 70, 76, 94, 100, 101, 102, 103, 131, 195, 237, 254, 262, 270, 271; founders of v., 25, 31
Violence, *see* Aggression
Virility, 179-80; medicines for, 140, 146, 179

Wall paintings, 29
Warthog, 40
Washing of hands, 81, 90
'Water' in sacrifice, 74, 90, 92, 95, 108
Wealth, 246, 255, 268, 272; display of, 117, 120, 122, 129, 272
Weber, Max, 227n., 259, 260, 261
Weltbild, 261, 262, 266, 267, 278
West Africa, 234, 245
White Man, 48, 50, 90, 163-4
Widows, 127-8, 182; remarriage of, 249-50, 257
Wife, role of, 174-5, 180
Wishfulfilment, in ritual, 112; in witchcraft beliefs, 178
Witchcraft, Witches, 4, 12, 18n., 22, 30, 33, 34, 66, 94, 112, chap. VI, 230, 267, 275, 278; accusations, 163, 166, 172, 186, 187, 188, 196, 205; becoming a w., 165; discovery of, 168, 170-1, 181-2, 188; female, 165, 169-72, 176-8, 201, 273; male, 169-71, 178; measures against, 168, 188 *et seq.*, 200-1; -medicines, 144, 151, 158-9, 166, 167, 170, 185, 188, 189, 190, 194; text on w., 165; w. trial, 163, 183, 188, 226
Women, imitation of, 82, 113, 218, 219; in Islam, 245-6; in ritual, 76, 81, 82, 91, 92, 93, 107, 111, 112, 118, 175, 272; social position of, 112, 167, 174-5, 245, 272
World, *see* Creation
World religions, 234
Worship, acts of, 3, 6-7, 149, 236, 254, 262, 271-2, 273, 276-7; climax in, 274; mood of, 273-4; *see also* Ecstatic, Excitement
Wrestling, 218

Yoruba tribe, 16, 18n., 38, 140, 189n., 197, 208, 210n., 213-14, 223, 228, 229-30, 249n.

žiba ritual, 72, 76-7, 87
žikinta ritual, 76, 84, 98, 220